ÇEMBERLİTAŞ HAMAMI IN ISTANBUL

Edinburgh Studies on the Ottoman Empire
Series Editor: Kent F. Schull

Published and forthcoming titles

Migrating Texts: Circulating Translations around the Eastern Mediterranean
Edited by Marilyn Booth

Ottoman Sunnism: New Perspectives
Edited by Vefa Erginbas

*Armenians in the Late Ottoman Empire: Migration, Mobility Control
and Sovereignty, 1885–1915*
David Gutman

The Kizilbash-Alevis in Ottoman Anatolia: Sufism, Politics and Community
Ayfer Karakaya-Stump

Çemberlitaş Hamamı in Istanbul: The Biographical Memoir of a Turkish Bath
Nina Macaraig

*Nineteenth Century Local Governance in Ottoman Bulgaria: Politics in
Provincial Councils*
M. Safa Saraçoğlu

Prisons in the Late Ottoman Empire: Microcosms of Modernity
Kent F. Schull

Ruler Visibility and Popular Belonging in the Ottoman Empire, 1808–1908
Darin N. Stephanov

edinburghuniversitypress.com/series/esoe

ÇEMBERLİTAŞ HAMAMI IN ISTANBUL

THE BIOGRAPHICAL MEMOIR OF A TURKISH BATH

∞

Nina Macaraig

EDINBURGH
University Press

For Cathy

Edinburgh University Press is one of the leading university presses in the UK. We publish academic books and journals in our selected subject areas across the humanities and social sciences, combining cutting-edge scholarship with high editorial and production values to produce academic works of lasting importance. For more information visit our website: edinburghuniversitypress.com

First published in hardback by Edinburgh University Press 2019

Edinburgh University Press Ltd
The Tun – Holyrood Road
12 (2f) Jackson's Entry
Edinburgh EH8 8PJ

Typeset in JaghbUni by
Servis Filmsetting Ltd, Stockport, Cheshire

A CIP record for this book is available from the British Library

ISBN 978 1 4744 3410 2 (hardback)
ISBN 978 1 4744 3411 9 (paperback)
ISBN 978 1 4744 3412 6 (webready PDF)
ISBN 978 1 4744 3413 3 (epub)

Published with the support of the University of Edinburgh Scholarly Publishing Initiatives Fund.

Contents

List of Tables   vii
List of Figures   viii
Preface   xii
Acknowledgements   xiii
Note on Transliteration   xvi

Introduction   1

1. Ancestry   24
   The Patroness: Nurbanu Sultan   24
   The Architect: Sinan   30
   Origins   32

2. Family   52
   The Atik Valide Vakfı   52
   The Atik Valide Mosque Complex   55
   The Endowed Hamams   64

3. From Birth to Breadwinner   73
   The Birth   73
   Getting Ready to Work   90
   The Hamam's Employees   92
   The Hamam's Customers   105
   Making Money   107

4. Impressions and Identity   116
   A Place for Ritual Cleansing   116
   A Place for Socialising   120
   A Place for Carnal Pleasure   132
   A Place for Healing   142
   Pride of the City   147

5. In Sickness and in Health   153
   Symptoms: Evidence for Renovations   153
   Causes: Fires, Earthquakes and Other Calamities   161
   Treatment: Repair and Renovation Work   168

6. Old Age   173
   Renegotiating Family Relations   173
   Mutilation   175
   A New Identity I: Emblem of Ottoman Heritage in the
     Nineteenth Century   179
   A New Identity II: Emblem of Ottoman Heritage in the
     Early Republic   185
   Survival   199

7. Second Spring   207
   A New Identity III: Tourist Attraction   207
   A New Identity IV: Object of Ottomania   222
   A New Identity V: The Hamam Managers' and
     Employees' Perspectives   227
   A New Identity VI: The Digital Age   234

Epilogue   241

Appendix: Endowment Deed of the Atik Valide Vakfı
  (VGM, D. 1766)   248
Notes   286
References   329
Index   361

Tables

3.1 Names, physical traits and place of origin of the attendants and servants working in Çemberlitaş Hamamı in 1752   95

3.2 Total endowment income, monthly rent income from the endowed hamams and the hamam's annual contribution to the total income, 1632–1832   110

3.3 Names of the renters of the Atik Valide Vakfı's endowed hamams in the seventeenth century   111

5.1 Dates, types and costs of repairs to Çemberlitaş Hamamı   160

Figures

I.1 Çemberlitaş Hamamı, 1583, Istanbul   2
I.2 Ground plan of Çemberlitaş Hamamı   3
I.3 *The Bather of Valpinçon*, Jean-August-Dominique
    Ingres, 1808   4
I.4 *The Bath*, Jean-Léon Gerôme, 1880–1885   5
I.5 Film poster of *Steam*, 1997   6
1.1 Nurbanu's funeral cortège leaving the Topkapı Palace,
    Lokman's *Şahinşahname*, 1597   29
1.2 Family tree tracing the ancestry of Çemberlitaş Hamamı   34
1.3 Bath of Gortys, third century BCE   35
1.4 Stabian Bath of Pompeii, phases III–IV, second century BCE   37
1.5 *Thermae* of Caracalla, between 206 and 216/17 CE, Rome   38
1.6 Schematic drawing of a Roman hypocaust system   38
1.7 Bath at Brad, *c.* 200 CE, Syria   40
1.8 Bath of Qasr al-Hayr al-Sharqi, first half of
    eighth century, Syria   41
1.9 Bath in the Dar al-'Amma, 836–884, Samarra   43
1.10 Bath at Nigar, date unknown, Iran   46
1.11 Sahib Ata Hamamı, 1258–1279, Konya   47
1.12 Orhan Gazi Hamamı, 1324–1362, Bursa   49
1.13 Tahtakale Hamamı, 1472–1473, Istanbul   50
1.14 Mahmud Paşa Hamamı, 1456–1461 or 1472/3, Istanbul   51
2.1 Ground plan of the Atik Valide Mosque Complex,
    c. 1571–1588, Istanbul   57
2.2 Aerial view of the Atik Valide Mosque Complex   58
2.3 Prayer niche of the Atik Valide Mosque   60
2.4 Istanbul's commercial areas in the sixteenth century   65
2.5 Atik Valide Hamamı, *c.* 1582, Istanbul   66
2.6 Büyük Hamam, *c.* 1583, Istanbul   68
2.7 Ground plan of the Büyük Hamam, *c.* 1583, Istanbul   69
2.8 Havuzlu Hamam, before 1582, Istanbul   70

Figures

2.9 Ground plan of the Havuzlu Hamam 70

3.1 Perspectival view of the Divan Yolu, westwards
from Hagia Sophia 74

3.2 Neighbourhood of Çemberlitaş Hamamı 74

3.3 Thomas Allom, *The Tcheenberle Tash, or Burnt Pillar* 76

3.4 Map of commercial areas and *han*s along Divan Yolu 77

3.5 Map of hamams and aqueducts along Divan Yolu 77

3.6 Dome lantern of Çemberlitaş Hamamı 78

3.7 Map of the water conduits belonging to the
Köprülü endowment, seventeenth century 79

3.8 Haseki Hamamı, 1553, Istanbul 80

3.9 Inscription above the entrance to the men's section of
Çemberlitaş Hamamı 81

3.10 Dressing room in the men's section of Çemberlitaş Hamamı 82

3.11 *Göbektaşı* in the men's hot room of Çemberlitaş Hamamı 84

3.12 Dome of the men's hot room of Çemberlitaş
Hamamı, interior 84

3.13 Dome of the men's hot room of Çemberlitaş
Hamamı, exterior 85

3.14 Men's hot room of Çemberlitaş Hamamı 85

3.15 Inscription in the men's hot room of Çemberlitaş Hamamı 86

3.16 Schematic drawing of a hamam's heating system 89

3.17 Guild of the *hamamcıyan*, *Surname-i Hümayun*, 1582 98

3.18 Guild of the *natıran*, *Surname-i Hümayun*, 1582 102

3.19 Guild of the *peştemalcıyan*, *Surname-i Hümayun*, 1582 104

3.20 Exterior of the Vezir Han, Istanbul, second half of
the seventeenth century 106

3.21 Ground plan of the Vezir Han, Istanbul, second half of
the seventeenth century 107

4.1 Ground plan of an Istanbul mansion with attached hamam 121

4.2 Ground plan of the Haseki Hamamı, 1553, Istanbul 125

4.3 Exterior of the Haseki Hamamı 126

4.4 Embroidered towel 127

4.5 Hamam bowl (*tas*), copper 128

4.6 Hamam clogs (*nalın*) 128

4.7 Wrapper (*bohça*) with hamam kit 130

4.8 Miniature from Lambert Wyts' *Iter factum e
Belgico-Gallica, Voyages de Wyts en Turquie, c. 1574* 131

4.9 Miniature from album titled *Ein Turggische Hochzeit,
c. 1582* 132

4.10 Folio from Album for Ahmed I, *c.* 1610 138

4.11 Hamam set piece for a Karagöz and Hacıvat shadow
puppet theatre 139
4.12 Abdullah Buhari, album leaf with bather, *c.* 1741 140
4.13 Hamam scene from Enderuni Fazıl Hüseyin's
Zenanname, 1793 141
4.14 Bathhouse attendant in Enderuni Fazıl Hüseyin's
Hubanname, 1793 142
5.1 Inscription in the men's hot room of Çemberlitaş
Hamamı, 1770 156
5.2 Ground plan of the men's hot room of Çemberlitaş
Hamamı, with 1766 earthquake damage indicated 158
5.3 Extent of the 1865 Hocapaşa Fire 164
5.4 Istanbul with buildings damaged by the 1766
earthquake indicated 166
6.1 Photograph of Çemberlitaş Hamamı, 6 June 1890 178
6.2 Leon Parvillée, drawing of the façade of the bath for
the 1867 World Fair, Paris 182
6.3 Leon Parvillée, ground plan of the bath for the 1867
World Fair, Paris 183
6.4 Maynard Owen Williams, 'Bathers in Istanbul', 1929 187
6.5 Ahmet Refik Altınay, 'İstanbul Hamamları', 1936 194
6.6 Kandemir, 'Eski Hamamlar', 1939 196
6.7 Ground plan of 'Tanzimat-box'-type apartment building 201
6.8 Jacques Pervititch, map of the neighbourhood of
Çemberlitaş, 1940 203
6.9 Jacques Pervititch, map of the neighbourhood of Çemberlitaş
south of the Divanyolu, 1923 204
7.1 *Le Bain Turc*, Jean-Auguste-Dominique Ingres, oil on
wood, 1852–1859 210
7.2 Women going to the bath, from Nicolas de Nicholay,
Nauigations 214
7.3 Şebnem İşigüzel, 'Waschtag im Reich der Sinne', 1998 217
7.4 Nancy Milford, 'Bathed in Tradition', 2000 218
7.5 Hamams as introduced in the *Eyewitness Travel Guide
Istanbul*, 1999 220
7.6 Cover of a travel supplement aimed at Turkish visitors 224
7.7 Page of a magazine supplement aimed at
Turkish consumers 225
7.8 Webpages of Çemberlitaş Hamamı in 2004 228
7.9 Customer brochure of Çemberlitaş Hamamı 230
7.10 Customer card for Çemberlitaş Hamamı 231

Figures

7.11 Business card of Çemberlitaş Hamamı   231

E.1 Hamam in the Sanda Day Spa, İstinye Park shopping mall,
Istanbul, 2007   242

E.2 State of preservation and restoration of the Kılıç Ali
Paşa Hamamı, 1578–1581   243

E.3 Site visit to the restoration of the Küçük Mustafa Paşa
Hamamı, 1477, Istanbul, 2016   244

E.4 Turkish Hamam Culture Museum in the bathhouse of
Bayezid II, Istanbul   245

E.5 Tea room in the bath-restaurant *Aux Gazelles*, Vienna, 2003   246

E.6 Hot room of *Aux Gazelles*, Vienna, 2003   246

Preface

The reason for writing this beautiful book, which resembles a perfumed veil adorning the beloved's face, is that one day our felicitous Çemberlitaş Hamamı, having become a frail old building, enticed me to record its history in prose in order to leave its fame and reputation on the pages of Time so that it may be remembered with well-wishing prayers. And I, Nina Macaraig, God's broken-hearted, meek, impoverished and humble servant, realised its wish by writing down this work to the best of my ability as a pitiful gift with which I entered into its happiness-causing presence. I subtitled it *The Biographical Memoir of a Turkish Bath* and humbly beg friends who read this epic to veil my shortcomings as much as possible with forgiveness, and not to turn this humble servant into a target of criticism with the saying 'The higher you reach, the harder you fall'.[1]

Acknowledgements

The making of this book has taken an embarrassing number of years, and in its course brought me to places I could never have imagined: university classrooms and library halls on the frozen tundra of Minnesota during its conception; the steam-filled chambers of Çemberlitaş Hamamı within Istanbul's stunning urban landscape during years of research and dissertation-writing; a verdant university campus near the Black Sea during the lengthy process of conducting more research, refining ideas and re-writing; many conference and lecture venues in Europe, Turkey and the United States, where listeners asked probing questions; and, finally, the sun-soaked beaches of Southern California during the very last stages. In all these different places I have encountered innumerable individuals and institutions who believed in the value of such an oxymoronic endeavour as writing the biography of an inanimate object and who pushed me forward through their support, help, advice and kindness. First and foremost is my adviser Catherine B. Asher of the Department of Art History at the University of Minnesota, whose brilliant teaching made it thinkable for me to pursue Islamic Art History as a scholar, whose own scholarship set standards of meticulous work, depth and nuance that I can only hope to have approached here, and whose unstinting support and wisdom as adviser I can only aspire to pay forward to my own students. Next to her, Fredrick M. Asher has always been another source of support, not only as an inspiring scholar and teacher, but also as a most effective administrator who would always find a small pot of money somewhere so as to make additional language training, conference attendance or other professional development activities feasible. Jane M. Blocker pushed me to think about the discipline of art history and the expressive qualities of writing beyond what I ever thought myself capable, and for that I will forever be grateful. Although I did not have the pleasure of studying under her, Amy Singer has been an excellent mentor and valuable friend, providing me with countless opportunities to develop my scholarship and to contribute to various shared endeavours.

The Department of Art History at the University of Minnesota was blessed with a wonderful cohort of graduate students during the time I spent there, and this book also owes a great debt of gratitude to them, whether it is because of sharing knowledge about Islamic Art History, about the exigencies of fieldwork, because of suffering together over seminar papers and grant applications, simply lending a sympathetic ear in difficult times, offering hospitality, or even taking over cat-sitting duties – foremost among them are Alisa Eimen, Jennifer Roberson, Jennifer Joffee, Hawon Kim and Kristy Phillips.

Dissertation research upon which this book is based was carried out with the financial support of the MacArthur Interdisciplinary Program on Global Change, Sustainability and Justice and of the William W. Stout Fellowship, both from the University of Minnesota. The eighteen months of research in Istanbul were both a trying and an enjoyable period, as I learned about the workings of Çemberlitaş Hamamı, navigated archives and libraries, and collected stacks of Ottoman documents. The biggest thanks are due to the managers of Çemberlitaş Hamamı, particularly Ruşen Baltacı. They patiently answered all my questions, showed me around and put up with my at first rudimentary Turkish speaking skills. The hamam attendants in the women's section adopted me, scrubbed me and fed me uncountable simits and glasses of tea, sustaining me emotionally as well as physically. The architect Halil Onur filled in many gaps in my knowledge and provided me with ground plans and examples from his rich collection of postcards and books. Ülkü Altindağ from the Topkapı Palace Archives generously extracted many precious documents from the stacks of the collection. The staff at the Prime Ministry's Archives and at the General Directorate of Endowments also provided me with their expertise. During the period of research, Hilal Kazan helped me greatly with finding literature, meeting scholars and translating Ottoman documents. Friends who made the research period enjoyable and productive include Boğaç Erozan and Ayşe Özbay, Tijana Krstic, Vera Constantini, Susan Francia, Richard Wittmann and Matthew Rascoff.

Dissertation writing was supported by a Doctoral Dissertation Fellowship from the University of Minnesota. At that time I also was a member of the Department of History at Istanbul Bilgi University, and I would like to thank Christoph Neumann, whose helpful comments can still be traced in the present text. Furthermore, I owe a debt of gratitude to the members of the Department of Art History at the University at Buffalo, New York, for their support during the last few months of dissertation writing and defence. A post-doctoral fellowship

Acknowledgements

at the Research Center for Anatolian Civilizations of Koç University, Istanbul, allowed me to conduct additional research and to take the first steps towards turning the dissertation into a monograph. At that juncture, Derin Terzioğlu generously shared with me her knowledge on the topic of biography in the Ottoman context. In the Department of Archaeology and History of Art at Koç University, I subsequently found myself surrounded by a most welcoming and supportive circle of colleagues, foremost among them Scott Redford, Günsel Renda and Lucienne Thys-Şenocak. They read through my writing, assisted with images and copyright permits, and propelled me forward with their sage advice. Scott Redford as the RCAC's director believed that a symposium on hamams would be a worthwhile endeavour, and was so trusting and kind as to hand over the organisationial reins to a very junior scholar. Aslı Niyazioğlu from the History Department provided valuable comments on the introduction, and Sooyong Kim from the the Department of English Language and Comparative Literature crucial assistance with translations of Ottoman poetry. Any mistakes are, of course, not their, but my own responsibility. Other cherished colleagues and friends at Koç University include Çiğdem Maner, Dikmen Bezmez and Suzan Yalman. Several graduate students assisted greatly in the last stages of the manuscript's preparation: Onur Engin, Yasemin Özarslan, Gonca Dardeniz and, especially, Sabiha Göloğlu. Sonja Sekely-Rowland from the Visual Resources Center at the University of California, Riverside, helped with her expertise on illustrations that were difficult to scan. Kent Schull as series editor was a great model of guidance as well as patience.

Finally, my deepest gratitude goes to close friends and family: Robert Cichocki, my father, who instilled a great love for travel, reading, language learning and Mediterranean cultures in me; Renate Cichocki, my mother, whose support has been indispensable; Lisa Cichocki, my sister, who has lent me her shoulder in dark moments and continues to believe in me; and Murat Ergin, my first husband – the book project may have outlasted our marriage, but his help with computers, digital cameras, transcribing interviews and translating texts from Turkish for the dissertation shall not be forgotten. Kiwi, Orzo, Biscuit, Hamsi and Miso occasionally took over the keyboard to contribute their own versions of the hamam's history, even if incomprehensible to humans, reminding me that there is life beyond books and computers. The last push to see the book through to completion was in no small way sustained by the affectionate love and unstinting generosity of my husband Milo Macaraig, whose indomitable spirit, boundless energy and sense of adventure continue to inspire me every single day.

Note on Transliteration

In an effort to make the present book easier to peruse for readers from outside the field of Islamic and Ottoman (Art) History, I have employed a transliteration system that approximates modern Turkish spelling, without indicating, for example, long vowels. However, where I have quoted from a previously published Turkish source text employing another transliteration system, that system has been kept.

Introduction

Do monuments have lives that justify writing down their life stories? And if they do, are their lives punctuated by events and structured by relationships, similar to human lives? Do they have an identity of their own, and does this identity change over time? This book has grown out of the desire to understand a particular monument, Çemberlitaş Hamamı in Istanbul, in its historical as well as its contemporary aspects, and the rich material collected and examined in this process – the architecture itself, archival documents, printed media, interviews and observations – suggests a resounding yes as answer to these questions. The hamam was never of the scale, magnificence or the legitimising power of either the Topkapı Palace or Süleyman the Magnificent's mosque complex, both of which are located within walking distance from the bathhouse. Yet it is exactly this relative modesty that permits the architectural historian to look beyond the building itself, into its complex relations with other monuments and humans, and to extend the timeframe of this study to the hamam's entire life span of more than four hundred years.

Located on the corner of the Divan Yolu – the main thoroughfare where now a stream of tourists wanders from the Hagia Sophia past travel agencies, souvenir shops and kebab restaurants towards the Covered Bazaar – and the small plaza around Constantine's Column, Çemberlitaş Hamamı today invites foreign visitors in search of the exotic and erotic as much as it invites Turkish visitors in search of a relaxing bath or an excursion into their own historical past (Figures I.1, I.2). As Istanbul has become a major tourist destination drawing visitors from around the world, the domes of Çemberlitaş Hamamı's dressing and bathing rooms resound with chatter in Turkish, English, German, French, Spanish, Italian, Japanese, Korean, Russian, Hebrew, Dutch and many other languages. For many tourists, the hamam visit is an activity fitted in between a visit to the whirling dervishes and the bazaar, into a hectic schedule meant to convey the splendour of a city whose name evokes the mysteries and pleasures of the Orient.

1

Figure I.1 Çemberlitaş Hamamı, 1583, Istanbul. *Source*: Author's photograph.

Çemberlitaş Hamamı's present role as a tourist attraction was certainly beyond the imagination of the monument's patron and architect. Nurbanu Sultan (*c.* 1525–1583), wife to Sultan Selim II and mother to Sultan Murad III, commissioned the imperial workshop under the direction of the Ottoman master architect Sinan (*c.* 1490–1588) to erect the bath, and Çemberlitaş Hamamı began to render services to the neighbourhood around Constantine's Column and the Atik Ali Paşa Mosque in late 1583 or 1584. With little modification in the actual bathing procedure, it has continued to provide service over the centuries. Yet its role and context have experienced numerous changes. During the fifteenth and sixteenth centuries, while the Ottoman Empire (1299–1922) was expanding and solidifying its power base, concerns about imperial legitimacy and the need to create economic and infrastructural networks motivated hamam construction. These concerns and needs also accounted for their particular manner of administration through pious endowments. The quest for a centralised fiscal policy in the wake of early modernisation efforts in the eighteenth century had the paradoxical effect of de-centralising hamam administration by allowing semi-private ownership for financial gains. The reformers of the Tanzimat period (1839–1876), in their zeal for transforming Turkish society and lifestyle and Istanbul's urban fabric, relegated bathhouses to a status insignificant and old-fashioned in comparison with the construction of wide boulevards connecting plazas around Byzantine

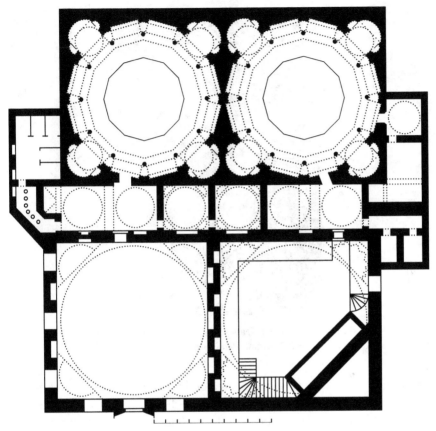

Figure I.2 Ground plan of Çemberlitaş Hamamı. *Source*: Sabiha Göloğlu, after Glück, *Probleme des Wölbungsbaues*, 1921.

monuments. With the establishment of the Turkish Republic in 1922, hamams as emblems of an old, non-Western lifestyle, were sometimes even deliberately destroyed and only survived by finding new functions.

Tourism has become one of the foremost functions that ensured the baths' survival, turning them into a locality to be marketed to foreign visitors in a global economy. The tourists' perceptions, in turn, have been shaped by the imaginative descriptions of travel writers past and present;[1] by the Orientalist paintings of Jean-Léon Gerôme and Jean-Auguste-Dominique Ingres (Figures I.3, I.4), for whom bathing scenes presented a most convenient pretext to display beautiful female forms in the nude; and by films such as *Steam* (1997) by the Turkish-Italian director Ferzan Özpetek (Figure I.5). Today, the bathhouse has become so emblematic of the Orient that most tourists enter Çemberlitaş Hamamı (or any other hamam) with a host of preconceived notions and expectations.

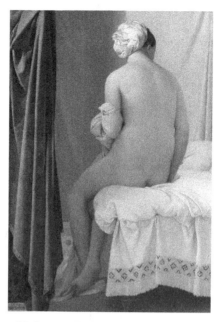

Figure I.3 *The Bather of Valpinçon,* Jean-August-Dominique Ingres, oil on canvas, 1808, Musée du Louvre. © RMN-Grand Palais/Art Resource, New York.

Accordingly, a full experience of authentic Turkish culture requires the sensuous bathing pleasure generally denied by their own culture, but emphasised by the other, exotic culture. When interviewing foreign tourists, I frequently asked why they visited the bath, and the lapidary remark of a New Zealander summarises the imperative nature of the hamam visit on a trip to Turkey: '[Visiting a hamam] is the thing to do when you are in Turkey. They have a famous reputation.'[2] While tourists come to enjoy the famous baths, some Turkish visitors today perceive the hamam as a repository of cultural identity and frame it as a representative example of 'our Ottoman heritage'. Thus, rather than possessing intrinsic, unchanging qualities and meanings, Turkish baths and bathing culture have assumed different and sometimes competing or conflicting identities with every major cultural transformation, as is exemplified in the life story of Çemberlitaş Hamamı.

Before delving further into the history and historiography of the bathhouse, it will be necessary to situate the term and the concept of the hamam.[3] The Turkicised word hamam, which I will use here, derives from the Arabic حمّام (ḥammām), meaning a bath, swimming pool, bathroom, bathhouse, spa or even watering place. The Arabic noun, in turn, derives from the verb حمّ (ḥamm), meaning to heat or to make hot.[4] The Arabic

Figure I.4 *The Bath,* Jean-Léon Gerôme, oil on canvas, 1880–1885, Fine Arts Museums of San Francisco, Mildred Anna Williams Collection. © Fine Arts Museum of San Francisco.

terminology thus suggests that a bathhouse is primarily qualified by the availability of hot water and a heated building. What makes a bathhouse Islamic, however, is a specific combination of a building dedicated to communal bathing, heated water and the religious requirement to ritually cleanse the body before entering a mosque. With the spread of Islam, the institution of the bathhouse migrated to virtually all regions of the Islamic

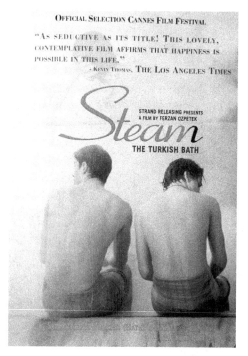

Figure I.5 Film poster of *Steam,* directed by Ferzan Özpetek, 1997. Artwork in the public domain.

world, from the Arab heartlands to Andalusia in the west and to Iran and the Indian Subcontinent in the east. This wide geographical distribution has diversified the concept of the hamam: as the various regions in the Sunni Islamic world adhere to four different rites, divergent requirements about canonical cleanliness account for the existence or absence of an immersion pool, for example. Where thermal water is available, bathhouses often include a sizeable pool to allow the bathers to soak; however, soaking in thermal water does not fulfil the criteria for canonical cleanliness according to the Hanefi rite prevalent in Turkey and Central Asia.[5] Linguistically, both Ottoman and modern Turkish clearly distinguish between a thermal spa (*kaplıca* or *ılıca*) and a bathhouse (hamam). Also, climatic differences determine the use of hot or cold water. In India's sweltering heat hamams mostly provided a cooling effect,[6] but some of the twelfth- and thirteenth-century baths in Anatolia – with its grim winter climate – had only hot running water.[7] The synonymous, but erroneous, usage of the name 'Turkish Bath' for hamams is to be attributed to foreign travel writers dating back to the sixteenth century, who collapsed ethnic and religious categories (to turn Turk meant to convert to Islam) and popularised the

6

hamam in Europe as something essentially Turkish. Ottomans themselves would not have described Çemberlitaş Hamamı in such ethnic terms, particularly because the word 'Turk' was considered derogatory (meaning provincial, uncivilised, ignorant) until the rise of Turkish nationalism in the nineteenth century. The term 'Turkish Bath', therefore, is problematic: if used in the travel writers' sense, it is Orientalist; if used in an ethnic or nationalist sense, it projects a nineteenth-century concept back onto previous centuries.

Hamams have long been prominent in the popular imagination, and coffee-table books treat the topic frequently, because of its 'exotic' and 'tantalising' nature.[8] Until recently, only few scholars have given these monuments the serious attention they deserve, especially when compared with the output on other historical monuments, such as mosques and palaces, even though interest has grown as the number of recent survey monographs, exhibitions, symposia and research projects suggests.[9] The number of recently restored hamams even within Istanbul – among them the Kılıç Ali Paşa Hamamı, the Küçük Mustafa Paşa Hamamı and the hamam of Bayezid II – also presents encouraging signs of a new appreciation. The latter monument has even been transformed into the country's first hamam museum, opening its doors in 2015.[10] Still, the volume of scholarly output is in stark contrast to the attention that has always been lavished on the bathing culture of Classical Antiquity.[11]

Literature on historical Islamic baths and bathing culture divides itself into four different strands. The first consists of empirical scholarship, often based on the archaeological and architectural examination of physical remains, resulting in monographic articles and books on the hamam architecture of a specific city or region. The earlier among these focused on the major civilisational centres and core regions of the Islamic world, such as Cairo, Damascus and Palestine, offering foundational surveys while at the same time devoting some space to a general interpretative treatment of their origins, usage, cultural significance and so forth.[12] Later studies of this kind also turned to regions that lie outside the Islamic heartlands and therefore may be considered more 'peripheral' to the history of Islamic architecture, such as Spain, Hungary and Greece.[13] A second strand of hamam scholarship may be termed text-centric, as it rests on a variety of textual sources – narrative, archival and legal – in order to understand the socio-cultural, religious and/or urban aspects of the monuments as they will be discussed in Chapter 4. A classic, often-cited example of this type is Heinz Grotzfeld's cultural history of the medieval Arab bathhouse based on an unpublished fifteenth-centuy manuscript, the *Kitab al-Hammamat* by Yusuf Abdalhadi.[14] Moreover, using archival sources, the eminent social historian André Raymond has contributed a large number of articles on the locations, furnishings, expenses and similar dimensions of hamams in the Arab-speaking world.[15] In contrast, Mohammed Hocine Benkheira has based his substantial study of nudity and moral order in medieval hamams on legal traditions as produced by the ulema.[16]

The third group of studies concerns sets of bathhouses or single monuments, with the aim of facilitating a greater understanding of cultural, social, urban, economic and religious changes, as well as architectural and artistic developments during the early Islamic centuries. These mostly discuss the rather unusual and outstanding examples of the bathhouses that form part of the so-called Umayyad desert castles,[17] to be discussed in Chapter 1 as Çemberlitaş Hamamı's ancestors. Foremost stands Oleg Grabar's discussion of these monuments, within the narrower framework of excavation reports, as well as in his ground-breaking *The Formation of Islamic Art*, which presents a broader perspective.[18] Following in his footsteps, Robert Hamilton examined the construction of Khirbat al-Mafjar, with particular attention given to the excesses of its patron, the Umayyad Caliph Walid II.[19] Most recently, Garth Fowden's thorough examination of Qusayr Amra, an eighth-century Syrian desert castle that includes a conspicuously decorated bathhouse, has shown the role of Romano-Byzantine culture in the formation of Arab bathing traditions.[20] Widening the focus from one to several monuments, Lara Tohme has also investigated the socio-political context of Umayyad Syrian baths in terms of the interplay between late Antique and early Islamic culture.[21]

A fourth strand of scholarship on the Islamic bathhouse emerges from the work of practising architects who are involved in the restoration of hamams and/or urban renewal schemes that include such monuments. Often, such restoration projects include some research to provide an ethnographic viewpoint of contemporary usage, as well as much needed historical context and depth; however, this research often remains wedded to a very practice-oriented perspective and is not always delegated to a historian who would be able to mine the existing archival and narrative sources. The papers guest-edited by Magda Sibley and published in a special issue of the *International Journal of Architectural Research* – the outcome of the EU-funded research project HAMMAM (Hammam, Aspects and Multidisciplinary Methods of Analysis for the Mediterranean Region), conducted under the auspices of the Vienna Institute of Urban Sustainability between 2005 and 2008 and focusing on the adaptive reuse of bathhouses[22] – exemplify such a perspective.[23] Overall, the literature on Islamic bathhouses appears to remain relatively stagnant at its core, with a limited number of surveys on their architecture and cultural dimensions in the Islamic heartlands continuing to provide the cornerstone around which new surveys in other locales are added.[24] Efforts to produce an authoritative account of hamams throughout the Islamic world are not forthcoming – maybe rightly so, given the enormous diversity of forms and practices, as well as the expansive knowledge of contexts and languages required. Yet one may also argue that this diversity and need for skills impossible to unite in a single scholar has not prevented the making of such an edited book on the contemporary mosque.[25]

The very first extensive scholarly investigation of Ottoman hamams dates to 1921, when the Viennese art historian Heinrich Glück published his typology and catalogue of Istanbul's bathhouses, meant to be part of a larger study on the development of vaulted architecture.[26] Based on the frequency with which he is cited, Glück's work still seems to be the canonical work on the topic. Unfortunately, in spite of its value as a first attempt to catalogue hamams, it contains many factual errors and reflects the Orientalist assumptions of its time.[27] In 1927, Karl Klinghardt followed in Glück's footsteps, proposing a chronology based on the evolution of ground plan types.[28]

Hamams in the geographical region of present-day Turkey have been the subject of art historical studies by Ahmet Süheyl Ünver, Yılmaz Önge and Semavi Eyice. Leaving aside his innumerable contributions to the popular press, Ünver's scholarly writing on hamams is commendable for his inclusion of Ottoman archival records. While Önge was particularly interested in the Seljuk era and in technical details,[29] Eyice has contributed numerous articles and encyclopaedia entries on Ottoman hamams and established a now widely accepted and reproduced formalist typology.[30] Likewise, he was the first historian of Ottoman architecture to go beyond an architectural survey and the historical context by examining the perception and treatment of Istanbul's bathhouses during the early twentieth century, based on newspaper articles and oral sources on neglect and demolition up to the 1950s.[31] A most valuable guide for the study of Istanbul's hamams is Mehmet Nermi Haskan's survey, representing the state of knowledge about each of the about 150 bathhouses at the time of its publication.[32]

Another body of literature relevant to the study of bathhouses is that of material culture and everyday life in the Ottoman Empire. This area has only recently begun to receive systematic investigation, and the few major publications that do exist treat hamams in a rather anecdotal manner.[33] Cengiz Kırlı's sophisticated study of late eighteenth- and early nineteenth-century Istanbul coffee houses as a site of sociability and confrontation between state and society examines one aspect of everyday life that shows significant parallels to public baths in terms of their place within the Istanbulites' practices of daily life.[34] Several edited volumes based on annual symposia on material culture have begun to treat topics such as food and drink, textiles, animals and reading culture in the depth they deserve;[35] it is to be hoped that water and body hygiene will one day appear on the agenda as well.

Given the central place that the hamam occupied in Ottoman culture and everyday life, why has it been largely ignored by historians of all stripes and colours? The nature of the relevant primary sources partially answers this question. Although the Ottoman bureaucracy has left us with what the Ottoman historian Amy Singer has called 'not a paper trail but rather a superhighway of documentation', there is a surprising dearth within that wealth of archival documents and narrative sources.[36] It seems that Ottomans took the hamam for granted, so much so that chroniclers and writers of narrative accounts rarely ever felt compelled to comment on it in detail. Archival records of charitable foundations – such as endowment deeds, accounting books and correspondence regarding repairs – and registers concerning prices and guild members provide rich quantitative data on social and economic aspects, but these tease rather than satisfy the historian wishing to reconstruct a history of baths that also encompasses their meanings.[37]

A second reason for the hitherto limited interest in the scholarly study of bathhouses might be found in the very fact that it figures so strongly in the popular imagination. Historians writing about bathhouses, then, might fear to participate in and perpetuate the Orientalist discourse about their exotic attraction, rather than contribute to its demise. One would hope, however, that more scholarly attention will help to demystify the hamam and its practices and rituals. Third, even if studies on Ottoman architecture in general and hamams in particular have greatly increased in number, there are still many more monuments that appear more worthy of study than hamams of lesser aesthetic value. Thus, the topic falls between two chairs: on the one hand, architectural historians turn their attention rather to mosques, palaces, mausolea and the like; on the other hand, few social and economic historians are equipped to interpret architecture.[38] Finally, studying a hamam that continues in use brings its own challenges, whether it is the fogged-up camera lenses in a hot room, the inaccessibility of rooms used by the opposite gender, or interviewees embarrassed to talk about a topic as private as washing.

The rich extant record employed to reconstruct the life story of Çemberlitaş Hamamı falls into several distinct categories that largely mirror its history's chronological periodisation. Inscribed on paper as well as in stone and dating to the first five years of its existence (1583–1588), the early textual record tells us of its establishment and initial operation. As Çemberlitaş Hamamı was built to generate revenue for Nurbanu Sultan's charitable foundation, the endowment deed (*vakıfname*) specifying the stipulations allows us a glimpse of the extensive network of buildings and economic and social relations of which this specific bathhouse was an important part at a particular moment in time.[39] While the endowment mentions the bathhouse only in a characteristically brief fashion and as a matter of course, the architectural inscription over the entrance is more descriptive. It advertises to hamam visitors and passers-by the building's imperial status and pleasant qualities in Ottoman-Turkish verse. A number of decrees issued by the imperial council (*mühimme*) concern the initial supply of water and firewood.[40]

A large number of accounting books dating to roughly the first century of the bath's operation – that is, to between 1596/7 and 1671 – make up a second group of documents that relates financial details, particularly the rent amounts.[41] At the same time, the accounting books put these numbers into the larger economic context of the charitable foundation. A register dating to 1640 and specifying officially fixed prices for certain consumer goods and service fees, in turn, helps to contextualise the rent amount in relation to the bathing fees in the middle of the seventeenth century.[42] Another group of accounting documents dating to between 1823 and 1833 proved to be particularly useful in juxtaposition to earlier financial records in order to observe fluctuations in the relation between total endowment income and rent amount.[43] Also relevant to the business operation is a register drawn up in 1751/2 to identify all male bath attendants and servants working in greater Istanbul, documenting the number, names and origins of Çemberlitaş Hamamı's employees and setting the scale of the business in perspective to other bathhouses.[44]

The third era in the history of Çemberlitaş Hamamı (and a distinct era in the history of Istanbul's bathhouses in general) was heralded by an imperial decree dating to 1768/9. This decree prohibited any further construction of baths in the city in order to preserve water and firewood.[45] From then on, no new bathhouses could be added to the admittedly already large number of establishments; thus, the maintenance of the existing buildings carried a greater significance. Coincidentally, the middle of the eighteenth century was a period of major seismic activity underneath Istanbul, and the badly repaired inscription in Çemberlitaş Hamamı's hot room in the men's section, dated to 1770, attests to the earthquakes' consequences. The number of documents referring to repair and renovation activities from 1786 to 1805 indicate that by the eighteenth century the constant wear and tear, the fires and earthquakes had started to take a toll on the building's fabric.[46]

I have not been able to find reference to Çemberlitaş Hamamı in documents kept in the archives after 1833, and it appears that the nineteenth century with its major socio-political re-organisations also constituted a fourth separate, transformative period in the life of the bath. The available sources now shift from handwritten to printed ones, such as the *Mecelle-i Umûr-ı Belediyye* (the records of proceedings of the Commission for Road Improvement) and newspaper articles.[47] As a result of the introduction of the Latin alphabet in 1928/9 and the subsequent government investment in literacy campaigns and education, the period after the 1930s saw a steep rise in the number of newspapers and popular magazines. The numerous articles on hamams published in these venues afford us insight into the perceptions and issues surrounding the role of the bathhouse in a society struggling to redefine itself as part of Western civilisation and a participant in modernity.[48]

As one would expect, the sources available for the last few decades of the twentieth century up to the present have increased exponentially both in volume and number of media, due mostly to the effects of global as well as local tourism. Çemberlitaş Hamamı and other bathhouses have been featured countless times in articles in foreign and Turkish newspapers and magazines,[49] on postcards, and in film and television.[50] The worldwide web has given the hamam managers the opportunity to represent Çemberlitaş Hamamı to a multinational audience.[51] Most importantly, the managers, employees and visitors of the bathhouse have generously offered their stories, memories, recollections and opinions about the recent past and the present. By observing and participating in the daily interactions between those working and bathing in the hamam, between foreigners and locals, between the building's users and its architecture, I have collected rich ethnographic texts.[52]

In addition to textual sources, the visual record so vital for art historical study also has much to offer. Obviously, the building itself is the most durable record, carrying the visible traces of its history on its body and face. Before the nineteenth century, only one single image can help us understand its original appearance and urban context and see the monument through the eyes of an Ottoman architect-engineer and/or painter.[53] With the much more facile and widespread printing of illustrated travel books and the emergence of photography and postcards, the representations of the bathhouse multiplied rapidly in the nineteenth century.[54] Similar to the chronological and thematic distribution of textual sources, the number of images and maps documenting the hamam's subsequent life periods is comparatively higher, as newspaper and magazine articles, coffee-table books and websites all include photographs and drawings. The quality and quantity of visual sources thus parallels those of the textual sources to a great extent, supporting the periodisation of the hamam's history into distinct life stations. Certainly, such a periodisation is contingent on the circumstances of research. More often than not, these circumstances reflect the researcher's abilities and predilections and include unfortunate failures to locate specific items, as well as happy coincidences.[55]

What began as an organisational tool to construct a chronological framework around the many documents I had collected soon became an avenue to consider a number of methodological questions: how far can archival documents and even material remains adequately encapsulate the multitude of forces, events and human actors that have made the hamam into what it is today? How can one trust the documentary value of archival documents when they themselves may be fiction – facts shaped into stories, true or untrue, about the progress of construction, about the disbursement and circulation of money for repair costs, about arguments between business partners, by Ottoman officials for a readership of other Ottoman officials? How can one craft a historical narrative around the documents and the material evidence, a narrative that at the same time does justice to the hamam's rich history and makes the fictional character both of its own and of the archival documents transparent?

The genre of history writing that seems most suitable to answer these questions and that therefore has inspired the present study is the biographical memoir (in Ottoman Turkish, *tezkere*). Hayden White has suggested that histories are about sets of events that historians put into relationship to each other; historians present these relationships in certain modes (myth, scientific knowledge, religion, literary art) and certain plot structures present in their own cultures.[56] Thus, historical narratives point towards both the set of events they intend to convey and the story type that the historian has chosen to structure the events. In selecting to tell the history of Çemberlitaş Hamamı in a form inspired by Ottoman *tezkere*s, my goal is to let the structure of an Ottoman mode of narrative history writing point towards the set of events that constitute the bath's history.

Grounding her discussion of the different biographies of a sixteenth-century Ottoman mystic, Aslı Niyazioğlu points out that:

> [b]iographical writing is always an exercise grounded in changing historical contexts. As new influences shape our perceptions of past figures, earlier biographies become inadequate. Since what we want to know does not equal what we have been told or how we want to say it, we produce new biographies

13

compatible with our new expectations. Along with these historical developments, personal experiences, affinities, and antipathies also influence the biographer.[57]

At this point, I should clarify that my own culture is not that of an Ottoman, but rather of a US-educated art historian with European roots, trained to work in the mode of a certain academic discourse and marked by a personal predilection for life stories. I do not presume to be able to sustain the historical idiom of a *tezkere* without breaking style or annoying readers less partial to flowery Ottoman-inspired prose; rather, paragraphs in the idiom of Ottoman memoirs will mark the beginning of each chapter.

One could argue that the plot structure of a life story or biography is not specifically Ottoman, but that it indeed characterises the history and literature of all of humanity, since the time span of a human being is one of the most universal and convenient units to measure and organise time. Historians and chroniclers have compared the life spans of empires and dynasties with those of individuals, in terms of gowth (rise), maturity ('golden age'), and decline and death (fall).[58] Writing the biographies of great men is as old as the exploit of writing history itself, whether to seek patterns and coherence in the individual life or to present models worthy of emulation. Indeed, the beginnings of the academic discipline of art history dates to the publication of the Florentine humanist Giorgio Vasari's *Lives* of Italian artists in 1550, which celebrated individual genius-artists and their achievements.[59] The biographical format has thus become an almost ubiquitous paradigm to organise art historical knowledge, whether in the form of the artist biography, the catalogue raisonnée or the solo exhibition of the individual artist's oeuvre.

In the Muslim Middle East, the biographical dictionary (*tabaqat*) emerged as a key genre in the ninth century, as part of the effort to evaluate the accuracy of information on the earliest period of Islam through verification of the transmitters' life dates. Soon the genre was extended to treat specific groups of people, from scholars and saints to poets and notables.[60] As heirs to both classical Islamic and Persianate literary traditions, Ottoman authors embraced the biographical format wholeheartedly, even if they did so comparatively late.[61] It was only in 1538 that Sehi of Edirne compiled the first Ottoman biographical dictionary, called *Heşt Bihişt* (*Eight Gardens*, in reference to the eight groups of biographical subjects discussed), establishing an Ottoman literary genre that lasted until the empire's demise. The biographic genre did not remain limited to Ottoman poets, as exemplified by Aşık Çelebi's *Meşa'ir aş-Şuara*, compiled in 1569.[62] The writing of official history equally utilised the life of the sultans as an organising principle in chronicling events.[63] The historian Mustafa Âli, in his *Künhü'l-Ahbâr* (*Essence of History*), expanded the use of the genre by including systematic biographies of the most important personages of the age at the end of each account of a sultan's reign.[64] Even if not explicitly preoccupied with the production of life narratives, other Ottoman literary genres also included biographic elements and provide fruitful source material for the historian interested in matters beyond official political and military events. Among them count the *menakıbname* (vitae of individual mystics),[65] the *seyahatname* (book of travels),[66] the captivity narrative,[67] self-reflexive diaries of Sufi mystics,[68] and the treatise (*risale*).[69]

In spite of this wealth of sources either of a biographical nature or containing information that facilitates the writing of biographies, few Ottoman historians have taken up this format to structure their own writing. Surprisingly few sultans have been the subject of a book-length study of their life.[70] Derin Terzioğlu has suggested that the lack of biographical studies is the result of two tendencies: first, Orientalist notions about individuality – or better the lack thereof – in the Muslim Middle East have precluded the scholarly attention that historians have given to Europeans from all walks of life, from kings and queens to millers and prostitutes; second, historians of the Ottoman Empire have emphasised the centrality and authority of the state and its power to absorb individuals into a larger, collective identity to the point of losing sight of the individual.[71] To these two I would like to add a third point: the nature of the sources and the dearth of information within a wealth of documentation that I have already addressed above. While there do exist personal writings, and still more are certain to surface in manuscript libraries, the overwhelming majority of biographical sources present themselves as lapidary lists of life dates and public offices that do not afford much insight into the individual as a human being. Little information is available on Ottoman experiences of childhood and early character formation, as Ottoman individuals achieved their place in society not so much by dint of their family origin, but through a complex mixture of geographic, linguistic, confessional and marital ties, as well as education and physical appearance. Foremost within this mixture stand the merits and offices accumulated during one's professional career; they constituted one of the most defining features of one's personality and individuality.[72]

A case in point is the structure and content of the five versions of the autobiographical notes of Sinan, the imperial architect who built Çemberlitaş Hamamı. In the later years of his life, he dictated these notes to a close friend, the poet-painter Mustafa Sai, so that we now have three draft versions preserved in the archives of the Topkapı Palace – the *Untitled Treatise* (*Adsız Risale*), the *Treatise on Architecture* (*Risâletü'l-Mi'mâriyye*) and the *Gift of Architects* (*Tuhfetü'l-Mi'mârîn*) – and two edited versions that circulated among the public– the *Biographical Memoir of Construction* (*Tezkîretü'l-Bünyân*) and the *Biographical Memoir of Buildings* (*Tezkîretü'l-Ebniyye*).[73] Each treatise is structured into three sections: (a) a brief biographical section describing the architect's recruitment, initial training and military career; (b) a section on his achievements as chief architect; and (c) a section listing his monuments in groups according to building types. To go behind the façade of Sinan's official persona requires a careful reading between the lines, an exercise masterfully demonstrated in Gülru Necipoğlu's *The Age of Sinan*.[74] The genre of biographical dictionaries of poets, however, is somewhat less stinting in its details, as the categories describing the poets and their oeuvre encompass many more sections, even if these are often presented rather briefly: (a) geographical origin; (b) ancestry; (c) birth and death; (d) education and teachers; (e) profession and career; (f) character and physical appearance; (g) additional biographical, anecdotal and incidental material; (h) literary activities; and (i) poetic citations.[75] These categories tell us much about how Ottomans conceptualised stations and shifts in the individual's life cycle, her or his defining characteristics, and achievements. Therefore, they provide a useful framework for what needs to be included in the life story of Çemberlitaş Hamamı.

This type of organisation of biographical material into categories clearly distinguishes Middle Eastern life narratives from Western autobiographies with their propensity towards linear narration in chronological order. As Dwight Reynolds has noted about pre-modern Arab life writing, the primary format for communicating information concerning human life was through categorisation and enumeration. Rather than introducing chapters that correspond to major developments and shifts in the subject's life, auto/biographers divided their texts according to rational criteria, such as full years, or according to thematic organisation, such as family history, teachers, publications and so forth.[76] The organisation of the present work will reflect these intellectual techniques to a certain extent. The chapters and sections refer to the categories found in Ottoman *tezkere* works and present a kaleidoscopic mix that supports the meta-narrative in a slightly askew manner, a manner that allows the arbitrariness of chapter divisions as well as the chaos, abruptness and indeterminacy of life to transpire.

Chapter 1 will discuss the patron, Nurbanu Sultan, and the architect, Mimar Sinan, as well as the ancestry of Çemberlitaş Hamamı, in terms of the formal origins of the architectural type of the bathhouse, from its ancient Greek and Roman over Early Islamic to Seljuk and Early Ottoman forebears. The family context in which the monument operated – that is, the extensive mosque complex that was funded by the charitable endowment that Nurbanu Sultan established, together with the other three endowed hamams – are the subject of Chapter 2. Chapter 3 then focuses on the birth or construction of the physical building and its water supply, and the various elements required to make the bathhouse into a successful business and breadwinner generating income for the endowment: the managers, attendants, servants and customers. Moreover, it examines in detail the economic history of this monument based on accounting books preserved in the archives. Chapter 4 considers the many different identities that Çemberlitaş Hamamı united within its physical space under the categories of religious, social, sexual, medical and urban significance. The successful operation of the bathhouse, together with Istanbul's frequent natural disasters in the form of fires and earthquakes, over time caused much wear and tear, necessitating repairs and renovation work. Chapter 5 takes up this aspect of the monument's history under the heading 'In Sickness and in Health'. As Çemberlitaş Hamamı aged while life in the Ottoman Empire underwent dizzying economic, administrative, political and social changes and finally gave way to the Turkish Republic, the monument also acquired a new identity as an emblem of Ottoman heritage, as discussed in Chapter 6. The final chapter will pick up the theme of heritagisation within the context of the more recent global phenomenon of tourism and the local phenomenon of Ottomania, which, due to a new-found appreciation, account for Çemberlitaş Hamamı's second spring. Particular attention is paid to the narratives of the different groups of people visiting and operating the hamam, from century-old Orientalist notions shaping tourists' experiences, over the employees' economic concerns, to the hamam managers' efforts to create experiences inclusive of both foreign and locals' expectations. The Epilogue will give a brief overview of developments in Turkey and Istanbul within the last few years and consider their implications.

As with any conceptual model, there are several points of criticism that could and should be raised against it, and I would be remiss if I did not enumerate some of them. Any biography or life story presupposes the existence of a *bios*, an animate being. Is it appropriate to impose the metaphor of the human life span onto inanimate objects and to anthropomorphise them? If I indeed err in doing so, I will not have erred alone, as many thought-provoking studies have laid the foundations upon which I build. In an essay on how commodities are produced not only materially, but also culturally, Igor Kopytoff has posed questions about objects, which in the field of anthropology are usually asked about human subjects:

> What, sociologically, are the biographical possibilities inherent in its 'status' and in the period and culture, and how are these possibilities realised? Where does the thing come from and who made it? What has been its career so far, and what do people consider an ideal career for such things? What are the recognized 'ages' or periods in the thing's life, and what are the cultural markers for them? How does the thing's use change with its age, and what happens to it when it reaches the end of its usefulness?[77]

While these questions lend themselves to studying any kind of material object, whether in the historical or social sciences, it is in particular European post-processual archaeologists who over the past decades have taken up Kopytoff's approach, repeatedly re-evaluated and expanded upon it. For instance, the express aim of a special issue of *World Archaeology* on *The Cultural Biography of Objects* was to 'address the way social interactions involving people and objects create meaning', predicated on 'the central idea . . . that, as people and objects gather time, movement and change, they are constantly transformed, and these transformations of person and object are tied up with each other'.[78] These social interactions, as Gosden and Marshall point out in their lead essay, can harbour tremendous variety – such as gifting, commodity exchange, recontextualisation in a colonial or museal context, rediscovery and reinterpretation – which in turn requires a panoply of theoretical and conceptual approaches relevant to each object under study. In a follow-up essay published a decade later, Jody Joy emphasised once again that the 'biographical approach provides a method to reveal relationships between people and objects' – relationships that have been referred to as 'entangled'[79] – but admitted that a comprehensive life history of a single object has rarely been attempted.[80] In the field of art history, two works that examine in greater depth the life story of art objects and monuments while paying ample attention to the people–object relations enveloping them come to mind here: in *Lives of Indian Images*, Richard Davis combines Kopytoff's seminal questions with the Hindu theological postulate that religious images *are* animate beings, even after people cease to worship them.[81] More recently, Paul Stephenson has employed the term 'cultural biography' to enframe his cross-civilisational history of the Ancient Greek Serpent Column on Istanbul's Hippodrome, located in walking distance from Çemberlitaş Hamamı – a study he qualifies as a combination of a cultural and reception history.[82]

Although Ottomans did not conceive of their architecture as animate beings that needed to be fed, bathed and clothed (as Hindu devotional images require), in their poetic imagination they sometimes liken buildings to persons. Vildan Serdaroğlu has provided convincing evidence that the three main figures in sixteenth-century Ottoman poetry – lover, beloved and rival – were often described with the help of architectural metaphors. In her own words:

> the beloved was metaphorically associated with sacred and well-proportioned monuments. Physical properties of the beloved, which are often the starting point in Ottoman poetry, resemble elements of the mosque complex in shape and meaning. His or her face resembles a mihrab with golden inscriptions on it. His or her body is tall and grand like a minaret. Likewise he or she is a hospital that provides healing for those who are sick with love, etc. The lover, too, is likened to architectural objects: his eyes, like a fountain, never cease flowing; his heart is a palace in which the sultan (the beloved) lives.[83]

Such imaginative likening of persons to monuments applied not only to love poetry. In his *Hevesname* (1493/4), the court poet Cafer Çelebi wrote about the Hagia Sophia in the following way:

> Although there are like [him] sacred temples
> [and] holy mosques with high domes
> [Hagia Sophia] is *the most victorious shah of them all*
> the prayer niche is his crown and throne[84]

Müstakimzade, in his account of a calligrapher's career, repeated this metaphor of the monument as an eminent leader among all mosques, when he described the calligrapher's workplace as the Hagia Sophia 'which is the commander of all mosques'.[85] Both of these two authors employ the metaphor of the exalted ruler, of the shah and of the commander, respectively, in order to convey the status of the Hagia Sophia as the foremost monument and place of worship in the imperial capital. By doing so, they imbue the building with a personality and an identity that was immediately recognisable to all Ottoman subjects: that of the Ottoman ruler.[86]

As for bathhouses, according to Serdaroğlu, Ottomans imagined them to be representative of the lover's condition, burning on the inside and crying constantly (that is, dripping water). The poet Zati's verses illustrate such a metaphor:

> Zati lies there like a hammam, with his eyes fixed on the sky,
> Burning inside like the bath-furnace with the fire of separation.[87]

Also, one of the present hamam managers in a personal conversation compared the hamam with a demanding woman who constantly needs maintenance and does not take kindly to any kind of negligence. However, I argue that it is not so much an interior and essential form of *bios* that makes Çemberlitaş Hamamı come alive; rather, it has come alive through the physical, mental and symbolic interaction of its users with its material structure, through forever changing social processes, experiences and understandings. And the life story approach allows us to see these contextual shifts in the use and meaning of monuments over time, privileging neither the past nor the present to the exclusion of the other.

Another point of criticism has to do with the argument that the genre of biography presupposes individuals that, as defined in eighteenth-century European Enlightenment thinking and celebrated by Romantic movements throughout Europe and America in the early nineteenth century, are conscious of themselves and their role as maker of their own universe. Hence, it may appear that the biographic model imposes upon the Ottoman context a concept that is not only anachronistic, but also culturally inappropriate, since Orientalist discourse has long denied the existence of such individuals in the East, claiming that the collective superseded the individual there. However, the extensive body of biographical and autobiographical writings from the Muslim Middle East predating European Enlightenment reports the falsity of a universal notion of the individual, and it is now well accepted that concepts of self-identity and individuality are historically constituted in language and society.[88] As long as the concept of the individual that underlies this biography originates from an Ottoman context, its usage here should pose no problems.

How, then, can we define the *homo Ottomanicus*? For obvious reasons, this rather essentialist question cannot be fully answered here, given that the expansive empire with a life span of seven centuries housed millions of persons belonging to different communities and undergoing transformations of self even within their own lifetimes. This diversity also emerges in one of the first publications to take in hand the idea of a *homo Ottomanicus*, which contains mostly portraits of specific individuals and smaller groups, such as the family Benakis, the Swiss community in Istanbul or a Kurdish emir.[89] By means of an 'anatomy' of one individual case, Maurits von den Boogert has attempted to define more concrete criteria, both constant and variable, for a more general concept of Ottoman identity:

A typical Ottoman was a man or a woman who was born in the Ottoman Empire and whose parents were Ottoman subjects, and who permanently resided in the Ottoman Empire. She or he could have had any of a number of skin colors ... Our model Ottoman belonged to one of the Empire's many confessional groups and spoke at least one of the Empire's many languages as his or her mother tongue. 'The' Ottoman also paid taxes to the imperial treasury.[90]

A more comprehensive and at the same time nuanced discussion and analysis in a chronological fashion can be found in *Living in the Ottoman Realm: Empire and Identity, 13th to 20th Centuries*, since its scope and breadth of contributions allows for giving ample space to the empire's diversity and longevity, and the specific political, social and cultural contexts.[91]

A few broad strokes may provide a sketch of the different possibilities of Ottoman self-definition, as they have been outlined also in these recent contributions. The most important way in which Ottomans formed their own identities and self-perceptions was in relation to others, in what Rhoads Murphey has called the reciprocal mode.[92] In this, Ottomans did not much differ from their European counterparts, as scholars now agree that complete autonomy is impossible. Even autonomous individuals do not emerge in isolation and need others to assert that they are apart from them; hence, identity is by necessity relational.[93] Ottomans defined themselves in relation to many types of 'other', encompassing concepts, groups and individuals. The resulting categories constituted pinpoints or circles of identity that, far from being static, could overlap, expand, contract or even disappear, and we should be mindful that our present categories may have made little sense to the people whom we study.[94] In the case of male Muslims, for example, these included such diverse possibilities as: God; the Ottoman Empire with its state apparatus;[95] the sultan and his family and officers; the region in which they had been born; the region, city and neighbourhood in which they lived;[96] their religious community, which could be as large as the House of Islam and as restricted as the people with whom they regularly prayed in the neighbourhood mosque, or the Sufi order where they practised mystic rituals;[97] their occupational group, often a guild, but sometimes as large as the international world of Islamic scholarship;[98] the people with whom they shared their native language;[99] their ethnic community;[100] their own gender group, to which they had to prove their masculinity; and their families, spouses and friends. This intricate web of social relationships not only worked horizontally – that is, in one's life-time – but also vertically – through genealogical connections in the family context and through intellectual or spiritual chains of transmission, as in the case of scholars or mystics.[101] In everyday life, Ottomans were able to express their multi-layered individual identities through a host of social practices and material objects: visiting a bathhouse together with friends; listening to a certain preacher; sharing meals; wearing a particular type of headgear; building mansions and mosques; establishing endowments for purposes close to their heart; reading or writing books. Ottoman culture provided many kinds of scripts and categories through which individuality could be achieved, but these necessarily were based on conventions one could push only so far without unpleasant repercussions. Thus, Ottoman individuality was formed in a field of tension between these conventions (such as literary or sartorial ones) and exceptional, non-conformist moments. To take an example from architecture, the structure of Ottoman mosques commissioned by a certain class of patrons had to adhere to certain fixed rules concerning the size and number of minarets and the like.[102] But this did not prevent patrons from expressing their perspective on religion or their status within that class by selecting certain architectural inscriptions or particularly beautiful tile revetments. In any case, the identity of *homo Ottomanicus* is arguably as much determined by symbolic, mental and physical interaction as is that of Çemberlitaş Hamamı. This life story, moreover, will add to the challenge to the generic category of the individual as a breathing human being that thinks of him- or herself as the center of his or her own universe.

A third point of criticism concerns Çemberlitaş Hamamı's status as the singular hero of the story. More often than not, biographies emphasise their subjects' exceptional character, their heroic deeds and cultural accomplishments, glorifying them for posterity and perpetuating a tele-ological concept of history ('the purpose of his life was to accomplish x'). In the field of Islamic Art History, it is usually the original appearance and the original context which are considered the most glorious period in a monument's life and as the one most worthy of in-depth study. In survey courses, monuments are generally presented in a way that emphasises their appearance at the time of their construction, rather than as the sum of additions over an extended period, each having value in its own right.[103] Even monographic publications on individual Islamic artworks focus on only one particular time or one particular aspect.[104] But this emphasis on a golden moment in the hamam's past need not be the case here. The less fortuitous events in its history will be given as much attention as its (purportedly) golden age. Moreover, Çemberlitaş Hamamı, interesting as its story is, hardly qualifies as one of the major monuments within the art historical canon. It is not a king or queen among monuments, but rather a commoner leading an 'ordinary' life, with an 'ordinary' story. And, as proponents of the New Cultural History have demonstrated, the lives of millers and maids are as interesting as those of their rulers, and likely even more conclusive about the experiences of much larger segments of societies past and present.[105] The biographical lens trained on the 'minor' monuments, then, allows us to critically re-examine two of the fetishes of Islamic Art History: the exceptional monument or masterpiece; and the monument's original appearance/context.

Introduction

The present work, then, can be read on two levels: on the one hand, I present an account of the history of Çemberlitaş Hamamı in narrative form, in the hope that the life story approach will make this narrative more accessible and enjoyable to read. This account will place the history of Çemberlitaş Hamamı within the larger history of the Ottoman Empire, by tracing its role within architectural, urban, social and economic history, as well as a history of mentalities. It will try to insert this rather 'ordinary' monument into the master narrative of Ottoman architectural master-pieces, an endeavour that, while paradoxically supporting that narrative, will hopefully at the same time unsettle it somewhat. On the other hand, this book is meant to be an exploration into the possibilities that the life-story approach opens up within the fields of Islamic Art History and Ottoman history.

1

Ancestry

It describes the most exalted valide sultan, *Nurbanu Sultan, wife to Sultan Selim Khan and mother to Sultan Murad Khan, her deeds and character and her benevolence and kindness, without which the hamam would not exist. And it briefly describes the most excellent of Ottoman chief architects, Sinan, and the architects of the imperial chamber who built this pleasurable hamam with a thousand efforts. And it describes the hamam's noble ancestry, its* şeref-i haseb ü neseb, *how its form – the three joy-giving halls, the lofty dome, the genial heating system – developed from the Roman to the Arab lands, from the domains of the Seljuks in Iran and Anatolia to the well-protected domains of the House of Osman.*

The Patroness: Nurbanu Sultan

Almost six decades before Çemberlitaş Hamamı came into being, in 1537, the Ottoman fleet under Admiral Hayreddin Barbaros raided the Greek islands of the Aegean and brought back to Istanbul 2,000 captured slaves. One of these slaves was to be Nurbanu Sultan, then a girl of no more than twelve years.[1] We know nothing certain about her early life, and historians have constructed two different versions of her biography. In the first version – and the one advocated by Nurbanu herself – she was Cecilia Venier-Baffo, the illegitimate daughter of the Venetian governor of Paros, Nicolo Venier, and the noblewoman Violante Baffo.[2] To bolster the story about her Venetian descent, Nurbanu claimed to remember her family's palace on the Grand Canal, but when the Venetian Senate tried to establish Nurbanu's ancestry on one occasion, their investigators could not arrive at any conclusive findings.[3] The inability of the Venetian Senate to find any evidence on Nurbanu's family origins points to the second version. According to that second version, she was a Greek girl from the Venetian-ruled island of Corfu, by the name of Kale Kartanou.[4] Once the Corfiote girl had entered the imperial harem, she might very well have elevated her status by claiming to be a member of Corfu's Venetian ruling elite.

A more recent study has called this second version 'rather far-fetched', and explains that her being described as Corfiote may derive from her being born on Paros but raised on Corfu.[5] Regardless of which version corresponds to actual historical fact, descent from Venetian nobility was of advantage to herself, since she could look down upon slave girls of less noble descent and ask for gifts from the Venetian ambassadors in exchange for political favours, as well as to Venice, which now had direct ties to the Ottoman ruler's immediate family.[6] Several surviving letters attest to this relationship of reciprocal favours.[7] In exchange for promoting trade relations and preventing an Ottoman invasion of Venetian-ruled Crete, Nurbanu received substantial sums of money and luxury items (such as cushions made of gold cloth).

The girl joined the imperial harem – then headed by Hürrem Sultan, wife to Süleyman the Magnificent (r. 1520–1566) – where she was given an Ottoman name and received education in reading, writing, music, dance, crafts and other feminine pursuits. The 'Princess of Light', as her name can be translated, soon became a favourite of Prince Selim on account of her beauty and intelligence. When Selim was posted to Konya in 1541/2 as a provincial governor in order to learn the craft of ruling as provincial governor, Nurbanu was inducted into the prince's harem. In rapid succession, she gave birth to four children, daughters Şah and Gevherhan in 1544, daughter İsmihan in 1545 and son Murad in 1546.[8] During her stay in the provinces, Nurbanu could observe the prince's philanthropic activities as they were expected from both male and female members of the sultan's family: the establishment of charitable endowments and architectural patronage. Her husband commissioned the imperial master architect Sinan to build a mosque complex at Karapınar, a village on the road between Konya and Adana. Supported by an endowment drawing an annual income of 11,000 *akçe* from eighty-four villages, the complex – according to a building inscription it was completed in the year 977 (1569/70) – included a Friday mosque, a caravansaray, a hospice, a bathhouse, a primary school, a public fountain and thirty-nine shops.[9]

When Sultan Süleyman the Magnificent died on 7 September 1566, on campaign in Hungary, Selim succeeded to the throne and moved his household, including Nurbanu, to the imperial capital and into the Topkapı Palace. Customarily, royal consorts ceased to be the sultan's sexual partner once they had produced an heir-apparent, as Nurbanu had done with the birth of Murad.[10] Yet Nurbanu had endeared herself so much to Selim that he formally married her in 1571 and gave her a dowry in the enormous sum of 110,000 ducats.[11] It seems that Nurbanu immediately set out to put this money to good use. In the same year, she instigated preparations for the construction of her own mosque complex in Üsküdar, on the Asian shore of the Bosphorus opposite the imperial palace.[12] In doing so, Nurbanu continued a long-standing tradition. Ottoman royal women had always participated indirectly in good government by commissioning mosques, caravansarays, hospitals, baths and other buildings that served the public good. With the construction of such buildings, they demonstrated to the Ottoman subjects that the ruler and his family cared about the well-being of the ruled; this strategy served to project imperial legitimacy. Hürrem Sultan, wife to the previous sultan and mother to Selim, had commissioned in her name mosques, hospitals, baths, *imarets* and schools in Istanbul, Edirne, Ankara, Jerusalem and Mecca.[13] What made Nurbanu's mosque complex unique was its conspicuous location on the hills of Üsküdar, where it would be visible from afar; its magnitude, both physically and in terms of the endowment that supported it; and its two minarets, a number that until then had been reserved for sultanic mosques. With her mosque complex, Nurbanu established a precedent for the royal women who would follow her: the endowment of imperial complexes in the capital became a prerogative of the sultan's mother, rather than of the sultan himself, with the notable exception of Sultan Ahmed I's mosque complex erected between 1609 and 1616.[14]

Only three years after Nurbanu's wedding, in 1574, Sultan Selim II drunkenly fell in the palace's bath and shortly thereafter died. Nurbanu immediately took matters into her own hands and concealed her husband's death until her son Murad could make his way to Istanbul from Manisa where he had served as governor. Thanks to his mother's secrecy, Murad ascended to the throne without being challenged by his half-brothers.[15] Nurbanu was motivated to such secrecy not only for the sake of her son; she also managed to cement her own position as the sultan's mother and, therefore, the most powerful woman in the Ottoman Empire. Her status and authority quickly became obvious with the ceremonial she established for her own processional arrival in the Topkapı Palace on the occasion of her son's enthronement. All members of the elite took part in a ceremony in which she distributed monetary gifts to the troops. The *yeniçeri ağası*, the head of the sultan's bodyguard, paid obeisance to her, as did the sultan himself, who received her at the palace not on horseback, as would have been customary, but on foot. Then she notified the grand vizier of her arrival and presented him with an honorary robe and a dagger. Her upward shift in status was not only marked by this novel ceremony, but also by the introduction of a new title later during her tenure as mother of the reigning sultan. Previously, women in her position had been referred to as 'mother of sultan X', as 'the Great Cradle' (*mehd-i ulya*) or as 'the nacre of the pearl of the sultanate' (*sedef-i dürrü-i saltanat*). Starting with Nurbanu, the sultan's mother held the formal title 'mother of the sultan' (*valide sultan*) and joined the highest ranks of officials in the Ottoman Empire.[16]

At the time of her husband's death and her son's accession, Nurbanu became the head of the imperial harem, and as such she was invested with the guardianship of the royal family and the administrative control over the harem household.[17] Together with the rising number of harem women (from forty-nine, excluding servants, in 1574, to 104 in 1581/2), her responsibilities increased, and so did her daily stipend. While regular harem women received a daily stipend of 40 *akçe*, Nurbanu's amounted to 1,100 under Selim II, and to 2,000 during Murad III's reign.[18] In addition to tending to the daily tasks of household administration, she forged political alliances by marrying her daughters to important court officials and guided her son in political matters.[19] Her extensive diplomatic correspondence with Venetian functionaries, as well as with the French dowager queen Catherine de Medici helped to promote good relations between the Ottoman Empire and the *serenissima*, as well as France. Her full purse allowed her to commission many architectural monuments that at the same time fulfilled philanthropic functions. The extensive mosque complex in Üsküdar (to be discussed in greater detail in the following chapter), including a far-flung and expensive network of water conduits, was completed in 1583, as were most of the commercial buildings generating income. Another small mosque complex in the town of Lapseki, near Edirne, which also benefited from her charitable foundation centred on the Üsküdar mosque complex, did not survive, and neither did a small mosque not connected to the foundation, in the village of Sarıgazi near Istanbul.[20] For her own enjoyment and leisure, Nurbanu maintained a private palace on the shore of the Sea of Marmara, near Yenikapı. But the *valide sultan* did not limit herself to architectural patronage alone. She also commissioned a wooden pulpit for the Yakup Ağa Mosque in Istanbul and more than one hundred manuscripts for her mosque complex's library.[21]

It was not only through her buildings that Nurbanu Sultan made herself eminently visible to Istanbul's populace. As her son increasingly withdrew into the palace, the *valide sultan* might have appeared in public more often than did the sultan himself. Her appearances, of course, took place in the form of processions of secluded carriages surrounded by bodyguards who scattered coins to the populace. These processions led from the palace to her mosque complex in Üsküdar, where she stayed overnight and attended Friday prayers.[22] Such ceremonial appearances were vital for the public image of the imperial dynasty, proving the benevolent presence of the ruler and his family. The fact that Nurbanu took over this function indicates her political significance within the empire as well.

Having sustained her active political involvement as *valide sultan* for about nine years, Nurbanu retired to her private palace in the Yenikapı quarter when her health began to fail. There, she died in agony on 6 December 1583, probably of stomach cancer.[23] Murad III was grief-stricken at the loss of his mother and closest political adviser, and arranged a funeral that was as remarkable as his mother's life and career. Indeed, Nurbanu's funeral cortege emerging from the palace is the only event in the life of a female member of the sultan's family to have been depicted in Ottoman manuscript painting (Figure 1.1). Contrary to custom, the sultan accompanied the coffin, draped in red-and-white cloth, on foot during its journey from Nurbanu's private palace to the mosque of Mehmed the Conqueror, all the while weeping inconsolably. Having passed a large number of bystanders who would pray for the soul of the deceased, the cortège then returned to the Hagia Sophia, where Nurbanu – in equally unusual fashion – was interred in Selim II's tomb, next to her husband. In keeping with the generosity the deceased had bestowed on the sultan's subjects during her lifetime, Janissaries and other palace officials distributed as alms 'the wealth of a Pharaoh'.[24]

Nurbanu's life story allows a number of conclusions about her character. If it is true that Nurbanu was a Corfiote girl of humble origins who fabricated a Venetian noble descent for herself, she was not above lying to advance her ambitions even at an early age. Her active involvement in politics – through her correspondence with European powers, the arrangement of her daughters' marriages, the forging of alliances at court and her role as adviser to her son – further strengthens a picture of Nurbanu as intelligent, ambitious, politically savvy and opportunist. Her many conspicuous building commissions in greater Istanbul and her regular appearances among the populace reveal that she understood the importance of maintaining good relations with the populace. She certainly liked to surround herself with luxury items, and she managed to amass large wealth from her daily stipend as well as through her charitable endowment's surplus revenues. One of the extant letters she wrote to the Venetian ambassador Morosini also shows her as quite demanding: 'Thus let it be known to the Baliyus [Venetian ambassador]! You have sent two lap dogs. Now, lap dogs that are not required, and they are big, also long-haired. Thus shall you know! Let them be white and let them be little!'[25] However one might interpret the evidence, the negative character traits that were emphasised in some of the historical sources commenting on her death need to be set against her charity,[26] which she bestowed upon

Figure 1.1 Nurbanu's funeral cortège leaving the Topkapı Palace, Lokman's
Şahinşahname, 1597, Topkapı Palace Library, B. 200, fol. 146a. *Source*: Topkapı Palace
Museum.

those benefiting from her mosque complex and her foundation and upon the members of her own household. For instance, at her death, 150 of her female slaves were manumitted and given 1,000 gold coins each.[27]

Setting an example for *valide sultans* to come, Nurbanu exercised great authority and power and decisively influenced the fate of the Ottoman dynasty. It was with her that the so-called Reign of Women began, a period during which a number of royal mothers acted as regents for their minor sons and thereby prevented the empire's collapse: Safiye Sultan, the mother of Mehmed III (r. 1596–1603); Kösem Mahpeyker Sultan, the stepmother of Osman II (r. 1618–1622) as well as mother of Murad IV (r. 1623–1640) and Ibrahim I (1640–1648); and Hatice Turhan Sultan, the mother of Mehmed IV (r. 1648–1687). During her own life time, Nurbanu Sultan combined many powerful personae: ambitious politician, philanthropist, and patron of art and architecture. In all of these three roles, her life is tied to that of Çemberlitaş Hamamı, which would not exist without her.

The Architect: Sinan

Sinan's story parallels Nurbanu Sultan's insofar as he too rose from humble beginnings outside the Ottoman court to one of the most exalted positions in the empire, being entrusted with the task of displaying the dynasty's might in his architecture. Born some time between 1489 and 1491 as a Christian in the Anatolian village of Ağırnas, near Kayseri, Sinan was recruited as a *devşirme* into the Ottoman army before or in 1514.[28] After arriving in the capital, he converted to Islam and was apprenticed to a carpenter's workshop, where he acquired a solid knowledge of applied geometry. As a soldier, he participated in Selim I's campaigns against the Safavids and the Mamluks – visiting numerous important monuments on the way – and then served in the households of several grandees. As a full-fledged Janissary, he took part in Süleyman the Magnificent's campaign to Belgrade in 1521 and thereafter quickly rose through various military ranks, particularly making a name for himself as a talented engineer in the construction of bridges, fortifications, catapults and other war machines. Over the next two decades, the many campaigns of Süleyman the Magnificent provided him with further opportunities to visit the borderlands of the empire and beyond, to acquire advanced skills in carpentry, stone masonry and engineering, and to become acquainted with different architectural styles and traditions. Sinan participated in the campaigns to Rhodes (1522), Mohacs (1526), Vienna (1529), Baghdad (1534–1537), Corfu and Apulia (1537), and Moldavia (1538). Having been promoted to the sultan's elite guard after the campaign to Baghdad, Sinan established a personal relationship with the grandee Lütfi Paşa, who after attaining the rank of grand vizier offered him the position of chief architect in 1539, now vacant on account of the death of Mimar Acem Alisi. Although Sinan seemed to have some qualms about leaving behind a flourishing career as a military engineer, the opportunity to build great Friday mosques rivalling famous ancient monuments and thus to secure himself a place in the next world was even more attractive.[29]

As *hassa baş mimarisi* – so the Ottoman title of the office of the imperial chief architect – Sinan had many duties and responsibilities. For major projects, he himself would select the building site, prepare cost estimates, draw up plans, procure materials and oversee the construction. Together with the *şehremini* (the administrative superintendent responsible for funding, building materials and construction) and the *bina emini* (the superintendent for larger projects), he headed a technical committee involved in all imperial building projects, a committee that included the minister of waterworks, the chief of lime kilns, the clerks of stores, the second architect and the chief of repairs. Sinan also supervised and trained the other court architects who were working on smaller projects, inspected buildings, and ordered repairs and renovations. At the end of his fifty years as a chief architect, Sinan could look back on a staggering number of 698 projects that he claimed to have built according to the autobiography he dictated to a close friend, the poet-painter Mustafa Sai (d. 1595/6), between 1584 and 1586.[30]

Considering the extensive nature of Sinan's duties and the range and geographical distribution of his architectural works, it is unreasonable to expect that he was personally involved in all aspects of the building process of every single monument for which he claimed authorship. More likely, this was only the case for large imperial commissions, while smaller projects were executed by his corps of architects based on his plans, or based on their plans but with his stamp of approval. The circumstances of the planning and construction of the Atik Valide Mosque Complex and Çemberlitaş Hamamı illustrate the likelihood of such a division of labour and concept of authorship. Because the patron of the mosque complex was a high-ranking member of the royal family, Sinan certainly carried out site selection, design and building supervision, at least in the project's early stages. The fact that the mosque complex and all its components are mentioned in each of the five versions of Sinan's autobiography underlines his claim to primary authorship. Çemberlitaş Hamamı, however, is a different matter. It is mentioned only in the *Tuhfetü'l-Mi'mârîn*, the most unreliable of all the five versions, since it was written in 1590, after his death, and lists among his works monuments constructed after his death date and in very distant geographical areas.[31] Thus, a careful consideration of Sinan's role in the bath's construction is in order.

The rank of the hamam's patron as well as its formal qualities – the harmonic relationship between the different building units, the novel arrangement of the hot rooms' niches to create a unified central space, and the subtle, understated decoration that foregrounds the impression of the space itself – all point to his authorship, or at least to the authorship of an architect trained and closely supervised by him. As Sinan was preoccupied with the planning and building of several smaller mosques in Istanbul and the provinces in 1583 and 1584, and possibly went on pilgrimage to Mecca early in 1584, he could very well have delegated Çemberlitaş Hamamı to the lower-ranking court architect Sedefkâr Mehmed Ağa. In fact, Sedefkâr Mehmed Ağa was appointed as Sinan's deputy during the master's absence fromt the capital.[32]

Like Sinan, Sedefkâr Mehmed Ağa had come as *devşirme* boy to Istanbul, where he was first trained as an imperial gardener and studied music before turning to the art of inlay with mother-of-pearl – a skill from which he derived the name Sedefkâr. In 1569/70, he finally turned his interest towards architecture and studied under Sinan's supervision. Filling the office of supervisor of waterways for several years, he was later appointed to the rank of imperial chief architect in 1606 and continued in this position until 1617. During his tenure, he built the Sultan Ahmed Mosque and became the subject of one of the most important Ottoman architectural treatises, the *Risâle-i Mi'mâriyye* (written in the second decade of the seventeenth century).[33] It is easy to imagine that Sinan trusted the promising young architect and man of many talents to contribute to the construction of a monument that, although imperial, was only of secondary significance in comparison to the mosque. The possibility that Sinan handed over responsibility for this construction project to a junior member of his workshop also accounts for Çemberlitaş Hamamı's conspicuous absence in the more reliable versions of his autobiography. However, until further evidence emerges, one can only speculate as to the exact roles that Sinan, Sedefkâr Mehmed Ağa and other imperial architects of lower rank played in the conception and construction of Nurbanu Sultan's bathhouse.

Origins

As humans have mothers and fathers, grandmothers and grandfathers, so does Çemberlitaş Hamamı have ancestors. In fact, the bathhouse on the corner of the Divan Yolu can look back on a long lineage from Ancient Greek baths to Roman *thermae*, Byzantine baths, early Arab-Islamic,

Perso-Islamic, Seljuk and, finally, Ottoman hamams. This lineage, however, did not devolve in a unilinear way and included a great deal of cross-fertilisation, similar to how the historian Mustafa Âli (1541–1600) describes the origins of his fellow Ottomans:

> Most of the inhabitants of Rum are of confused ethnic origins. Among its notables there are few whose lineage does not go back to a convert to Islam ... either on their father's or their mother's side, the genealogy is traced to a filthy infidel. It is as if two different species of fruitbearing tree mingled and mated, with leaves and fruit; and the fruit of this union was large and filled with liquid, like a princely pearl. The best qualities of the progenitors were then manifested and gave distinction, either in physical beauty or in spiritual wisdom.[34]

An alternate way of conceptualising the hamam's variegated ancestry – which, however, is not mutually exclusive with the notion of cross-fertilisation – can be found in the words of Isom-Verhaaren: 'the formation of an Ottoman identity was a layering process, superimposing another identity rather than obliterating a former one'.[35]

The complex origins of Çemberlitaş Hamamı are best expressed with the help of a pictorial device used in Ottoman *silsilenames* (genealogical histories) of the late sixteenth and seventeenth centuries: a family tree.[36] Genealogical histories had long been part of Islamic history writing, primarily as a tool to evaluate the veracity and reliability of the chain of transmission of religious traditions. In the fifteenth century, the Timurid dynasty (1370–1507) adopted this genre and imbued it with political significance, in an effort to demonstrate that the rule of Timur (r. 1370–1405) and his successors was indeed legitimised through his indirect descent from the legendary Genghis Khan (r. 1206–1227). After the writing of genealogical histories had been abandoned for almost two centuries, the Ottomans revived the genre – a Timurid genealogical scroll preserved in the Topkapı Palace Library likely served as a model. It has been suggested that the Ottoman *silsilenames* were meant to spread the news of Mehmed III's accession in 1595 to officials in the provinces; at the same time, they stressed the perpetuation of Sunni heritage by the Ottoman dynasty and conveyed the dynasty's religio-political legitimacy particularly in the recently conquered eastern territories of the empire.[37] Ottoman court painters even enhanced the genre's visual impact by adding the sultans' portraits in the form of illuminated medallions to the family tree, annotated with the most important life dates and achievements. It is only proper, then, to direct this Ottoman preoccupation with genealogy towards a bathhouse commissioned by a member of the sultan's family and to trace its noble ancestry, its *şeref-i haseb-ü-neseb*, via the development of its architectural form and function (Figure 1.2).

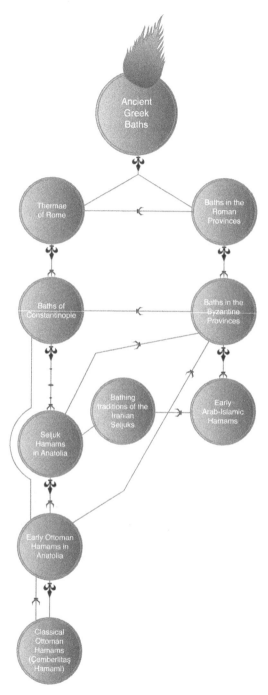

Figure 1.2 Family tree tracing the ancestry of Çemberlitaş Hamamı. An arrow with a fleur de lis indicates a direct descendant or influence, a plain arrow an indirect one.

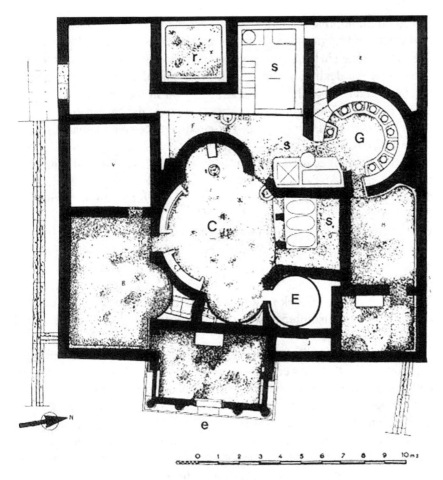

Figure 1.3 Bath of Gortys, third century BCE. *Source*: Courtesy of Fikret Yegül.

The oldest traceable forefathers are Ancient Greek baths, found since the fifth century BCE: in sanctuaries, small public *balaneia* and *gymnasia*. Particularly *gymnasia* provided the context for one of the earliest forms of communal bathing in ancient society. One of the earliest preserved examples is the one in Gortys, Arcadia, dating to the third century BCE (Figure 1.3). Baths typically consisted of a suite of irregularly shaped rooms, equipped with a water supply system, basins, tubs and a drainage system. The rooms were clustered around a sweating chamber. This architectural organisation hints at an attempt to differentiate elements of the bathing procedure by separating them and housing them in distinct units, even if no fixed definition of the order of use was achieved yet.[38] Ancient Greek baths fulfilled many diverse functions which by no means remained monolithic and unchanged over the centuries. One can discern a physical and hygienic function, as bathing was an integral part of the exercise regimen in the *gymnasia*; a social function that gathered in importance with the decline of the athletic ideal and the increasing emphasis on intellectual rather than physical education in the first century BCE; a medical function, as hydrotherapy became a popular treatment for many types of diseases starting in the first century BCE; and a ritual function, since bathing often preceded religious ceremonies.[39] Because physical education held little significance in Islamic societies (polo, hunting, wrestling and other war-like sports played by elite males being the exception), this aspect was not carried over from Greek bathing culture. However, the connection between cleanliness and ritual remained, in spite of its weakening due to the Christian ascetic ideal of *alousia* – the state of being unwashed as a negation of the body and for the achievement of a higher state of spirituality, which was propagated by certain monastic communities in the fourth and fifth centuries.[40] Much of Islamic medicine is based on Ancient Greek medicine and, therefore, the medical function of bathing was transmitted as well (for a discussion of Ottoman medicinal bathing, see Chapter 4).

The Hellenistic tradition of public bathing became the parent of a Roman bathing culture that was central to social life and cultural identity.[41] The building of large *thermae* and small *balneae* was not restricted to Rome, but also brought Roman bathing culture to the provinces, from England in the northwest to Asia Minor and the Fertile Crescent in the east. A clear definition of rooms in accordance with the order of their use and with temperature gradation (as well as a true hypocaust system) can be observed for the first time in the second century BCE. This is also the time to which the earliest and best-preserved bath of the Republican Period dates, phases III and IV of the Stabian Bath in Pompeii (Figure 1.4). The Stabian Bath consists of a row of rooms arranged along a single axis. According to Yegül, 'the disposition of a number of functionally interrelated rooms in a straight sequence reflects the order of usage, a direct progression from the unheated areas to the heated ones . . .: *apodyterium* [dressing room], *tepidarium* [warm room], *caldarium* [hot room]'.[42] This Roman room arrangement clearly influenced the tripartite ground plan of later Islamic baths.

Remains more impressive than the simple and modest neighbourhood baths of Pompeii have survived with the imperial *thermae*.[43] These colossal establishments, seven of which were constructed in Rome between *c.* 25 BCE and 300 CE, added unprecedented splendour to communal bathing. Accommodating as many as 3,000 bathers, *thermae* housed not only a large number of rooms for bathing – the *apodyterium* (dressing

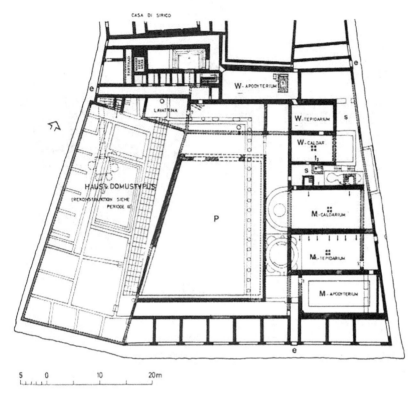

Figure 1.4 Stabian Bath of Pompeii, phases III–IV, second century BCE. *Source*:
Courtesy of Fikret Yegül.

room), *frigidarium* (cold room), *tepidarium* (warm room), *caldarium* (hot room), *sudatorium* (sweating room) and the *piscina* (pool) – but also many secondary facilities. Bathing rooms, libraries, halls, cult shrines, porticoes, promenades, gardens and sports fields were often arranged in a bilaterally symmetrical fashion along a cross-axis. The conspicuous dome over the hot room, which would later on become the hallmark of Ottoman baths, makes its first appearance as a monumental feature in the imperial Thermae of Caracalla, dating to between 206 and 217 CE (Figure 1.5). No less important is the symmetrical arrangement that many Islamic architects later applied to bathhouses. A further technical detail of Roman baths that determined later architectural traditions elsewhere is the heating of both air and water (Figure 1.6). A furnace (*praefurnium*), consisting of a low brick arch opening to the hollow space underneath the bath's floor, heats the water as well as the building. The fire heats a water boiler as well as the bath's floors through a hypocaust system: the floor is suspended on brick pillars, and this creates a hollow space through

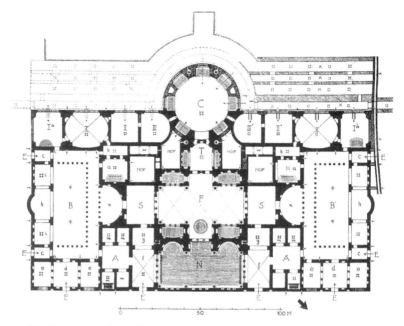

Figure 1.5 *Thermae* of Caracalla, between 206 and 216/17 CE, Rome. *Source*: Courtesy of Fikret Yegül.

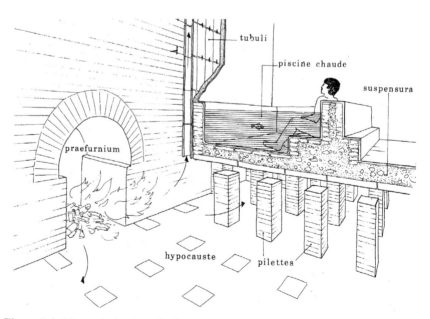

Figure 1.6 Schematic drawing of a Roman hypocaust system. *Source*: Courtesy of Fikret Yegül.

which hot gases and smoke circulate.[44] This ingenious system still heats Çemberlitaş Hamamı today.

Whether located in the capital or in the provinces, the functions of Roman baths included physical, social, ideological-symbolic, economic and urban aspects. Romans considered bathing to be part of a physical exercise regimen necessary to stay healthy, or in case of illness to regain health.[45] Bathing was a socially satisfying experience, as one met friends there before dinner and could flaunt expensive jewellery, costly bathing equipment and a retinue of handsome slaves. Fagan describes the baths as 'a noisy, vibrant place, with dinner parties meeting; bathers eating, drinking and singing; . . . to visit the baths was not only to touch a nerve center of ancient urban life but to participate in a complex social convention defined by fashion'.[46] It comes as no surprise, then, that Roman emperors emerged as important patrons of this type of building and institution so well liked by the public. By building *thermae*, emperors demonstrated their concern for public welfare, and dynastic rivalry and propaganda must certainly have motivated bathhouse-building to a great extent, too. The *thermae* as a place where the social order was reproduced *en miniature* also reinforced and emphasised the stability of the empire. Baths expressed the emperor's power over vast resources, and even over nature, with the creation of artificial heat and the supply of copious water.[47] Hygiene was considered part of the civilising process, and baths located in military outposts and provincial regions allowed Roman soldiers and locals to partake in the same ritual of daily life as the citizens of the capital.[48] Bathers could visit free of charge those imperial *thermae* supported by an endowment, whereas small neighbourhood baths usually generated profit for private entrepreneurs. The existence of small *balneae* and colossal *thermae* alike were a matter of civic pride for cities. Most of these functions and meanings of Roman baths found their way into Islamic bathing culture, although some were suppressed or forgotten at times. Hamams were as much a noisy and vibrant place with people socialising, gossiping and eating as Roman baths had been, and both rulers and city inhabitants considered them an integral part of urban life.

Together with the expansion of the Roman Empire, bathing culture and architecture travelled to the provinces. Although Roman bath-gymnasium complexes at Sardis, Milet and Ephesus and the famous Byzantine *thermae* of Constantinople assured the continuity of bathing tradition in Asia Minor,[49] when regarded from the vantage point of later Ottoman baths, they proved a *cul-de-sac* in terms of formal development.[50] It was the provincial Romano-Byzantine baths in Syria, Jordan and Palestine that provided a matrix for Islamic bath architecture. One

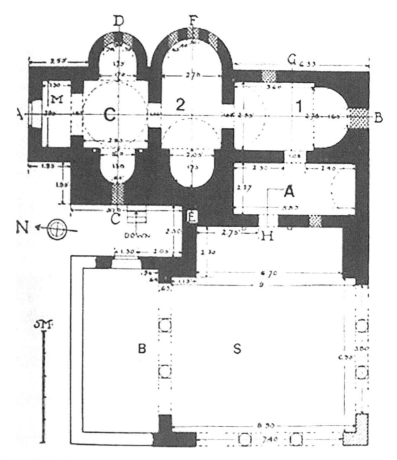

Figure 1.7 Bath at Brad, *c.* 200 CE, Syria. *Source*: Courtesy of Fikret Yegül.

example of a bath in northern Syria that illustrates the link between Roman, Byzantine and early Islamic baths is located at Brad and dates to about 200 CE (Figure 1.7). In this small bathhouse, three rooms – the vaulted cold and warm rooms and the domed hot room, all heated by hypocausts – have been connected in a row and grafted onto the dressing room and the reception area. Dow has argued that, although larger municipal *thermae* with a more formal, symmetrical layout remained in use in Late Antiquity, smaller, modest baths with only three washing rooms – like the one at Brad – contributed most to the development of the early Arab-Islamic bath type.[51] It was here in Syria that the first Muslims encountered Romano-Byzantine bathing tradition.[52] One particularly poignant example of continued use is the bathhouse of Hammat Gader, fed by the thermal springs near Lake Tiberias. Its Hall of Fountains boasts

40

a Greek inscription, still *in situ*, informing the visitor that it was restored under the Umayyad caliph Mu'awiyah (r. 661–680).[53] The inscription asserts that the balneal tradition of Hammat Gader continued, as did the epigraphic tradition of pre-Islamic culture. The early Muslim community not only visited medicinal baths such as the one at Hammat Gader, but, more importantly, made ritual purification an element of religious practice and firmly integrated communal bathing into their lifestyle (for a more detailed discussion of ritual purification, see Chapter 4).

Muslim Arabs erected one of their first baths at Qasr al-Hayr al-Sharqi, an Umayyad walled settlement of the first half of the eighth century, between Palmyra and Damascus (Figure 1.8). The settlement consisted of residences, a mosque, a public building, oil presses, a grazing enclosure, a fortified caravansaray, an elaborate water supply system and two baths – one *intra muros*, one *extra muros*.[54] By the time of construction – barely one century after the beginning of the Muslim calendar – a bath was already considered

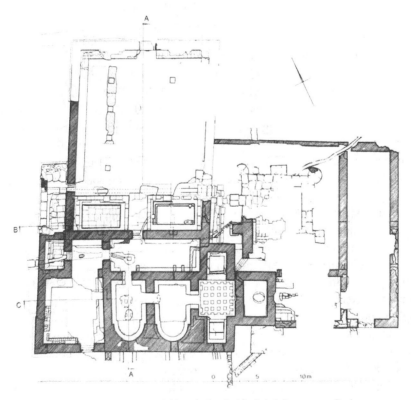

Figure 1.8 Bath of Qasr al-Hayr al-Sharqi, first half of eighth century, Syria.
Source: Courtesy of Fikret Yegül.

an essential urban amenity,[55] even if the water supply required extensive planning. The hamam at Qasr al-Hayr al-Sharqi did not remain an isolated instance: currently we know of nineteen Umayyad baths preserved well enough to be identified as such.[56] The Umayyad desert palaces at Qusayr 'Amra (*c.* 712) and Khirbat al-Mafjar (built between 724 and 743) included most extraordinary bathing facilities, built less with religious requirements in mind than with providing luxurious gathering spaces for elite visitors.[57]

The ground plan of the *extra muros* bath at Qasr al-Hayr al-Sharqi shows a fundamental similarity to the earlier bath at Brad.[58] In Brad, the visitors entered the bath through a porticoed reception area. In Qasr al-Hayr al-Sharqi, a basilical hall with two decorative pools marks the entrance area. From there, the visitors continued to a vaulted room. In Brad, this vaulted room certainly fulfilled the function of a dressing room, whence the bather would proceed directly to the first bathing chamber, the cold room. At Qasr al-Hayr al-Sharqi, there were two dressing rooms, the first one possibly functioning primarily as a foyer and the second, L-shaped room as the dressing room proper.[59] Both of these rooms had benches where visitors could sit down to disrobe. The bathing chambers consist of a series of three rectangular or square rooms. In the cold and warm rooms, the bathers would sit down on the benches along the walls to rest, to get acclimatised to the higher temperature, and maybe also to perform cosmetic procedures. In the hot room, two projections on the north and south walls contained marble-lined immersion tubs. At Brad, the bathing procedure was very similar, progressing through three rooms and culminating in the hottest room containing a pool. Both baths were heated by means of a furnace and hypocausts. The basilical hall at Qasr al-Hayr al-Sharqi can be interpreted as a reception hall or lounge, and in comparison with the bathing rooms proper, this hall was much larger in size and even sported geometric and vegetal designs as decoration. This decorated reception hall hints at the increasing significance of the social aspect of bathing culture, since an attractive environment invited bathers to linger and to enjoy conviviality.[60]

The baths of the desert cities and desert palaces were primarily an Umayyad tradition, but the Abbasid dynasty (750–1258) also erected bathhouses in their palace complexes, for example, in the one at Ukhaidir (late eighth century).[61] Made of baked brick and built into the complex's outer fortification walls, the bath's room arrangement resembles the one favoured by Romano-Byzantine and Umayyad builders. The bathers entered first a cross-vaulted reception room before proceeding to the bench-lined dressing room. From there, they accessed the cold, the warm and the hot room. The latter contained a semi-circular niche in the west wall and adjoined the furnace and hot water tank in the east. While baths such as the one at Ukhaidir give witness to the continuity from Umayyad to Abbasid balneal culture outside cities, it was under the Abbasids that bathing on a more monumental scale became an inextricable part of Islamic city life. Unfortunately, nothing remains of Abbasid hamams in Baghdad, except for textual evidence, such as *The History of Baghdad* by al-Khatib (1002–72). Al-Khatib claims that in the era of the caliph al-Muqtadir (r. 908–932) 27,000 baths served the residents of the Abbasid capital.[62] Of course, this boastfully inflated number tells us more about the hamams' significance as an emblem of civic pride than about the actual number of baths.

There are several hamams in Samarra, the city built about 90 km north of Baghdad in 836 when the caliph wanted to escape the political intrigues and riots of the capital. Not all the baths of Samarra have been excavated or properly documented, but there were at least five.[63] The bath in the public palace where the caliph spent most of his days, held public audiences and received visitors is of particular interest because of its formal characteristics betraying a strong Iranian influence (as does the rest of the complex).[64] Located in the southeastern corner of the first courtyard straight behind the ceremonial entrance gate (Bab al-'Amma), the bath's hot room is arranged in the form of four large vaulted recesses around a central space (Figure 1.9). The available documentation of the

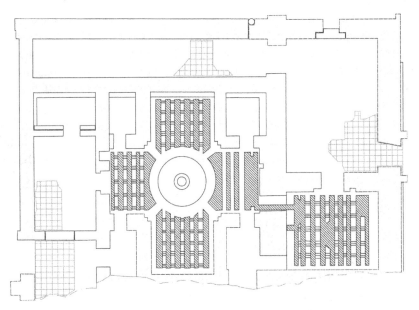

Figure 1.9 Bath in the Dar al-'Amma, 836–884, Samarra. *Source*: Courtesy of Alasdair Northedge.

bath's excavated portion suggests that bathers entered the hamam from a door to the west, undressed in a room to their left-hand side and then proceded to the four-*iwan* bathing hall, which was heated by hypocausts. Small chambers inscribed into the corners between the recesses afforded more privacy, if desired. Another door in the east wall led to a square room also heated by hypocausts, a second, probably even warmer hot room.[65] Common features of both pre-Islamic and Islamic Iranian architecture, vaulted recesses (*iwan*) are often arranged in four around a central space with a decorative pool. As an element of palatial architecture – such as the throne hall at Ctesiphon, built under the Sassanian dynasty (r. 224–651) – *iwan*s were very well suited to a bath integrated into a public palace, a bath that could double for an audience hall in a more relaxed and convivial setting. The Abbasid builder's integration of the four-*iwan* plan into bath-house architecture points to a lively exchange in terms of both bathing and building tradition.

In fact, public baths had already travelled to the border area of Iran via Sassanian Iraq prior to the Muslim conquests, due to the forcible settlement of Syrian and Greek captives in the region in the sixth century. New Antioch, a city that Khusraw Anushirvan built for the captive population of Antioch after 540, had several public baths. The introduction and spread of public baths, supported by royal Sassanian patronage, was one of the most significant results of western influence in sixth-century Iraq.[66] Although baths had existed in pre-Islamic Iran, they were not widely spread, because of the Zoroastrian belief that the holy element of water should not be polluted. In the second half of the seventh century, the arrival of the Islamic faith, together with its prescriptions on ritual cleanliness, overruled Zoroastrian objections. Investigating the acceptance of Islamic bathhouses into Iranian culture could tell us much about the changes in lifestyle accompanying conversion. Unfortunately, there are very few archaeological or historical studies on the early Islamic baths of Iran.[67] This dearth of information changes with the ninth century, when baths are more frequently mentioned in Persian literature, illustrating that by that time the concept had been absorbed into Iranian-Islamic tradition (and probably influenced Abbasid hamams at Samarra in reverse). The author of an eleventh-century mirror for princes, the *Qabusnama*, devotes an entire chapter to bathing procedure and etiquette. He recommends taking a bath every other day, to leave enough time to digest between a meal and the bathhouse visit, and to avoid during the bath sexual intercourse and the consumption of alcohol – except for a small draught to alleviate hangover. The correct washing procedure was to remain in the cold chamber for a while, and then to linger in the warm room before entering the hot room.

The author also cautions moderation in that the bather should not stay too long or use water that is either too hot or too cold. Bathers should slowly acclimatise to the room temperature, both when entering and leaving. In conclusion, the author extols the hamam: 'The baths in themselves are an excellent institution and from the time when wise men began to erect buildings nothing better than baths has been built.'[68]

It is also to Iran that one may turn in order to explain some features of Ottoman hamams – such as the integration of *iwan*-like niches around a centralised space. After all, some of the first groups of Muslims who came to Anatolia to stay permanently were from Iran and could thus look back on the bathing traditions and hamam architecture outlined above. (Still, one needs to acknowledge that many of the architectural developments leading up to the typical form of Ottoman hamams took place in Syria, and the cultural exchange between northern Syria and southeast Turkey did much to spread bathing culture and bath architecture into Anatolia from Roman times.[69] For instance, the Arabic name for the hot room, *harara*, has been adopted into Turkish as *hararet*, giving evidence of the Arab origin of Anatolian-Islamic bathing tradition and of how terminology travelled together with this tradition.) Yet it was the Seljuks who were responsible for the convergence of Anatolian Romano-Byzantine, Arab and Iranian bathhouse architecture in Anatolia.

The preserved monuments of the Seljuk dynasty (1038–1194) afford us insight into how Iranian bathhouse architecture developed after the ninth century, which Arab elements were transmitted and which innovations were added. Not surprisingly, the four-*iwan* plan, having become a central feature of Iranian Seljuk architecture adorning mosques, palaces, caravan-sarays, schools and residences, also anchors the layout of a Seljuk bath at Nigar, south of Kirman (Figure 1.10). The dressing room consists of four *iwan*s around a central space with a decorative pool. The arrangement of the cold, warm and hot rooms diverges from Umayyad and early Abbasid ground plans, but is reminiscent of the ninth-century Abbasid bath in the Dar al-'Amma at Samarra. Rather than lining up the rooms in a row and grafting them onto the reception area and dressing room, the architect has centralised and connected them in a way similar to a honeycomb pattern. In all likelihood, this was done in order to facilitate a centralised four-*iwan* scheme while at the same time maximising the use of space.

When the Seljuks moved into eastern and central Anatolia following their victory at the battle of Manzikert in 1077, they found an already many-centuries-old and well-established bathing tradition; however, they also brought with them their own conceptions of hamam architecture and notions of hygiene and bathing etiquette, all of which would enrich and

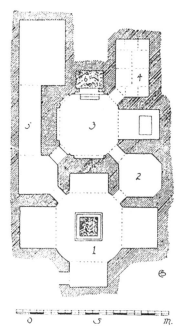

Figure 1.10 Bath at Nigar, date unknown, Iran. *Source*: Pope, *A Survey of Persian Art*, 1964/5.

Islamicise the Anatolian tradition. The *Qabusnama*, for example, was translated into Turkish in the fourteenth century, but its original, Persian version probably circulated among the Seljuk elite in Anatolia long before that.[70] Anatolian Seljuk builders continued to apply the four-*iwan* plan to their hamams, but with one important alteration. They now integrated *iwan*s into the hot room, rather than into the dressing room. In his survey of twelfth- to thirteenth-century hamams in Anatolia, Önge argues that Seljuk baths emerged as a fixed building type and that their form barely changed afterwards.[71] This indicates that the building type had already been formulated and codified in Iran. The building type, as exemplified in the Sahib Ata Hamamı in Konya (built between 1258 and 1279), included the following characteristics: the sequence of bathing rooms consisted of four chambers, the dressing room, the cold or mediating room, the warm room and the hot room (Figure 1.11). This sequence of rooms could be doubled to form a so-called *çifte* hamam, with parallel sections for men and women. The quadripartite sequence of bathing rooms still bears resemblance to the Seljuk hamams' ancestors, the Arab hamams as seen at Qasr al-Hayr al-Sharqi. The hot room was built with four *iwan*s, with the resulting corner spaces used as separate, more private bathing chambers.

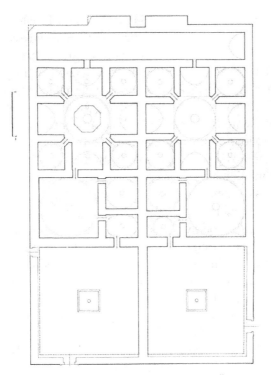

Figure 1.11 Sahib Ata Hamamı, 1258–1279, Konya. *Source*: Önge, *Anadolu'da XII.–XIII. Yüzyıl Türk Hamamları*, 1995.

Thus, the Iranian element of the four-*iwan* plan was still present, but in a different location within the structure.

Seljuk baths continued to fulfil many of the functions of their ancient predecessors. They not only provided water for washing, but also a place to enjoy good company. Seljuk hospitals had facilities for thermal bathing, since hydrotherapy was a common cure for all kinds of ailments.[72] The religious significance of hamams as a place for performing ablutions carried particularly strong significance in a borderland of Islam, and baths were usually erected together with and in close proximity to mosques. Another setting in which hamams were found consisted of the caravansarays that served travellers of all ranks.[73] The patrons considered them an integral element of Islamic urban culture and a beacon of civilisation, very much like the Roman *thermae* in the provinces. In a city like Konya, a Seljuk capital between *c.* 1115 and 1308, the baths must have been a matter of civic pride. Maybe the hamams also contributed to attracting local non-Muslims to partake in the Seljuk lifestyle and to eventually convert to the new faith. Baths were familiar to Hellenic

Anatolians (even if they existed on a much reduced scale during the Late Byzantine period), and such similarities in lifestyle and everyday practice made assimilation into a new culture and religion easier. In fact, Seljuk baths were often erected over the remains of ancient and Byzantine baths, where a water source existed and building material lay ready in the rubble of the ruins.[74] The visitors to Seljuk baths, regardless of whether they were Hellenic Anatolians or Seljuks, usually contributed to the revenue of a charitable pious endowment, as their bathing fee ultimately financed the building and upkeep of charitable institutions and the distribution of free food and medicine to the poor.

By the time the Ottomans emerged as a major military force from among the many small warring principalities of fourteenth-century Anatolia, the Seljuks had already codified the architectural and cultural tradition of the bathhouse. Some Seljuk baths, such as the Sahib Ata Hamamı at Konya, were simply taken over by the Ottomans, with their endowment intact and without any major disruption to the bathing business.[75] The earliest hamams built by the Ottomans themselves, however, reflect the dynasty's humble origins in that they were of simple structure and building technique. In spite of their simplicity, the ten hamams erected under Orhan (r. 1324–1362) incorporated the four-*iwan* plan. The hot room of the Orhan Gazi Hamamı in Bursa, for example, shows the characteristic cross-shape on the ground plan and the small domed units inserted into the corners (Figure 1.12). In this bath, the large central dome, the hallmark of the Ottoman hamam, was already fully formulated.

Tracing the architectural development of Çemberlitaş Hamamı's 185 Ottoman ancestors built especially in the earlier capitals of İznik, Bursa[76] and Edirne before the conquest of Constantinople in 1453 lies outside the scope of this book.[77] For our purposes, it suffices to note that the early Ottoman hamams already had a very long, complex and venerable lineage. Thus, in 1453, Mehmed the Conqueror (r. 1444–1446 and 1451–1481) brought an architectural type and bathing concept with a centuries-old Anatolian tradition to the vanquished Byzantine capital whose once splendid monumental public baths had lain in ruins for the past few centuries, after communal bathing had fallen out of fashion (see Chapter 4).[78] The first Ottoman hamam of the newly conquered city, the Çukur Hamamı close to Mehmed's mosque complex, has not survived.[79] Instead, two hamams built in the first two decades after the conquest can stand in as parents to Çemberlitaş Hamamı. Located in a commercial area on a main traffic artery, the imposing Tahtakale Hamamı was erected around 1472/3 in order to generate revenue for the charitable endowment supporting the Hagia Sophia (Figure 1.13).

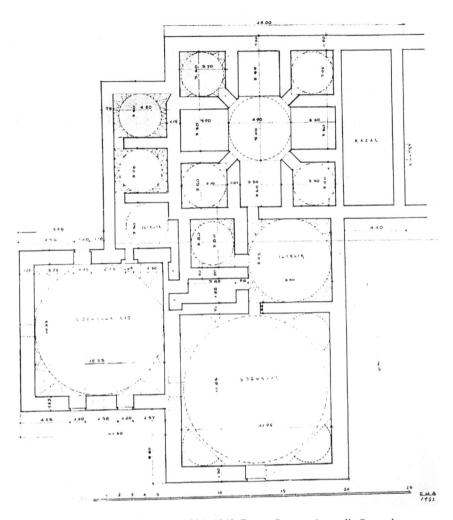

Figure 1.12 Orhan Gazi Hamamı, 1324–1362, Bursa. *Source*: Ayverdi, *Osmanlı Mimarisinin İlk Devri*, 1966.

This major landmark attracted many visitors, as is attested by its high income.[80] Equally imposing was the Mahmud Paşa Hamamı, commissioned by Grand Vizier Mahmut Paşa (r. 1456–1468 and 1472–1473).[81] The size of its dome surpassed that of any other Ottoman building in the capital until the completion of Mehmed the Conqueror's mosque (Figure 1.14).[82] Both of these buildings share a tripartite ground plan, with a large square dressing room followed by a small warm room and a four-*iwan* hot room. The four-*iwan* plan, however, has been turned by 45 degrees, so that the *iwan* niches have become inserted into the corners of

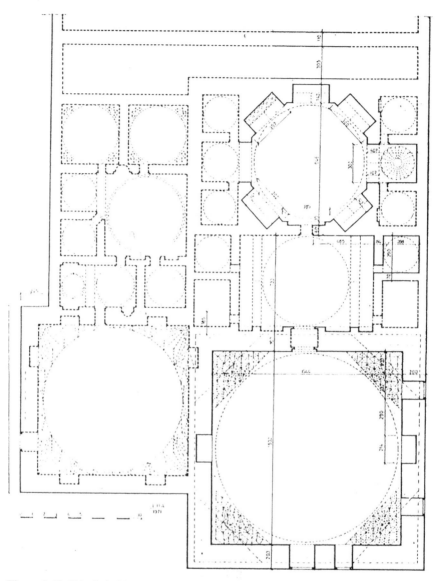

Figure 1.13 Tahtakale Hamamı, 1472–1473, Istanbul. *Source*: Ayverdi, *Osmanlı Mimarisinde Fatih Devri*, 1989.

the hot room's square area – a feature that would appear in Çemberlitaş Hamamı as well as in an even more softened version to effect a unified centralised space.

In sum, Çemberlitaş Hamamı inherited from the Roman *thermae* the

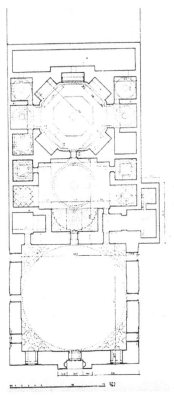

Figure 1.14 Mahmud Paşa Hamamı, 1456–1461 or 1472/3, Istanbul. *Source*: Ayverdi, *Osmanlı Mimarisinde Fatih Devri*, 1989.

hypocausts as the heating system, the order of use from the cold to the hot room, and the dome over the hot room. To these basic formal characteristics, its Arab-Islamic ancestors contributed the large dressing room equal in size to the hot room, and its Iranian-Seljuk ancestors the four-*iwan* plan, while its Anatolian-Seljuk ancestors moved the four *iwan*s into the hot room and contributed the doubling of the bathing rooms into a *çifte* hamam. Its Ottoman ancestors again moved the four *iwan*s by rotating them to the hot room's corners. Like a sixteenth-century Istanbulite whose mother might have been a Circassian slave girl and whose father a tribute child (*devşirme*) taken from his Albanian home, who would have been educated in the palace school, hardened on military campaigns to Hungary and Iraq, and elevated to the rank of a vizier, Çemberlitaş Hamamı is quintessentially Ottoman in that it looks back on a complex mixed heritage of architectural and balneal traditions.

2

Family

It describes how the aforementioned, most exalted valide sultan *established
her endowment to lavish her benevolence on the people of Istanbul
and Üsküdar, and the many lofty buildings she erected: a noble Friday
mosque with many dependencies on the hitherto empty hills of Üsküdar,
including schools, a hospital, an inn for weary travellers, and the like.
And it describes what sums were needed and what expenses were made
for the upkeep of these charities and where the money for the upkeep of
these charitable buildings came from – it came from Çemberlitaş Hamamı,
together with the Atik Valide Hamamı and the Büyük Hamam and the
Havuzlu Hamam, all of which the wise* valide sultan *built in such a way as
to invite many visitors.*

The Atik Valide Vakfı

Already before 1571, when the designing and procuring of building materials for her mosque complex began, Nurbanu had planned to establish
a *vakıf*, a perpetual charitable endowment to support the construction
and maintenance of the buildings.[1] Such endowments had tied (and held)
together economic, religious, social and cultural life in the Ottoman
Empire since its inception, following Byzantine, Arab and Seljuk models.[2]
The sultan who conquered Constantinople, Mehmed II (r. 1444–1446,
1451–1481), very well understood the utility of endowments for urban
development, establishing two of the largest *evkaf* in the entire empire,
one in his own name, the other in that of the Hagia Sophia. At the same
time, he urged officials and dignitaries of his court to do the same and
to construct buildings with commercial, social and religious purposes.
That the resulting mosque complexes provided durable focal points for
urban development is still evident in those neighbourhoods that carry
the mosque founder's name – such as Davutpaşa or Mahmutpaşa. The
building complexes provided an urban infrastructure in the form of water
supply, roads and canalisation; employment opportunities through their
hiring of personnel; business opportunities through the creation of market

52

space, baths and inns; and social and cultural facilities in the form of schools, convents, public kitchens and hospitals. Although the foundation's income was not subject to taxes and therefore promised no profit for the state's coffers, endowed complexes had other advantages for governing Ottoman subjects. They could work as control mechanisms for the state, as they preserved unity in religious practice and offered food and other basic services to their employees as well as to the poor, thereby preventing discontent among the populace. Thus, mosque complexes constituted a nexus where a patron–client relationship between the ruler and his extended family on one side, and the individual subject on the other side, came to be enacted through the giving and receiving of food and services needed to live a proper Muslim life.[3] These institutions advertised the power and wealth of the Ottoman ruler and his family even abroad, when travellers stayed in endowed inns for three days without having to pay for lodging, food or feed for their animals. Returning to their home countries or moving on, these travellers were likely to pass on word about the charity they had received.

Endowment-making was such a widespread practice that by 1596 well over three thousand pious foundations existed in Istanbul – although most of them were small in scale and did not necessarily involve architectural patronage.[4] More than a third of the founders were women.[5] In this context, Nurbanu distinguished herself from other female endowment-makers only by dint of her foundation's unprecedented scale. In order to establish her *vakıf*, she first had to accumulate capital in the form of money and real estate in her private possession. Since most real estate in the Ottoman Empire was considered public (*miri*) and therefore de facto belonged to the sultan, she had to turn to her husband (and later on, her son) to receive the property rights (*mülk*) over the lands she wished to endow. Once the property rights were transferred to her, as documented in a *mülkname*, Nurbanu could have a scribe draw up a deed of trust (*vakıfname*).[6] The deed lays out the endowment's major components in the following order: the charitable buildings where services and goods are to be dispensed to the designated beneficiaries (*mavkûf aleyhi*, including a mosque, a primary school, a secondary school, a seminary for the study of Qur'an recital, a seminary for the study of the Prophet's sayings and traditions, an *imaret* (soup kitchen), a convent and a hospital in Üsküdar, and a small mosque, primary school and *imaret* in the village of Lapseki near Edirne; the revenue-generating properties (*mavkûf*); the staff to be employed in the foundation's administration and the mosque complexes in both Üsküdar and Lapseki, together with their necessary qualifications and their salaries; the amount and type of medicine, clothes and money distributed to the needy and to several of Nurbanu's former slaves; the types of food to be cooked in the *imaret*s and distributed to the staff and the poor; and, finally, the details of the administration. The document concludes with a description of how Nurbanu's son, Murad III, disputed the endowment. This was a standard procedure to test its legal validity before a judge.

The revenue-generating components of this sizeable operation were equally extensive in order to provide the funds necessary to construct, maintain and operate the mosque complexes in Üsküdar and Lapseki. The entire district of Yeni İl in eastern Anatolia, a land grant (*has*) yielding an income of more than 100,000 *akçe*, made up a large portion of revenue, bolstered by the rent income from smaller commercial property in Istanbul and Üsküdar: one inn (*han*) with twenty-two rooms; 122 residential structures; eighty-one shops; three hamams; one stable; three slaughterhouses; six tanneries; one shop where sheep heads and trotters were cooked and sold (*serhane*); one shop where candles were produced and sold (*şem'hane*); and three plots of land. Agricultural and commercial property outside the capital consisted of three bread ovens in Bursa, six farms, four fields, four mansions (*menzil*), three vineyards and three pastures. The income of nine entire villages also went straight into the endowment's coffers, as did the fees collected in Üsküdar's horse market and the head tax (*cizye*) on non-Muslims living in Yeni Mahalle near Nurbanu's mosque complex. In addition, the endowment's sheep – which were exempt from any kind of taxation – had the right to graze freely on twelve different pastures, and the income accrued from their lambs, wool and milk also belonged to the *vakıf*.

Considering the size of the endowment of which it was a part, Çemberlitaş Hamamı was but a small cog in a large machine, a pinpoint-sized node in an extensive economic network that tied together urban buildings and gardens in the imperial capital with the farms, pastures, inns and bread ovens in the far-flung provinces, from present-day Bulgaria to eastern Anatolia. The people using the endowment's buildings, working in them, providing income for them and moving in between them were just as diverse as the endowment network itself. Hamam managers, merchants, artisans and craftsmen, bakers, gardeners, shepherds, farmers, Jewish and Christian taxpayers, and many others generated money that went towards paying the salaries of administrators, imams, Qur'an reciters, seminary students, dervishes, doctors and other mosque complex employees, as well as money to maintain buildings and waterways and to feed the urban poor. As Singer has observed for another foundation in the empire's Arab provinces, the ties between villages and urban endowments were all but superficial; rather, they refashioned the villagers' identity, regardless of physical distance, by aligning them with the endowment's purposes through their payments.[7] In the case of Nurbanu's endowment, the payments, as they were recorded in the foundation's accounting books (*muhasebe defterleri*), were of such a size that the total annual income ranged from 2,985,596 *akçe* in a meagre year (1632) to 4,561,310 *akçe* in a fat year (1644/5).[8]

The amassing of wealth through surplus revenue was certainly a strong motivation for endowment-making, but so were less tangible benefits. Whoever founded a *vakıf* for the common good went beyond the religious obligation of giving charity (*sadakat*) and thus could aspire to a place in Paradise. Though formulaic and prescriptive in nature, like most endowment deeds, the beginning section of Nurbanu's *vakıfname* describes her hopes for reward in the afterworld:

> The *valide sultan* wanted to join the blessings of the transitory world with the blessings and the joys of the eternal afterworld, because a smart person would not tie his hopes only to the uncertain possessions of the world. With this in mind, the abovementioned *valide* opened her generous hand to everybody and wanted to bestow a gift that is always open to the entire public, in order to attain good deeds and to escape the sufferings of a terrible day when not possessions and children, but only embracing Allah with a clean heart will be beneficial.[9]

Implying that Nurbanu is a very intelligent person and a faithful Muslim, this passage clearly lays out the dual purpose of endowment-making in joining together material as well as spiritual blessings.[10] Material gains, in this context, also came in the form of enhanced status and power. The beneficiary who accepted the charity bestowed on the giver his gratitude and well-wishing prayers in return and – in the case of an imperial or sub-imperial endowment – also accepted the donor's political legitimacy. One just needs to imagine a snippet of conversation between two Ottoman residents of Üsküdar: 'Yesterday I went to pray in the mosque of the old *valide sultan*. It is such a beautiful mosque! Then I received a meal from her *imaret*, rice and bread and a piece of meat. God bless her and her son's soul!'

The Atik Valide Mosque Complex

Çemberlitaş Hamamı was brought to life in order to generate income for its family, Nurbanu's mosque complex. Located on a hilltop in Üsküdar, on the Asian side of the Bosphorus, the complex today almost vanishes among the surrounding residential buildings. Originally, the area had been uninhabited, and the complex not only served as a visual reminder of the Ottoman dynasty's power and the *valide sultan*'s benevolence – its imposing structure was easily visible from across the Bosphorus, from Galata and the Topkapı Palace – but also as an incentive to settlement. The deed of trust specified that 358 staff positions should be filled, and although not every one of these posts required the employee to work at the mosque complex, much less reside there, the majority of employees did settle in its vicinity. This vigorous urban development is also noted by a contemporary observer, the geographer Aşık Mehmed, in the 1590s: 'Before the above-mentioned lady established these charitable buildings, their site and environs had been vacant plots. With the construction of new housing, they attracted around them a large population, and they augmented Üsküdar's inhabited region by at least on third.'[11]

One of the first archival traces of the mosque complex dates to 20 February 1571, when Nurbanu's husband, Selim II, issued an imperial decree ordering the procurement of marble for the building project.[12] Further decrees and other records capture the progress of building material procurement and construction in great detail, from the sultan's donation of land and villages to the endowment, to the instructions to transport quarried stones to the prospective construction site.[13] Although the religious core of the complex had been finished by 1579, the foundation inscription over the mosque's main door carries the date of AH 991 (1583), the year of the *valide sultan*'s death and of the first Friday preacher's appointment.[14] At that date, the dependencies of the mosque complex and the revenue-generating buildings were still in the stages of planning or under construction, and would continue to be so until 1588. Even the mosque itself was remodelled and enlarged between 1584 and 1586 with two domed side wings and a gallery along the walls of the prayer hall.[15]

When the din of construction work finally stopped in Toptaşı, as the neighbourhood is now called, the complex that sprawled over the terraced hill boasted not only a mosque with twin minarets in a large courtyard (Figure 2.1, No. 1), but also a secondary school (*medrese*, No. 2), a primary school (*sıbyan mektebi*, No. 4), a convent (*tekke*, No. 3), a seminary for Qur'an reciters (*darülkurra*, No. 5), a seminary teaching the traditions of the Prophet (*darülhadis*, No. 5), a soup kitchen (*imaret*, No. 10), a hospital (*darüşşifa*, No. 12), an inn for travellers (*han*, No. 11) with a stable (No. 8) and a hamam (No. 13). This large number of dependencies meant that Nurbanu's complex approached the size of Mehmed II's and Süleyman I's foundations in Istanbul.

While the complex today is called Atik Valide Külliyesi, 'Old Mother's Complex', until the seventeenth century it was known as the Valide Sultan Cami. In 1640/1, another mosque complex was completed in Üsküdar,

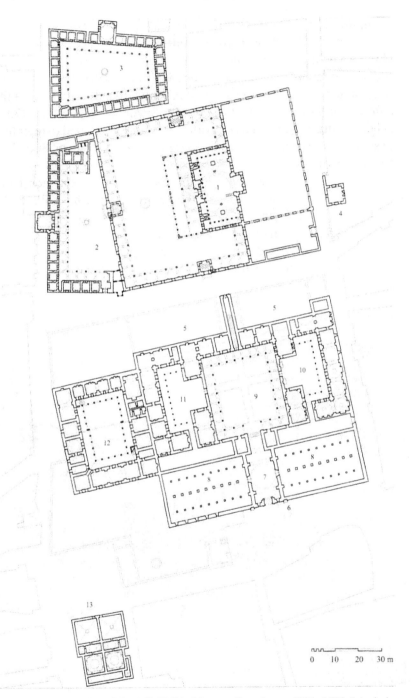

Figure 2.1 Ground plan of the Atik Valide Mosque Complex, *c.* 1571–1588, Istanbul.
Source: Courtesy of Gülru Necipoğlu.

commissioned by Mahpeyker Kösem Sultan – mother to Mustafa I
(r. 1617–1623), Murad IV (r. 1623–1640) and Ibrahim I (r. 1640–1648) –
and it became necessary to distinguish between these two *valide sultan*'s
mosques. Contrary to Kuran's and Goodwin's claims that Nurbanu's structure became the 'Old Mother's complex' only around 1710, when a third
valide sultan – Emetullah Gülnüş, mother to Ahmed III (r. 1703–1736) –
had her mosque added to the area, official documents started to refer to the
oldest of the three complexes as Atik Valide, Valide-i Atik or Eski Valide
Cami as early as 1666.[16]

Befitting its status among the complex's components, the mosque and
its courtyard occupy the terrace on the very top of the hill (Figure 2.2).
In its original shape, the mosque consisted of a nearly square prayer
hall capped by a hexagonal baldachin made up of a central dome with
a diameter of 12.7 m and four abutting semi-domes, which in turn were
supported by two free-standing columns. The projecting prayer niche is

Figure 2.2 Aerial view of the Atik Valide Mosque Complex. *Source*: Courtesy of Gülru
Necipoğlu.

equally capped by a half-dome. The five-bayed portico – surrounded by a second, outer portico – served as overflow space for worshippers during Friday prayers (*son cemaat yeri*). The two minarets once rose from the two corners where the prayer hall walls meet the inner portico; however, with the addition of two lateral wings with two domes each, the architect elongated the prayer hall to meet the corners of the outer portico and thus awkwardly embedded the minarets in its façade. Over the *muqarnas*-capped marble portal, an inscription in *ta'lik* script praises the patron and her architectural achievement:

> Nurbanu, that person full of purity,
> resolved to perform charitable works.
> She built this charming place of worship.
> Wonderful sight, most beautiful and charming!
> This peerless work of charity is an imperial foundation.
> Its date was 'Excellent, sublime paradise!' 991 [1583/4]

The exterior decoration of Qur'anic inscriptions on rectangular Iznik tile lunettes over the doors and windows is continued in the interior, culminating in the dazzling calligraphic and floral panels in the *mihrab* recess (Figure 2.3). The colourful tiles, the *minbar* with its intricate carving, the wooden window shutters and doors with their fine inlay work, and the painted decoration all work together to help worshippers imagine the paradise evoked in the inscription over the entrance.

The worshippers' experience of the mosque was not a quiet, contemplative one; rather, at any given time the prayer hall was teeming with people in the employ of the endowment. Salaried worshippers prayed for the soul of the Prophet and his family, of the sultan and of Nurbanu. More than one hundred Qur'an reciters and readers were hired, so that the verses of the holy text resounded almost continually in the domed space.[17] Librarians made sure that Qur'an copies were in good condition and available to both hired and regular worshippers. Sweepers and cleaners saw to it that tiles and marble sparkled and the carpets were clean and straight. Another employee took care of curtains and wall hangings. On Fridays, when a sermon accompanied the noon prayer and additional Qur'an verses were recited, a so-called *buhurcu* burnt incense in order to perfume the mosque.[18] In fact, the mosque was much less a place for quiet, solitary prayer than a stage for religious performances involving a large community as much as the five senses: worshippers listened to the chanted Qu'ran and the clicking of prayer beads, heard the rustle of fabrics, beheld the architecture and the decoration, felt the pile of the carpet underneath their hands and feet, smelled the rich

Figure 2.3 Prayer niche of the Atik Valide Mosque. *Source*: Author's photograph.

fragrance of incense, and bodily communicated with God by prostrating in prayer.

Across from the entrance to the mosque, on the other side of the courtyard, a gate in the domical arcade leads down a stairway into the *medrese*, where sixteen male students lived and studied with their teacher (Figure 2.1, No. 2). Located on a lower terrace, the school sits at an angle against the wall of the mosque courtyard. Sixteen cells and three further rooms around a courtyard with a fountain housed the students, one doorman, one janitor and the teacher. The classroom opposite the entrance is set off from the remaining rooms and juts out over the next-lower terrace, forming an archway with a fountain over the street underneath. Since she assigned 'much value and importance to the reputation of science and education, and in order to elevate and ennoble the scholars among the people', Nurbanu determined in her deed of trust the following condition:

[S]ixteen students of those who are capable and desiring of the acquisition of knowledge and who are currently studying in the medrese and who are studying the customary books shall reside [there]. And from among [these sixteen students], a *muid* [tutor] shall be appointed, who is the best in knowledge and virtue, who is most inclined to remove ignorance and acquire knowledge.

And this student shall not stop to continue the lessons in this way without any rightful excuse. And the salary of the *muid* shall be five, the salary of the others two *dirhem*.[19]

While the *medrese* was an institution of secondary education, primary education also took place in the mosque complex, in the small elementary school once located behind the mosque and the cemetery. In this simple, no longer extant, building – a square room covered by a single dome – children learned how to read the Qur'an and to write under the watchful eyes of a teacher (*muallim*), his assistant (*kalfa*) and a calligraphy teacher (*hüsnühat muallimi*). In her endowment deed, Nurbanu shows much concern for the teacher's treatment of the youngest among the mosque complex's beneficiaries, as she set the condition that 'to the children he will open the wings of gentleness' and that 'he will look at them as if they were his own children'.[20] In addition to free education, thirty of the poorest among the *mekteb* students also received clothes and shoes – to a total value of 1,500 *akçe* – twice a year, on the occasion of the Prophet's birthday (*mevlid*) and during the month of fasting.[21]

The seminaries for teaching the traditions of the Prophet (*darülhadis*) and the art of Qur'an recital (*darülkurra*) were not accommodated in buildings constructed of stone masonry, probably because the students did not reside within the confines of the complex and came only to meet on days appointed for lessons. Instead, lessons took place in a wooden building – no longer extant – located between the south wall of the mosque courtyard and adjacent to the north wall of the *imaret*.[22] In the *darülhadis*, twelve students studied not only the traditions and saying of the Prophet (*hadis*) that guide Muslims in daily life, but also Qur'an exegesis (*tefsir*). In the *darülkurra*, ten select students met four times a week to learn how to properly chant the Qur'an in the ten canonical styles. The *vakıfname* devotes much space to the quality of the recitation teacher, the styles to be taught and even to the textbooks used for the lessons. Neither for the *medrese* nor for the *darülhadis* did Nurbanu pay such detailed attention to the specifics of teaching, and this emphasis – together with the high number of reciters employed in the mosque – seems to indicate that she (or her son) had a particular fondness for Qur'an recitation.[23]

The inn for travellers, the *imaret* and the hospital are all located in a large roadside complex to the south of the mosque-cum-*medrese*. The hospital, however, was a self-sufficient unit with a separate entrance, so that the patients would not be disturbed by the hustle and bustle of travellers, guests and service personnel. The hospital's courtyard was sur-rounded by irregularly distributed cells, capped with domes and fronted by porticoes. Most of the rooms housed the patients, while others functioned as a pharmacy and as treatment rooms for the doctors, surgeons and ophthalmologists. For those patients whose treatment required hydrotherapy and massages and for those who wished to take a regular bath, a small hamam provided services. Also, a small mosque allowed the sick and the convalescing to pray or to give thanks for their recovery.[24] As with the treatment of children in the elementary school, the gentle and kind treatment of the sick appears to have been of particular importance to Nurbanu. The *vakıfname* stipulates that the doctors – in addition to being well trained and knowledgeable in both the theory and practice of medicine – shall 'never use hard words when seeing the patients; they will treat every patient with kindness and politeness, as if they were their nearest family and relatives'.[25] Diagnosis and treatment were given free of charge to all patients and included the administration of different kinds of medicines – herbs, potions, a medicated, slightly narcotic confection called *macun*, and salves, all to the worth of 200 *akçe* per day – as well as surgery, bathing and massage in the hospital's *hamam*, and dietary food prepared by the hospital's own cook.

Certainly, the weary travellers for whom Üsküdar was the final stop on a journey that might have led them over the westernmost stretches of the Silk Road to Istanbul took advantage of the hospital to cure sore feet and many other travel-related ailments. Travellers and their animals could stay in the adjacent inn for three days for free. The inn (*han*) welcomed guests through a gate on the south side that leads into a large domed reception hall opening to the two side wings where the stables were located. North of this reception hall lies a large arcaded courtyard with the entrance to the guest house and the refectory (*tabhane*) to its left, and to the kitchens and various storage rooms to its right. The building has undergone a great many changes over the last two centuries in order to accommodate functions as diverse as a military barrack, a prison, a mental institution and a tobacco warehouse, so that its present state tells only little about life in a late sixteenth-century *imaret*. The deed of trust, however, allows us to imagine the now empty rooms populated by a *şeyh* who acted as a sort of innkeeper, storage clerks who recorded incoming and outgoing foodstuffs, cooks and bakers, waiters and dishwashers, porters, janitors and garbage collectors – a staff of sixty who in total earned a salary of 190 *akçe* per day – as well as guests and charity recipients. Every day, the cooks and bakers prepared enormous quantities of food. On any given weekday, 32 kg of mutton was cooked, 300 kg of flour was made into *fodula* bread, 84 kg of rice into rice soup and 150 kg of wheat into wheat soup. The guests of the inn and the personnel of the mosque entitled to meals from the *imaret* received one morning meal and one evening meal each; the dinner consisted of 'one ladle of soup or some other stew, a piece of meat in the amount of 50 *dirhem* [150 gr] and a piece of bread in the amount of 200 *dirhem* [600 gr]'.[26] After the recipients mentioned in the deed of trust were served, what remained went to the poor who waited in front of the entrance to the *han*. The remainders were seldom enough to feed all the destitute hoping for a morsel and were fought over furiously, so much so that three doormen had to be hired 'to prevent crowding and chaos and to ensure order while the food is distributed to the poor and the orphans'.[27]

On feast days – Thursday nights, during the month of fasting, on the Feast of Sacrifice and on the birthday of the Prophet – particularly delicious food was prepared and distributed. For example, on the latter occasion, the employees of the mosque complex were invited to banquet tables bending under the load of sixteen different dishes and three kinds of sherbets (made of enormous quantities of honey, sugar, candied fruit and rose water), while the poor and needy received special rations of *dane* (a dish made with spiced rice and mutton) and *zerde* (a starchy dessert of sweetened rice with saffron). Evliya Çelebi, a seventeenth-century traveller who was greatly interested in the food of the regions he visited, noted that *zerde* was also distributed on Thursday nights, which according to the Muslim calendar belongs to Friday, the holiest day of the week.[28] *Zerde* was one of the most popular foods among Ottomans of the fifteenth and sixteenth century, both commoners and palace residents,[29] and the distribution of such a delicacy was certain to draw attention to Nurbanu's charity.[30]

On the other side of the mosque, across the street and far away from the busy *han* and *imaret*, another dependency offered a quieter and introspective atmosphere – the dervish convent (*tekke*). The irregular structure, consisting of thirty-three cells and one ceremonial hall (*tevhidhane*) around a trapezoidal courtyard with a central fountain, is only accessible from a door in the south corner. Its high solid walls sheltered the resident ascetics from the bustle outside. This design was the result of – and, in turn, enhanced – the devotional practice of seclusion favoured by the Halvetiyye order to which the thirty-two dervishes and their spiritual leader (*şeyh*) belonged.[31] The *şeyh* of the convent also acted as the mosque's Friday preacher, and even though the dervishes should be 'content with few worldly possessions',[32] as the endowment deed stipulates, they all received a small daily stipend in addition to food from the *imaret*.

Water supply was vital to the functioning of the mosque complex, and since no waterways existed prior to its construction, Nurbanu's pious foundation also financed the necessary infrastructure. The *Atik Valide Suyolu*, erected in 1582/3 and extended in 1584, provided the water necessary for the worshippers' ablutions, for quenching the thirst of the travellers and their animals, for cooking and cleaning, and for the bath-house. With a length of 15 km and a flow of 676,000 litres per day, the *Atik Valide Suyolu* brought the precious commodity from several springs located on the hills northeast of Üsküdar and supplied not only Nurbanu's own complex, but also other mosques, *imarets*, schools and fountains in its environs.[33] Merely constructing the waterway was not enough: constant maintenance work kept the water flowing in such abundance. Thus, the endowment employed seven waterway engineers and their apprentices, who looked after the *Atik Valide Suyolu*, as well as after other waterways that provisioned endowed properties elsewhere in Istanbul, even if those had been built by a different patron. The endowment deed specifies that two of the engineers were 'responsible for looking after the waterways leading to the hamam of the exalted founder in the vicinity of Dikilitaş [i.e., Çemberlitaş Hamamı] and to the hamam in the vicinity of Ayakapı [i.e., the Havuzlu Hamam]'.[34]

The Endowed Hamams

Financing the daily stipends of the foundation's employees, the food distributed by the *imaret*, the treatment dispensed in the hospital and the maintenance of the buildings and waterways required a steady, substantial income. While agricultural revenue could fluctuate considerably due to natural disasters or rebellions, rent income from urban commercial property in the form of the masonry buildings constituted a relatively secure source of income. The four hamams endowed to the Atik Valide Vakfı were all built in strategic locations in Istanbul and Üsküdar, not only to contribute to a relatively even distribution of these amenities for the populace,[35] but also to ensure a constant stream of paying customers. While the Atik Valide Hamamı next to the mosque complex served the employees, the travellers staying in the inn and the residents of the immediate neighbourhood, the other three bathhouses were all erected in commercial areas (Figure 2.4). Since Üsküdar was the point of arrival for trade goods coming to Istanbul from Asia Minor and, therefore, the westernmost end of the Silk Road, the Büyük Hamam on the main road down the hill to the Bosphorus was in a particularly well-suited location to attract travelling merchants. Indeed, Evliya Çelebi writes in his *Seyahatname* that the Büyük Hamam belongs to travellers.[36] Those arriving from the far ends of the Ottoman Empire and beyond dismounted from their mules, horses or camels and entered the hamam to wash off the dirt and dust of the journey.

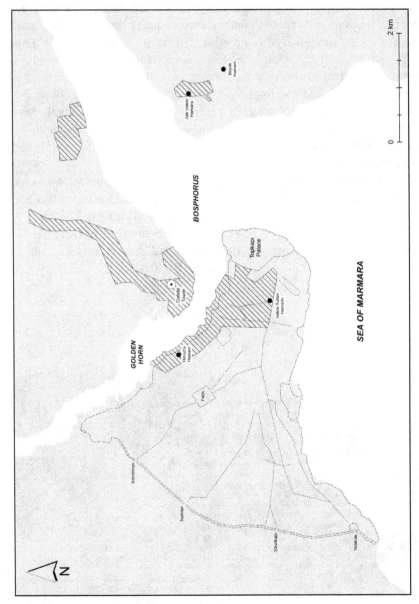

Figure 2.4 Istanbul's commercial areas in the sixteenth century. *Source*: Yasemin Özarslan.

The Havuzlu Hamam on the Golden Horn served a rather different clientele: the tradesmen and craftsmen living and working in the shops and wharves along the shoreline, where timber was traded and ships caulked and readied for sea. Çemberlitaş Hamamı, however, had the most advantageous location, on one of Istanbul's main traffic arteries. This main road, following the old Byzantine *mese*, led from one of the major gates in the city wall, the Topkapı, to the mosque complex of Mehmed the Conqueror, to the Covered Bazaar, and to the old hippodrome in front of the Hagia Sophia and the Imperial Palace. The bath's proximity to two of the most important commercial centres of the city – Tahtakale with its many markets and *han*s to the north, and the Covered Bazaar to the west – promised not only a large crowd of local bathers, but also visits from foreign travellers and merchants.

The endowment deed describes the Atik Valide Hamamı as 'two adjacent hamams, one for men, the other for women and heated by a furnace, in the abovementioned neighbourhood [i.e., Yeni Mahalle in Üsküdar]'.[37] The small double hamam is located across the street from the roadside complex containing the inn and the *imaret*, and thus grants easy access from the mosque complex (Figures 2.5). Both its rubble masonry and

Figure 2.5 Atik Valide Hamamı, *c*. 1582, Istanbul. *Source*: Author's photograph.

simple ground plan reflect the building's modest character. The men's and women's section each contain a dressing room, a warm room and a minuscule hot room, the latter being capped by a dome that sits directly on the walls, without any transitional elements. In spite of the structure's unpolished appearance, Sinan claims authorship to the building in the *Tuhfetü'l-Mi'mârîn*.[38]

An imperial decree of Selim II ordered the procurement of timber for this bathhouse as early as 1574, and both the structure's simplicity and the mention in the endowment deed make the year of the deed's writing (1582) a safe *terminus ante quem* for its completion.[39] The rent income produced by the Atik Valide Hamamı fluctuated between 2,500 and 4,166 *akçe* per month over the following three centuries, a small but steady revenue (see Chapter 3, Table 3.2). In the early nineteenth century, its roof tiles required extensive repairs, and by the early twentieth century the hamam, now no longer part of the dissolved endowment, fell into disrepair while it doubled as a carpenter's workshop.[40] In 1985, the Atik Valide Hamamı was restored to its original function and is now mostly visited by local residents.[41] Embedded between apartment buildings, the bath is no longer recognisable as a part of the mosque complex it once served.

The deed of trust of 1582 does not mention the Büyük Hamam in the centre of Üsküdar; therefore, it is likely that it was built after that date, around 1583 (Figures 2.6, 2.7).[42] That it indeed belonged to the Atik Valide Vakfı is without a doubt. In his eighteenth-century guide book to the Muslim monuments of Istanbul, the Ottoman author Ayvansarayi wrote: 'Among [the Atik Valide Mosque's] *vakıfs* are the nearby double hamam, the Yeşil Direkli Hamam near the Valide-i Cedid Congregational Mosque in Üsküdar, the well-known Çifte Hamam on the Divan Yolu in Istanbul and the single hamam with a pool, located inside the Yani Kapı of Langa.'[43] As with many monuments, this bathhouse had several names that changed over the centuries. Depending on which of the hamam's features mattered most to the person who uttered its name, it could be identified based on its size (Büyük Hamam, large bathhouse), a characteristic mark in its interior architecture (Yeşil Direkli Hamam, bathhouse with the green column), its location (Çarşı Hamamı, market bath), its founder (Valide Sultan Hamamı) or its architect (Mimar Sinan Hamamı).

The parallel sections with a dressing room, warm room and hot room each are inscribed within a rectangular building block. From the square domed dressing room, the bathers proceeded through the small warm room, made up of three domed bays, into the hot room. The latter was built over a ground plan that approximates the shape of a star. Here, Sinan rotated the four-*iwan* plan so that the deep niches have come to lie in the corners

Figure 2.6 Büyük Hamam, *c.* 1583, Istanbul. *Source*: Author's photograph.

of the outer square and form private bathing chambers (*halvet*) capped by small domes. Between these deep niches, Sinan added deep rectangular recesses that make for an interesting interplay between the space's central unity and its sectionality. As a very large hamam and the most frequented in Üsküdar, the Büyük Hamam brought a monthly income of between 3,000 and 6,000 *akçe* during the seventeenth century (see Chapter 3, Table 3.2). By the nineteenth century, the monthly rent had increased to 10,820 *akçe*, and while this increase was also due to inflation, it shows the hamam's popularity and profitability during the 1800s. However, with the building of the railway on the Anatolian side of the Bosphorus, the commercial centre shifted from Üsküdar to the Haydarpaşa train station (erected in 1908), and the Büyük Hamam lost a good number of customers. By 1917, economic difficulties forced its private owner to close the hamam, only to be reopened to have its marble interior removed and sold for quick cash. Thereafter, it was used as warehouse and workshop. After the bathhouse came under state ownership in 1959, it was renovated and turned into a shopping centre, with small stores fitted into the *halvet*s and additional doors broken through its exterior walls in order to allow shoppers to enter from all sides.[44]

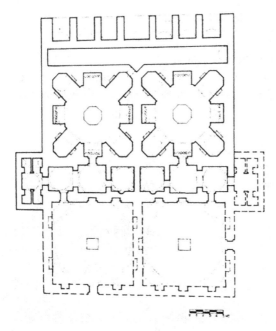

Figure 2.7 Ground plan of the Büyük Hamam. *Source*: Ünsal, 'Sinan'ın Son Bir Eseri Üsküdar Büyük Hamamın Aslı Şekline Dönüşümü', 1986.

The Havuzlu Hamam on the shore of the Golden Horn was already well known by 1582, as the deed of trust describes: 'Located in the vicinity of Aya Kapu in the neighbourhood of the Gül Cami, a single hamam; there is no need to describe it, because its connection to the founder is well-known.'[45] Like the Büyük Hamam, it carried several different names: Havuzlu Hamam after the decorative pool in its dressing room; Aya Kapı Hamamı after the nearby gate of Hagia Theodosius in the old Byzantine city wall; and, later, Yeni Kapı Hamamı after the new gate broken into the city wall in even closer proximity. Built in the spring of 1582 under the supervision of Sinan, this new gate must have become necessary because of the increased volume of traffic and commerce in the area – a flow of people that also guaranteed customers for the hamam.[46] Not only the city gate, but also the bath's completion fell under Sinan's supervision, since his memoirs unequivocally list the building among his achievements.[47]

Although the hamam's entrance has been destroyed, Ayvansarayi mentions the text of the building inscription and chronogram originally decorating the lunette over the door in his *Mecmu'a-i Tevarih*:

Praise be to God, this pleasant place,
it was with a thousand efforts that it was completed.

It was said about the date of this lofty building
'that this hamam was the pride of the city'. [1582][48] '

The exalted inscription stands in stark contrast to the modest size of the single bath, squeezed into an irregularly shaped plot of land (Figures 2.8, 2.9). The bathers entered the building from its shortest side,

Figure 2.8 Havuzlu Hamam, before 1582, Istanbul. *Source*: Author's photograph.

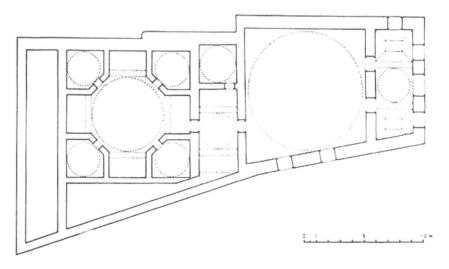

Figure 2.9 Ground plan of the Havuzlu Hamam. *Source*: Cantay, 'Mimar Sinan'ın Az Tanınan Bir Eseri', 1987.

through a *rüzgarlık*, a small rectangular room designed to prevent wind from the Golden Horn from sweeping into the dressing room. Passing under the *rüzgarlık*'s miniature dome, the visitors entered a trapezoidal, dome-capped dressing room of no more than 10 m length. A minuscule warm room led to a triangular side room – created by the need to inscribe a square hot room into a trapezoidal building – and to the hot room proper. The latter is an interesting variation of the dome-over-square ground plan. Deliberately kept small, the central dome rests on the octagonal support system created by the walls of the surrounding niches and chambers. Sinan used the four-*iwan* plan to anchor the hot room's ground plan and added domed pentagonal *halvet*s in the resulting corners – an arrangement that gave the space an enclosed and intimate quality.

Although located in a lively commercial area, the hamam's small scale and its clientele, which, because of its single bathing unit, excluded the female part of the neighbourhood's population were reflected in the rent income. In 1628, the Havuzlu Hamam brought a monthly rent of no more than 1,000 *akçe* to Nurbanu's endowment, and during most of the seventeenth century, the rent amount fluctuated between 1,666 and 2,865 *akçe* per month. With few exceptional months, this made it the least profitable of the foundation's baths. It might be its lesser value to the endowment that in the long run contributed to the present state of the hamam. After the building had fallen into disrepair in the 1920s, the private owner used it as a storehouse for timber in the 1940s, a function it continues to serve.[49] In 2000, the owner attempted to sell the ruin, praising in the for-sale advertisement its resistance to earthquakes, its storage capabilities and its potential for renovation into a bathhouse, but the high asking price deterred any buyers.[50]

Çemberlitaş Hamamı's family consisted of a parent (the Atik Valide Mosque Complex), that parent's smaller sibling (the mosque complex in Lapseki, Thrace), three siblings of its own kind (the Atik Valide Hamamı, the Büyük Hamam and the Havuzlu Hamam), as well as many other siblings of a different kind (the revenue-generating buildings around Istanbul and the empire at large). Çemberlitaş Hamamı and its siblings had all been brought into the world to work for the parent. Like a large, immobile grandee who lived a pious life in his mansion, distributing charity in the form of food, money and medicine to his *kapı halkı* (his retinue of dependants living in the neighbourhood), the mosque complex itself was not able to generate the revenue necessary to sponsor its charity. Rather, it sent out its offspring (the four hamams, as well as the residences, shops, workshops, mansions, farms and pastures) to do business on its behalf and to generate the large sums of money it needed to sustain itself and its philanthropic activities. Indeed, Çemberlitaş Hamamı and its siblings worked hard to satisfy the parent who, large of girth, always clamoured for more. Yet the children were not merely breadwinners for their parent; they also constituted symbolic capital, announcing the fecundity, the hard work and the philanthropy of the family as a whole, which in turn reflected on the patron, Nurbanu, and the dynasty to which she belonged.

3

From Birth to Breadwinner

*It describes how the aforementioned hamam appeared when it was first
erected and before it lived through the vicissitudes of fires and earthquakes
and the addition of ignoble lean-to buildings to its attractive front. And
then it describes how this humble servant, this poor one, determined the
very exact date of construction of the aforementioned hamam, with the
help of the many orders that the servants to the Sublime Porte and their
descendants kept for posterity. It describes how this pleasurable hamam,
after its completion, began to take up work and how it was readied – with
water and wood – to render its joy-giving service to the people of the
Protected City. And it describes the people who expended all their zeal
humanly possible on making this bathhouse a most pleasurable one – the
hamamcı, the attendants, the furnace stoker – and how these people come
together in guilds. And then, who the people visiting the hamam and, by
paying their akçes for the most excellent services given there, contributing
to the* valide sultan's *charitable foundation were. And it describes how the
aforementioned hamam worked hard, together with its siblings, in order to
support the* valide sultan's *noble Friday Mosque and its dependencies in
Üsküdar, and in detail how much money it earned in this quest.*

The Birth

At birth, Çemberlitaş Hamamı presented an appearance very different
from the one visitors experience today. During Byzantine times, the Forum
of Constantine occupied the area, its centre marked by a porphyry column
with a statue of Constantine the Great as Apollo Helios. The column had
been erected in 330 to commemorate the dedication of Constantinople as
the new capital of the Roman Empire. Through the forum ran the *mese*, the
major road leading from the Hippodrome to the main gate in the city wall.
The Ottomans subsequently continued to use large portions of this road,
which in the eighteenth century came to be officially called Divan Yolu,
as a major traffic artery and processional route and turned the forum into
a market space and land for a new mosque complex (Figures 3.1, 3.2).[1]

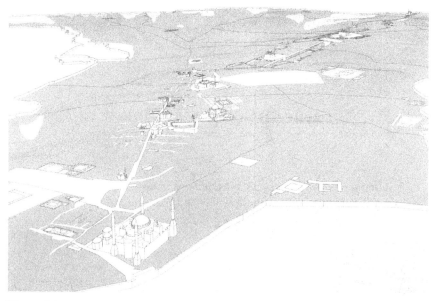

Figure 3.1 Perspectival view of the Divan Yolu, westwards from Hagia Sophia.
Source: Cerasi, *The Istanbul Divan Yolu*, 2006.

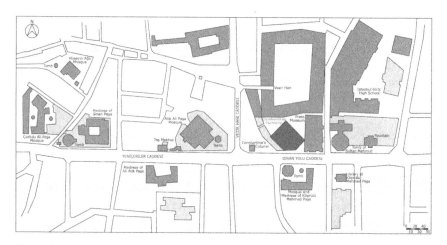

Figure 3.2 Neighbourhood of Çemberlitaş Hamamı. *Source*: Sabiha Göloğlu.

In 1496/7, the vizier Atik Ali Paşa – who would later go on to serve as grand vizier to Sultan Bayezid II twice, from 1501 to 1503 and from 1506 to 1511 – celebrated the completion of his mosque, *medrese*, hospice and dervish convent on a plot just northwest of the column. At the end of his second term as grand vizier, he added to his complex an inn for travellers on the south side of the Divan Yolu. This inn, which has not survived, routinely housed foreign ambassadors until 1645 and was therefore known as the Ambassador's caravansaray, Elçi Han. Another no longer extant monument, the Dikilitaş Mescidi, was completed around the same time as the Atik Ali Paşa Mosque and, according to Ayvansarayi, was located on the road that ran in front of the hamam and intersected with the Divan Yolu.[2] Still, these monuments were few enough to allow an open space within the as-of-yet rather loose urban fabric, and Çemberlitaş Hamamı stood in grandeur as an isolated building, towering much higher than today's street level allows.

In spite of its relative isolation, Çemberlitaş Hamamı was part of an urban architectural ensemble that was anchored by Constantine's Column. The Ottomans called the column Dikilitaş (erect stone) until the nineteenth century, when iron bands were added for stabilisation and it became Çemberlitaş (hooped stone). This ensemble of mosque complex, caravansaray, *mescid*, column and hamam owed its coherence not so much to an axial alignment of its separate constituents, but rather to the visual links between the monuments that the users of this space experienced and the resulting theatrical quality (Figure 3.3).[3] Çemberlitaş Hamamı's location was well chosen, because of the availability of an empty, flat plot of land on the former forum, allowing a free-standing and symmetrically designed building, and because it is adjacent to – or rather even with its southern corner intruding into – the symbolically charged and very prestigious Divan Yolu. The city's main processional route, frequently travelled by the sultan and his officials, connected the Topkapı Palace and the Hagia Sophia with the mosque complexes of Beyazid II and Mehmed the Conqueror and, beyond that, the major city gates.[4] Over the three centuries following the hamam's completion, many high-ranking patrons of architecture – Koca Sinan Paşa in 1593, the Köprülü family in the seventeenth century, Kara Mustafa Paşa in 1690 and Çorlulu Ali Paşa in 1708 – erected building complexes along the road.[5] In addition to its symbolic significance as some of the most sought-after real estate in Istanbul, the hamam's plot had great economic advantages. It was located next to a mosque without a bathhouse of its own, close to an inn for travellers and within the commercial hub of the city, in walking distance from the Covered Bazaar (Figure 3.4). Of course, Çemberlitaş Hamamı was not the only bathhouse along the Divan Yolu, but as Figure 3.5, based on the thirteen extant hamams, illustrates, these establishments were spaced relatively evenly along the route, so that they did not compete unfairly with each other.[6]

Today, Çemberlitaş Hamamı's façade is enveloped by many smaller buildings and shops and no longer resembles the distinguished,

Figure 3.3 Thomas Allom, *The Tcheenberle Tash, or Burnt Pillar. Source*: Pardoe, *City of the Sultan,* 1837.

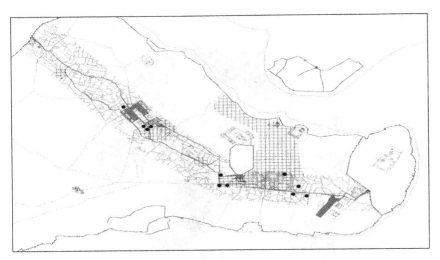

Figure 3.4 Map of commercial areas (hatched) and *han*s (dots) along Divan Yolu. *Source*: Cerasi, *The Istanbul Divan Yolu*, 2006.

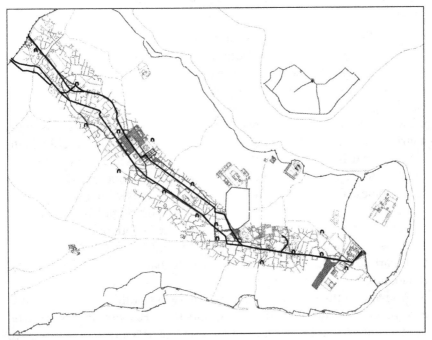

Figure 3.5 Map of hamams and aqueducts along Divan Yolu. *Source*: Cerasi, *The Istanbul Divan Yolu*, 2006.

Figure 3.6 Dome lantern of Çemberlitaş Hamamı. *Source*: Author's photograph.

free-standing imperial monument it once was. Often, architects had to fit bathhouses into tight spaces between already existing structures, resulting in an asymmetrical and irregular layout; because a very high-ranking member of the sultan's household commissioned Çemberlitaş Hamamı, this was not the case here. While the ground plan does show a very minor axial irregularity, the overall arrangement is symmetrical, with the men's and women's sections side by side inscribed into a rectangular block of about 38 × 38 m. Each dressing room's and hot room's location within the building is indicated on the exterior by four large domes. Originally, both lead-covered domes over the hot rooms carried lanterns with eight small columns supporting pointed arches and a crown-shaped miniature dome. Now only the lantern over the women's dressing room has remained in place (Figure 3.6). Very likely, the lanterns carried standarts (*'alem*) to indicate the bath's status as an imperial foundation.[7]

A seventeenth-century map of the waterways of the Köprülü family's endowment includes a drawing of Çemberlitaş Hamamı that, schematic as it is, allows a reconstruction of the façade's original appearance (Figure 3.7). Since no plaster was applied to most of the exterior walls, the building stone was visible, as indicated by long horizontal and short vertical lines on the right of the building front The right half of the façade, fronting the women's section, consisted of a blind wall that drew

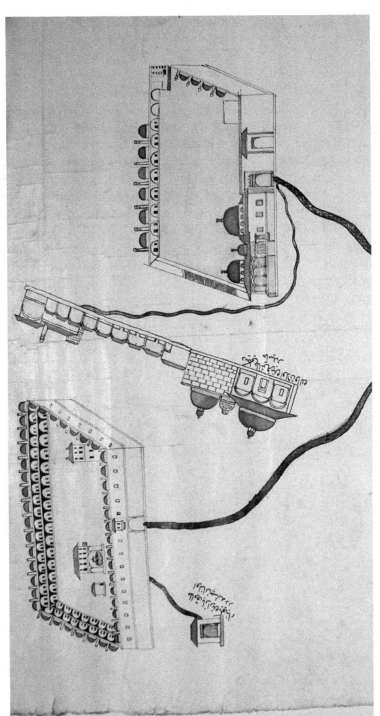

Figure 3.7 Map of the water conduits belonging to the Köprülü endowment, seventeenth century, Süleymaniye Library. Köprülü İlave 197, *Source*: Süleymaniye Library.

attention away from the women visitors – who entered through an inconspicuous door on the side – in order to protect their modesty. The façade of the men's section was fronted by a portico, one of Sinan's innovations in hamam architecture.[8] According to the draftsman of the waterway map, the portico consisted of three arches supported by four columns. Elsewhere in the building, in the hot rooms, and for his other imperially commissioned monuments, Sinan favoured marble columns with lozenge capitals, and there is little reason to believe that his workshop would have chosen a different style of columns for Çemberlitaş Hamamı's portico. The portico carried a shed roof; on the drawing the draftsman combined this roof with the dome above to a hat-like shape. This portico in many ways must have resembled that of the Haseki Hamamı, a bathhouse that Sinan built for Sultan Süleyman's wife in 1553, some thirty years before Çemberlitaş Hamamı (Figure 3.8). There, the portico counts five pointed arches resting on marble columns with lozenge capitals and is covered by a small central dome and two flat brick vaults to each side. Both at the Haseki Hamamı and Çemberlitaş Hamamı two windows flanked the central door. In both bathhouses, a gold-on-green inscription over the door greeted the customer.

Figure 3.8 Haseki Hamamı, 1553, Istanbul. *Source*: Author's photograph.

Figure 3.9 Inscription above the entrance to the men's section of Çemberlitaş Hamamı. *Source*: Author's photograph.

In Çemberlitaş Hamamı's inscription, the poet-painter Mustafa Sai – whom we have already encountered as personal friend of Sinan and poet who helped him write his memoir – welcomed the visitor, explained Nurbanu's motivation for erecting the building and extolled its beauty (Figure 3.9):

> Thanks be to God, today is Sultan Murad's ...
> This pleasurable hamam is a wonderful place.
> As the world stands still, it bestows blessings on the deceased [patron]'s name.
> Its atmosphere is pleasant, its building is attractive, its front clean.
> Sai-i Dai saw the perfection and told the date.
> The Valide Sultan Hamam was made and became noble.
> 992 [1584][9]

Thus greeted, male visitors entered the dressing room, or *soğukluk*. A square of about 13 m in length, the room supports a dome with a diameter of 12.5 m (Figure 3.10). An oculus in the dome's centre, once covered by the abovementioned lantern to keep precipitation out of the interior, allows daylight in. Grooved squinches decorate the transition zones in the

Figure 3.10 Dressing room in the men's section of Çemberlitaş Hamamı.
Source: www.cemberlitashamami.com, artwork in the public domain.

corners. Today, the dressing room's walls are lined with wooden cabins up to the height of these squinches; it is not certain whether the same arrangement already existed in the sixteenth century. The *soğukluk* traditionally functions as a dressing room where bathers disrobe and store their belongings for the duration of the bath, and as a lounge for resting, taking refreshments and entertaining afterwards. While chatting and sipping sherbet or coffee, visitors would have reclined on low couches (*divan*) and enjoyed the water games of a decorative marble fountain in the room's centre. That a fountain was part of the original context is proven by a document mentioning a *şadırvan* (fountain).[10]

After undressing and wrapping themselves in flat-woven towels (*peştemal*), male visitors leave the dressing room through a door opposite the main entrance and proceed to the warm room (*ılıklık*). In this long room, which Sinan arranged horizontally to the square dressing room and covered with three small domes, bathers can spend some time to slowly accustom their bodies to the bath's higher temperature. The warm room contains several basins set against the marble-panelled walls and a decorative wall fountain that must be dated to a later century, based on its baroque ornaments. Two doors lead out of this room: one sideways to the toilets, and the other opposite the entrance to the heart of the hamam, the hot room (*sıcaklık*).

The hot room consists of one primary large space covering a dode-cagonal area of a diameter of 12.5 m, and four secondary spaces. In order to solve the architectural problem of transitioning from a square area to a domed elevation and at the same time to create a unified, centralised space, Sinan handled the room's composition quite innovatively: the four niches of the four-*iwan* plan have been rotated by 45 degrees, so that they now occupy the corners. Separated by dividing walls of slightly more than human height and crowned by small domes, these more secluded niches (*halvet*) with their three basins each can accommodate bathers who desire more privacy. Two shallow niches each between the four *halvet* entrances form the background to the twelve columns supporting the central dome. These twelve columns, all with lozenge capitals, are placed in equidis-tance to and connected with the exterior walls, so that they distract from the differing angles and depths of the *halvet* entrances and niches and enhance the room's unified appearance.

In the centre of the room, an elevated marble slab (*göbektaşı*) gives the bathers a place to lie down and to wait for the skin's pores to open in the humid air. After about half an hour, bathers are ready for a scrub with the rough massage glove (*kese*), which they can either apply them-selves or have an attendant do. In 1916 or 1917, when Glück visited Çemberlitaş Hamamı, the *göbektaşı* still boasted a magnificent, geomet-ric inlay in black on white marble, which bathers could have traced with their eyes while lying belly-down (Figure 3.11). The small holes pierced into the masonry of the whitewashed dome above, covered with glass cups of a diameter of about 20 cm (*filgözü*), admit daylight to the space (Figures 3.12, 3.13).

Due to the many restorations and renovations over the centuries, the marble basins (*kurna*) have been replaced. However, some of the divid-ing walls, with their carved ornamental bands of palmettes and finials, still give a sense of the hamam's original decoration (Figure 3.14). Male bathers were also able to enjoy an ornament that the women's hot room did not have: a lengthy inscription of twenty verses running along the dividing walls, inscribed in stark black on the soft grey marble in cartou-ches of varying form (Figure 3.15). Only verses 1–9 and 17–20 date to Çemberlitaş Hamamı's time of birth. The remaining verses were destroyed and replaced in the eighteenth century, as will be discussed in Chapter 5. Once again, the painter-poet Mustafa Sai exhorted the bath's qualities, but this time he also added a mystic dimension in his poem:

A lovely hamam brings pleasure and
its pleasant atmosphere is an elixir for the soul.

Figure 3.11 *Göbektaşı* in the men's hot room of Çemberlitaş Hamamı. *Source*: Author's photograph.

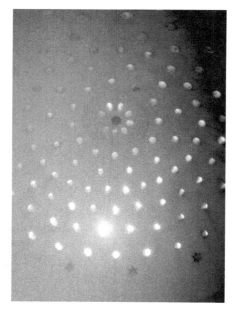

Figure 3.12 Dome of the men's hot room of Çemberlitaş Hamamı, interior. *Source*: Author's photograph.

Figure 3.13 Dome of the men's hot room of Çemberlitaş Hamamı, exterior. *Source*: Author's photograph.

Figure 3.14 Men's hot room of Çemberlitaş Hamamı. *Source*: Author's photograph.

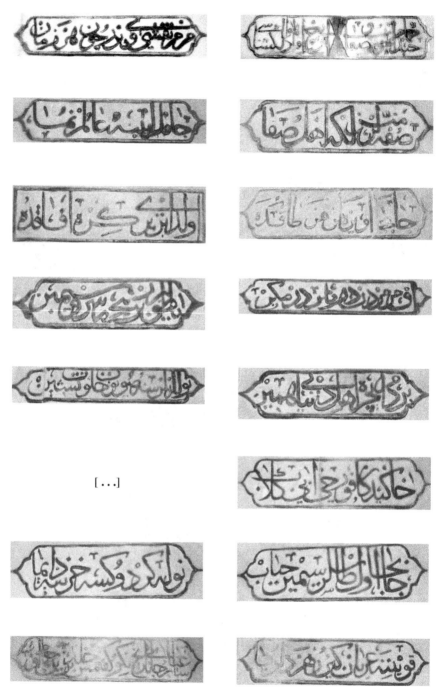

[...]

Figure 3.15 Inscription in the men's hot room of Çemberlitaş Hamamı. Reading direction of the panels is from right to left. *Source*: Author's photograph.

Its marble adornments drink water
like the beautiful waves of the sea.
To the men of pleasure *sofas* [i.e., bench-lined halls] are the place of
    destination.
Windows are the mirror showing the world.
Here and there chandeliers in every dome
are overflowing on the horizon.
Unless those are marble columns,
they [must be] tall silver-skinned graceful youths.
The men of the world chatter on all the same,
what does it matter if they understand those who sit in the seclusion of water?
. . .
The floor [of the hamam] is camphor-white, the water of life rose-water.
Here and there those bowls [resemble] silvery water bubbles.
What does it matter if [the water] always returns to the reservoir?
Every beloved comes into his lover's arms naked.
It was granted to Sai the request to utter a beautiful dated inscription for that
    earthly paradise, the hamam. 992 [1584][11]

As customary in Ottoman building inscriptions, chronograms and poetry in general, several of the lines can be read in more than one way and carry additional connotations that require explanation. For example, the line 'they [must be] tall silver-skinned graceful youths' can be alternatively read as 'they must be traces of moonlight on the calm sea'. In another instance, the lines 'The men of the world chatter on all the same, what does it matter if they understand those who sit in the seclusion of water?' refer to the ritual practice of seclusion in Sufism. The Ottoman term *halvet-nişin* can mean both somebody who sits in a private bathing chamber (*halvet*), as well as someone who sits in a secluded cell (also *halvet*) for the purpose of meditation in an environment of sensory deprivation. Thus, Çemberlitaş Hamamı is more than merely a place for idle entertainment and chatter. Equally, in the line 'what does it matter if [the water] always returns to the reservoir?' Mustafa Sai alluded to the hamam's purity – although water once used is not supposed to flow back to the reservoir, this bath is so pristine that even its used water retains its cleansing power – as well as to the mystical notion that humans always return to God, their creator. In the following line, the image of the naked beloved coming into his lover's arms is a metaphor for the (almost) naked bather coming into the hamam's embrace. As discussed in the Introduction, equating the hamam with the figure of the lover was a common conceit in the Ottoman poetic imagination, and therefore the inscription evoked a well-known metaphor.

87

Literate bathers could read the poem, progressing from one *halvet* to the next and then ponder its layered meanings while resting on the *göbektaşı*. Bathers unable to read could ask someone else to read the verses to them, and the attendants – even if not literate – may well have memorised the verses. Did the women's hot room have a similar inscription that allowed female bathers the literary pleasures of reading and meditating on its meanings? The women's *sıcaklık* has undergone so many repairs that nothing of its original interior decoration remains; however, the relatively lower rate of literacy among Ottoman women, the parallel lack of inscriptions in other women's sections of Sinan's hamams and even on Çemberlitaş Hamamı's façade point to a negative answer.

With the lengthy inscription, the men's hot room contains the most elaborate decoration in the bath's interior, even if its stark quality gives it a rather sombre note. Similar to the *sıcaklıks*, the remaining rooms are almost bare of decoration, except for the few ornaments on the marble panels and the architectural elements themselves. This restraint in decoration leaves the architectural volume unencumbered so as to allow a strong, clear impression on the builiding's users while they move through the space; an impression of fine understatement, as is so often affected by Sinan's most successful creations.

Those parts of a bathhouse that few visitors ever see or consider, but without which it cannot function, are tucked away at the back of the building and hidden inside the walls: the water reservoir with its distribution system, the furnace and the heating flues. Located behind the hot rooms, the furnace (*külhan*) heats the air that circulates through the hypocaust system in order to warm the interior (Figure 3.16). The furnace opens up into a hollow space (*cehennemlik*) underneath the bath's floor which is suspended on pillars. Like blood coursing through the arteries and veins of a living creature, hot air, smoke and gases circulate through these open spaces, rise through the flues embedded in the walls and are finally released through chimneys on the roof. The furnace also heats the water in a metal boiler mounted directly above it. The metal boiler is fed from a water reservoir at roof level, whose high location facilitates the gravitational flow of the water. The hot water leaving the boiler is instantly replaced by cold water from the reservoir, which due to the difference in temperature sinks to the bottom where the fire immediately heats it. The metal boiler feeds hot water to the faucets in the hamam, while the cold water comes directly from the water reservoir.

A furnace stoker, or *külhancı*, looks after the heating system and fuels the fire with wood from the storage also located at the back of the building.

Figure 3.16 Schematic drawing of a hamam's heating system. A: furnace, B: hypocaust, C; water reservoir, D: flue, E: copper boiler. *Source*: Author.

The stoker's duty is to keep the fire going permanently, so that the hamam's walls remain dry in spite of the constant humidity. If the fire extinguishes and the building cools down, re-heating the entire system requires efforts lasting several days. The problem of how to preserve heat while economising fuel greatly influenced the design of Ottoman bathhouses: the walls of the warm and hot rooms have few openings – the glass-covered windows in the domes are deliberately kept small – and the building's compact form minimises heat loss through the exterior walls.

Reconstructing Çemberlitaş Hamamı's date of birth appears easy enough thanks to the dated inscriptions on the façade and in the men's hot room, which provide a *terminus ante quem*. Yet there is an abundance of records with various contradicting completion dates that need to be reconciled. The endowment deed in Ottoman Turkish, dated to April 1582, lists the bathhouse among the endowed properties and laconically adds: 'There is no need to describe and define it, because its connection to the founder is well-known among noble and lowly people'.[12] Accordingly, the hamam should have been in business by 1582, two years before the inscription's date. Scribal practices of endowment administration can explain this discrepancy: originally, a scribe had penned the deed of trust, in its function as a legal document, in Arabic in 1582. Several years later, the day-to day administration of the *vakıf* required a more readily usable document in

Ottoman Turkish, and in the process of copying, the second scribe merely transposed the earlier date onto the new version.

More helpful for a precise dating are the entries in the *mühimme deft-erleri* that deal with the hamam's water supply. Two records – the first dating to 29 Zilhicce 990 (24 January 1583), the second to 28 Safer 991 (23 March 1583) – mention the status of the construction.[13] The first entry concerns 'the hamam that *will be erected* in front of the Dikilitaş', suggesting that the construction work had not yet begun.[14] The second entry indicates that construction was now in process by referring to 'the hamam that *she began to build*'.[15] Thus, the beginning date of the construction falls into the two-month period between 24 January and 23 March 1583. Taking into consideration that inscriptions often predated the actual completion of the rest of the building, a construction period of one to two years (between January/February/March 1583 and 1584) still seems ample time for the birth of a monument of Çemberlitaş Hamamı's scale.

Getting Ready to Work

After the interior walls had been plastered and whitewashed, the domes covered with lead and glass cups, the hot rooms furnished with marble panels, basins and a *göbektaşı*, and the faucets connected to the internal water supply, Çemberlitaş Hamamı was still not entirely ready to begin work. It needed water. Since Istanbul is a city notoriously poor in immediate fresh water sources,[16] the Ottoman imperial administration closely monitored the water supply, regularly discussed its details in the imperial council and meticulously recorded its decisions and orders in the *mühimme defterleri*. According to an entry dating to 29 Zilhicce 990 (24 January 1583), Çemberlitaş Hamamı's water came from a well in the valley of İvadlu and was conveyed through the waterway of Kağıdhane, which runs towards the north end of the Golden Horn.[17] One *lüle*, equaling 0.6 litres per second (i.e., 51,840 litres in a 24-hour day), was drawn from the well and three-quarters of it was assigned to the hamam.[18] For the right to these 38,880 litres of water daily, the endowment had to pay the hefty sum of 30,000 *akçe*.

Only two months later, on 23 March 1583, the imperial council again discussed Çemberlitaş Hamamı's water supply and approved the bath's being connected to the waterway supplying the mosque and *imaret* of Sultan Bayezit II.[19] This waterway – whose exact construction date is unknown – brought water from the Belgrade Forest north of Istanbul to the city *intra muros*.[20] The supervisor of Bayezit's endowment, however, claimed that the waterway was in need of repair, the costs being estimated at 1 million *akçe*. While 600,000 *akçe* had already come out of the sultan's coffers, the remaining 400,000 *akçe* should be covered by money from the net accrual of the Atik Valide Vakfı. Furthermore, the water that would flow through the newly repaired Bayezit waterway to Çemberlitaş Hamamı had to be augmented by water drawn from a well in the countryside.

Supplying a bathhouse with the necessary water was a lengthy and expensive procedure. First, water rights had to be purchased, legalised through a petition to the imperial council and registered with the *kadı* in charge. Second, the water had to be transported to the hamam. There was an extensive network of waterways in Istanbul, but the permission to connect any building to that network was often tied to stipulations such as financing renovations and repairs to the waterway in question. Waterways were usually part of endowments, and this meant that the *vakıf* erecting the new building – whether that new structure was a chari-table building such as an *imaret*, or a commercial building such as a row of shops – at the same time contributed to another endowment. Hence, endowments were not financially self-contained units, but forged eco-nomic ties with and profited from each other: in exchange for the water supply of Çemberlitaş Hamamı, the Atik Valide Vakfı contributed to the older Sultan Bayezit Vakfı.

Only about one year into Çemberlitaş Hamamı's working life, water supply became an issue again, since the previously assigned 38,800 litres per day had proved to be insufficient. On 2 December 1585, the imperial council ordered that four *lüle* (207,360 litres per day) from a spring or well close to a village called Petnahor should be assigned for the hamam's use.[21] These 207,360 litres flowed into Sultan Süleyman's waterway of Kağıdhane, north of the Golden Horn. Çemberlitaş Hamamı then drew the allotted water from the underground channel next to the bachelors' boarding house (*bekar odaları*) opposite Ibrahim Paşa's palace on the Hippodrome, with the help of a water wheel. According to a 1588 *mühimme* entry, this water wheel was powered by horses, whose yearly upkeep of 6,000–7,000 *akçe* was paid by yet another endowment that received for its fountain the water not needed by the hamam.[22] To compli-cate matters even further, superfluous water from that endowed fountain flowed to the houses of one Ahmed Ağa and one Çeri Kethüda, who paid 100,000 *akçe* to the Atik Valide Vakfı for their water rights. Çemberlitaş Hamamı was thus integrated into an ever-growing web of economic ties between endowments and individuals, a web whose threads consisted of waterways.[23]

In addition to water, Çemberlitaş Hamamı needed fuel to work, and the necessary wood – which in the form of shavings and sawdust still heats the bathhouse today – had to be transported from the forest into the city. The imperial council concerned itself with the question of provisioning the newly established bath on 12 March 1583, in the same month as it discussed the water supply.[24] The order went to the *kadı*s of the Mediterranean and the Black Sea regions to acquire wood at the going rate in their respective areas of jurisdiction and to send it to Istanbul on the boat belonging to a certain Ali Reis. Once the requisite water and fuel had arrived, Çemberlitaş Hamamı was almost ready to begin work; now only employees and customers were needed to breathe life into it.

The Hamam's Employees[25]

It was the duty of the bath's manager (*hamamcı*), who rented the building from the endowment, to furnish the bath's dressing room with rugs, mats, pillows and wooden chests for safekeeping valuables, with towels and clogs and bowls for those customers who came without their own hamam kit, and to hire the attendants and other employees necessary.[26] Large bathhouses, like Çemberlitaş Hamamı, bustled with people. The *hamamcı* oversaw a team consisting of a *meydancı* (supervisor and fee collector); a group of attendants (*tellak*s) who washed and scrubbed the customers, supervised by the *ser-nöbet tellak*; a group of bathhouse attendants in training (*çırak*, or *şagırd*); a group of servants (*natır*) who helped bathers to undress and dress, handing them towels and other items;[27] a barber; a keeper of towels (*peştemalcı*); a cook who prepared coffee and other refreshments (*kahveci*); a laundryman (*çamaşırcı*, or *came-şuy*); and a furnace stoker (*külhancı*).[28] In the women's section, the *hamam anası* (literally, 'mother of the hamam') oversaw the female bathhouse attendants.

The most important among the employees providing services was the *tellak* who scrubbed and massaged the bathers. Apprentices to this profession were selected as boys, based on their physique and character. Ideally, a *tellak* was handsome, strong enough to withstand the hard labour in the humid air of the hot room, and personable in character, so as to make customers feel at ease. The apprentice received his training on the job and learned how to wash the customers' hair, how to soap, scrub and massage them with the scrubbing glove (*kese*). On the day he graduated to master attendant (*usta*), he was girded with a black silk towel which distinguished him from the bathers. The salary of a *tellak* usually consisted of the customers' tips.[29] Many of them lived in the bathhouse permanently, because they were bachelors or migrant workers from the provinces who did not set up a household in the capital, but sent a portion of their salary home to their families or saved up their income.[30]

Until the late eighteenth century, most *tellaks* were of Albanian origin, and generation after generation of men followed in the professional footsteps of their fathers, brothers, uncles and cousins – a pattern of professional choice that still exists today. However, in 1730 the Patrona Halil rebellion, named after the eponymous Albanian bathhouse attendant working in the Bayezid Hamamı, shook Istanbul and the Ottoman Empire. The rebellion was a reaction to the continued debasement of currency, changes in the guild system due to the influx of Anatolian and Rumelian migrants into Istanbul, and the burdensome taxes extracted from the guilds to mobilise the army against the Safavid Empire. It ended with the deposition of Sultan Ahmed III in October 1730 and the execution of Patrona Halil in November.[31] As a public space that allowed people to gather and to discuss the issues of the day, bathhouses now increasingly appeared to the imperial administration as places with dangerous potential for creating social unrest. They needed to be policed much more carefully, and in 1734/5, in an effort to control this professional group, an imperial decree ordered that from that year on all bathhouse attendants working in Istanbul should be registered.[32] It comes as no surprise that the administration was particularly weary of Patrona Halil's countrymen and required scribes preparing these registers to indicate *tellaks* of Albanian origin in red ink. By actively discriminating against Albanian bathhouse attendants, the administration intended to push this ethnic group out of the guild. Once an Albanian returned to his province of origin, he could no longer work in a hamam upon his return, and all new attendants should hail from Istanbul or Anatolia. Indeed, following these regulations, hamam managers recruited more and more attendants from eastern Anatolian towns, and Sivas and Tokat soon distinguished themselves by producing generations of *tellaks* migrating to Istanbul[33] – a tradition that continues today.

The impact of the new regulations was not as immediate as the administration probably had hoped for. By 1752, the *tellaks* still constituted a very colourful group in terms of their ethnic origins, as a register compiled for purposes of policing the hamams of Istanbul and the districts of Eyüp and Galata shows.[34] The *defter* enumerates every single one of the recorded 2,400 *tellaks* and *natırs* by name, home town, non-Muslim status (*zımmi*) if applicable, and a one-word physical description. The latter generally referred to the degree of maturity as indicated by facial hair. *Sabi* meant a boy, *taze* a beardless youth, *çar-ebru* a youth whose beard had just started to grow; *sakallı* (bearded) and *bıyıklı* (mustachioed) connotated an adult, and white-bearded or the word *ihtiyar* (old) an elderly man.[35] Sometimes also distinguishing marks such as a missing eye figured in the records. In several instances, patronymics also indicate that the bathhouse attendant had completed the pilgrimage to Mecca (*hacı*) or was affiliated with a Sufi order (*derviş, pir*).

Çemberlitaş Hamamı employed forty-four *tellak*s and fourteen *natır*s (Table 3.1). To this staff of 58 providing services directly to the male bathers, there need to be added the employees of the women's section as well as the keeper of towels, laundrymen, coffee cook, furnace stoker and other persons ensuring the smooth functioning of the hamam—that is, if the *tellak*s did not take over some of these duties as well. In any case, a staff of about seventy persons is reasonable to assume. Compared to the number of *tellak*s and *natır*s of the other registered bathhouses, only the Tahtakale Hamamı located in the commercial district down the hill towards the Golden Horn employed more male attendants and servants, that is, 63. Ranking third after Çemberlitaş Hamamı, the Mahmut Paşa Hamamı in the same commercial district provided work for 51 *tellak*s and *natır*s. Hence, Çemberlitaş Hamamı was the second-largest bathhouse business of mid-eighteenth-century Istanbul.[36]

According to the register, all the *tellak*s and *natır*s at Çemberlitaş Hamamı in 1752 were Muslims and hailed exclusively from the central and western Balkan peninsula, from provinces such as Manastır (present-day Bitola), Bihlişte, Görice (present-day Korçë), İstarova (present-day Starovë), Opar, Elbasan and Avlonya (present-day Vlorë). Unfortunately, the scribe disregarded the 1734/5 decree's order to use red ink, and ethnic identity can now only be ascribed based on the geographic location of the provinces. İstarovans were a particularly strong presence: out of the fifty-eight male empolyees, twenty-nine called this little town on Lake Ohrid (or the surrounding province) in central eastern Albania their home. Very likely, the İstarovan employees were all members of an extended family that upheld ties to the bathhouse and routinely sent off its young unmarried males and those without local means to sustain their nuclear family off to work in Istanbul. Most of the *tellak*s and *natır*s were young: seven boys, fourteen beardless youths and thirteen slightly bearded youths. Many of them probably worked as apprentices alongside the twenty-one adult *usta*s. Only one *tellak* seems to have been past his prime, with a grey moustache. This age distribution is not surprising, given that many of the men returned to their hometown after having saved up enough money to marry and set up a household. Also, the heavy physical labour involved in working as a bathhouse attendant made the profession undesirable after a certain age.[37]

Like most artisans and craftsmen, bathhouse employees organised themselves in the form of guilds (*esnaf*). The guild of hamam managers (*hamamcıyan*) was the wealthiest in the bathing business; all other related guilds depended on it and therefore were considered assistant

Table 3.1 Names, physical traits and place of origin of the attendants and servants working in Çemberlitaş Hamamı in 1752, according to BOA, Kamil Kepeci Müteferrik Defterleri 7437

	Tellaks		
	Name	**Physical traits**	**Origin**
1	Yakub Ahmed	black beard	Görice
2	İbrahim Mehmed	slight facial hair	İstarova
3	İsmail Halil	whitish moustache	İstarova
4	Abdi Ali	blond moustache	Elbasan
5	Şahin Osman	slight facial hair	Elbasan
6	Ahmed Hasan	no facial hair [young]	İstarova
7	Süleyman Osman	no facial hair [young]	Opar
8	Mustafa Ali	no facial hair [young]	Opar
9	Ahmed [illegible]	blond moustache	İstarova
10	Haseki Mustafa	old	Opar
11	Bekir Mustafa	slight facial hair	Opar
12	Ömer Ali	no facial hair [young]	İstarova
13	Yakub Ali	black beard	Avlonya
14	Süleyman Ümmi Ali	no facial hair [young]	İstarova
15	Osman Hüseyin	slight facial hair	Görice
16	Ali Bekir	blond moustache	Opar
17	Bekir Mustafa	slight facial hair	Opar
18	Ali Hasan	slight facial hair	Görice
19	Ömer Hasan	blond beard	Opar
20	Mustafa Ali	black beard	Premedi
21	Ahmed Mustafa	black moustache	Opar
22	Hamza Mehmed	black moustache	İstarova
23	Süleyman Hasan	boy	İstarova
24	Ahmed Hasan	blond moustache	Elbasan
25	Süleyman Resul	moustache	Görice
26	Osman Ömer	no facial hair [young]	Görice
27	İsa Hüseyin	boy without facial hair	Opar
28	Mehmed Osman	no facial hair [young]	İstarova
29	Hüseyin Ali	no facial hair [young]	İstarova
30	Bekir Ahmed	boy without facial hair	İstarova
31	Deli Ali Hasan	black beard	İstarova
32	Latif İsmail	no facial hair [young]	İstarova
33	Osman Ali	[illegible] beard	İstarova
34	Bekir Süleyman	boy without facial hair	Avlonya
35	Ahmed Süleyman	boy without facial hair	Elbasan
36	Hasan Osman	blond moustache	Opar
37	Halil Ahmed	no facial hair [young]	İstarova

(Continued)

Table 3.1 [Continued]

	Name	Physical traits	Origin
38	Abdullah Hasan	no facial hair [young]	İstarova
39	Ali Ömer	no facial hair [young]	İstarova
40	İbrahim [illegible]	no facial hair [young]	İstarova
41	Hüseyin Hasan	no facial hair [young]	Bihlişte
42	Süleyman Mehmed	boy without facial hair	İstarova
43	Hüseyin Hasan	boy without facial hair	İstarova
44	Hüseyin Ahmed	black moustache	Manastır
		Natırs	
1	Hüseyin Receb	black moustache	[not recorded]
2	Hasan Musa	blond moustache	İstarova
3	Mustafa Ali	(illegible)	İstarova
4	Murad Hüseyin	slight facial hair	Elbasan
5	Ömer Bekir	blond moustache	İstarova
6	Ahmed Bektaş	slight facial hair	İstarova
7	Osman Ali	slight facial hair	İstarova
8	Mahmud Hasan	slight facial hair	İstarova
9	Ali Mustafa	blond moustache	[not recorded]
10	Bayram Hasan	black beard	İstarova
11	Osman Mehmed	black beard	İstarova
12	Seyyid Ali	slight facial hair	İstarova
13	Ömer Ahmed	slight facial hair	İstarova
14	Mustafa Hasan	slight facial hair	Bihlişte

guilds (*yamak*). This elevated status and role also finds its expression in one of the richest visual sources on the identity of professional groups in the Ottoman capital, the *Surname-i Hümayun* (*Book of Imperial Processions*).[38] In 1582, Nurbanu's grandson (and Sultan Murad III's son) Mehmed was circumcised, and in his honour the capital celebrated a festival that lasted fifty-two days. The *Surname*'s text and the hundreds of accompanying miniatures, painted by the famous court artist Nakkaş Osman, record this extraordinary event in great detail. Most of the extant miniatures show the different guilds parading in the Hippodrome in front of the sultan and his guests.

Like many other guilds, the *hamamcıyan* displayed their craft with the help of a sophisticated model transported on wheels and drawn by pairs of oxen (Figure 3.17). The *hamamcıyan* even went so far as to have a small-scale bathhouse constructed, complete with water reservoir and furnace, and to staff this fully functional miniature hamam with customers and *tellak*s. One side of this model was left open so as to reveal the interior with the bathers pouring water over themselves, the attendants in their dark silk towels waiting for customers and the *peştemal*s drying on lines. The model builders carefully rendered those architectural features that helped viewers identify the contraption as a bathhouse. Although windows would have been unnecessary because of the removed wall, the model builders pierced the domes and covered the holes with the typical glass cups. Behind the parade float, the hamam managers followed on foot, dressed in particularly colourful and magnificent kaftans for the occasion. They brought with them a horse carrying the fuel necessary to keep the miniature furnace going. The sultan handsomely rewarded this spectacle by sending a group of his chamberlains to climb onto the parade float and enter the hamam, paying for their admittance with a pouch of gold coins.[39]

Several decades later, in the seventeenth century, on the occasion of another festival the *hamamcıyan* again put on a similar display, as described by Evliya Çelebi:

> In this guild procession, a total of 151 *hamamcı* clad in armour passes; they are rich and righteous men . . . All of the *hamamcı* are mounted on pure-bred Arabian horses, and their servants pass on wagons on which baths made of felt and decorated with illuminated glasses [have been installed] and call: 'Come to the Vefa Hamam, my darling, enter the Hacı Kadın Hamamı, my lady, see the Çinili Hamam, my darling.' Thus shout the beautiful *tellak*s who are naked but for a dark blue towel wrapped [around their waists].[40]

The elaborate parade floats, expensive as they must have been, expressed the corporate identity of the hamam managers and the pride that the members of this very wealthy and respected guild felt about their trade.

The first among the assistant guilds dependent on the *hamamcıyan* was the guild of bathhouse attendants, the *tellakan*. In the 1582 procession, the attendants did not form a separate group with a display of their own, but participated in the hamam managers' parade float by providing service in the miniature hamam. In the seventeenth-century imperial procession, however, they organised their own display immediately following that of their employers:

> The guild of the *tellak*s [is comprised of] a total of 2,000 persons . . . All these *tellak*s are naked, and with the silk towels the beautiful ones dishevel their hair; they pass with the *kese* in their hands and with the pumice stone and the musk-scented soap on their waists, rubbing each other with the stone and the soap.[41]

Figure 3.17 Guild of the *hamamcıyan, Surname-i Hümayun,* 1582, Topkapı Palace Library, H. 1344, fol. 336b–337a. *Source*: Topkapı Palace Museum.

Figure 3.17 [Continued]

This much more modest display of the guild's craft focused on the customary dress and emblematic tools of the profession – silk towel, pumice stone, soap and *kese* – and on the guild members' skill.

In the assistant guilds' hierarchy below the *tellak*s were the bathhouse servants, the *natıran*, who in the 1582 processions also demonstrated their craft with the help of a miniature bathhouse on wheels (Figure 3.18). Consisting only of a dressing room with a functioning fountain in the centre, the *natıran*'s miniature bathhouse did not require the power of oxen to pull it, but only that of two humans. Nevertheless, it was big enough to allow a *natır* to show how he removed dried towels and bath bowls with a long pole from the lines and handed them to a customer. Other guild members accompanied the mobile dressing room, carrying a folded towel over a shoulder as a mark of their professional identity. This magnificent display was much reduced in the seventeenth-century procession described by Evliya. Marching right after the *tellakan*, the 1,000 *natıran*s displayed their skills which included girding swords around their aprons and handing to each other bathing clogs of ebony and boxwood, inlaid with mother-of-pearl.[42]

During the 1582 circumcision festival, the guild of towel-makers (*peştemalcıyan*) marched right behind the hamam managers, a position indicating their dependence on the bathing business (Figure 3.19). They offered a display no less spectacular than that of the functioning miniature bathhouse on wheels. The *Surname*'s painting shows seven guild members carrying long poles, some of them with standards made from the expensive wrappers (*bohça*) that women used in order to carry their bath kits (Figure 4.7); some were topped by almost man-sized birds fashioned from towels. The colourful birds seemed alive, flapping their wings, opening their beaks or turning around on the pole. The *peştemalcıyan* accomplished this feat by hiding a system of pulleys inside the birds, connected by cords to wheels at the lower end of the pole.[43] Thus, the guild proudly presented their products to the sultan, his guests, and all other spectators in a very imaginative and creative fashion, transcending the usual craft displays that merely demonstrated the production process.

Neither the *Surname-i Hümayun* nor Evliya Çelebi's account give the names of guild members participating in the processions. However, the temporal proximity between the 1582 circumcision festival and the opening of Çemberlitaş Hamamı makes it likely that some of the persons depicted in the miniatures would later produce towels used in that very hamam, started to work there as an attendants or servants, or even became its manager. The seventeenth-century procession most certainly included

Çemberlitaş Hamamı's manager, *tellak*s and *natır*s who proudly showed the wealth they had acquired and the skills they had developed to the festival audience.

It goes without saying that the function of the guilds went beyond that of presenting a corporate professional identity to the sultan and his guests during festivals and processions. As administrative bodies, guilds permeated a large segment of the Ottoman workforce and determined rules and regulations based on the consensus of their members. Furthermore, they provided a link between the state and the workforce through the intercession of the guild representatives; for example, by aiding in the collection of taxes. On a more mundane level, guilds regulated the professional training of their members, determined fees and prices, made sure that certain quality standards for products and services were maintained, and secured the purchase of raw materials at fixed prices.[44] In an order dated 17 March 1592, the sultan responded to a complaint, evidently lodged by a representative of Istanbul's *hamamcıyan* guild, concerning the price regulation of materials needed to run a hamam.[45] Apparently, tradesmen selling firewood, towels, soap and other bathing items had tried to cheat hamam managers, and the petitioners now asked for a stricter application of the price regulations determined by the government.

Maintenance of the quality of the services offered in Istanbul's bathhouses was effected by a code of guild regulations called *nizamname*. These codes, which the guild steward needed to register with a *kadı*, determined not only standards of service and hygiene, but also the hierarchy of employees, prices and fees, and rules of behaviour for non-Muslim customers. A 1630/1 *nizamname* describes what was expected of a *tellak*:

> The *tellak*s shall be strong and agile; they shall be masters in shaving the head and keep their razors sharp; they shall provide services with heart and soul and they shall use the scrubbing glove powerfully and they shall wash [the customers] well with soap, and they shall always keep their scrubbing glove clean.[46]

Another *nizamname* written ten years later as part of an official price register (*narh defteri*) paid more attention to the interaction between the customer and the hamam staff:

> Whoever gives the hamam manager more [money] because he is satisfied shall not be hindered from doing so. When the customer gives to the *tellak* and the *natır* an *akçe* out of satisfaction, he shall still give to the hamam the customary fee. When the customer, especially the poor and [out-of-town or foreign] guests, does not give an *akçe* out of satisfaction, [then] the *tellak* and *natır* shall not demand an *akçe*. When the *tellak* shaves the customer, he shall put a towel around his neck so that the *tellak*'s sweat will not drip on the customer; the

Figure 3.18 Guild of the *natıran, Surname-i Hümayun,* 1582, Topkapı Palace Library, H. 1344, fol. 260b–261a. *Source*: Topkapı Palace Museum.

Figure 3.18 [Continued]

Figure 3.19 Guild of the *peştemalcıyan, Surname-i Hümayun,* 1582, Topkapı Palace Library, H. 1344, fol. 338b–339a. *Source*: Topkapı Palace Museum.

tellak shall obey the customer's wishes and give him a clean and dry towel and wiping cloth after the bath; the *tellak* shall wear a silken *peştemal*; the customer shall employ the *tellak* he desires; the *tellak* shall wash the customer and not follow [and pressure] him.[47]

Since rules and regulations usually responded to undesirable circumstances and were meant as a corrective to improve service and hygiene standards, the 1640 *nizamname* implies that bathhouse attendants and servants at times pestered the customers, either to hire them or for tips, and that servants did not give the bathers towels or, if they did, that these were dirty and wet.

Merely registering a *nizamname* with the *kadı* was not enough to enforce rules and regulations. It was up to the market inspector (*muhtesib*) to find and punish those hamam managers who did not run their business properly or who could not prevent their attendants and servants from harassing customers. The *muhtesib*, who was mainly responsible for controlling weights and measures in the marketplace, inspected bathhouses for their cleanliness, monitored the quality of service and checked whether the hamam equipment was in working order. He also checked to ensure that the *tellak*s and *natır*s dressed properly and that the customers complied with the rules concerning proper behaviour.[48] For example, bathing

naked was strictly prohibited, and non-Muslim customers were not supposed to share equipment – whether clogs, towels, bowls or razors – with
Muslims.[49]

A rule for business activities that concerned bathhouse managers in the
seventeenth century demanded that they acquire a licence (*gedik*) to run
a business.[50] There is no scholarly consensus on when the *gedik* system
first emerged, but Yi has suggested the seventeenth century, with the cautious addition that it was later modified.[51] The emergence of this system
guaranteed the survival of the established businesses of guild members in
the face of an excessive influx of military elements and immigrants into
some trades.[52] Obviously, there could exist only as many licences as there
were hamams in Istanbul, and licences either devolved from generation
to generation (if the children had acquired the necessary skills in the
same trade) or were sold to the highest bidder. The system allowed the
guild to foster continuation of the trade from generation to generation
and to protect its trade, since it was possible to withdraw a licence from a
disreputable hamam manager.[53]

The Hamam's Customers

Who were the bathers whose money passed through the hands of the
manager of Çemberlitaş Hamamı to finally land in the coffers of the Atik
Valide Vakfı? Some of the Muslims coming to pray in the Atik Ali Paşa
Mosque on the western side of Constantine's Column visited the hamam to
take the full-body ablution canonically required after major pollution and
before prayer (on such requirements, see Chapter 4). Many major mosque
complexes included a bathhouse of their own, but the Atik Ali Paşa's did
not. Its congregation would have frequented other nearby hamams. The
neighbourhoods north of the Divan Yolu housed many workshops, store-
houses and shops, and the shop owners, artisans, porters and other menial
workers were among those who came to Çemberlitaş Hamamı to relax
and wash away the sweat and dust of a hard day's work. Furthermore, two
inns, the Elçi Han and the Vezir Han, gave shelter to Ottoman subjects and
foreign travellers and traders alike.

The Elçi Han, built in 1510/11 by Atik Ali Paşa, provided hospitality to
foreign ambassadors until the eighteenth century, when embassy buildings
started to mushroom throughout the district of Pera, across the Golden
Horn.[54] As a residence to ambassadors and their retinues, the *han* often
figures in travel accounts that also describe a visit to a bathhouse. In the
1670s, the Vezir Han was added to the north side of Çemberlitaş Hamamı
(Figures 3.2, 3.20, 3.21).[55] Commissioned by Grand Vizier Fazıl Ahmed

Figure 3.20 Exterior of the Vezir Han, Istanbul, second half of the seventeenth century. *Source*: Author's photograph.

Paşa Köprülüzade – whose family also erected a small complex including a library and a tomb on the south side of the Divan Yolu – the *han* was, and still is, one of the largest in Istanbul. Rows of small rooms on two stories encircle one large and one small irregularly shaped courtyard, the larger with arched porticoes. While the lower storey housed small shops, the rooms on the upper storey served as residences for the merchants selling goods in the *han* and for travelling merchants and traders.

Like the temporary residents of the Elçi Han, the inhabitants of the Vezir Han found Çemberlitaş Hamamı most conveniently located for a refreshing bath at the end of the working day or after a long trip. Goodwin claims that a passage provided direct access from the southern wall of the Vezir Han to the northern lateral wall of Çemberlitaş Hamamı's men's section.[56] Indeed, an outlying portion of the Vezir Han, its latrines, joins the toilet area of the men's section. The purported passageway would thus have led from latrine to latrine, creating a rather undignified manner of entering. More likely, both of the buildings' latrine areas abutted here because they shared a connection to the sewer system.

The experiences of local hamam visitors virtually never found their way into Ottoman sources, whether narrative or documentary. Thus, there are many more questions than answers: were the bathers aware of the contribution their entrance fees made to the Atik Valide Vakfı? Did they

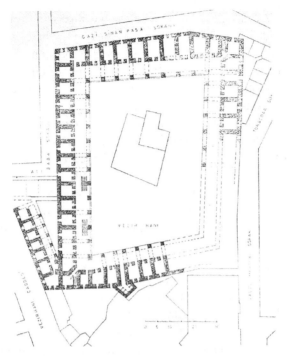

Figure 3.21 Ground plan of the Vezir Han, Istanbul, second half of the seventeenth century. *Source*: Güran, *Türk Hanların Gelişimi ve İstanbul Hanları Mimarisi*, 1976.

know that their money would, over several detours, land in the hands of the Atik Valide Mosque Complex's employees, buy foodstuff that would feed the complex's employees and the poor of Üsküdar, or purchase the ingredients for the medicine dispensed in the Atik Valide hospital? Would visitors choose Çemberlitaş Hamamı because it was conveniently located and provided good service in a beautiful building, without even knowing that it was connected to an endowment, or would they come because they felt the Atik Valide Vakfı deserved their entrance fees?

Making Money

The entrance fees paid to Çemberlitaş Hamamı made it possible for the bath to work as a breadwinner for the Atik Valide Vakfı. The relationship between the customers' entrance fees, the bathhouse rent paid to the endowment and the endowment's total income becomes visible in a comparative analysis of the endowment's accounting book (*muhasebe defteri*) dating to 1639, and the 1640/1 official price register (*narh defteri*). In this price register, the fee for using a hamam in order to perform a full-body ablution (*gusül*) was fixed at 1 *akçe*. If the customer wanted a scrub (*kese*) and a shave (*traş*), he had to add 2 *akçe*.[57] The tips expected by the attendant and the servant, if the customer chose to use their services, were not included in this amount; in any case, tips varied in amount based on what the customer could afford to give. Thus, the poorest among the city residents were still able to bathe in a hamam, even if they could not afford to employ a *tellak* or a *natır*, or to leave an extra tip for the *hamamcı*. Regular customers using full services spent a minimum of 6 *akçe* – 3 *akçe* for ablution, scrub and shave, and 1 *akçe* each as tip for attendant, servant, and *hamamcı*. In the middle of the seventeenth century, an unskilled labourer working on a construction site (*ırgad*) earned 15 *akçe* per day;[58] the ratio of bathing fee to daily salary made a weekly hamam visit with full services affordable even for the humblest among the Ottoman subjects.

Given that customers left an average of 3 *akçe* for their visit – services provided by *tellak*s, *natır*s and others not included – how many customers were necessary to make Çemberlitaş Hamamı a profitable business? In the year 1639, the *hamamcı* Hızır Çelebi paid to the Atik Valide Vakfı a monthly rent of 5,833 *akçe*.[59] Leaving aside expenses for firewood, towels, soap and other incidentals, a monthly minimum number of 1,944 customers paying the amount of 3 *akçe* was necessary to cover the the rent expense alone. Distributed over a month, this minimum number requires sixty-five customers per day. Çemberlitaş Hamamı's status as the second largest bathhouse in the city and its advantageous location makes it likely that the clientele easily numbered 100–150 persons per day. Based on this estimate, the hamam manager – even after subtracting money for expenses other than rent – made a profit of several thousand *akçe* per month.

The Atik Valide Vakfı's profit from Çemberlitaş Hamamı's rent must be seen within the larger context of the endowment's net accrual. In the year 1639, the same year that Hızır Çelebi paid a monthly rent of 5,833 *akçe*, the scribe recorded in the accounting book a total annual income of 3,994,040 *akçe*.[60] While Çemberlitaş Hamamı certainly earned more than its siblings – the Havuzlu Hamam's monthly rent was 1,833 *akçe*, the Atik Valide Hamamı's 3,333 *akçe* and that of the Büyük Hamam 3,666 *akçe* – its income still appears diminutive in comparison with the endowment's annual income of almost 4 million *akçe*. In other words, its contribution amounted to no more than 1.31 per cent of that year's budget. In general, it was not so much the rental income from the endowment's real estate in Istanbul, but businesses in the city and landholdings elsewhere that provided the bulk of revenue. The economic value of Çemberlitaş Hamamı and of its siblings as breadwinners for the Atik Valide Vakfı was limited;

yet, because the bathhouses played an important role in the daily life of Istanbul's inhabitants, they carried great significance as symbolic capital, as emblems of the imperial family's largesse and benevolence, and as contributors to the capital's architectural splendour.

Economic relationships between family members are never static; while small children are dependent on their parents, this relationship changes once children mature and begin to work. It may even become inverted once parents age and are no longer able to provide for themselves. Occasionally, grown children may revert to a position of dependence if they lose their employment or fall ill. The economic relationship between Çemberlitaş Hamamı and the Atik Valide Vakfı did not undergo such drastic changes; nevertheless, it fluctuated over time, with the hamam contributing sometimes less and sometimes more, and sometimes even requiring from the endowment a contribution towards repairs and renovation (to be discussed in Chapter 5). Table 3.2 gives a general overview of the fluctuation of rent amounts between the years 1632 and 1832, and thus the varying contribution of the hamams to their extended family, the *vakıf*, in the long term. Table 3.3 lists the names of the hamam managers and therefore permits some conclusions about the persons who ran the businesses and took care of the bathhouses.

Between 1628 and 1639, a Hızır Çelebi rented Çemberlitaş Hamamı at what appears to have been a fixed rent of 5,833 *akçe* per month. This amounted to an annual contribution to the endowment of approximately 1.75 per cent. Around the year 1645, the hamam passed into the hands of one Bekir Çelebi, and the rent increased to 7,083 *akçe* per month. This increase probably reflected the endowment trustee's (*mütevelli*) decision to adjust the rent according to the bath's profitability. In other words, Hızır Çelebi had made so much money that the *mütevelli* thought a larger portion of this profit should go to the *vakıf* when he negotiated the rent contract with a new bathhouse tenant and hamam manager, Ebu Bekir Çelebi. During Ebu Bekir Çelebi's tenure, Çemberlitaş Hamamı's rent accounted for 1.86 per cent and 2.04 per cent in the years 1645 and 1646, respectively. In the middle of the century, the rent reached a peak amount of 11,677 *akçe* per month under the new manager el-Hac Mustafa Hammami. This translated to 4.37 per cent of the total income in 1652 and to 4.12 per cent in 1655, a significantly larger share than in previous years. Even if inflation is taken into consideration, the bath's profitability for the endowment increased steadily in the first seven or so decades after its birth.

This changed in the second half of the century: in 1658, the rent amount decreased to 8,934 *akçe* per month, or an annual contribution of 3.2 per cent, paralleling general economic difficulties in the Ottoman Empire.[61]

Table 3.2 Total endowment income, monthly rent income from the endowed hamams and the hamam's annual contribution (%) to the total income, 1632–1832

Year	Total annual *vakıf* income	Çemberlitaş Hamamı	Havuzlu Hamam	Büyük Hamam	Atik Valide Hamamı
1632 1041 AH	3,869,975	5,833 (1.8%)	1,833 (0.57%)	3,666 (1.14%)	4,166 (1.29%)
1632 1041–2 AH	2,985,596	not recorded	not recorded	3,666 (1.47%)	4,166 (1.67%)
1639 1049 AH	3,994,040	5,833 (1.75%)	1,833 (0.55%)	3,666 (1.1%)	3,333 (1%)
1645 1054–5 AH	4,561,310	7,083 (1.86%)	2,166 (0.57%)	3,833 (1.01%)	3,333 (0.88%)
1646 1056–7 AH	4,170,698	7,083 (2.04%)	1,666 (0.48%)	3,333 (0.96%)	3,833 (1.1%)
1652 1062–3 AH	3,203,570	11,677 (4.37%)	1,666 (0.62%)	3,800 (1.42%)	3,333 (1.25%)
1655 1064–5 AH	3,399,916	11,677 (4.12%)	1,666 (0.59%)	5,833 (2.06%)	3,333 (1.18%)
1658 1068–9 AH	3,349,996	8,934 (3.2%)	1,666 (0.6%)	4,584 (1.64%)	3,333 (1.2%)
1663 1073–4 AH	3,047,594	5,000 (1.97%)	2,865 (1.13%)	3,765 (1.48%)	2,500 (0.98%)
1666 1076 AH	3,748,667	5,000 (1.6%)	1,265 (0.4%)	3,765 (1.2%)	2,500 (0.8%)
1666 1076–7 AH	4,275,343	5,000 (1.4%)	2,865 (0.8%)	3,765 (1.06%)	2,500 (0.7%)
1667 1077–8 AH	4,704,181	5,000 (1.27%)	1,250 (0.32%)	3,750 (0.96%)	2,500 (0.64%)
1669 1080–1 AH	3,770,744	5,000 (1.59%)	4,761 (1.51%)	3,333 (1.06%)	2,500 (0.8%)
1823 1238 AH	4,390,237	12,882 (3.52%)	not recorded	10,820 (2.96%)	3,435 (0.94%)
1828 1243 AH	4,385,877	12,882 (3.52%)	4,166 (1.14%)	10,820 (2.96%)	3,435 (0.94%)
1832 1248 AH	1,756,319	12,882 (8.8%)	4,166 (2.85%)	10,820 (7.4%)	3,435 (2.35%)

Sources: BOA, MAD 3002, pp. 83–4, 170–1, 44–5; 987, pp. 2–3; 5742, p. 2; 5886, p. 1; 5273, p. 2; 1672, p. 2; 2263, p. 4; 2105, p. 4; TSA, D. 1901, pp. 1–2; D. 1781, p. 1; E. 246/61; E. 246/62; BOA, EV.HMH.VLSA 6/102.

Five years later, the rent further plummeted to 5,000 *akçe* per month, when Çemberlitaş Hamamı was turned over to one Abdi Çelebi. While also fluctuating somewhat, the rent of the other endowed hamams did not experience such a sharp decrease, and this makes it likely that external

Table 3.3 Names of the renters of the Atik Valide Vakfı's endowed hamams in the seventeenth century

Year	Çemberlitaş Hamamı	Havuzlu Hamam	Büyük Hamam	Atik Valide Hamamı
1628 1037–8 AH	Hızır Beg	Mehmed Çelebi	Hüseyin Çelebi	Hüseyin Çelebi
1632 1041 AH	Hızır Çelebi	Mehmed Çelebi	Hüseyin Çelebi	Hüseyin Çelebi
1632 1041–2 AH	not recorded	not recorded	Mehmed Beg	[?] Çelebi
1639 1049 AH	Hızır Çelebi	[?] Çelebi	Hüseyin Çelebi	[?]
1645 1054–5 AH	Ebu Bekir Çelebi	Ayşe Hanum	Mustafa Çelebi el-Hac	Hüseyin Çelebi el-Hac
1646 1056–7 AH	Bekir Çelebi	Abdullah Beg Hammami	Hüseyin Çelebi Hammami	Hüseyin Çelebi
1652 1062–3 AH	el-Hac Mustafa Hammami	Receb Başe Hammami	Mustafa Çelebi	el-hac Mehmed Hammami
1658 1068–9 AH	Mustafa Beg	Mehmed Çelebi	Mustafa Çelebi	el-Hac Mehmed
1663 1073–4 AH	Abdi Çelebi	Osman Çavuş	Mustafa Çelebi	el-Hac Mehmed
1666 1076 AH	Abdi Çelebi	Osman Çelebi	Hacı Mustafa	Hacı Mehmed
1666 1076–7 AH	Abdi Çelebi Hac	Osman Çavuş	Mustafa Çelebi Hac	Hüseyin Beg
1667 1077–8 AH	Abdi Çelebi	Osman Çavuş	Mustafa Çelebi	Hacı Mehmed

Sources: BOA, MAD 5827, p. 2; 3002, pp. 83–4, 170–1, 44–5; 987, pp. 2–3; 5247, p. 2; 5273, p. 2; 1672, p. 2; 2263, p. 4; 2105, p. 4; TSA, D. 1910, pp. 1–2.

factors were responsible, factors that had no influence over Çemberlitaş Hamamı's siblings. An explanation for the sharp decrease in monthly rent from more than 11,000 *akçe* to less than half that amount can be found in the damage that the Big Fire of 1660 (*İhrak-i Kebir*) inflicted (as will be discussed in Chapter 5). In order to be able to rent out the hamam at all, the *mütevelli* would have negotiated a rent contract particularly favourable to the tenant, if Abdi Çelebi pledged to contribute to the repairs, for instance. Since the endowment in general continued to earn an amount between 3 and 4 million *akçe*, Çemberlitaş Hamamı's share of the family income also plummeted to no more than between 1 and 2 per cent.

In the early nineteenth century, not surprisingly due to then rampant inflation, the rent rose to 12,882 *akçe* per month, whereas the endowment income still remained approximately the same as in the second half of the seventeenth century. However, this changed in 1832, when the *vakıf*'s total income did not even amount to 2 million *akçe*, reflecting the dire economic situation of the Ottoman Empire and maybe also due to the imperial treasury's new policy of tapping into endowment funds. Consequently, Çemberlitaş Hamamı's contribution rose from 3.52 per cent to 8.8 per cent, a staggering increase that hints at the growing economic significance of the bath *vis-à-vis* other forms of urban real estate and landholdings.

Also interesting to note here is the identity of the renters in the early nineteenth century. It was not a single individual tenant, but a business partnerhip that leased the *vakıf* property. An 1805 petition (*arzuhal*) concerning a dispute about repairs mentions that the hamam's licence (*gedik*) had been divided into twelve shares, held jointly by Ayşe bint es-Seyyid İsmail (one share), es-Seyyid Mehmed Tahir (who also managed the Şifa Hamamı in Sultanahmet, one share), the unnamed wife of one Salih Paşa, the governor of Trabzon (four shares) and Feride Naile Hanım, the wife of the manager of the Yenikapı Hamamı (six shares).[62] The unequal distribution of shares suggests that this was a partnership of the *inan* type – where investment amounts may differ and profit may be divided at will – or of the kind called *vücuh* – where profit shares were based on each partner's original investment.[63] The exact type cannot be deduced from the wording or information contained in this source. Such a business partnership was not without its problems, as is clearly evident from the licence-holders' squabbling over the timing of and payment for repairs to Çemberlitaş Hamamı, which they could resolve only by appealing to the judges of the imperial *divan* and the sultan. Nevertheless, the partnership continued over decades, even if it changed somewhat in composition. In 1830, el-Hace Ayşe Sıdıka, Seyyid Mehmed Tahir Ağa, Emin Efendi and el-Hac Hüseyin Efendi together paid a monthly rent of 12,500 *akçe*.[64]

The social status of hamam managers is reflected in their titles, even if scribes used them rather inconsistently. The name *Çelebi* implies a well-bred and educated gentleman and notable, as did the title *beg*. *Hacı* or *el-Hac* meant that the person had completed the pilgrimage to Mecca, and it seems that quite a few among the hamam managers had the spiritual inclination, the time and the financial resources to fulfil this religious duty. Only two of the scribes – one registering the income and expenditures in 1646, the other in 1652 – used the title *Hammami* to describe the tenants' professional identity, a usage that might reflect the scribe's personal opinion about their reputation and standing in society. For at least five *hicri* years, from 1663 to 1667, the Havuzlu Hamam was rented by a certain Osman Çavuş, the latter part of his name qualifying him as a sergeant of the imperial army. Although he seems to have remained the only member of the military who participated in the Atik Valide Vakfı's hamam business, his tenure reflects the argument that military elements became a presence among guilds in the seventeenth century.[65] By the eighteenth century, young applicants (*civelek*) to the Janissary corps apparently also worked as *tellak*s at the same time.[66]

Women also constituted a significant presence among the tenants. In 1645, a certain Ayşe Hanum rented the Havuzlu Hamam, and between 1786 and 1790 a Fatma Kadın bint Abdullah (the latter part of the name may denote her status as convert to Islam) leased Çemberlitaş Hamamı under conditions that made her responsible for extensive renovation and repair work.[67] At the beginning of the nineteenth century, a business partnership of four persons holding shares of the bath's licence included three women. Together, these women held eleven out of a total of twelve shares. One of these women, Feride Naile Hanım, is qualified as the wife of the manager of another hamam, and this points to the social network that existed between members of the hamam managers' guild in Istanbul. Had Feride Naile Hanım's father been a *hamamcı*, and did she receive her shares in the *gedik* as an inheritance from him? Had she married a *hamamcı* whom her father had chosen for her, maybe the son of a fellow guild member who later on inherited his own father's *gedik*? Or was Feride a newcomer to the bathing business and bought the shares with her own dowry money (*mehr*), thinking that her husband's expertise would help in her own dealings? However these women acquired their licence or bathhouse tenancy, they were rather wealthy in their own right and held high social status – in fact, one of the 1805 *gedik* shareholders was the wife of a provincial governor. Clearly, the hamam business was deemed suitable for women. Women invested their own money – which they could have received through inheritance, gifts or dowry – in order to secure an income and, as a result, economic autonomy from their family.[68] However, their social status and gender meant that these business women entrusted the day-to-day management to a proxy (*vekil*), who was often mentioned by name in official documents. For example, Ayşe Hanum's tenure of the Havuzlu Hamam did not entail her presence at the bathhouse, since it served only male customers. This would have made it quite unacceptable for her to be on the premises during the bath's opening hours.

This question of direct involvement can also be extended to the hamams' male tenants. Particularly in the eighteenth century, it became more commonplace to rent out *vakıf* property on a perpetual lease (*icareteyn*) to contractors (*mutassarrıf*) who could act like property owners. These contractors then leased either the entire property or parts of it to further tenants, making themselves into nothing but brokers or financing middlemen between the endowment and those who actually ran the business. Also, given that *hamamcıs* often rented more than one bathhouse – for instance, Hüseyin Çelebi rented both the Büyük Hamam and the Atik Valide Hamamı at the same time from 1628 to 1632 and then again in 1646 – the managers had to divide their time between different business locations and could not attend to the daily affairs of each in person.

The length of the tenure also tells much about the leaseholders. Clearly, the endowment administrators were interested in entrusting the bathhouses to a person who would maximise profit (which, in turn, would increase the use-value of the property and, therefore, the rent amount they could demand), who was reliable and in good standing in the community, who was punctual in their payments and who took good care of the *vakıf* property. Frequent changes among tenants and managers – something that the customary one- to two-year contracts for endowed property actually encouraged – could disrupt the smooth functioning of the bathhouses. Indeed, even when considering the gaps in date between the sources employed here, all indications are that most of Çemberlitaş Hamamı's seventeenth-century tenants held their contracts for longer periods of time or had them frequently renewed in their names. Hızır Çelebi rented the bathhouse for at least eleven years between 1628 and 1639, if not longer; Mustafa for at least six years from 1652 to 1658; and Abdi Çelebi for at least four years from 1663 to 1667, as did Fatma Kadın from 1786 to 1790.

Like an Ottoman craftsman working in the nearby Covered Bazaar, Çemberlitaş Hamamı also had to go through a number of preparatory stages before it could begin to earn money. The time spent in acquiring the necessary items for business was rather short and hardly comparable to that of an Ottoman craftsman who had to undergo years of training, first as an apprentice and then as a journeyman, before finally becoming a master. It took only a few months for the hamam to secure the necessary water supply, fuel, soap, towels and the like. Like an Ottoman craftsman employing apprentices and assistants to help with the work, so Çemberlitaş Hamamı employed *tellaks*, *natırs* and others to render services – not for a fixed salary, but for the customers' tips only, akin to payment for piece work. However, as the second-largest bathing business of eighteenth-century Istanbul, with fifty-eight employees in the men's section alone, Çemberlitaş Hamamı surpassed by a wide margin the number of employees that most Ottoman craftsmen could ever need or afford.

Like a craftsman, so did the hamam develop a network of customers who decided to frequent this rather than any of the other bathhouses in the vicinity. Such a decision could be based on quality (the excellent services rendered by the hamam's employees), beauty (the well-appointed building and its pleasant atmosphere, as advertised in the foundation inscription), convenience (the close proximity of the hamam to the Atik Ali Paşa Mosque, the nearby *han*s, and the surrounding residences, shops and warehouses), and maybe also status (the hamam, after all, was an imperial foundation). It was the customers who allowed Çemberlitaş Hamamı to gain enough income so as to make it a business venture attractive to hamam managers who would maintain and represent it. Although the rent that the hamam managers paid did fluctuate over time, it permitted Çemberlitaş Hamamı to fulfil one of the two purposes for which it had been created: securing revenue for the Atik Valide Vakfı. The other purpose was to broadcast the benevolence of the imperial family who cared about the Ottoman subjects' well-being. Therefore, in its connection with the Ottoman dynasty, Çemberlitaş Hamamı was much like a craftsman belonging to one of the imperial guilds (*ehl-i hiref*) at court, doing the empire proud with the quality of its work.

4

Impressions and Identity

---

*It describes how all hamams, among them also the aforementioned
hamam, help the believers to carry out their religious duties as they are
described in the Qur'an and the Hadith; how all people of the protected
City, noble and lowly, men and women, rejoice in visiting the baths, for
they offer them the opportunity to meet with each other and to exchange
good and bad news alike and to engage in many matters, sometimes even
carnal pleasures; how Ibn Sina and those who follow in his footsteps
consider bathhouses to be a well-spring of health; and how Sultan
Mehmed Khan, Conqueror of the Protected City, deemed it one of his
most important duties to decorate the city with splendid and costly baths,
among other exalted buildings.*

A Place for Ritual Cleansing

Because Ottomans were deeply affected by their relationship to God,
Çemberlitaş Hamamı's religious identity as a Sunni Muslim adhering to
the Hanefi rite, prevalent in the Ottoman Empire and modern-day Turkey,
deserves to be discussed first. Islam places great emphasis on cleanliness
and purity (*taharet*), both internal and external.[1] Internal purity means to
be clean of pride and of the love of self and the world, whereas external
purity refers to physical cleanliness. A Muslim cannot possess one without
the other; the two are inseparable. The following text passage from the
Sahih Muslim, for Hanefi Muslims after the *Sahih al-Bukhari* the second
most important collection of the sayings and traditions of the Prophet
Muhammad, draws a quite explicit connection between washing and the
purification from sins:

> Abu Huraira reported: Allah's messenger (may peace be upon him) said: When
> a bondsman – a Muslim or a believer – washes his face [in the course of ablu-
> tion], every sin he contemplated with his eyes will be washed away from his
> face along with water, or with the last drop of water; when he washes his hands,
> every sin they wrought will be effaced from his hands with the water, or with

the last drop of water; and when he washes his feet, every sin towards which his feet have walked will be washed away with the water or with the last drop of water with the result that he comes out pure from all sins.[2]

In fact, a pure Muslim is easily recognisable by the external marks of purity – such as trimmed clean fingernails, clean teeth, plucked armpits and shaved pubes, a carefully washed body, and – in the case of a male – a clipped moustache and circumcised genitalia.[3]

When in a state of ritual impurity (*cenabet*), Muslims should not perform the canonical prayer, unnecessarily enter a mosque, or touch or read the Qur'an. States of ritual impurity can be caused by defilement with urine, excrement, vomit, blood, semen, sleep, skin contact with members of the opposite sex, and contact with beings or substances deemed inherently impure, but not every type of defilement is of the same gravity.[4] Sura 5:6 differentiates:

> O ye who believe! When ye prepare for prayer, wash your faces, and your hands (and arms) to the elbows; rub your heads (with water); and (wash) your feet to the ankles. If ye are in a state of ceremonial impurity, bathe your whole body.[5]

The smaller ablution (*wudu'* in Arabic, *abdest* in Turkish) described in this Qur'an verse becomes obligatory after urinating, defecating, breaking wind, bleeding, vomiting, sleeping and fainting, and includes a washing of the feet, of the hands up to the elbows, of the face, a wetting of the hair, and rinsing of mouth and nose.[6] Such an ablution would not have required a visit to the bathhouse, unlike a greater ablution (*ghusl* in Arabic, *gusül* in Turkish). The latter, required after sexual activity, menstruation, childbirth, touching a dead body and before Friday prayers, the two major Muslim holidays, and departure on the pilgrimage to Mecca, consists of a careful scrubbing and rinsing of the entire body. The *Sahih al-Bukhari*, the most authoritative Hanefi *hadith* collection, relates the Prophet's manner of taking a full-body ablution in the following way:

> Narrated Maimuna bin al-Harith: I placed water for the bath of Allah's Apostle and put a screen. He poured water over his hands, and washed them once or twice . . . Then he poured water with his right hand over his left one and washed his private parts. He rubbed his hand over the earth or the wall and washed it. He rinsed his mouth and washed his nose by putting water in it and blowing it out. He washed his face, forearms and head. He poured water over his body and then withdrew from that place and washed his feet. I presented him a piece of cloth (towel) and he pointed with his hand (that he does not want it) and did not take it.[7]

The Hanefi rite considers only running water or water that is being poured as ritually purifying.[8] The absence of an immersion pool, which one finds in hamams in North Africa where the Maliki rite with its different ritual requirements is prevalent, clearly indicates Çemberlitaş Hamamı's religious identity as a Hanefi Muslim.[9]

Even if Muslims find themselves in a situation where there is no water available for the ablution before prayer or where contact with water could be harmful to health, the Qur'an gives instructions to use clean sand or earth instead of water, a practice called *tayammum* in Arabic, or *teyemmüm* in Turkish:

> But if ye are ill, or on a journey, or one of you cometh from offices of nature, or ye have been with women, and ye find no water, then take for yourselves clean sand or earth, and rub therewith your faces and hands. Allah doth not wish to place you in a difficulty, but to make you clean, and to complete his favour to you, that ye may be grateful.[10]

The practice of bathing before Fridays and major holidays, a time when communal prayer in crowded mosques takes place, originated from one specific event in the early history of Islam. A group of believers who worked in menial jobs and traditionally wore heavy woollen garments came to Friday prayer without having cleaned themselves of their sweat. It did not take long before the Prophet noticed the unpleasant odour emanating from them. He told them to wash and perfume themselves before joining the community, so as not to disturb their fellow Muslims in prayer.[11] Because of this specific injunction, repeated many times throughout all *hadith* collections, there were always hamams built close to mosques or as part of mosque complexes. Thursday nights and Friday mornings before the obligatory noon prayer were always the busiest times for bathhouses, and even today Çemberlitaş Hamamı experiences a peak in the number of local visitors the night before major holidays, when it keeps its doors open all night in order to accommodate the flow of bathers.

Although the religious identity of Çemberlitaş Hamamı, like that of most other bathhouses in Istanbul, was Muslim, this did not mean that it exclusively catered to a Muslim clientele. There were some baths that catered to a specific denomination, such as the *Yahudiyyin/Yahudiler Hamamı* belonging to Mehmed the Conqueror's endowment, which, as its name indicates, catered to the Jewish community and must have provided its customers with a *mikveh* for ritual bathing.[12] Generally, however, it appears that the clientele was mixed: an imperial decree (*hüküm*) dated AH1003–1018/1594–1609 reveals that, although Jews and Christians continued to frequent Islamic bathhouses, the interaction between Muslims and non-Muslims was now regulated by specific rules that imply a negative view of such mixing. Accordingly, bathhouse attendants 'shall not mix up the towels of the Muslims and the non-Muslims. The barbers also shall not shave the Muslims with the blade with which they have shaved non-Muslims.'[13] Therefore, while they were allowed to use the same space, bathers were prevented from 'contaminating' each other.[14] Close contact, even if only through the shared use of towels and grooming utensils, was undesirable, at least from the perspective of the city administration. This was once again emphasised in the already mentioned price register of 1640: 'Infidels shall undress themselves next to the *kafes* [lattice screen] and shall not be given clogs and shall put on their towels a [distinguishing] sign for the public. There shall be a special basin outside the *halvet* for the infidels and they shall not annoy and disturb the Muslims in any way and enter the *halvet*.'[15] Thus, by the seventeenth century, the state even tried to preclude inter-confessional social interaction by dictating how Muslims and non-Muslims should share the space inside the bathing chambers. One may speculate that the fundamentalist Kadızadeli movement, first consisting of discontented low-class members of the religious establishment who violently reacted against the heterodox practices of Sufism as well as against non-Muslim communities, played a role in creating an atmosphere that encouraged religious segregation, supported by decrees of this sort.[16]

As for the hamams' religious identity, those aspects of bathing culture deemed to be objectionable on religious grounds also require consideration. One issue that had already proved to be problematic during the Prophet's lifetime was nudity. The Ancient Greek and Roman traditions of communal bathing, from which the Islamic tradition stems, had no such qualms about the naked body and permitted men and women to bathe together in the nude. The Prophet, however, preferred to have the privacy of a curtain drawn around him,[17] and forbade seeing the private parts of someone else.[18] A *hadith* included neither in the *Sahih al-Bukhari* nor in the *Sahih Muslim*, but in the Maliki collection *Mishkat al-Masabih*, claims that:

> Ya'la told of God's messenger seeing a man washing in a public place, so he mounted the pulpit, and when he had praised and extolled God he said, 'God is characterized by modesty and concealment and loves modesty and concealment, so when any of you washes he should conceal himself.'[19]

While the Prophet clearly encouraged hygiene as a prerequisite of the faith, he was not favourably disposed towards communal bathing. Nevertheless, the Islamic bathing tradition gradually overcame orthodox resistance by appropriating and codifying certain standards of modesty – such as covering one's private parts and not looking at others' genitalia if they happen to be visible – both in *hadith* and *fiqh*, the canon jurisprudence.[20]

For Ottomans visiting Çemberlitaş Hamamı or other bathhouses, the notion of *avret* circumscribed what was permissible in terms of revealing one's body.[21] *Avret* literally means the parts of the body that modesty requires to be concealed, particularly in the presence of the opposite sex.[22] For men, this area is between the navel and the knees; for slave women, it is the area between the waist and knees as well as the back; and for free women, it is the entire body with the exception of hands and feet. Other meanings of the word include 'wife', or the time period during which one is in a state of undress. As bathhouses were segregated by gender – either by having separate sections or by assigning different bathing times to men and women – modesty was often relaxed. Certainly, attitudes towards modesty and nudity varied among bathers, both male and female, based on how strictly individuals viewed Islamic rules: the strictest bathers who had the necessary financial resources could rent an entire *halvet* and close it off with a towel draped over its entrance; the modest ones could make sure that the parts of their bodies considered *avret* were at all times covered by a towel; and the most permissive ones would neglect wearing a *peştemal* and see nothing shameful about their bodies – a custom among female bathers in the eighteenth century that Lady Mary Wortley-Montagu commented upon with great wonder at the time.[23] However, in the same century, female nudity in the hamams of Ottoman Aleppo provoked a great deal of anxiety: in response to the mingling of naked Muslim and non-Muslim women bathers, the local shari'a court ruled that non-Muslim females counted as unrelated males who were barred from looking at nude Muslim women, thus gendering their gaze as male. As a result, segregated schedules were instituted to put an end to mixed confessional bathing in the women's sections.[24] Whether in the provinces or the imperial capital, male bathers were always required to keep at least their private parts covered, a practice done away with only in hamams of a certain ill-repute, to which Çemberlitaş Hamamı does not belong.

A Place for Socialising

Ottomans would hardly let a week pass without a visit to the bathhouse, not only for hygienic and religious, but also for social reasons. Even notables who possessed private hamams attached to their mansions (Figure 4.1) frequented the large public hamams every once in a while.[25] Both men and women went with groups of friends of the same sex, enjoying an

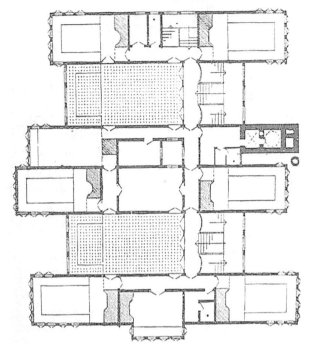

Figure 4.1 Ground plan of an Istanbul mansion with attached hamam. *Source: Eldem, Türk Evi Plan Tipleri*, 1968.

atmosphere of relaxation and entertaining each other with gossip, stories, songs and poetry. One sixteenth-century Arab scholar who lived in the provinces of the Ottoman Empire wrote in his treatise on bathing that 'one should go to the bath with an educated group of friends who know stories and anecdotes, because they will make you forget your worries and make your heart rejoice'.[26] Without a doubt, the hamam presented a *locus* for leisure.[27]

More than merely being a place for convivial entertainment, hamams served as a public forum where one met with friends as much as with strangers, exchanged and spread news, formed opinions about the events of the day and mobilised groups of people for action. In this, they very much resembled the many coffee houses of Istanbul where adult males gathered; their social topography has been more extensively studied.[28] Thus, Lady Mary Wortley-Montagu remarked about the bathhouse: 'In short, 'tis the women's coffee house, where all the news of the town is told, scandal invented etc.'[29] The city's administration was well aware of the dangerous potential of these dense information networks and tried to establish control over spaces where people sat together idly, where they disregarded the existing social order and rules of morality, and possibly planted the seeds of sedition through their rumours. Already in the seventeenth century, a special undercover troop of Janissaries (*salma çukadari*) patrolled both coffee houses and bathhouses.[30] Later on, in the nineteenth century, the sultan received spy reports based on the oral reports of informers located in coffee houses, hamams and many other similar places.[31]

That hamams as public forum could indeed constitute the starting point of major socio-political unrest is evident in the Patrona Halil Rebellion of 1730, which has been discussed in Chapter 3. It is not difficult to imagine that Patrona Halil's constant interaction and conversations not only with members of his own guild, but also with the many hamam customers – who were very much affected by the economic, social and military situation, and probably vented their anger in the public forum that the bathhouse provided – did contribute to him taking matters into his own hands. Thereafter, the Ottoman administration kept an ever-watchful eye on Istanbul's bathhouses, in the mid-eighteenth century going so far as to record in the previously mentioned register each and every male bathhouse attendant in great detail for the purposes of tighter control. By the early nineteenth century, the government had even planted a network of spies listening in on conversations in dressing rooms and around *göbektaşı*s; in 1809, several women who were discussing the political state of affairs were arrested based on a spy's report.[32]

A civil unrest of smaller scale than the Patrona Halil Revolt, but directly related to the life story of Çemberlitaş Hamamı, was the so-called *Çemberlitaş Hamamı Baskını Vak'ası* (Case of the Raid at Çemberlitaş Hamamı) in 1810. Janissaries from a nearby police station kidnapped a young (and probably handsome) male bathhouse attendant with the intention of having him dance for them. When the Janissaries of a second police station were called upon to intervene, a riot ensued. In the end, the ten Janissaries responsible for the kidnapping of the young bath attendant were hanged in front of the bathhouse.[33]

Such disruptive events, however much attention they received because of their extraordinary nature, were still of minor significance in terms of the hamam's sustained role in Ottoman social life. Much more important and meaningful were the little day-to-day rituals, often related to the transition from one specific station in the life cycle to another. In fact, the very first outing that an Ottoman infant made on the fortieth day after birth led to the bathhouse, where the women of the family organised the so-called *kirk hamamı* or *lohusa hamamı* (*lohusa* meaning a woman recovering from childbirth). Abdülaziz Bey (1850–1918) described the ceremony in his book on the customs and traditions of the Ottomans in great detail:

The *lohusa* is undressed and wrapped into Bursa towels, the ends of which are embroidered with silk and silver thread. Towards her are turned bath clogs with straps made of silver thread, their surface decorated with flower designs made from silver or mother-of-pearl. The midwife takes her under her arm to the right and the *hamamcı* to the left, and together they slowly walk to the interior door of the hamam. Either the *lohusa*'s mother or mother-in-law steps inside first. If neither of them is present, then she enters by herself and sits down next to a *kurna*, while the other women sit down in front of the other *kurnas*. On the other *kurnas*, white towels have been hung, yellow bowls set out, clay has been pounded and musk-scented soap prepared. Before the tap of the *kurna* where the *lohusa* sits no other tap may be opened. This is done by the oldest woman present. Once the *kurna* is filled with water, a gold coin is thrown into it – so that the child's destiny will be bountiful – and given to the midwife.

The *lohusa* is washed carefully with lukewarm water by the master of the hamam attendants, the child by the midwife. A gold coin that has been passed on as inheritance is dipped into the water forty times. This water is then little by little poured over the *lohusa* and the child forty times, with a tortoise shell being used as bowl. In the ladies' parlance, this is called *kırklanma* [repeating something forty times, from the word *kırk* for forty; hence the name *kırk hamamı*]. Afterwards, the child is quickly wrapped into heavily embroidered precious towels and immediately taken outside to a protected spot. After the *lohusa* has been washed, clay is smeared on her head and body, according to an old custom, and after leaving it for a while, it is washed off. Later, the *lohusa* is taken by two skilled master bath attendants to the *göbektaşı* in the centre of the hamam and laid on her back on towels that have been spread on top of each other. A *peştemal* is tied around her waist, each of the ladies grabs one end and, pulling hard, she is quartered [*çaryeklenir*], as the women say. Finally, a few bowls of water are poured over her and, once again she is wrapped into a precious embroidered *peştemal* and towels, and then she is taken outside, to where her child is. Following her, the women, having washed and smeared themselves with clay, go outside. During that time, the hamam master and the *natır*s sing sad songs and poems while lightly beating a *def* [tambourine-like instrument]. The ladies drink coffee and smoke a pipe. After having amused themselves in this manner for a while, the invited ladies together with the *lohusa* start to get dressed. During that time, the child is perfumed with incense made of *çörek otu* [black sesame seeds]. A small amount of *çörek otu* is also poured between the child's swaddling clothes. Afterwards, each and every woman is given sincere good wishes and thanks as she leaves the hamam, first of all the mother of the *lohusa*. At the end, as the child is carried outside through the hamam entrance, a splash of red sugary sherbet is poured on the threshold while uttering the prayer: 'May they [the *jinns*] be at an auspicious moment, God save them and the community of the religion from their evilness.'[34] Following this, the women return to the mansion.[35]

123

With this ceremony, the mother, who had remained in a liminal and vulnerable state for the forty days following childbirth, returned to her normal life, and the infant, having survived the equally vulnerable first forty days, entered society.

Another most significant stage in the life cycle of an Ottoman was marriage,[36] and the wedding itself was preceded by the bride's bath (*gelin hamamı*) on the woman's side and the groom's bath (*damat hamamı*) on the man's. This bathhouse visit was accompanied by a lively party with music, dance and food. If the families of the bride and groom could afford to do so, they would rent an entire hamam for the occasion. During the *gelin hamamı*, the bride was wrapped into particularly beautiful towels and garments, paraded around and washed at the bride's basin (*gelin kurnası*), which was distinguished by its particularly beautiful ornamentation. Other liminal experiences involving a bathhouse visit included the return from a journey, recovery from an illness, release from prison and the wearing of new clothes, as well as joining the army (*asker hamamı*). As has been discussed in relation to the hamam's religious identity, sexual activity necessitates a canonical cleansing in order to restore the social order that has been disturbed by the act; the hamam visit serves this function and therefore is 'an epilogue to sexual conduct', to use Boudhiba's phrase.[37]

Although the notion of the hamam as a place for socialising might give the impression that bathers freely mingled with each other regardless of their status in society, this was not entirely the case. Social differentiation did exist in various forms. To begin with (and to state the obvious), men and women were strictly segregated, as was reflected in the architectural form. Some hamams exclusively served women, and these were called *avret hamamı* – as discussed above, *avret* literally means the part of the body that modesty requires to be concealed, and more broadly also a family's womenfolk whom modesty requires to be secluded. Other hamams exclusively served men, and these were called *rical hamamı* – the bathhouse of the gentlemen. These hamams had only one set of dressing, warm and hot rooms (Figure 2.9, above). A third group of baths also had only one set of dressing, warm and hot rooms, but still served both men and women, by offering alternate bathing times for men and women. In some cases, men and women would bathe on alternate days, while in others the establishment would be open to men in the morning and to women between the noon and evening prayers. This type of bathhouse was called *kuşluk hamamı*, because the morning time reserved for the male bathers was known as *kuşluk*. In order to indicate that it was the women's time in the bath and to prevent men from stealing a glance, a cloth would be draped over the entrance during the women's hours. The fourth group of bathhouses consisted of *çifte* (double) hamams and could serve both sexes at the same time. While many of these offered equal facilities for men and women, there also exist double hamams where the women's section is smaller, maybe based on the demographics of the neighbourhood (compare Figures 1.13 and 2.5, above). Considering these four groups, gender segregation could be organised based on either space or time, depending on the architectural form of the hamam.

Social interaction between men and women was furthermore prevented by placing the entrance to the women's section away from that to the men's section. While the men's entrance was often the exterior focus of the building, sometimes with a domed portico and/or an inscription panel over the door, the women's entrance was a simple, much smaller door without any ornamentation, easy to overlook. In the Haseki Hamamı, the men entered the bath over a porch, while the women's entrance was tucked away on the opposite end of the building, below the street level and reached over a flight of stairs (Figure 3.8, above, Figures 4.2, 4.3). However, as one can imagine, attempts to transgress these boundaries did occur, as I will discuss in the following section.

Ethnic, professional and religious belonging may have played a role in the decision as to which hamam to visit. Evliya Çelebi, in the Istanbul section of his famous *Seyahatname*, offers a list of baths together with the groups who frequented them:

> Now, as a joke among brethren of noble disposition, [this section] assigns all the hamams to a class of persons each and lists them, claiming an attribution of hamams appropriate to the characteristics [of] the groups of persons . . . For

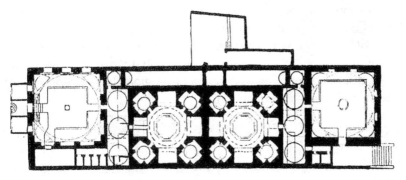

Figure 4.2 Ground plan of the Haseki Hamamı, 1553, Istanbul. *Source*: Glück, *Probleme des Wölbungsbaues*, 1921.

Figure 4.3 Exterior of the Haseki Hamamı. *Source*: Author's photograph.

the sick, the bath of Eyüp Sultan; for the sheikhs, the bath of Aya Sofya; for the Sufis, the bath of the Sufis [*sofular hammâmı*]; for strangers [*azeb*], the bath of the strangers [*azebler hammâmı*]; for the gardeners [*bostancı*], the garden bath [*bostan hammâmı*]; for the market-people [*bâzârcı*], the Friday market bath [*cum'abâzârı hammâmı*]; for heretics, the pit bath [*çukur hammâm*]; . . . for the painters, the tiled bath [*çinili hammâm*]; . . . for the surgeons [*cerrah*], the bath of the surgeon paşa [*cerrahpaşa hamâmı*]; . . .[38]

The list continues, but even without reproducing it in full, Evliya's text offers a glimpse into a certain mindset. His text does have to be taken with a grain of salt, especially since his express aim is to assign baths 'in an amusing way'. Nevertheless, given that Istanbul's neighbourhoods were organised along ethnic, professional and religious lines, there may be a kernel of truth contained in his list.

Class also constituted a major dividing line, even if people of different strata – from the well-off to the poorest, from the educated to the illiterate – did come together in one place, which made it possible to interact with persons of relatively higher or lower status and to expand one's personal network.[39] However, whether they in fact wanted to do so was another matter. The bathers' class was easily recognisable from

the hamam kit that they brought with them or, if they did not have one
of their own, the kit that the hamam manager would allocate them.[40]
Towels to wrap around the waist (*peştemal*) and the head (*peşkir*) were
of a wide variety of qualities, from simple monochrome cotton to lavishly
embroidered silk (Figure 4.4).[41] The bowls used for pouring water (*tas*)
came in silver, copper and brass, and ranged from very simple to having
embossed ornaments and figural designs (Figure 4.5). The bath clogs
(*nalın*) protecting the feet from the hot and slippery floor varied from
a simple wood version with attached leather straps to clogs inlaid with
mother-of-pearl and other precious materials (Figure 4.6). Furthermore,
there were many other accoutrements – such as mirrors, jewellery boxes,

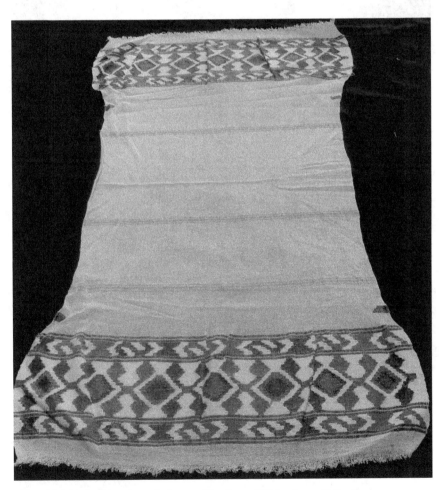

Figure 4.4 Embroidered towel. *Source*: Courtesy of Naim Arnas Collection.

Figure 4.5 Hamam bowl (*tas*), copper. *Source*: Courtesy of Naim Arnas Collection.

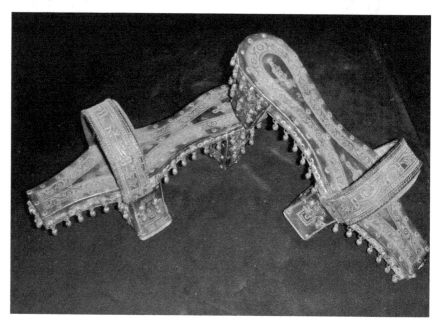

Figure 4.6 Hamam clogs (*nalın*). *Source*: Courtesy of Naim Arnas Collection.

flacons for perfume and rose water, containers for kohl, henna and pumice stones, and even bars of soap with imprinted decoration or in fanciful shapes – that permitted especially female bathers to communicate their wealth and status and establish certain boundaries, even in the intimate atmosphere created by the state of undress and the communal cosmetic procedures (such as hair care, removal of body hair and the application of henna and make-up).[42]

The need for privacy and seclusion that wealthier women desired in the bath is beautifully expressed in İrfan Orga's account of his grandmother visiting the bathhouse in the first decade of the twentieth century: 'She always engaged private rooms for herself at the hamam, a room for disrobing and another for washing herself, feeling quite definitely that she could not be expected to mix entirely with the common herd. Sociability could only go so far.'[43] The private room for washing mentioned here refers to the smaller chambers (*halvet*) inserted into the corners of the hot room, sometimes with the help of dividing walls, sometimes in the form of more distinct spatial units. The opening to the *halvet* could also be closed by hanging a large towel over it. Ottoman hamam architecture thus beautifully accommodated divergent social needs: the centralised layout of most *sıcaklık*s encouraged sociability, while the *halvet*s offered privacy.

Religion constituted a further dividing line that influenced the way in which bathers interacted, as has been discussed above. However, this may have been less so in the first decades after the Ottoman conquest of the city, when its population was still very mixed and had not organised itself into neighbourhoods primarily based on confessions. According to Çiğdem Kafesçioğlu's study on the transformation of post-conquest Constantinople, the unprecedented monumental scale of the bathhouses built in the late 1400s – their domes loomed much larger within the urban landscape than those of their contemporary mosques, and neither their size nor their large number can be explained by ritual necessity alone – suggest that these buildings were 'nonconfessional urban foci [and] centers of interaction, . . . public spaces in which all could partake'.[44] The bathhouses in the lively commercial areas, such as the Tahtakale Hamamı and the Mahmud Paşa Hamamı, might indeed have been inviting to and accepting of Muslim and non-Muslim bathers alike, especially given that the latter at the time still constituted the majority of Istanbul's inhabitants.

The one social group for whom the hamam was one of the very few accessible spaces for social interaction and the only public forum consisted of secluded women (*muhaddere*). Seclusion was only practised by the higher strata of society, as it was not feasible for women without recourse to servants to do domestic chores outside the home for them.[45] The diversions and amusements available to secluded women included visiting female relatives and friends, occasional outings during festive days, and visits to tombs and other sacred spaces on religious holidays.[46] Visiting the hamam, usually once every week or every other week, was the only time when they could meet women outside their immediate circle of friends and relatives. Husbands sometimes tried to curtail their secluded wives' bathhouse visits, since this was the one of the few occasions when they could not control their spouse's whereabouts. Still, the right of secluded women to visit the hamam was confirmed by a jurisprudential opinion (*fetva*) of Ebussuud Efendi, the highest legal authority (*şeyhülislam*) of the Ottoman Empire from 1545 to 1574. To the question of whether women who visited the bathhouse counted as respectable and modest (*muhaddere*), he answered: 'Yes, as long as it is in a chaste and demure manner and with her retinue of servants.'[47] Going to the hamam alone and without permission, however, could be grounds for divorce.[48]

Figure 4.7 Wrapper (*bohça*) with hamam kit consisting of towels, mirror, comb, soaps and pumice stone. *Source*: Courtesy of Naim Arnas Collection.

Hamam-related sociability did not start at the door of the building, but extended backwards in time and space and included other sets of activities. Nowhere is this more evident than in the way in which women organised their bi-weekly visit. Women usually went to the hamam in groups together with female relatives, children, friends, servants and slaves, thus ensuring that they were still *muhaddere*, and for them the visit involved much more preparation than simply a walk to the bathhouse. Usually, food – such as stuffed grape leaves (*dolma*) and meatballs (*köfte*) – was cooked and packed, to be consumed picnic-style during the day-long bathhouse visit. Clean clothes, towels, bathing clogs, soaps, cosmetics and other necessities were packed into big bundles and tied into wrappers called *bohça*, often beautifully embroidered (Figure 4.7). The group then proceeded through the streets to the hamam, often highly visible, as can be seen from two paintings in Lambert Wyts' *Iter factum e Belgico-Gallica, Voyages de Wyts en Turquie* from *c.* 1574 (Figure 4.8), and in the album titled *Ein Turggische Hochzeit* from *c.* 1582 (Figure 4.9). Thus, female hamam sociability was an affair that began, sometimes several

Figure 4.8 Miniature from Lambert Wyts' *Iter factum e Belgico-Gallica, Voyages de Wyts en Turquie*, c. 1574, Österreischische Nationalbibliothek Vienna, Codex Vindobonensis, 3325, fol. 82r. *Source*: Österreischische Nationalbibliothek Vienna.

Figure 4.9 Miniature from album titled *Ein Turggische Hochzeit, c.* 1582, Sächsische Landesbibliothek, Mscr.Dresd.J.2.a. *Source*: Staats- und Universitätsbibliothek Dresden (SLUB).

days earlier, with women contacting each other to determine the day of the visit, sitting down in groups within the household to prepare *dolma* and *köfte*, and packing up their bundles. These shared activities strengthened the bonds within this specific group of women, while setting boundaries against those not included.

A Place for Carnal Pleasure

Bonds of a sexual and sometimes illicit nature were also part and parcel of bathing culture.[49] Well before European travellers and Orientalist painters imagined the hamam as a place of sexual encounter, the Ottomans had already very much thought of and used it as such. To begin with, while the bathhouse primarily constitutes a place for purity and ritual ablution, like similar dark spaces with running water it is also a liminal place where deceitful evil spirits (*jinns*) gather and provoke lust.[50] Thus, it may house danger and sin. Moreover, the hamam was where one went after intercourse in order to restore ritual purity (see above); as an epilogue to sexual activity, it was simultaneously an integral component of it.[51] Finally, for many male children it was the site where they consciously experienced the difference between the sexes for the first time, as small boys accompanied their mothers to the hamam until the *hamam anası* decided that the child had become cognisant and would no longer be admitted. This she did by asking a question such as the price of bread.[52] The very last hamam visit in the women's section as a liminal experience between the end of childhood and the beginning of manhood was incisive

Figure 4.9 [Continued]

enough in men's consciousness so as to become a literary *topos*.[53] Beneath the conscious, the hamam continued to figure as a symbol of femininity, 'a warm, enclosed, humid receptacle', occasionally emerging in dreams that Ottoman dream interpretation literature equated with a sign foretelling heterosexual intercourse.[54]

It is not only manuals on dream interpretation, but also many other types of Ottoman literature, shadow theatre plays, erotic paintings and legal documents that tell of the hetero- as well as homoerotic aspects of the hamam. Quite explicit in its condemnation of the latter, a sultanic decree dating to 1585/6 addresses the judges of Bursa, ordering them to take charge:

> I [previously] issued a decree that smooth-cheeked young men should not be in the bathhouses in order that nothing contrary to the sharia might issue from them. It has recently come to my attention that there are again boys in some bathhouses and [that] they are engaged in all manner of [morally] disruptive activities. Therefore, I have sent the conveyor of royal commands, 'Amr Aga, in order to decree that each of you should see to the inspection of the bathhouses under his jurisdiction and that, if such boys are found [therein], they should be chastised; you should take care in this regard to manage this [situation] and to reprimand the vile youths ... Cemadi I [890 AH].[55]

This decree implies that the judges of Bursa had been aware of immoral sexual activities in the city's bathhouses, that they had already been given orders to rectify this situation, but then once again had turned a blind eye – and, one may venture, in some cases they even may have visited these establishments themselves.

Although the imperial decree does not explicitly mention prostitution – morally disruptive activities contrary to the shari'a may also happen on a consensual basis, after all – its existence in hamams throughout the centuries, the widespread knowledge of its existence, and the constant struggle of the Ottoman administration in contending with the trade in carnal pleasure are indisputable.[56] The scholar and historian Mustafa Ali (1541–1600) implies that, as places where women gather, bathhouses generally may constitute a 'marketplace' for such trade.[57] The abovementioned Evliya Çelebi was even more specific in that he named in his early seventeenth-century account of Istanbul the Ortaköy Hamamı in relation to (female) prostitutes.[58] To the later seventeenth century dates a manuscript titled *Dellakname-i Dilküşa* (*The Heart-Breaking Book of Masseurs*), purportedly authored by Derviş İsmail, the steward of the guild of hamam managers.[59] Eleven chapters are devoted to eleven individual *tellak*s, who sell their (homo)sexual services in different hamams, mentioning their life stories, what makes their services unique and the prices they ask. Thus, the *Dellakname-i Dilküşa* reflects the perspective of someone who not only condones but encourages male prostitution. In contrast, another text – the so-called *Risale-i Garibe*, written by an anonymous author and dated to the end of the seventeenth or early eighteenth century based on internal textual evidence – passes a negative value judgement by enumerating male bath attendants and barbers who sell their bodies and those who procure them among the swelled ranks of ne'er-do-wells in the Ottoman capital.[60] For the first half of the eighteenth century, the chronicler Mü'minzâde Seyyid Ahmed Hasîb Efendi in his *Ravzatü'l-Küberâ* (*Garden of the Grandees*) mentions *tellak*s acting as prostitutes, even if only in passing.[61] A very specific, illustrative case of several young *tellak*s affiliated with the Janissary corps, while also working as prostitutes in Istanbul's hamams, dates to 1709; the authorities dealt with it by making the hamam managers promise that they would expel said youths from their establishments.[62] Sünbülzade Vehbi (1719–1802) in his humourous pornographic poem *Şevk-Engiz* (*Desire-Provoker*, dating to between 1789 and 1798/9) describes 'bad-tempered bath-attendants' (*natura*) as women most likely to be approachable for sexual intercourse, even though elsewhere he cautions against illegitimately consorting with women.[63] Even into the twentieth century, prostitution continued to be an issue that, although sometimes treated humourously by poets, was not taken lightly by the administration. A legal document dating to 1908 decrees that hamam managers who henceforth continue to sell sexual services in their establishments shall be punished according to the penal code.[64] Today, bathhouses may still serve as meeting points for men seeking homoerotic pleasure.[65]

A particularly interesting case explicating a sixteenth-century hamam's identity as place for carnal pleasure – whether in the form of prostitution or sexual activity without financial compensation – revolves around Deli Birader Gazali (d. *c.*1535), the author of the *Dâfi'ü'l-Gumûm ve Râfi'ü'l-Humûm* (*The Repeller of Sorrow and Remover of Anxiety*).[66] A *medrese* teacher, Sufi and poet enjoying patronage by the elite, he retired to Istanbul later in life, where he established a mosque, dervish lodge and hamam in the Beşiktaş neighbourhood. A fellow poet wrote about Deli Birader Gazali's establishment that he 'staffed it with bath boys each of whose bodies was a silver cypress', and continues to describe its commercial success:

> The beloveds of Istanbul streamed to that bath from all directions, and the lovers came, burning hotly in fires of separation [from their beloveds], and in that bath they enflamed the wild horses of their hasty desire in the waters of lust. The most elegant of both noble and common, when they failed to find room [in the bath], climbed up on the roof and looked on through the windows. Birader filled casks with silver bullion; the [other] bathhouse keepers, [overcome] by desire, put on bath towels [and joined in], and the bath boys stuffed their purses.[67]

Deli Birader Gazali's major oeuvre (and at the same time one of the first examples of erotic Ottoman literature) is the abovementioned *Dâfi'ü'l-Gumûm ve Râfi'ü'l-Humûm*, which in prose and occasionally in poetry describes and comments on male sexual practices under seven different headings, not without reminding readers of their sinful nature. Apparently, this work was well received and steadily reproduced over the centuries, even though it was not included in the Ottoman literary canon, for obvious reasons.

A hamam figures as a setting in six different passages of this text. While three stories refer to it only in passing – as a place where one goes after intercourse,[68] as a place for 'lathered masturbation' with soap,[69] and as a place where a woman may find an accomplice for her scheme to meet her secret lover[70] – two stories more explicitly describe the bathhouse as a site for sexual activity. In an anecdote in the section titled 'How to Enjoy the Company of Boys', a man washing in a hamam tricks a one-eyed boy he encounters there into homosexual intercourse by persuading him that this act will 'open his eye'.[71] The second, more elaborate passage praises baths in the following manner:

> Even though it can be performed in almost any place, the ideal setting for masturbators is the bathhouse. There they can watch beautiful boys with ornate asses, white and soft bodies and feel as if they are dying out of pleasure. Then they can immediately go to the depilatory chamber [where one customarily removes all body hair] of the bathhouse and start performing their craft.[72]

Yet not everybody felt comfortable with such behaviour or turned a blind eye to it, as the brief anecdote immediately following the passage above reveals:

> One day a man got into the depilatory chamber and, leaning his head forward, started jacking off. All of a sudden a beautiful and young masseur poured cold water over him. The man opened his eyes and said, 'I haven't reached the point of performing ablutions [as is required after ejaculation], wait until I become soiled'.[73]

While a great many literary works focusing on sensuality and sexuality were rather crude and to the point when evincing the homoerotic aspects of the hamam's identity,[74] various other genres show much more restraint and a general preference for metaphoric language circumscribing the physical beauty of young male bath attendants. This is true of *divan* poetry as much as of etiquette books and biographical dictionaries that mention adolescent *tellak*s as objects of homoerotic imagination.[75] A poetic genre that can be considered a sub-category of *divan* poetry and shares its restrained character, even though it exclusively deals with bathhouses and the beauties who work there, is that of the *hamamiye* or *hamamname*. In his comprehensive survey of this type of Ottoman poetry, İ. Güven Kaya has extracted four main themes that usually follow the order in which they are listed here (although the poet may occasionally change them): introduction of the specific bathhouse or arrival of the poet or beautiful beloved at the hamam; the beautiful beloved undresses and enters the hot room; various aspects of the bathhouse architecture as well as the bathing experience – for instance, the dome, basins, spouts and fountains, as well as the water, steam, towels and bowls – receive praise; and, finally, the beautiful beloved dresses and leaves.[76]

A typical *hamamiye* by Tâcîzâde Cafer Çelebi is included in its entirety in the following section, but excerpts from two other well-known poets exemplify the sensual and sexual longings that visitors could experience in the hamam. The sixteenth-century poet Fuzûlî captures the image of a male bathing beauty in the following way:

> He wrapped his naked body in an indigo-coloured towel[,]
> Like a peeled almond falling into a violet [blossom.]
> The lip of the pool became exalted from kissing the foot in reverence[,]
> The glass eye [i.e., the glass cups in the hot room's dome] found light from the charming sight [of the beloved.][77]

Even more so than Fuzûlî, Yenişehirli Beliğ Mehmed Emin (d. 1760) uses a language that invites a reading of his *hamamiye* on a homoerotically highly charged level:

The glass [cups] gathered together with the splendour of the crystal[-like]
  neck[.]
The hamam got hot [referring to temperature as well as sexual arousal] from
  the yearning and hope for an embrace[.]
The exterior turned from a curtain into a silvery-limbed mirror[,]
[as] the sweet almond took off its peel in heat [referring to temperature as
  well as sexual arousal].

In both these examples, the beloved and various architectural elements
– the pool or fountain, the glass cups in the *sıcaklık*'s dome, even the
building as a whole – are interacting with each other, so that the hamam
itself becomes a character capable of emotion and of reacting to a male
bathing beauty.

Homoerotic attraction in the bathhouse emerged as a theme not only in
written words, but also in combination of text and image. This has been
argued for the Album of Ahmed I, which contains a folio juxtaposing two
paintings, of a bath scene and a scene in a lunatic asylum (Figure 4.10).[78]
Dating to around 1610, the album offers its readers an entertaining array of
calligraphic pieces, drawings and miniature paintings collected between its
covers.[79] Reconciling the poems speaking of unrequited love on the facing
page with the images of bathers and madmen, Emine Fetvacı convincingly
posits that there exists an integral connection between the three, that what
is erotic in the bathhouse – youngsters with elegant bodies and white skin
admire, groom, flirt with and embrace each other in and around a central
pool, but all in tasteful restraint and without exposing themselves – becomes
grotesque in the insane asylum, where grown men with exaggerated, cari-
cature-like features, grimacing and exposing their private parts, have to be
chained down.[80] Here, the image of the hamam (or, rather, the *kaplıca* as evidenced by the pool) parallels the tone of the refined *hamamiye*s in its subtle
references to male–male love affairs of a socially more acceptable nature.

More for the common people than for the elite, who had access to
books and was literate enough to read *hamamiye*s (or listen to recitations
thereof), were the widely popular Karagöz and Hacıvat shadow puppet
plays (Figure 4.11).[81] In these ribald comedies, a subversive pleasure
enjoyed by high and low alike, the two heroes forever hatch schemes to
ogle naked ladies bathing. One way of achieving this is by sneaking into
the dressing room in the disguise of an old hag, but more often than not are
they found out and receive a good beating with bath clogs from the women
present.[82] Another way is by climbing onto the roof and peeping through a
window or the glass covers on the hot room's dome, or by opening a hole
between the men's and women's sections;[83] however, it is doubtful they
would have seen much of what they had imagined.

Figure 4.10 Folio from Album for Ahmed I, *c.* 1610, Topkapı Palace Library, B. 408, fol. 18a. *Source*: Topkapı Palace Museum.

The imagination of Ottoman men is captured well in a miniature painting that presents a striking parallel to European Orientalist bathing scenes. The miniature is part of an album kept in the Topkapı Palace Library, dated to *c.* 1610 (Figure 4.12). Painted by the famous master Abdullah Buhari, it shows a female bather seated on a wooden bench next to a *kurna*, daintily pouring water over herself from a *tas*. As she lifts her arms, she offers a full view of her round, firm breasts and her plump belly; the dark blue embroidered *peştemal* has slipped down so as to reveal her ample hips and thighs as well as her hairless genital area. The tips of her fingers and her toes have been dyed red with henna, and she wears several rings and an armband. Her long black hair, swept back over her shoulders, frames a rounded face with wide, well-defined black eyebrows and dark eyes. Her gaze suggests that she is lost in thought, maybe absent-mindedly humming a tune through closed lips as she performs her ablutions. The background against which this Ottoman beauty is displayed consists of nothing more than the plain paper standing for the whitewashed walls of the hot room, allowing the viewer to focus without any distraction on her fashionably pale flesh. Much like the bathers depicted by Ingres

Figure 4.11 Hamam set piece for a Karagöz and Hacıvat shadow puppet theatre. *Source*: Yapı Kredi Collection.

or Gerôme (Figures I.3, I.4, above and Figure 7.1, below), the *topos* of the bather serves Abdullah Buhari as an excuse to turn his gaze on the ideal female form. Album leaves displaying beautiful females as well as males, made in the Ottoman and Safavid empires of the seventeenth and eighteenth centuries, present the equivalent of twentieth-century pin-up postcards and posters. While European Orientalist painters usually did not show in such obvious and explicit manner the bather's genital area – most of the time the bathing women either turned away from the viewer or they held their legs tightly closed – Buhari left little to the imagination, demonstrating beyond a doubt that the subject matter of the album leaf was of an erotic nature.

Equally explicit is a miniature in Enderuni Fazıl Hüseyin's *Zenanname* (*Book of Women*), dated to 1793 (Figure 4.13).[84] This is in keeping with the nature of the manuscript as a whole, since it was something like a dating manual detailing in poetic form the character and the advantages and disadvantages of different women to be found in Ottoman Istanbul, from Greeks to Circassians, from Turks to Austrians, illustrated with the occasional miniature. (Women and men of homosexual inclination could find parallel information in the *Hubanname*, the *Book of Young Men*, which also included the painting of a young *tellak* (Figure 4.14).[85]) The

139

Figure 4.12 Abdullah Buhari, album leaf with bather, *c.* 1741, Topkapı Palace Library, YY. 1403. *Source*: Topkapı Palace Museum.

hamam scene shows a total of eleven women bathers, two children and a female bath attendant, dressed in full attire and teetering on dangerously high bathing clogs while serving a cup of coffee. The five bathers seated on the *göbektaşı* merrily chat with each other; one is about to be served coffee and another eats what appears to be a halved lemon to refresh herself. It is a scene of amicable, intimate interaction, and none of them bothers to cover up their breasts or pull the towel tightly around her body. While the painter's emphasis in the foreground is more on the social aspect of the bathhouse visit, the figures in the background display a more obviously erotic character. Left and right of the central *kurna* squat two bathers washing themselves: one scrubs her torso with a *kese* on one hand while filling her bathing bowl from the tap with the other; the second washes her hair with the help of another bather standing behind her. The bather washing her hair has removed her *peştemal* and folded it over her left thigh, revealing not only a pear-shaped belly reminiscent of Abdullah Buhari's bather – clearly a beauty ideal of the time – but also genitalia of exaggerated proportions. Once again, the hamam scene becomes an

Figure 4.13 Hamam scene from Enderuni Fazıl Hüseyin's *Zenanname*, 1793, Istanbul University Library, T. 5502. *Source*: Istanbul University Library.

Figure 4.14 Bathhouse attendant in Enderuni Fazıl Hüseyin's *Hubanname*, 1793, Istanbul University Library, T. 5502. *Source*: Istanbul University Library.

excuse for depicting the female form in all its details, although in the *Zenanname* illustration nothing is left to the imagination.

A Place for Healing

Even though it did not have the explicitly medicinal benefits of bath-houses with thermal water supply (*ılıca* or *kaplıca*), the urban hamam – as the so-called 'silent doctor' (in Arabic, *al-tabib al-bakkush*) of Islamic medicine – nevertheless fulfilled a number of functions in the prevention and treatment of diseases. These functions need to be contextualised within the different etiological systems that existed in the early modern Ottoman Empire, as its inhabitants practised three separate medical traditions that at times overlapped, at other times complimented and sometimes competed with each other: Galenic humouralism, religious medicine and folk medicine.[86] Although humouralism was consulted only by certain groups – elite patients and those who received treatment in urban *vakıf* hospitals because they lacked a social network to take care of them – it is this branch that has produced the most concrete textual evidence about the medical role of bathing and hence will be the focus of discussion.

Humoural medicine, the learned tradition passed on in the imperial medical schools and practised by doctors (*hekim*) and in the imperial hospitals, was based on Galen's principles as transmitted by the eleventh-century *Canon of Medicine* (*Kanun fi't-Tibb*) of the Persian physician Ibn Sina (*c.* 980–1037), also known by the Latinised name Avicenna.[87] As a science taught and practised in elite circles, the humouralist tradition was kept alive in the Ottoman Empire through its own literary genre of medical treatises written in Ottoman Turkish or in Arabic. Preventive rather than curative in nature, Galenic medicine aimed at maintaining or restoring the balance of the human body's four humours or fluids – that is, blood (warm and moist), black bile (cold and dry), yellow bile (warm and dry) and phlegm (cold and moist). A deficiency or excess in one of the humours would result in imbalance and illness, which the physician was to diagnose and counteract with the help of a regimen that included, for instance, exposure to light and air, consumption of specific foods and drinks, rest or activity, sleep and bathing.

According to Ibn Sina, the benefits of bathing are manifold for balancing the humours. A patient who needs to gain weight should visit the hamam after having eaten; this will produce a moderate increase of weight.[88] Because the humid atmosphere in the hamam opens the pores, the skin can be cleansed most thoroughly. Furthermore, the humidity aids in the maturation and dispersal of waste matters in the body and gives physiological assistance in the excretion of these poisonous matters.[89] Different types of massage also shaped the specific beneficial aspects of the bath: while hard massage makes the body firm and consequently removes fatigue, soft massage relaxes the body and induces sleep. The application of moderate massage helps to develop muscle tone, and prolonged massage is recommended to reduce the bather's weight. Rough massage with a *kese* or loofah sponge briskly draws the blood towards the skin and assists the body in the elimination of waste products.[90]

In order to enhance the beneficial effects of bathing, Ibn Sina laid out a number of rules. First of all, bathers should be rested and not enter the hamam immediately after having exerted themselves. While in the hot room, they were recommended to sprinkle water on the floor, so that the atmosphere would remain sufficiently moist. In terms of duration, Ibn Sina suggested a stay of moderate length in the hot room, for he warns that 'those who remain in the bath for a long time develop excessive heat in the heart from exertion and suffer nausea followed by fainting'.[91] After the bath, one should stay in the dressing room until the body temperature returned to normal. The application of oil to the skin and the consumption of drinks such as barley water and donkey's milk enhanced the therapeutic effects. Adverse effects,[92] on the other hand, resulted from prolonged exposure to heat, which could weaken the heart and the nerves and predispose to putrefaction if the stagnant and morbid matters in the body were disturbed. Massage in the hot environment could also disperse matters towards the flexures and weaker organs and thus produce inflammation; therefore, a person suffering from fever, injury or inflammation was advised against a long hamam visit including a massage. Even in a healthy person, exaggerated bathing could cause the body to become overly loose and lax, impair the appetite and cause sexual debility.

Ibn Sina also had something to say about the form of hamam architecture most conducive to medicinal bathing. He argued that 'there should also be proper arrangements for regulating the temperature according to individual temperaments [in other words, humours] . . . The first room of a hammam is cold and moist, the second hot and moist and the third hot and dry.'[93] (Given that Ottoman hamams did not continue the Ancient Greek and Roman tradition of having a dry hot room as well as a moist hot room, such a recommendation pertains more to pre-Ottoman arrangements; either tenth- and eleventh-century Perso-Islamic bathhouse architecture still kept this tradition alive, or Ibn Sina merely repeated what Galen had said about the desired qualities of Roman baths of the second century CE.) Moreover, the building should be spacious, with a supply of fresh but not cold air and clean, fresh water.[94]

Ibn Sina's rules and recommendations were further elaborated upon and shaped to fit more properly into the Ottoman context in medical treatises such as Emir Çelebi's *Enmüzecü'l-Tıbb* (*Summary of Medicine*), originally composed in 1625. Emir Çelebi was an Anatolian physician who worked in a famous hospital in Cairo and later on advanced to the position of imperial head physician under Murad IV (r. 1623–1640). His work includes a short chapter on the hamam, which is worth reproducing here in full, in order to illustrate not only his debt to Ibn Sina and Galen, but also Ottoman doctors' views and opinions about their 'silent colleague':

> A good bathhouse is one which is spacious and whose building is aged, so that its air is pleasant and its water moderate. He who goes to the bathhouse should sit in such a sultry *caldarium* [*halvet*] long enough so that sweat should pour out [of his body]. The sultry *caldarium* is beneficial to phlegmatic people of cold temperament. The first of the previous chambers of the bathhouse is cold and humid; the second one is hot and humid; and its sultry *caldarium* is hot and [*yab?*]. The effects of a bath on the human body are evident. Essentially it

heats up [the body], [while it also] affords a cooling down. It has a resolving influence [upon inflammations and the like]. Exceedingly hot water irritates the skin; since it does not penetrate into the body, it does not have any regulating effect either. If the intention is [to induce] perspiration, it is easiest in the first and second chambers. Excessive perspiration should be avoided, lest one be over-hydrated instead. If one does need excessive sweat – that is, the healing effect of humidity – he should sit only in the sultry caldarium as long as he could, until sweat diffuses [all over the body]. Yet he should not pour much water over himself, nor should he eat, until the bathhouse becomes moderate [in temperature]. Going to the bathhouse with a full stomach makes one grow fat. But one should fear [having] a belly [*sürre*, meaning navel]. A symptomatic belly is one which [... ?]. If it is so, the person should obtain oxymel seeds and enter the bathhouse without having eaten anything hot. If what he has eaten is cold, on the other hand, it can cause thirst [*mucib-i istika*, can also be translated as vomiting]. It is preferable that neither does it cause thirst [or vomiting], nor does the person enter the bathhouse with an empty stomach; instead, [it is better] to go to the bathhouse after having eaten some food and after the signs of digestion become apparent. Even though a bath is constipating, it conducts cold winds to the feeble organ, and thus a [... ?] temperament is brought about, especially in those who linger too long [in the bathhouse]. Bathhouse waters are also varied. For instance, if it includes sulphur, gunpowder [*barut*, probably meaning potassium nitrate], and sulphate, it is a resolvent and increases exfoliation. It is beneficial to many maladies. Above all, it removes skin diseases and is beneficial to scabies and [... ?] . Copper, iron, and lead – waters that come out of all these mines are beneficial to cold and humid temperament. They are also beneficial to joint pain, muscle laxity, contraction [*zıyyık*, can also be translated as shortness of breath] and kidney disease. They give strength to those with broken health. They are beneficial to boils and swellings. [Yet] it is necessary to adhere to moderation.[95]

Emir Çelebi's advice certainly would have been applied in the hamams that were built as part of the imperial hospitals. The Atik Valide Mosque Complex also included a minuscule bathhouse exclusively reserved for the patients of its *darüşşifa*, within the latter's walls (Figure 2.1, above). It was so small that its staff consisted of one person only, according to the endowment deed: 'one *külhancı* [furnace attendant] shall be appointed in order to heat the hamam prepared for the patients and to massage the patients in the hamam and to look after other tasks related to the hamam; and his salary shall be two dirhem ...'[96] Probably the *külhancı-tellak* gave massages to the specifications of the treating doctor – soft, moderate or rough, based on the guidelines of Ibn Sina's humoural medicine. This was a task he accomplished in addition to the washing, shaving and nail-clipping which maintained the patients' personal hygiene and therefore the sanitary conditions of the hospital's environment overall.[97] More than just serving physical health and cleanliness, hamams were also expected to restore mental health and well-being, much like the ornamental fountains and small but pleasing gardens contained in hospitals.[98] Having recourse to such a facility within the building, patients did not have to leave the hospital in order to use the complex's close-by public bathhouse for washing or hydrotherapy. This was probably as much for the convenience of the patients, especially for those who were not ambulatory, as for the prevention of the spread of communicable diseases to the healthy visitors of the Atik Valide Hamamı.

How far did public bathhouses outside the imperial hospitals, like Çemberlitaş Hamamı, serve medical purposes? According to popular lore, a bathhouse visit was meant to maintain health and well-being in addition to personal hygiene, and therefore may be considered a preventive cure. Ottomans were aware that cleanliness could prevent the spread of diseases and that the wide availability of public baths could preclude their occurrence to begin with. In Istanbul, baths were usually build close to *imarets*, where cooks, bakers and other workers daily prepared and served food to as many as thousands of beneficiaries. An unclean *imaret* employee might have cause hundreds of cases of food poisoning or other illness, and it is quite possible that, prior to the start of a work day during which large quantities of food were handled, bathing was, if not compulsory, then at least expected in order to ensure hygienic conditions in the kitchens.[99]

Visiting the public hamam as curative treatment depended on the bather's cultural horizons and social and economic realities. The above-mentioned learned treatises by Ibn Sina and Emir Çelebi suggested bathing as a cure to restore the balance of humours – but were elite patients who knew about humouralism inclined to use public bathhouses for that purpose? Certainly, the lower segments of Ottoman society who may not even have had recourse to doctors or imperial hospitals would have used the hamam as a folk medicine remedy, whether in consultation with healers or on the basis of common-sense knowledge – sweating in the hot room was probably one of the few avenues of relief easily available to treat fevers, aches and pains. In some cases, a more invasive procedure such as blood-letting was on the list of services offered by the *tellaks*, as the sixteenth-century traveller Solomon Schweigger reported.[100] With its abundant water supply, smooth and easy-to-clean surfaces, comfortable temperature and the *göbektaşı* as a convenient place to lay out patients, hamams constituted an ideal place for surgical interventions.[101] The same can be claimed for bathhouses as a place for deliveries, as the warm air temperature and the application of warm water could not only speed up labour,[102] but also ease birth pains.[103]

Today, medical doctors, bath attendants and bathers are still very much aware of the medicinal effects of traditional hamams. The physiological effects of a visit with a typical washing procedure have been investigated in a small-scale study in Çemberlitaş Hamamı: a slight if significant increase in heart rate and body temperature indicative of a mild hyperthermia during the washing in the hot room, followed by a decrease in blood pressure after the hamam session. Although the study found no statistically significant increase in beta endorphin, which plays an important role in pain mechanisms, the study participants' responses showed a decrease in mean bodily pain scores and great improvement in psychological scores.[104] These effects resonate with the personal observations of Sefer Yüce, a *tellak* in Çemberlitaş Hamamı, who described the beneficial qualities of bathing as detoxifying, widening the blood vessels, enhancing circulation and preventing colds in people who have caught a chill but immediately thereafter come to bathe.[105] In fact, as I was able to observe during the winter months of my fieldwork, many Turkish visitors come to Çemberlitaş Hamamı in order to rid themselves of a cold or flu. The hot, humid air opens congested passages, alleviates coughs and raises the body temperature high enough to sweat out fever. In the early modern period, a hamam visit was probably the most easily accessible and effective medicine against these winter ailments. Ottoman residential architecture in that period consisted of wood, and heating was done with the help of coal-fuelled braziers (*mangal*) which diffused little warmth. During the cold and rainy winter months in Istanbul, only hamams and a few other buildings were thoroughly heated spaces where someone chilled to the bone could find relief.

Pride of the City

For the Ottoman sultans and their family as well as for the inhabitants of Istanbul who felt pride in their capital – one of the most populous and splendid cities in the world in the sixteenth century – Çemberlitaş Hamamı and the many other baths there also took on the identity of monuments contributing to that splendour. This side to Çemberlitaş Hamamı's multifarious identity was inherited from its predecessors, as Ancient Roman *thermae* and the hamams of Abbasid Baghdad or Seljuk Konya had equally added to the grandeur of their cities and the patrons that had commissioned them. Therefore, this aspect of hamams' identity has to be viewed in the larger context of Istanbul's urban development and image.

After the conquest of Constantinople in 1453, Sultan Mehmed II (r. 1444–1446, 1451–1481) set out to endow the partially destroyed city with new public buildings that would restore its former glory, transform it into a Muslim rather than Christian city, and serve the needs of the populace in order to legitimise his rule.[106] Mehmed II's court historian, the Greek Kritovoulos, describes the sultan's building and reconstruction activities, including his mosque complex (erected 1462–1472), his old palace – later to be abandoned for the Topkapı Palace – and the Grand Bazaar (built in the 1450s and 1460s, but subsequently enlarged over the centuries), as well as caravansarays, roads and bridges. Kritovoulos also notes the building of new baths:

> He also ordered [the workmen] to construct splendid and costly baths, and through aqueducts into the City from the countryside an abundance of water. Many such things he also ordered to be done for the building up and beautifying of the City, and for the benefit and needs and comfort of the inhabitants.[107]

Mehmed II did not content himself with the monuments erected under his patronage, but also enjoined his officials and dignitaries to embellish the city:

> [H]e called together all the wealthy and most able persons into his presence, those who enjoyed great wealth and prosperity, and ordered them to build grand houses in the City, wherever each chose to build. He also commanded them to build baths and inns and marketplaces, and very many and very beautiful workshops, to erect places of worship, and to adorn and embellish the City with many other such buildings, sparing no expense, as each man had the means and the ability.[108]

The first bath built under Mehmed II, in the immediate vicinity of his mosque complex between 1462 and 1472 and named Çukur Hamamı because of its location in the depression of an old cistern, was according to Evliya Çelebi meant to serve the construction workers building the mosque complex.[109] While the Çukur Hamamı has disappeared,[110] the largest among the baths built by Mehmed II's dignitaries still stands: the Mahmud Paşa Hamamı, erected in 1466 by the eponymous grand vizier in a commercial area south of the Hippodrome, with its dome of a diameter of 15.5 m dominates the neighbourhood.

The hamams commissioned by Mehmed II and his dignitaries fulfilled several functions in the urban context. First, as parts of charitable endowments, they secured income that would be re-invested into the city's infrastructure and monuments. For example, Mehmed II's endowment supporting the Hagia Sophia – now turned into a mosque – included no less than thirteen hamams.[111] Secondly, these hamams as washing facilities were 'for the benefit and needs and comfort of the inhabitants', to use

Kritovoulos' words. Thirdly, the hamams symbolised the power of the sultan over vital resources through the restoration of waterways and the provisioning of the city with water for drinking and washing.[112] Finally, the bathhouses as non-confessional public spaces extended the sultan's benevolence to his non-Muslim subjects.[113]

Within the context of the neighbourhoods (*mahalle*), hamams quickly became focal points, even providing the name for several.[114] A *mahalle* constituted an administrative unit for tax purposes, with its tax-paying inhabitants (*re'aya*) registered in survey books (*tahrir defterleri*).[115] Such neighbourhoods were organised along ethnic–religious groupings, within geographical boundaries, or sometimes according to professional groups; this resulted in demographic concentrations that, to a certain extent, are still visible in Istanbul's urban fabric today. Neighbourhoods were rarely separated according to income, but housed rich and poor alike. The loyalty of *homo Ottomanicus* belonged first and foremost to her or his community of the *mahalle*, and only second to the sultan.[116]

Istanbul's neighbourhoods of early modern times usually encompassed about 150 residences, constructed from wood and ranging from *konak*s (large mansions with gardens, owned by dignitaries) to *menzil*s (composite dwellings made up of one or two houses, shops and a courtyard), from *beyt*s (one- or two-storey houses) to *hücre*s (individual rooms built in rows, generally inhabited by unmarried men).[117] Small inward-turned streets that terminated in cul-de-sacs connected these residential buildings. Amid this sea of wooden houses, stone monuments marked the neighbourhoods' focal points where social life was concentrated: the mosque, the *mekteb*, the *medrese*, the *meydan* (a small public space for neighbourhood markets and other gatherings), the public fountain and the hamam.[118] These stone monuments were the only buildings that could withstand the frequent fires that would erase entire neighbourhoods around them (see Chapter 5). In many cases, their permanency within the urban fabric and memory was such that neighbourhoods adopted the names of the most frequented or most outstanding monument. An eighteenth-century description of the mosques of Istanbul, Ayvansarayi's *Garden of the Mosques*, mentions hamams sixty-six times; Ayvansarayi refers nineteen time to hamams as points of references when locating a mosque; and in six instances the mentioned hamams have acted as name-patron to either a mosque or an entire neighbourhood.[119]

It was not only in residential districts that baths constituted proud emblems of the Ottoman capital city. Commercial districts as centres of economic, political and religious life showed a higher concentration of stone buildings; yet the hamams erected under imperial or sub-imperial patronage still figured among the largest ones there. The scale of the so-called market baths (*çarşı hamamı*) was not only due to the higher number of customers to be expected from among the men working in the markets and shops, but their size and splendour also demonstrated the sultan's grandeur and generosity to the foreign merchants housed in the surrounding caravansarays and *hans*. Many travelogues – among them those written by the sixteenth-century travellers and ambassadors Nicolas de Nicholay, Reinhold Lubenau, Hans Dernschwam, Solomon Schweigger and Ogier Ghiselin de Busbecq – show that the intended foreign audience was duly impressed and spread the reputation of Turkish baths to Europe.[120]

The Ottomans themselves expressed admiration for and pride in the bathhouses of Istanbul in their literature. *Şehr-engiz* poetry, a genre that extols the beauty of specific cities, often devoted some space to one or more hamams considered to be particularly splendid. In his *Hevesname* (1493/4), the court poet Tâcîzâde Cafer Çelebi praises the beauty of the Hagia Sophia, the Fatih Mosque, the Yedikule Castle, of Istanbul's hospitals and *imaret*s, as well as the remarkable character of an unidentified bathhouse:

On this square, there is a marvellous hamam[,]
no one living today has seen the likes of it[.]
Its building is heart-captivating[,] its space bright[,]
its water and air pleasant and mild[,]
its floor crafted with artistry of different [kinds of] marble[.]
So much money was spent on it that its weight was [measured] in gold[.]
The water from the earthen reservoir resembles [the paradisiacal drink]
    Kevser[.]
Its plaster smells intensely of saffron and musk[,]
What is burnt in the furnace are sandal- and aloeswood[,]
the rising smoke reproaches the musk of Hatay [i.e., imported from China] [.]
The great powerful master of the treasure
keeps his door open to visitors night and day[.]
He spends water abundantly like silver [;]
what pure water is that pouring silver[!]
It reconciles fire and water and creates balance between them[.]
This building brings opposites together[.]
Its exterior is a stoke-hole[,] its interior a joy-giving rose garden[,]
it is like paradise on top of hell[.]
Such a paradise is rarely found[.]
Every one of its stone benches is so refined,
The heavens that know it envy it [so much that]
from wrath its blood has turned to water[.]
Every halvet is warm like a heart in love

its interior is clean and light, the conversation there passionate[,]
its taps are gilded and its basins of greenish stone[.]
Those who see it take off their clothes[,] offering thanks[,]
whoever sees it is at ease and his soul rejoices[.]
The clouds are the towel, sun and moon are the bowls,
they make the Ninth Sphere of the firmament jealous[.]
The Shah [the beloved] enters with a few cypress-like beauties,
a jasmine-breasted, rosebud-lipped, rosy-cheeked bathhouse attendant,
not one of them has [even] the smallest defect[.]
Everyone who will enter the hamam is naked[,]
their reflection fills heavens and earth of the hamam[.]
The tulip-coloured window glass is from the light of the soul[.]
When its fountains look at the stature of the beauties,
their mouths water in excitement[.]
When the water sees the young and soft [body,]
it spreads heat and kisses their feet.[121]

Cafer Çelebi's encomium interweaves different strands of appreciation: for the artistry and high-quality construction material with which the hamam was built, the fact that no expense was spared, the resulting architectural space, the fresh and plentiful water dispensed from the reservoir, and the attendants' physical beauty. Although only few visitors to this and other baths would have possessed the level of literacy to formulate a response to their bathing experience in the same way as the court poet, they still would have been able to appreciate particularly well-built and -appointed establishments and to reflect in one way or another on the impression they generated. In fact, Ottomans expected any town of repute to have at least one hamam – if it did not, then this was a sign of the town's backwardness, or it required explanation, such as its population being composed mostly of Christians.[122]

Given the many different aspects of identity and the various roles and functions that Ottoman baths united, it is little wonder that Istanbul boasted so many of them – Evliya Çelebi counted a total of 302 public hamams, mentioning 124 by name, and adding the fantastical number of 14,536 private ones, with the comment that the number of public baths is rather small for a city of Istanbul's size.[123] As in all the other baths, each user of Çemberlitaş Hamamı had a different impression of the building and ascribed one or more functions to it. The hamam's identity as breadwinner – as discussed in Chapter 3 – took centre stage for officials connected to the Atik Valide Vakfı, to the *hamamcı* and to the employees working there, but this function was of lesser significance to the majority of the Muslim bathers who came, for instance, to fulfil the canonical requirements of body hygiene. To be sure, most bathers came for multiple purposes and considered Çemberlitaş Hamamı as much a place for canonical ablutions as a site of sociability, a well-spring of health and a monument that bestowed pride on the city.

The identity of Çemberlitaş Hamamı, as Eric Dursteler has argued generally for individuals in the early modern Mediterranean, did not possess a primordial and essential character, nor was it the sum total of its constituent parts – such as 'nation' in the form of regional origin, religion, a sense of a shared history and culture, political status, gender, family and so on, which existed as broad organising categories.[124] Rather, 'early modern identity was multilayered, multivalent and composite'.[125] These various layers and valences, furthermore, continuously shifted and moved along a spectrum, contingent on specific situations and interactions. As Christine Isom-Verhaaren and Kent Schull point out, 'categories and attributes that were not viewed as salient for Ottoman identity in 1350 might be so in 1650, and others that were salient in 1350 might be of little consequence for categorisation in 1750'.[126] The abundance of syncretic practices in the early modern Mediterranean meant that even religious identity was much less fixed than is commonly assumed.[127] For Çemberlitaş Hamamı, this meant that it served Muslims and non-Muslims alike, parallel to the practice of Ottoman Christians and Muslims venerating the same saints and seeking a cure at the same holy waters. On different occasions, specific constituents of identity came to the fore or receded into the background, even for one and the same customer. One may envision, for example, an Ottoman merchant who arrived in the Vezir Han on a Saturday, went to Çemberlitaş Hamamı to wash off the dirt of the road on the same day, then returned on Monday in order to find reprieve from a cold he had caught while on the road, and then finally visited again on Friday morning for ritual cleansing before congregational prayer in the Atik Ali Paşa Mosque – each time he would leave the bathhouse having interacted with a different aspect of the monument's identity and with a different impression.

5

In Sickness and in Health

---

*It describes how this pleasurable hamam has suffered over the course of
time and what the marks of these sufferings are; how it has been injured
by the earthquakes and fires that ravaged Istanbul; as how the atmosphere
inside, pleasant to the bather, is harmful to the noble building; and how the
imperial orders penned by the servants of the Sublime Porte allow this poor
one to understand how the architects of the imperial chamber went about to
restore health to this lofty hamam.*

Symptoms: Evidence for Renovations

By the late eighteenth century, the continual use and the fires and earthquakes that so frequently afflict Istanbul had begun to take a toll on
Çemberlitaş Hamamı, as the inscription inside as well as the accumulation
of archival documents about repairs and renovations suggest. Certainly,
improvements to the structure and particularly to the waterways supplying the hamam had been made earlier (and continued to be made
later); however, the late eighteenth century constitutes a distinct station in
Çemberlitaş Hamamı's life cycle, marked by the first signs of ageing and
more extensive and frequent renovations. Taking better care of the existing bathhouses of Istanbul, rather than building new ones, also became
an imperative after 1768. In July 1768, an imperial decree prohibited the
construction of any new hamams in the city, because of the serious strain
on the urban water and fuel supply:

> I order the head of the court architects that[:]
>
> Although the existing hamams built in Istanbul and Üsküdar and Galata
> and in the connected provinces and in Eyüp on the Golden Horn and in the
> villages on [the shores of the] Bosphorus are sufficient for the people of the
> present neighbourhoods, for some time some people have built several single
> baths and several double baths, which are unnecessary, in the previously men-
> tioned neighbourhoods in Istanbul and Üsküdar and Galata and the connected
> provinces, with the intention of generating income for themselves[.] And since

the abundance of unnecessary hamam[s] causes a shortage of water in the hot season and, in addition, since it is obvious that this condition causes, together with the unnecessary destruction and waste of fuel brought to Istanbul, a scarcity [of fuel] for the men of God, there shall henceforth no architect or other person give in any way permission or licence for building a double or single hamam, neither in Istanbul and Üsküdar and Galata and the connected provinces, nor in the villages of Eyüp, [along] the Golden Horn and the Bosphorus[.] When my honoured imperial decree regarding the complete prohibition and removal [of these buildings] is issued [the following shall be enforced:] As soon as you, the abovementioned head of the Imperial Architects, are aware of the circumstances, no permission and licence to build either a single or double hamam in the abovementioned places shall henceforth be given by you under any circumstances[.] If, contrary to my imperial order, [someone] sets out to build a hamam in Istanbul or the abovementioned places, an inquiry shall be made and continuously great care and attention shall be paid to immediately carrying out my imperial order to demolish [the bath] . . . In the first ten days of Rebiülevvel 1182[1]

From the verbiage of the imperial decree, one can gather that operating a hamam was such a profitable trade that businesspeople built more bath-houses than strictly needed by Istanbul's population. Already before the decree, no one had been able to build a hamam without petitioning the head of imperial architects for permission, but now the head of impe-rial architects had to decline all such requests. Sultan Mustafa III felt so strongly about the hamams' waste of the city's resources that he ordered the demolition of baths built without permission. However, this strict attitude begs the question as to whether it was really the hamams that were responsible for water and fuel shortages, or whether they just served as scapegoat. Moreover, one has to question the efficacy of the imperial decree. Were Istanbulites aware of the decree, and did it affect their atti-tude towards the bathhouse buildings? Was there a way around the new rules, maybe by means of an extra payment to the relevant authorities? Did official circles really put more emphasis on renovating the existing build-ings since no new baths could be erected, or did they go about business as usual, thinking of the restriction as temporary? While there may never be answers to these questions, it is still remarkable that so many documents concerning repair work to Çemberlitaş Hamamı date to the years after the decree's date of issuance.

The earliest document referring to repair work, however, is dated 100 years before the decree, to 1667/8.[2] In addition to recording the endowment's income from different real estate properties, as well as the food and salary expenses of the mosque complex, the accounting book mentions expenditures for repairs. Between 25 February 1667 and 13 February 1668, the Atik Valide Vakfı spent a total of 280,771 *akçe* on repairs to its properties – that is, 5.96 per cent of its total income. Most of these expenditures went towards the maintenance of revenue-generating properties, with the intention of keeping them in good working order so as to garner greater profits in return. Çemberlitaş Hamamı was one of these revenue-generating properties being repaired. For the most part, the account-book entries do not specify the nature of the repairs – except when waterways were involved – but record the amounts of money only: 2,306, 3,175, 135, 4,760 and 5,590 *akçe*. Thus, the endowment spent a total of 15,966 *akçe*, or 0.34 per cent of its 1667/8 revenue. Although the summarily given information precludes any understanding of whether these sums covered both building materials and labour costs, or only one of these, the nature of the record shows that the scribe considered such expenses a regular part of the endowment's finances, as the entries are in no way singled out and take their place between routine expenditures.

The inscription on the marble room dividers in Çemberlitaş Hamamı's men's hot room also indirectly tells of renovation work, thanks to inconsistencies in the inscribed poem's content and calligraphic rendering (Figure 5.1). Beginning with the verse on the exterior marble panel of the *halvet* immediately to the right-hand side of the entrance, one can count twenty cartouches with a line of poetry each (Figures 3.14, 3.15, above). While lines 1–9 and 17–20 constitute the original inscription penned in 1584 by the same Sai responsible for the inscription over the entrance, lines 10–16 are a later addition. Lines 11–15, adorning the walls of one single *halvet*, make up one entity visibly different from the rest: within the cartouches, the calligrapher has arranged the syllables on two levels, rather than on one. The content matches the preceding and following lines insofar as it also exhorts the bathhouse's physical beauty:[3]

> Its surface is as if made of mirrors and crystal[,]
> the basins are from mother-of-pearl[,] the bowls from porcelain[.]
> Is there any place more pleasant[?]
> Friends flow into [the hamam] like water, to watch[.]
> Its windows look like budding hollyhock blossoms[,]
> the golden pieces in it like tulips[.][4]

Clearly, this portion of the inscription was added later, with the intent to approximate the content of Sai's lines and to give an appearance of continuity. However, lines 10 and 16, placed on the lateral walls of the two *halvet*s right before and after lines 11–15, disrupt the flow of the poem.

Figure 5.1 Inscription in the men's hot room of Çemberlitaş Hamamı, 1770.
Source: Author's photograph.

Between Sai's and the later poet's exhortations of the bath's beauty, line 10 reads:

The beloved at the beginning of the path is expecting[,]
good news to you, sir, the supreme help of Selim arrived 1184 [1770][5]

This line was intended to commemorate the date of the renovation's completion – a renovation sponsored by Prince Selim, later to become Sultan Selim III (r. 1789–1807). The image of the beloved waiting full of hope and expectation alludes to a delay in securing financial means for the repair.

Line 16 appears equally disjointed compared to the rhythm of the remaining poem. Not only does its calligraphic rendition differ considerably, it also describes, in between two lines referring to the bathhouse architecture, a bath attendant and compares him to the mystical figure of a dervish:

Its clean and shaven *tellak*
reminds of the [hairless] dervish who does not care about the world[.][6]

These disjointed lines of different date help to construct a scenario related to the major earthquake that hit Istanbul in 1766. During the quake, the marble room dividers inscribed with lines 10–16 were destroyed, and it took four years for the renovation to be completed, as indicated by the panel dated 1770 (Figure 5.2). After such a long time, no one could remember the exact words of the destroyed original inscription, and the endowment administrator or *hamamcı* asked a calligrapher to pen a similar text, substituting lines 11–15; however, neither content nor calligraphic style were a perfect match. Line 10 was added with the explicit intent of commemorating the patron and the renovation date. Finally, line 16 was meant to fill the gap between lines 15 and 17 – a line possibly plagiarised from another poem, since the artistic quality of this line is comparatively higher.[7]

While accounting books give only the most summary information on repair expenses, other documents occasionally describe in greater detail the costs for material and labour. One such document tells about the cost of repairs to the water conduits of the Atik Valide Vakfı and Sultan Bayezid's endowment outside Istanbul, as well as those supplying the fountain in Çemberlitaş Hamamı, probably located in the men's dressing room.[8] Written between March or April 1786 and March 1787, the earlier, upper portion of the sheet contains an estimate listing the following expenses: 5,400 *akçe* for new water pipes, ledges and bricks; 3,600 *akçe* for a stone cover; 3,564 *akçe* for 170.2 kg of linseed oil (together with

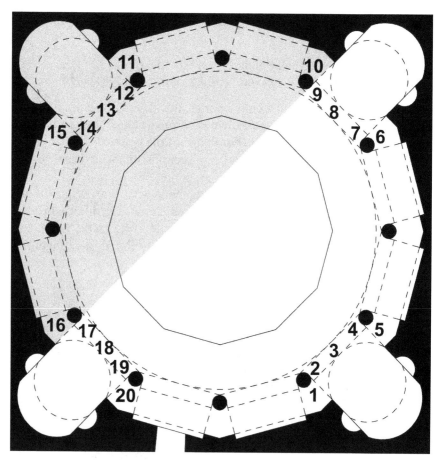

Figure 5.2 Ground plan of the men's hot room of Çemberlitaş Hamamı, with 1766 earthquake damage indicated. *Source*: Sabiha Göloğlu.

cotton used to waterproof pipes); 1,800 *akçe* for transportation costs; 9,600 *akçe* for 80 days of labour by sewermen (*lağımcı*); 4,200 *akçe* for 35 days of labour by waterway engineers (*suyolcu*); and 4,236 *akçe* for an unidentifiable item. Thus, the total sum of this repair work amounted to 32,400 *akçe*, the equivalent of 270 *kuruş*. The lower portion of the document, added a year later, explains that the renter of Çemberlitaş Hamamı, Fatma Kadın, had requested from the state permission to renovate the ruined waterways, since they supplied the (now probably dry) bathhouse fountain. The original estimate of costs had amounted to 280 *kuruş*; however, after the work's completion – cleaning the sewers as well as laying and waterproofing new pipes under the supervision of Bölükbaşı Seyyid Hasan Ağa – the expenses totalled 10 *kuruş* less. A second sheet referring to the same renovation work – though undated, it must have been written in or soon after 1787 – asks the Atik Valide Vakfı's accountant to pay these 270 *kuruş* to Fatma Kadın, in order to reimburse her for the money she had advanced for the repairs.[9] Fatma Kadın must have been a wealthy woman indeed to be able to front such a considerable sum. With the reimbursement, a major renovation of Çemberlitaş Hamamı's water conduits had been completed in all of its aspects, including the administrative one.

Documents such as the estimate/correction of costs not only give valuable information about building material and practices; they also confirm the argument that Çemberlitaş Hamamı was not an isolated, self-contained building, but rather part of an extensive economic and symbolic network that tied together different endowments. The threads of this web were not merely of a legal or financial nature; they literally consisted of the water conduits both inside and outside the city walls, which supplied more than one monument and whose construction and maintenance was carried out by multiple endowments. Whenever repairs to the water conduits became necessary, the renter of Çemberlitaş Hamamı – in this case, Fatma Kadın – became deeper and deeper entangled in the web of legal, financial and architectural relations and obligations across different endowments.[10]

Fatma Kadın's involvement in repair work did not end here; only three years later, in 1790, she instigated another major renovation, this time not only to the waterways, but also to the interior and the roof of Çemberlitaş Hamamı. On 16 January 1790, Veliyüddin, the trustee of the Atik Valide Vakfı, sent a petition (*arzuhal*) to the imperial council in which he requested that, in accordance with the conditions set in the deed of trust, the endowment should pay for the repairs to the waterways and the roof, while Fatma Kadın would meet the cost of repairs to the interior (*derun*) of the bathhouse in their entirety.[11]

The request was granted, and another petition written by Veliyüddin in 1790/1 states that the necessary repairs by far exceeded the orginal estimate of 825 *kuruş* and 42 *akçe*.[12] In the end, the architect had spent 1,721 *kuruş*, due to the extensive damage resulting from the long-term neglect of the building.[13] The request to pay for the difference was granted, too, in April 1792.[14] As with so many administrative documents dealing with renovations, so does this set of documents mention the types of repairs only in the most summarily fashion. Nevertheless, the amount of 1,721 *kuruş* (206,520 *akçe*) gives an idea of their scale. Çemberlitaş Hamamı's roof and water conduits must have been in a very ruined condition indeed to warrant such a sum. In fact, in the eighteenth century Istanbul lived through several major disasters – massive earthquakes in 1719, 1754 and 1766, and an all-consuming fire in 1782 – that all affected Çemberlitaş Hamamı in one way or another. The resulting structural damage and economic hardship would send the hamam's business into a downward spiral: fewer people had money to spare for things not strictly necessary, such as fees and tips for bathing; a bathhouse in a bad state of repair attracted fewer wealthy customers; and less income meant that the hamam looked less and less like a lucrative business venture to potential investors willing to advance repair costs.

Fatma Kadın's efforts to restore the Çemberlita Hamamı to structural and economic health seemed to have had a positive effect, if not a very long-lasting one. Only fourteen years after her renovations, in 1805, the bath's water conduits and roof (as well as other unspecified parts) were once again in such desparate need of repair that Ayşe bint es-Seyyid İsmail – one of four renters sharing the licence – petitioned the imperial council to order her business partners, who seem to have procrastinated over the work, to see to these repairs.[15]

The archival documents and inscription allow composing the outline of a chronology, summarised in Table 5.1. When constructing such a chronology, however, it is imperative not to forget that the sources used reflect only the administrative dimension of renovation projects. On the ground, things might have looked quite different. Any kind of renovation or repair work to endowment property had to be done with the approval and under the supervision of the endowment trustee (*mütevelli*); yet the amount and processing time of the paperwork needed when going through official channels – requests for permission, estimates of cost, imperial decrees ordering the work, receipts detailing the actual costs, adjustments of the

Table 5.1 Dates, types and costs of repairs to Çemberlitaş Hamamı

Date	Type of Repair	Cost
February 1667–February 1668	Unspecified, water conduits	15,966 *akçe*
1770	Inscribed marble panels in the men's hot room	Not documented
Before March 1786	Water conduits outside Istanbul, water conduit supplying the hamam's fountain	32,400 *akçe*
1790–1	Interior	Not documented
1790–1	Roof, water conduits, other unspecified places	206,520 *akçe*
In/after 1805	Lead cover of domes, water conduits, other unspecified places	Not documented

costs and so forth *ad nauseam* – probably made bathhouse managers think twice about informing the trustee of minor repairs to Çemberlitaş Hamamı. Therefore, a great many small changes to the structure could have gone, if not unnoticed, then undocumented. In other words, the symptoms – that is, the growth of paper accumulating in the archives – do not necessarily always match the illness.

Causes: Fires, Earthquakes and Other Calamities

As a city consisting of densely built wooden houses interspersed with stone and brick structures – such as mosques, bathhouses, fountains and commercial buildings – Istanbul was very prone to fires. The absence of an effectively working fire brigade further complicated the task of extinguishing fires. Most of the fires were localised and consumed only a few houses, but some turned into truly cataclysmic events that lasted for several days, killing many inhabitants and turning vast stretches of the city into ashes. The suffering of the victims who lost their homes, their household goods and often also family members, as well as the economic consequences of the incinerated shops and workplaces had an enormous impact and touched even those who had survived the con-flagration relatively unscathed.[16] No archival documents tell in explicit terms whether and what kind of damage Çemberlitaş Hamamı sustained in those fires, but there is no doubt that it was affected both structurally and economically.

The first fire in the life of Çemberlitaş Hamamı occurred within four years of its birth, on 23 July 1587. At that time, a German traveller and member of Emperor Rudolph II's embassy, Reinhold Lubenau, stayed in the Elçi Han on the Divan Yolu, across from the bathhouse. He describes the destruction in vivid detail:

> On July 23, after midnight, a big fire broke out and burnt down everything around Constantine's column, across from our serai [the Elçi Han], especially three large beautiful caravanserais, all the dyers' workshops, and about 3,000 houses and shops, where a lot of burning oil, lard and soap fuelled the fire even more. Also, many precious goods and large amounts of cypress wood and finished products which are usually sold around the Constantine's Forum [were burnt]. And thus enormous damage occurred. The caravanserais were all covered with lead, and nobody trying to extinguish the fire could reach them, because the molten lead dripped down on the people, and our serai was so hot that one could not put his hand on the walls. We closed our house tightly. Also, the Janissary Ağa sent many Janissaries to our house, who had to protect it [against looters]. There is also a beautiful church or mosque next to the column,

called Ali Bassa [*sic*, the Atik Ali Paşa Mosque], which was the first Turkish church or mosque built in Constantinople. There, the lead melted off the roof, so large was the fire and so horrible to watch.[17]

It is hard to imagine that this raging inferno hot enough to liquefy the lead on the roofs of nearby mosques and *hans* did not in some way also damage Çemberlitaş Hamamı. Even if by some miracle the bath's roof was not stripped of its lead covers and the walls cracked from the intense heat, the fire would at least have blackened the exterior and made a thorough cleaning necessary.

On 20 December 1652, another fire devastated the area stretching from Çemberlitaş Hamamı to the Bayezid Mosque and the Covered Bazaar. According to Naima's chronicle, it originated in the Esir Han in the neighbourhood of the Atik Ali Paşa Mosque.[18] Although Naima mentions that the 'Valde Hamam' was engulfed by the flames, he leaves the aftermath to the reader's imagination: molten roofing lead, and the walls blackened by soot and possibly cracked. The fire's economic consequences on the bathhouse are not measureable in any reliable way; yet the customers who mostly consisted of merchants and workers whose workshops and goods had now vanished could spare no money for bathing fees and tips for bath attendants and servants. Before the fire in December, Çemberlitaş Hamamı's monthly rent had increased from 7,500 to 11,677 *akçe*; but now the renter, el-Hac Mustafa Hammami, found himself with a seriously damaged business.[19]

The seventeenth century saw another major fire that one that the chronicles came to call *İhrak-i Kebir*, the Big Burning. It started in a timber shop near where the Byzantine city walls meet the Golden Horn, on 24 July 1660, and raged for two days. Thousands of Istanbulites perished, their houses, shops, 360 mosques, 40 hamams, a great number of churches and other stone buildings were either destroyed or rendered unusable.[20] A popular rhymed history of the event, signed 'Katipzade', describes at length how the dreadful fire consumed neighbourhood after neighbourhood and monument after monument:

From God it came first, the poisonous fire,
[it was] as if it set on fire the whole of Istanbul[.]
When it shimmered, the exemplary fire became like a dragon[.]
They were not strong enough to drive it away, it wanted to swallow every
    creature[.]
All hell broke loose, it suddenly surprised mankind[.]
First they stood as if resurrected from the tomb, with bare head, naked[.]
Everybody shouldered haircloth sacks on their backs[.]

It turned into the Day of Judgement, with a great many people on the
    Atmeydanı[.]
They stood bewildered from head to toe, everybody was in awe,
what shall the helpless creatures do, the fire caught them from right and left,
they gathered and everybody crowded unto an open piece of land for rescue[.]
It burned their clothes [until] they were like rags on the back of a porter[.]
How many of their possessions, precious things, rarities were burnt,
one could not calculate in money the unfathomable number of goods[.]
They had not been in such a fire since the beginning of mankind,
it engulfed [them], it was as if the inner city was full of ovens[.]
How many pavilions and palaces were destroyed by this giant,
it scattered stones and earth, no place was left where it did not pass,
hans and hamams and big medreses and storage buildings
did not gain any advantage from their iron doors[.]
Mosques and mescids burned and also imarets on that day[.]
It burned so that the ashes rose to the highest point of heaven with the wind[.]
Not a place to stay was left for the poor[.]
  . . .
The surroundings of Dikilitaş burned together with the Women's Market[.]
It stayed there and two arms of the fire were cut off,
and another remaining arm proceeded from the Little Market,
it came to the Small Arasta [market], it burned Tahtakale,
it turned and burned to the end of the Uzunçarşı[.][21]

The poetic description of the fire and its economic and psychological effect
on the populace at the beginning of the poem sharply contrasts with the
lapidary account of the fire's damage to the urban fabric in the latter part.
Again, Çemberlitaş Hamamı is not specifically mentioned, but Katipzade
states that the area around Constantine's Column was destroyed. In the first
half of the poem, he points out that not even their iron-clad doors could
protect monuments from the spreading fire and that many of the stone
buildings, including mosques, schools and *hans*, succumbed. Istanbul's
commercial areas suffered greatly, and so did Çemberlitaş Hamamı. The
bathhouse's rent plummeted by more than half after 1660, from 11,677 to
5,000 *akçe* per month.[22] It is all too likely that the hamam manager Abdi
Çelebi succeeded in negotiating with the endowment trustee such a low
sum because of Çemberlitaş Hamamı's and the neighbourhood's ruined
condition.

In the eighteenth century, the Greatest Fire (*Harik-i Ekber*) devastated
an enormous portion of Istanbul's historic peninsula. Once again originat-
ing on the shore of the Golden Horn, on 22 August 1782, it spread from
there all the way to the Sea of Marmara.[23] Luckily, the area immediately
around Çemberlitaş Hamamı was left unscathed. However, in the next few

decades the neighbourhood was less fortunate, and two major fires – both called Hocapaşa fire after the eponymous area they destroyed – affected the hamam, on 2 August 1826 and on 19 September 1865. In both instances, the fires ravaged the city from the Golden Horn in the north to the Sea of Marmara in the south, from Sultanahmet in the east to the Bayezid Mosque in the west, including the area around Çemberlitaş Hamamı (Figure 5.3). The 1865 Hocapaşa Fire marked a turning point in the urban history of Istanbul as well as in the life of Çemberlitaş Hamamı. In its wake, the Commission for Road Improvement (*Islahat-ı Turuk Komisyonu*) was established to undertake an extensive urban planning and reconstruction scheme based on European models. This would entail the hamam's mutilation, to be discussed in Chapter 6.

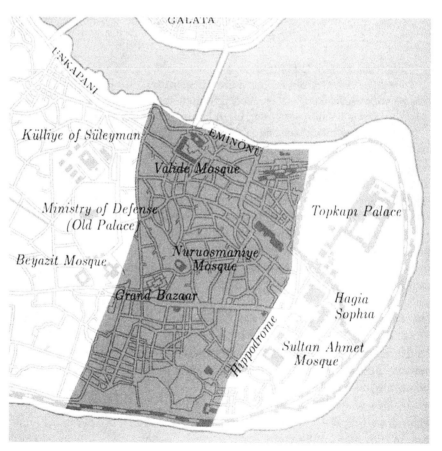

Figure 5.3 Extent of the 1865 Hocapaşa Fire. *Source*: Çelik, *Remaking of Istanbul*, 1986.

The fires were not the only recurring disasters to which Çemberlitaş Hamamı was subjected. Located in an area of high seismic activity, Istanbul did and still does experience frequent earthquakes that terrorise its inhabitants and damage buildings to varying degrees, from mere cracks in the walls to collapsed houses, mosques and minarets. Mosques, *hans*, hamams and other stone monuments suffered from earthquakes more than from fires, since they were more susceptible to the shocks than the wooden houses. Between its completion in 1584 and 1912, Çemberlitaş Hamamı experienced forty major shocks, and on four occasions – in 1719, 1754, 1766 and 1894 – buildings in close proximity were severely damaged.[24] Again, the dearth of documents related directly to the earthquakes' effects on the bathhouse forces one to turn to evidence about these neighbouring buildings (such as the Vezir Han or the Atik Ali Paşa Mosque, as well as the water conduits) in order to speculate about the damage to the hamam.

On 25 May 1719, Istanbul and the villages and towns around the eastern Marmara Sea shook violently, and an eyewitness present in the capital reported:

[M]any chimneys and ruined buildings and some of the boathouses in the vicinity of an old kiosk in the Palace, and the castle walls opposite the mosque at the Edirne Kapısı, and the walls on the land side of the Istanbul city walls, especially from Yedikule to Ahur Kapısı, and most of the walls on the sea side, and some towers (on the sea side) were destroyed . . . and in addition to these destroyed places, the dome of the Edirne Kapısı mosque and the domes of its medrese and many mescids and places of worship and the domes and arches of baths were cracked, countless windows and parts of buildings fell off and very many of the people's houses collapsed, and walls were destroyed . . .[25]

According to this witness, the earthquake affected stone and brick buildings by cracking domes and arches and collapsing walls. Both the Hagia Sophia and the Bayezid Mosque received damage; since Çemberlitaş Hamamı is located halfway between these two monuments, it is all too likely that it sustained some damage as well. Yet because the shock's effect on domes decreases relative to their diameter, the small bath's domes would have suffered less than those of large mosques.

Another shock occurred on 2 September 1754, and badly damaged the mosque of Sultan Mehmed the Conqueror, the Bayezid Mosque, Küçük Ayasofya, many other smaller mosques' minarets and numerous *hans*, including the Vezir Han next to Çemberlitaş Hamamı.[26] Many wells in the city dried up due to the shifting earth. The earthquake affected Çemberlitaş Hamamı in three ways: first, structural damage could disrupt the business and require costly repairs; secondly, the neighbouring Vezir Han, rendered uninhabitable for a period of time, no longer provided a large number of customers; and, finally, dried-up wells and blocked water conduits meant that the water supply system failed at least for a while. A short earthquake of less than one minute, such as this, could easily destroy not only the bath's building itself, but also its economic base for weeks to come.

Only twelve years later, another major earthquake hit the city. On 22 May 1766, shortly after morning prayer, the ground moved so violently that not only the domes and walls of a great many masonry buildings completely collapsed, killing an estimated 4,000–5,000 victims, but also the quays and docks along the Golden Horn and in Galata were partially submerged under the sea (Figure 5.4).[27] A second major shock on 5 August flattened many already damaged buildings. The central dome and the

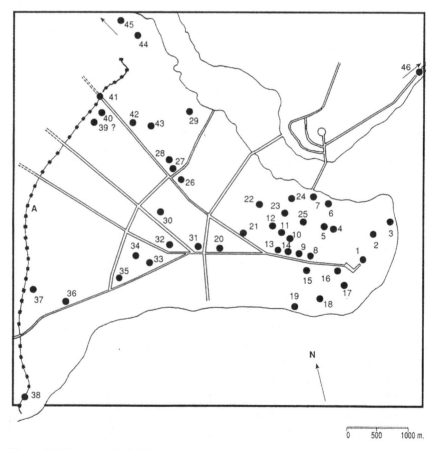

Figure 5.4 Istanbul with buildings damaged by the 1766 earthquake indicated.
Source: Ambraseys and Finkel, *Seismicity of Turkey*, 1995.

minarets of the Atik Ali Paşa Mosque opposite Çemberlitaş Hamamı collapsed, and the Vezir Han adjoining the bath was almost completely overturned.[28] Probably due to its sound structure and small height in relation to the thickness of its walls, Çemberlitaş Hamamı survived, even if quite injured, as the abovementioned epigraphic symptom shows.[29] The *halvet* walls in the men's hot room's northeast corner needed replacing. The tremors could have caused the marble panels to separate themselves from the walls and crash onto the floor, shattering into a thousand pieces, or maybe a part of the dome collapsed and crushed the marble panels with the inscriptions. Which other parts of the hamam sustained damage is not clear, but the water conduits supplying it required extensive repairs, both inside and outside the city walls.

Thanks to the report prepared by an investigative committee as well as newspaper coverage, the earthquake on 10 July 1894 is the best documented one before the twentieth century.[30] The shock registered between 6.5 and 7 on the Richter scale and damaged 387 masonry buildings, 1,087 residences and 299 shops. Within Istanbul, 474 persons died and 482 were injured.[31] The detailed report mentions even minor damage and records the devastated buildings one by one – including twenty hamams in the greater area of the city, which sustained cracked domes at best or were completely collapsed at worst. Çemberlitaş Hamamı does not figure in the report and hence must have gone undamaged, a quite remarkable feat considering that the Ali Paşa Medrese was completely ruined and that part of the neighbouring Vezir Han fell down, killing several of its residents. Another *han* down the street was destroyed, and many waterways became blocked.[32] Although the hamam itself escaped destruction, the terror felt by those inside at the time of the earthquake is vividly depicted in a newspaper article: throughout Istanbul, bathhouse attendants and bathers ran into the streets in panic, wearing nothing but a *peştemal* around their waist.[33]

Earthquakes continue to afflict Istanbul, the most recent major one occurring on 17 August 1999. While tens of thousands of people were buried under the rubble of shoddily built apartment blocks in nearby towns, none of the Ottoman monuments of Istanbul sustained major damage. This may also be due to good fortune, but, more importantly, the credit goes to the Ottoman architects' engineering skills. Alternating layers of brick with layers of stone masonry help to absorb sudden violent movements within the walls and to make structures more resistant. Çemberlitaş Hamamı is a good example of this type of shock-resistant building method, having survived more than four centuries of intermittent minor and major earthquakes.

Maybe even more detrimental to the bath than the occasional earthquakes and fires, slow deterioration through daily use rarely finds its way into documentary evidence. The 1667/8 accounting book, which records expenses for repairs to Çemberlitaş Hamamı as well as to its three siblings, seems to indicate that such expenditures were quite frequent and nothing out of the ordinary, probably made to counteract the regular wear and tear. Wear and tear to the structure was (and still is) aggravated by the humidity to which every bathhouse is constantly exposed. High humidity causes the plaster on the walls to become discoloured and mouldy, so that it has to be replaced at frequent intervals. Humidity can also soften the adhesive matter between marble panels and walls, so that panels may fall off and shatter.[34] Moreover, while marble itself is very durable, the force of an inadvertent blow can chip or crack it.

On the exterior, both walls and roof needed regular cleaning and maintenance, and every once in a while the domes' lead covers and glass cups had to be replaced. In one instance, an archival document even pinoints a specific cause for the damage to the roof: the response to Ayşe bint es-Seyyid İsmail's 1805 petition mentions that high winds and hail had ruined the lead covers.[35] The waterways supplying the hamam also suffered from regular wear and tear, as one document dating to 1787 states that they had become ruined over the course of time.[36] The specific wording of the source – *mürur-ı ezmine* connotes a passing along in time – suggests that it was not so much a specific event causing violent damage (such as an earthquake), but merely that the pipes had eroded, perhaps to the point of leaking.

Treatment: Repair and Renovation Work

Having surveyed the symptoms and causes of the diseases and calamities afflicting Çemberlitaş Hamamı, this chapter also needs to address the treatment meant to cure it. Who decided when renovations became necessary? What was the procedure for requesting permission to conduct repair work? Who paid for the material and labour? Who were the craftsmen executing the repairs? While the answers to these questions provide the necessary background,[37] the example of one problematic request for renovation will show that, in spite of an extensive administrative framework meant to ensure the proper maintenance of endowed buildings, procedures did not always go smoothly.

Whenever Çemberlitaş Hamamı – or any other endowed building in Istanbul or elsewhere – needed repairs, an extensive network of people and institutions became involved. Since all endowed property was under the supervision of the respective trustee (*mütevelli*), any kind of renovation or repair work had to be performed with his approval and under his scrutiny.

It could have been the endowment inspector who noticed the need for repairs on one of his tours of *vakıf* properties or, more likely, the renter of the revenue-generating property who contacted the trustee for permission. Given the large amount of paperwork and delay involved in asking for permission, it is probable that some renters took it upon themselves to make minor repairs and paid out of their own pocket, without informing the trustee. Large-scale work to be financed by the *vakıf*, however, certainly needed approval, and once the trustee deemed the work fit and necessary, an architect surveyed the property and estimated the cost. The status of the *vakıf* also determined the status of the architect: for an imperial endowment, such as the Atik Valide Vakfı, no less than a member of the organisation of imperial architects (*hassa mimarları*) saw to this job. After the architect had determined the extent and cost of the repairs, he wrote a report to the head of the imperial architects, who in turn submitted the report to the *defterdarlık* (Office of the Director of Finance). Finally, after the construction material and labour had been procured by means of an imperial decree, the actual work could begin.

Under the technical supervision of the surveying architect, workmen carried out the actual renovation work. For the most part, these workmen belonged to the permanent salaried staff of the endowment. The hiring of permanent staff illustrates the importance that founders and trustees of endowments assigned to keeping the endowed buildings – both beneficiaries and revenue-producers – in good shape. Most endowments employed *meremmetçi*s (restorer artisans),[38] *su yolcu*s (waterway engineers) and *kurşuncu*s (roofers). The Atik Valide Vakfı employed a permanent maintenance and repair staff of ten: one *kurşuncu*, two *meremmetçi*s, seven *su yolcu*s, and one person whose job, curiously, was to clean offensive graffiti off the walls of the mosque complex.[39] Two of the waterway engineers were under orders to take care of the water conduits leading to the endowment's hamams within the city: 'Two of [the *su yolcu*s] shall be responsible for looking after the waterways leading to the hamam of the exalted founder in the vicinity of Dikilitaş and to the hamam in the vicinity of Ayakapı.'[40] Thus, Çemberlitaş Hamamı's waterways had a caretaker of their own.

All of the repairmen received a regular, daily salary, amounting to a total expenditure of 43 *akçe* per day for the endowment. This meant that, as long as their services alone sufficed to carry out regular repair work, no further expenditures for labour had to be made. But if more manpower than that kept on the payroll proved to be necessary, the endowment hired additional temporary workers for a lump sum or a daily wage. The investment in a permanent maintenance staff very likely prevented larger damage that would eventually call for more expensive renovations and the hiring of additional staff. The permanent repairmen's immediate response to any problem, minor or acute, precluded the snowballing effect of neglected damage or delayed repairs. This approach to maintenance work is also reflected in a passage in the endowment deed: 'greater damage shall not be caused as a result of delay and negligence in this matter'.[41]

In any case, it was the endowment that usually carried the costs of both labour and material, unless special arrangements were made in the form of a double rent (*icareteyn*) contract.[42] The surveying architect had to decide which and how much material and labour would be necessary and estimate the cost accordingly. In order to prevent misuse of funds and material, the architect was obliged to keep an accounting book and to submit it to the *başmuhasebe kalemi* (Office of Chief Treasurer) after completion. In the end, the expenses for maintenance and repair also appeared in the endowment's accounting books.[43]

A successful completion of repairs according to all procedural rules, however, was an ideal scenario that did not occur all too often. Disputes arose concerning estimates, payments or the responsibility for costs, delaying the execution of desperately needed repairs. Such was the case with Çemberlitaş Hamamı in 1805. In that year, the hamam's renters consisted of a partnership of four who jointly held the twelve shares of the bathhouse licence (*gedik*).[44] Ayşe bint es-Seyyid İsmail, who held one share, wanted to repair the hamam whose roof had been damaged by hail and high winds, but the other shareholders refused to give their consent. Their excuse was that 'the time was not theirs [that is, not right for the repairs]'.[45] In the meantime, water leaked into the unprotected domes, and Çemberlitaş Hamamı fell into further disrepair, until Ayşe decided to take a drastic step, probably because any attempts at extrajudicial negotiation had failed.[46] She took her three business partners to court where they were judged according to the shari'a in front of two supervising officials responsible for the Atik Valide Vakfı, the *nazır-ı vakıf* and the *haremeyn-i şerifeyn müfettişi*. Still, they procrastinated. Finally, Ayşe petitioned the sultan to issue an imperial decree ordering the negligent shareholders to repair the exactly specified parts of the hamam. In response to her petition, the sultan pointed out that the hamam's ruined state was harmful (*muzırr*) to the endowment as a whole and ordered them to renovate the roof. This case illustrates all too well that renovation work was not merely a matter of deciding to undertake repairs, having an estimate done and then doing the actual work. Rather, it was also contingent on business practices and interpersonal relationships between the licence's shareholders. The more shareholders that were involved in running a hamam, the more opportunity there was for conflict – and this type of conflict could affect Çemberlitaş Hamamı's structure as much as a fire or an earthquake.

Art historians usually focus on recovering the original condition and appearance of buildings. Yet, from the first day, the building substance of a hamam – or any other given monument – changes in small increments, in the form of subtractions and additions. Subtractions can be as small as scratching a graffiti onto a wall or as large as the destruction of parts of the building. Additions can range from a wooden lean-to shack for storage space to substantial enlargements of the structure. Although it is impossible to follow every single addition or subtraction – either with the help of a structural examination, which would necessitate a partial dismantling, or with the help of documents, which reflect only admin-istrative dimensions and are incompletely preserved in any case – one can perceive of Çemberlitaş Hamamı as a palimpsest: layer upon layer of construction, repair and renovation make it into the structure it is today. In David Lowenthal's words, 'Traces of cumulative creation . . . engender a sense of accretion where each year, each generation adds more to the scene. Accretion results from temporal asymmetry: the cumulations of time gen-erally surpass its dissolutions, and yield sums greater than their parts . . . It is accretion, in particular, that generates the past's enrichment.'[47] Thus, the frequently recurring repairs, renovations and structural changes have created the unique physical appearance and character of the hamam as it stands today. From this viewpoint, it becomes a constant work-in-progress, and repairmen play a most significant role in its life story, since over time they, too, shaped its appearance, perhaps as much as its architect.

The conscious emphasis that the endowment deed of the Atik Valide Vakfı placed on renovation and repair, as well as the care bestowed upon Çemberlitaş Hamamı confirms the conclusions that historians of Islamic architecture have already drawn concerning the issue of preservation in pre-modern Islamic cities. In European architectural history, the concept of preservation in an institutionalised framework owes much to nineteenth-century developments. The rise of nationalism sparked interest in the mate-rial culture of the past, as the newly emerging nation-states strove to create a coherent cultural heritage on which to centre their identity. Furthermore, ever-accelerating change due to technological advances spawned a more conscious approach to history and its physical remains.[48] However, in the Ottoman capital conservation and restoration had already achieved an impressive scope during the sixteenth century.[49] As Meinecke puts it:

[t]he idea of protecting historical buildings is not an invention of the twen-tieth century, but an integral part of Islamic architectural history. The extant

monuments – particularly the most important monuments, the appearance of which has shaped our understanding of architectural development in the Islamic World – are still there because they have been restored many times over.[50]

Renovation and preservation were already an integral part of the philanthropic tradition and the construction industry, from the endowment founders and imperial architects at the top to the construction workers at the bottom. The *vakıf* system constituted the institutional apparatus through which renovation work was requested, organised and paid. Not only religious or imperial buildings benefited from this apparatus, but all structures that were of value to endowments. Commercial buildings such as *han*s, shops and bathhouses provided income for the *evkaf*; therefore, it was most important to the family, the Atik Valide Vakfı, that Çemberlitaş Hamamı be taken care of and remain healthy.

6

Old Age

It describes how the aforementioned hamam began to show signs of ageing, how it became a burden to the exalted valide sultan*'s pious endowment and how, because of that, its familial ties to the noble Friday mosque in Üsküdar became loosened. And it describes how the Protected City changed after the Hocapaşa Fire of 1865 and the novel ways of street building that mutilated the poor hamam, yet how bathhouses came to show to the Franks the wonderful achievements of the Domains under the House of Osman. And it describes how the Domain of the House of Osman gave way to the Republic of Turkey and how many noble architectural masterpieces became old doddering folks in the eyes of many Republican citizens, being neglected and even destroyed in many instances; how newspapers talked about the hamams of Istanbul, making them into emblems of a past long gone, but also decrying their destruction; and how this pleasurable hamam survived these indignities and continued to give services to the people of Istanbul, providing cleanliness and entertainment.*

Renegotiating Family Relations

The Ottoman state of the eighteenth century was an empire weakened by military defeats and territorial losses.[1] These failures led to an increased cultural exchange between Europe and the Ottomans, who felt the need to reform military technology and state organisation. In the second half of the eighteenth century, administration was transformed into a more centralised apparatus supported by a growing bureaucracy. Symptomatic of the state's financial problems, fiscal policy and increasing centralisation was the treatment of endowments and their properties during that time. Abdülhamid I (r. 1774–1789) established the Superintendence of Imperial Endowments (*Evkaf-ı Hümayun Nezareti*), to which he annexed the endowments of the imperial harem – that is, the endowments founded by imperial women, including the Atik Valide Vakfı.[2] The purpose of the new ministry – which due to the maneouvering of the Chief Black Eunuch whose powers and interests it directly challenged soon became ineffective – was to create a legal and administrative framework to channel the endowment revenues into the near-empty state coffers, rather than back into the endowments. In order to attract more renters willing to invest capital into endowed revenue-generating property – now no longer supported by its own revenues – the ministry encouraged the already widespread practice of double rent (*icareteyn*) as the norm rather than the exception.[3]

The practice of *icareteyn* had existed since the sixteenth century as a legal loophole around the conditions laid out in endowment deeds and to rent out property in the long term rather than for the customary one-year periods.[4] The possibility of leasing property in the long term was meant to attract renters who were willing to invest money. The recurring fires in Istanbul destroyed revenue-generating property so often that the endowments soon became incapable of financing their reconstruction and renovation, and short-term renters tended to abandon the destroyed property rather than to rebuild a house, workshop or hamam which they could use only for several months afterwards. Allowing renters to effectively become co-owners – that is, to use endowed property for life and to bequeath it to their offspring – in exchange for a large initital payment that financed the property's reconstruction and a nominal monthly or yearly rent was a way to fill the *evkaf*'s drained reserves and to ensure renovations without the endowments actually having to finance them.[5]

The double rent consisted of two payments: a lump sum paid initially when the renter signed the lease for a period of 200 or 300 years (*icare-i mu'accele*, immediate rent); and the monthly or yearly rent of a rather negligible amount (*icare-i mü'eccele*, postponed rent). The latter served as a reminder that ultimately the property still belonged to the endowment and that it would return to the endowment, if the renter defaulted on the payments or died without heirs.[6] This practice paved the way to private ownership of formerly endowed property in the twentieth century. When in 1936 the practice of *icareteyn* was legally abolished, several imperial monuments – including numerous hamams – became the private property of the previous renters or their descendants, rather than reverting to the state. This also happened to Çemberlitaş Hamamı: the bath had been rented out under the conditions of an *icareteyn* contract before November 1786. Fatma Kadın, the female renter so actively engaged in renovation work, was according to one document a *bi'l-icareteyn müstaceresi*, a 'renter by way of double rent'.[7] Although Fatma requested from the endowment the sum she had advanced for the cost of repairs to the water conduits and the hamam's exterior, she financed the work on the interior herself. Most likely, such were the conditions of the arrangement

174

between herself and the endowment's trustee in the framework of the *icareteyn* lease.

The arrangement of repair costs being counted towards the immediate rent certainly was part of the contract between the endowment and the partnership of four (rather negligent) licence shareholders already encountered in the previous chapter. The sultan's response to Ayşe bint es-Seyyid İsmail's 1805 petition confirms 'that the renters repair and renovate [Çemberlitaş Hamamı], counting the repair and renovation costs from their own property towards the *mu'accele* [i.e., the immediate rent], is [according to] the conditions of the abovementioned endowment'.[8] Thus, the four renters paid for renewing the roof, and this amount was subtracted from the initial lump sum that constituted the immediate rent. Clearly, here the objective of leasing out revenue-generating endowed property on double rent was to shift the financial responsibility for specific renovations from the Atik Valide Vakfı's shoulders to those of wealthy individuals. Çemberlitaş Hamamı's state of health and the expenses that its condition incurred had become such a burden to its family that it had to be farmed out, at least for a while.

By 1829, Çemberlitaş Hamamı no longer needed financial help through *icareteyn* payments and regained its role as fully functional breadwinner within the family. In July, October and November 1829, and January and May/June 1830, the Atik Valide Vakfı's trustee, Ali Haydar, received rent payments each in the amount of 12,500 *akçe*, documented by five stamped and signed rent receipts.[9] Still, the hamam was operated by a partnership of four – Hace Ayşe Sadıka, Emin Efendi, Hacı Hüseyin Efendi and Mehmed es-Seyyid Tahir Ağa – but now the archival sources no longer speak of double rent, immediate rent or postponed rent. An accounting book dated to 27 July 1832, equally states that the yearly rent of the 'Hamam of Dikilitaş in Istanbul' amounted to 154,584 *akçe*, suggesting that the *icareteyn* had only been a temporary fix, until Çemberlitaş Hamamı got back on its feet. Nevertheless, in the long run the ever more common transfer of endowed property into the hands of individuals – together with the sale of *vakıf* properties in the economically dire years of the Republic, as will be discussed below – opened the doors to private ownership, which also led to Çemberlitaş Hamamı's status as private property today.

Mutilation

Attempts at reform and modernisation can be observed in the Ottoman Empire beginning with the eighteenth century, but it was the nineteenth century that saw the most effective measures to transform the empire into a Europeanised state.[10] In 1839, Sultan Abdülmecid (r. 1839–1861) issued the *Hatt-ı Şerif* of Gülhane, the Imperial Rescript of the Rose Pavilion, which redefined the relationship between state and subjects as well as between subjects. The aim was to create citizens with specific rights and duties to the state, equal to each other regardless of their confessional or ethnic identity. The concepts of equality, liberty and civic rights had already been points of discussion before 1839; the Imperial Rescript now codified equality before the law. In spite of the reiteration of these points in another charter issued in 1856 (*Hatt-ı Hümayun Islahat Fermanı*), the reforms that came to be labelled as *Tanzimat* did not lead to the expected outcomes. Instead of creating equal access to education and employment, universal military conscription and a centralised state apparatus, the reforms resulted in an ever-widening gap between a Europeanised elite and a majority living according to long-established values. The reforms also resulted in an almost dogmatic belief in Europe's superiority and the rather naive notion that eliminating old institutions and substituting them wholesale with imported European ones would solve all of the empire's problems.[11]

In the sphere of urban policy-making, the introduction of European-style administrative bodies, building types and architectural styles paralleled the socio-political aims of the *Tanzimat* charters.[12] Beyond the adoption of theatres, apartment buildings and similar new structures, Ottoman reformers imported design principles on a larger scale, as well as laws and regulations about urban planning. An influential person in this matter was Mustafa Reşid Paşa, one of the authors of the Imperial Rescript of the Rose Pavilion. He had seen and greatly admired Paris, Vienna and London on his diplomatic missions and wished for Istanbul to meet European standards.[13] The earliest concrete plans to regularise Istanbul's urban fabric date to between 1835 and 1839, when the Prussian general Helmuth von Moltke was hired to survey the city and produce maps, and when an anonymous document (dated 1839 and found in the State Secretariat's archive) proposed 'planning policy directions and specific design features for the built environment'.[14] These schemes did not come to fruition, and neither did most of the large-scale plans in the following two decades,[15] although several regulations somewhat improved transportation, communications and the condition of the streets.[16] In order to achieve a city with straight and uniformly wide streets, flanked by rectangular blocks of masonry or brick buildings, which the *Tanzimat* planners dreamed of, it would have been necessary to eliminate the existing urban fabric. But a wilful wholesale destruction of a large urban area was too radical even for the most zealous reformers.

What the urban reformers could not bring themselves to destroy on the historical peninsula, the Hocapaşa Fire of 1865 did within a matter of 32 hours (Figure 5.3, above). The devastated area included many important mosques, commercial buildings and major thoroughfares, and Çemberlitaş Hamamı was right at its centre. Insofar as it created a *tabula rasa* on which to rebuild the city according to European urban planning principles, the fire was quite advantageous for the proponents of urban reform. In its wake, the *Islahat-ı Turuk Komisyonu* (Commission for Road Improvement) was established on 10 May 1866, primarily in order to see to the repair of roads. Comprising nine government officials educated in the best *Tanzimat* manner (such as Mustafa Reşid Paşa and Server Paşa), the commission completed an astonishing amount of work within a short time, building sewers and wide streets and repairing sidewalks until its dissolution in 1869.[17]

A significant portion of the commission's work focused on the Divan Yolu, which, as a major traffic artery, was widened from an average of 3.8 metres to 16.75 metres.[18] In order to ensure its appearance as a straight street lined by regular blocks of masonry buildings, the commission interfered with many historic monuments in the neighbourhood of Çemberlitaş Hamamı: it demolished the *medrese* of the Atik Ali Paşa Mosque complex, half of the Köprülü Medrese (erected 1659) and the Elçi Han (which had housed Reinhold Lubenau, witness to the 1587 fire), removed the wooden huts accumulated around Constantine's Column and reinforced the column's shaft with iron hoops. Furthermore, the commission dismantled, moved and reassembled the mausoleum of Köprülü Mehmed Paşa, so that it now neatly lined the street.[19] According to Nur Altınyıldız, this was the first instance of 'monuments being surrendered to roads in a quest for modernisation'.[20]

In 1868, Çemberlitaş Hamamı itself was partially demolished to accommodate the street's new width: the commission cut off the southwest corner of the women's dressing room at a 45-degree angle, including the dome (Figures I.1, I.2, above). The resulting opening was then filled with a brick wall, and the blind arches and star-shaped windows show that the commission still wanted to preserve a certain ornamental quality to the building. The architect responsible for this design was the Italian Giovanni Battista Barborini.[21] The demolition, which reduced the square women's dressing room to an irregular shape, led to the women's section being closed down as a whole in the long run. In a photograph taken before or in 1890, an awning in front of the former women's dressing room indicates that the space had been converted into a shop or some other type of commercial establishment (Figure 6.1). When Glück surveyed the hamam in

Figure 6.1 Photograph of Çemberlitaş Hamamı. *Source*: *Servet-i Fünun*, 6 June 1890.

1916 or 1917, the women's section had not welcomed bathers for a long time, and two connecting doors had been broken into the wall between the men's and women's section.[22] Only after a major renovation in 1988 did the hamam open its doors to female customers again.[23] The women's dressing room still remained a commercial space until 2011, housing a restaurant marketing Anatolian fare to tourists. Today, all parts of the women's section are fully functional once again.

The physical changes that the Commission of Road Improvement undertook amount to the amputation of a limb no longer deemed necessary. For the urban reformers, the value of Çemberlitaş Hamamı had declined so significantly that they did not hesitate to sacrifice part of the then 285-year-old monument to construct a straight and wide street, implying that it had reached an age at which it had become partially obsolete.

A New Identity I: Emblem of Ottoman Heritage in the Nineteenth Century

The act of tearing down part of Çemberlitaş Hamamı (and other historic monuments) to make space for a street wide enough to accommodate sidewalks and a tramway reflects a shift in the urban planners' administration and perception of the Ottoman built heritage. From now on, hamams acquired a new layer of meaning – in addition to their religious, social, economic, political and medical significance – in that they became a symbol of traditional Ottoman lifestyle. As such, hamams could be viewed either negatively or positively, depending on how the Ottoman beholders positioned themselves *vis-à-vis* modernisation.[24]

The concrete result of the reformers' negative attitude towards Çemberlitaş Hamamı was its mutilation, as discussed above. The Commission of Road Improvement strove to create an urban space conforming to the planning principles of Georges-Eugène Haussmann's design for Paris: straight, wide, tree-lined boulevards with sidewalks cutting through the urban fabric and leading the gaze towards grand historic monuments that stand in splendid isolation.[25] In Istanbul, the decision as to which historic monuments are worthy of the gaze and deserve preservation and presentation in the grand manner of Haussmann often privileged the ancient (including Byzantine) period over the Ottoman. For example, Cemil Paşa – Istanbul's mayor (*şehremini*) from 1912 to 1914 and from 1919 to 1920 – attempted to demolish the Haseki Hamamı while clearing the immediate environs of the Hagia Sophia, but his plan was thwarted.[26]

The commission's activities around the Divan Yolu clearly illustrate this preference. The wooden huts around Constantine's Column were removed in order to create a triangular plaza that was centred on the ancient monument. From there, the Divan Yolu led directly to the former entrance of the Byzantine Hippodrome (today's Atmeydanı), passing the Byzantine Empire's zero-mile marker (*million*), and to the newly created square in front of the Hagia Sophia. Had the aim of creating long, straight streets connecting ancient monuments been less urgent, an angled version of the Divan Yolu could have preserved Çemberlitaş Hamamı, the Atik Ali Paşa Mosque complex and the Köprülü Mehmed Paşa complex as a harmonious ensemble of Ottoman monuments in its entirety and in its original location. However, the commission envisioned straight and uniformly wide boulevards, ideally tree-lined, as the road to progress. For them, the Ottoman monuments – including Çemberlitaş Hamamı, which now symbolised a non-Classical, Islamic heritage and traditional city life – would in the long run only stand in its way.

This emphasis on ancient monuments had important ideological under-pinnings.[27] The *Tanzimat* reforms attempted to fashion a modern state out of an empire and to bring the Ottomans closer to Western civilisation. This approximation also necessitated an appropriate historical narrative that proved that the Ottoman Empire did indeed share the same roots with European civilisation. In Europe, historical narratives in the service of emerging nation-states depended on an interpretation of history as a linear cultural development from Ancient Greece to the current point in time. This supposedly universal interpretation not only appeared on the pages of scholarly books, but also became visible in the display and exhibition strategies of European museums. In the great museums of Paris, London, Vienna and Berlin, visitors could retrace the development from prehistoric to ancient, medieval, Renaissance and contemporary civilisation, as they walked from art object to art object and from gallery to gallery. In this scheme, civilisations outside the Western world primarily figured as back-ground onto which Europeans could project the image of an inferior Other, for the purpose of self-identification. Moreover, European imperialist domination over these territories and peoples was justified by demonstrat-ing that they fell outside the purportedly universal, humanist narrative that centred on Ancient Greece's heritage.

Ottoman reformers were fully aware of this narrative; if the empire should be part of modern Western civilisation, it also needed to share in the history and cultural heritage that had led Europe to the point where it now was. Thus, in an anachronistic twist the existence of Hellenistic and Byzantine antiquities on Ottoman soil could demonstrate that the Ottoman Empire was an integral part of modern European culture, bypass-ing Islamic history. In Wendy Shaw's words:

> members of the Ottoman elite hoped to become acknowledged as a seminal site for European culture rather than be excluded from the narratives of its supremacy. Moreover, an association with ancient Greece would link the empire with modern science and distance it from the narrative of irrationalism associated with religion, particularly Islam, which had not entered a secular phase, in contemporary European discourse.[28]

In the light of the Ottoman elite's aspirations, it is not surprising that Ancient Greek and Byzantine monuments and art objects gained superior symbolic value. Placed in opposition to the Ancient Greek and Byzantine heritage were contemporary Ottoman and Islamic monuments – and they were assigned inferior value. Çemberlitaş Hamamı fell victim to this categorisation, accounting for its mutilation, while at the same time Byzantine monuments were incorporated into and glorified within the urban planning schemes.

Yet the tampering with and deliberate destruction of Ottoman monuments along the Divan Yolu did not go unchallenged, particularly where religious buildings were concerned. A brainchild of several members of the Commission for Road Improvement, which represented the Ottoman elite, the necessary demolitions along the new Divan Yolu were not warmly embraced by the local populace.[29] An anecdote recorded by Osman Nuri Ergin in his *Mecelle-i Umûr-ı Belediyye* relates the public opinion about the construction work. While the commission member Keçecizade Fuad Paşa supervised the demolition of the Köprülü cemetery across from Çemberlitaş Hamamı, an elderly man addressed him: 'Paşa, you are demolishing these mosques, *medreses* and tombs, but tomorrow the people will shit onto your grave.' Determined to create a modern city that would be appreciated by future generations, Fuad Paşa retorted: 'If the people shit on my grave, [then] their children will come and clean it, collect it, and throw it into the sea.'[30]

Of course, even within the ranks of the Ottoman elite the attitude towards Islamic monuments was neither static nor unisonous, but exhibited changing and divergent views as early as in the nineteenth century. Even one and the same person could exhibit an ambivalent attitude: the famous architect and father of the revivalist First National Style, Mimar Kemalettin (1870–1927), on the one hand, worked for the re-established Ministry of Pious Foundations (*Evkaf-ı Hümayun Nezareti*) to protect and repair endowed properties, and harshly criticised Cemil Paşa's and the *Islahat-ı Turuk Komisyonu*'s practices; on the other hand, he tore down *medreses*, *imarets* and other historic buildings to make room for his own creations.[31] While urban planners fully or partially demolished hamams in the Ottoman capital, the Ottoman Empire at the same time presented itself at the 1867 World Fair in Paris and the 1873 World Fair in Vienna with pavilions that included baths. This inclusion very well reflected the great interest that Europeans and Americans now had in these institutions, an interest that even resulted in the 'Turkish bath movement', the building of hamams in major European cities for socio-political and medical purposes.[32] Representing an Ottoman cultural identity in an essentialised summary form, the pavilions of the 1867 fair consisted of a mosque, a residential building, a fountain on a plaza and a bath.[33] These buildings and the activities they housed were intended to convey to the European visitors a sense of Ottoman social and cultural life. The Ottoman exhibition committee commissioned the French self-trained architect Léon Parvillée to design the temporary structures. Parvillée had gained first-hand experience of Ottoman architecture when documenting and analysing the monuments of Bursa.[34] Most of the architects designing the fair's pavilions for the different empires and nations were Frenchmen, as not only in Islamic countries it was believed that the conception and design of the architectural emblems of cultural identity should best be left to foreigners (who could also communicate more easily with the exhibition administration and the local construction workers).

The Ottoman bath at the 1867 World Fair was a longish, rectangular building block with three rooms lined up in a row: the dressing room (A), the warm room (B) and the hot room (C) (Figures 6.2, 6.3). Domes on octagonal drums capped the dressing room and the hot room, and the façade reflected the tripartite arrangement of the interior rooms. The exterior of the dressing room consisted of a high portal flanked by two windows on each side; the warm room's exterior wall had two blind arches circumscribing latticed windows; and the hot room's façade was

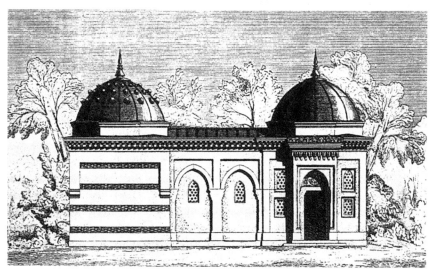

Figure 6.2 Leon Parvillée, drawing of the façade of the bath for the 1867 World Fair, Paris, *Gazette des Architectes et du Bâtiment*, special issue, 1867. *Source*: Çelik, *Displaying the Orient*, 1992.

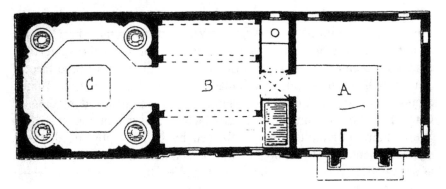

Figure 6.3 Leon Parvillée, ground plan of the bath for the 1867 World Fair, Paris, *Gazette des Architectes et du Bâtiment*, special issue, 1867. *Source*: Çelik, *Displaying the Orient*, 1992.

nothing but a solid wall of alternating layers of *faux* brick and stone. The hot room had an octagonal ground plan, with four pools in the corners resembling washing basins. A bench lining the walls all around invited visitors to sit down and contemplate the 'Oriental' atmosphere under the pierced dome. The ground plan of this non-functional exhibition bath was quite faithful to the functional hamams in the Ottoman Empire. In fact, one can achieve the same layout by cutting Çemberlitaş Hamamı's ground plan in half lengthwise between the men's and women's sections. The same building layout was recycled as part of an Ottoman residence at the 1873 World Fair in Vienna, where it represented Ottoman culture together with several other structures, among them a coffee house and the Sultan's Treasury.[35] Keeping close to reality while still emphasising the more exotic aspects of Ottoman architecture, the designers of the World Fair baths could make 'a claim to scientific authority and accuracy while nourishing fantasy'.[36]

The hamam and the other buildings representing the Ottoman Empire at the World Fairs also stood for the past cultural heritage – beyond the ancient heritage – that the empire needed to possess if it wanted to be on par with contemporary Europe. If the appearance of this heritage conformed to the perceptions and expectations of European viewers, it was all the better. Adopting the tropes of colonialist representation (or, in other words, European stereotypes about them), the Ottomans enaged in what Mary Louise Pratt has called 'auto-ethnography'.[37] Ottomans depicted their own past, their own traditions as an ethnographic Other. They did so in order to show that they had re-evaluated and re-defined their own identity according to Western views; that they had adopted

European conventions; and that Ottoman civilisation had reached the same stage as European civilisation. While proving that the Ottoman Empire was part of Europe, the exhibition displays at the same time asserted the empire's regional difference and uniqueness in the face of a universalising modernity that emanated from Europe and the United States.[38] As Ahmet Ersoy has argued in his sophisticated reading of Ottoman scholarly and architectural activities surrounding the 1873 World Fair, 'Orientalism was embraced by its very objects, the self-styled "Orientals" of the modern world, as a marker of authenticity and as a strategically located aesthetic tool to project universally recognizable images of cultural difference.'[39] Hence, the Ottoman contributions to the fair challenged 'the established vision of Orientalist representations as a closed and univocal tradition that prescribes fixed positions of alterity and opposition'.[40]

It is interesting to note here that the Ottoman Empire was the only Islamic country to include a hamam in its exhibits, maybe because the Western popular imagination had already known these building types as 'Turkish baths' for several centuries and thus considered hamams an essential and distinctive characteristic of 'Oriental' lifestyle.[41] In this sense, the hamam as an emblem of a long-standing Ottoman tradition respected by both locals and foreigners alike acquired a positive meaning, also for those reformers who looked towards Europe – that is, as long as the emblem was dead and under control and could be presented like a taxidermied animal in a museum.[42]

In the reformers' minds, hamams and their symbolic value must have been a vexing issue indeed: on the one hand, hamams represented Ottoman 'backwardness', since the norm among the Europeanised elite was to have washing facilities in one's residence. Such a view not only disregarded the fact that not everybody could afford to have a bathroom, but also that Western norms of body hygiene were actually much less stringent.[43] On the other hand, hamams were the kind of cultural patrimony that was crucial for a nation's cultural identity and gave it a certain cohesiveness and legitimacy. It was a traditional institution – and traditional institutions and ceremonies were of such utmost significance that fledgling European nation-states often had to invent them.[44] What complicated the matter further was that bathhouses continued to have great use-value as providers of hygiene and as centres of social life (see the section 'Survival', below). Çemberlitaş Hamamı's new identity as an emblem of Ottoman Heritage in the nineteenth century was thus a most conflicted and contradictory one.

A New Identity II: Emblem of Ottoman Heritage in the Early Republic

The establishment of the Republic of Turkey in 1923, as proclaimed at the Grand National Assembly in Ankara on 29 October, heralded a new age for the inhabitants of the former empire, in spite of the many continuities in everyday life.[45] It also heralded a new phase, and with it a new identity, in Çemberlitaş Hamamı's life story. This was a phase of old age, as the hamam continued to be a symbol of traditional Ottoman lifestyle. The Republican reformers – who declared most things Ottoman as hopelessly outdated and backward – would often have preferred that this institution should die out and be showcased only in a museum context, like so many art objects losing their original function. Indeed, by 1943 only 86 of the originally 150 hamams of Istanbul were still operating.[46] In the following, I will examine how Republican reforms – in particular, secularism and nationalism – shaped attitudes towards the bathhouses.

In the making of the Turkish Republic, Mustafa Kemal Atatürk played a role that can hardly be overestimated. Born in Salonica in 1881, he entered military school where he became a member of the Committee of Union and Progress (CUP). This political organisation had been founded in 1889 with the aim of strengthening the empire and reintroducing the constitution that Sultan Abdülhamid II (r. 1876–1908) had suspended. Eventually, in 1909, the CUP succeeded in forcing the sultan to resign during the Revolution of Young Turks. In the late nineteenth and early twentieth century, the empire's elite attempted to conceptualise a new Ottoman identity, especially since one province after another declared independence and formed new nation-states. One suggested rallying point for a new national identity uniting all Ottoman subjects was Ottomanism, based on loyalty to one shared government carried by the sultan. Another was pan-Islamism, based on loyalty to the Islamic religion. A third option was Turkism (*Türkçülük*), which promoted loyalty to an ethnically homogeneous nation of Turks.

The masterminds behind Turkism were the Russia-born intellectual Yusuf Akçura (1876–1935) and the sociologist and writer Ziya Gökalp (1876–1924), who also served as the official ideologue of the CUP. Their ideology greatly influenced the leaders and intellectuals of the Turkish Republic, and Mustafa Kemal espoused it wholeheartedly. Defending Gallipoli against the Allied troops during the First World War, Mustafa Kemal distinguished himself as a war hero and went on to become an important leader in the liberation war against the Greeks and the post-First World War allies (1920–1922). In 1920, he established an opposition government in Ankara, challenging the Istanbul-centred sultan's power. Two years later, the sultanate was effectively abolished and the Ankara government, as the sole representative of the new republic, signed the Treaty of Lausanne on 24 July 1923. The treaty determined the shape of the Turkish Republic as it is today.

Atatürk himself was not much of an ideologue; rather, he introduced reforms according to practical considerations, concentrating heavily on political, cultural and intellectual renewal. Only at a later stage, in 1937, were his reforms codified in the constitution as consisting of six principles under the term 'Kemalism'. These six principles – secularism, nationalism, populism, etatism, republicanism and reformism – were aimed at shaping the Ottoman Empire into a Turkish nation-state and Ottoman subjects into Turkish citizens who in their daily life would act like their European contemporaries. Institutions of daily life – bathhouses included – experienced the impact of these principles to varying degrees. The two principles that affected hamams most were secularism and nationalism.

Secularism led to the re-organisation of Istanbul's urban structure and social life, which in the neighbourhoods not inhabited by the Europeanised elite still worked along religious lines.[47] Mosques, churches, synagogues, religious schools, Sufi convents, coffee houses (with an exclusively male clientele) and bathhouses still constituted the primary public spaces for social interaction. Instead of these mostly religious spaces, new secular spaces increasingly occupied important points in the urban fabric: cinemas, theatres, cafés (for a mixed clientele), restaurants, plazas in front of state-sponsored buildings and, later on, public parks with Atatürk busts or statues at the centre. Already in the nineteenth century, the elite had started to break the norm of Islamic gender segregation, but now segregated sites of sociability became even less attractive to the secularised citizens of the new republic. Women's increased freedom of mobility also meant they now had options other than hamams to meet with friends and to socialise.[48] And while in the late nineteenth century a young Muslim woman still had to fear for her reputation if she visited a café with a male companion not related by blood, in the early 1930s young men and women clad in swimsuits together flocked to the beaches around Istanbul during the summer months in order to enjoy sun and sea (Figure 6.4).[49]

Not only public spaces changed, but also private residences. In the 1930s, German architects working in the modernist idiom of the Bauhaus brought the concept of the 'modern house' to the new republic.[50] Although only the upper classes could afford to have concrete apartment buildings constructed, this new type of building soon appeared in many parts of the city. Most of the modern apartments had bathrooms that made a visit to

186

Figure 6.4 Maynard Owen Williams, 'Bathers in Istanbul', 1929. *Source*: National Geographic Creative.

the hamam for hygienic reasons more or less redundant. If the inhabitants of these new, well-equipped apartments did visit Friday prayers at all, they would perform the required full-body ablutions in their home rather than in the hamam. How quickly secularisation changed people's relationship to bathhouses even before the advent of the 'modern house' was recorded by the art historian Karl Klinghardt in 1927. Between 1911 and 1913, Klinghardt had surveyed the bathhouses of Istanbul and other parts of the Ottoman Empire; when he returned fifteen years later, he found bathing habits dramatically changed:

> The contrasts between the life of yore [1911–1913] and of today [1927], particularly in the cities, are surprising and cannot be grasped by the Western imagination of the Orient . . . The tranquil life of Turkish baths, which had allowed the old customs of Asia and of the classical tradition to live on, can today only be found in villages, and there it will not last much longer either.[51]

While Klinghardt in his nostalgia for the good old days may well have exaggerated when he claimed that physical exercise in new sports facilities now substituted for the benefits of hamam massage, his observation that bathers spent less time in the hamam and that the quality of the service suffered probably had a basis in fact.[52]

Secularism also changed the administrative context of endowed hamams. As discussed above, the endowments had already come under the government's centralised control and management with the re-establishment of the Ministry of Imperial Pious Foundations (*Evkaf-ı Hümayun Nezareti*) in 1826, and had therefore seen their administrative and financial independence severely curtailed. One major impetus behind the reform of the *vakıf* system can be located in the desire to bring the Ottoman economy more in line with the European version of modern capitalism, which had little place for an institution that straddled public good and private property in the way in which the endowments did.[53] (One should keep in mind that in 1923, three-quarters of Turkey's arable territory belonged to charitable endowments.[54]) The considerable decline in revenue especially over the last decades of the empire had already led to ministry officials selling endowed property, especially ruined buildings, or replacing them with new, revenue-generating buildings,[55] such as the office blocks (*vakıf han*) designed by the abovementioned Mimar Kemalettin.[56] The introduction of the Turkish Civil Code (*Türk Medeni Kanunu*) on 4 October 1926 spelled an end to the endowment system as it had functioned for many centuries before; the already existing foundations were transferred to the General Directorate of Endowments (*Vakıflar Genel Müdürlüğü*), an instituiton directly answering to the prime minister. Several further laws enacted over the following decade enabled the state to take over the assets of endowments considered 'expired' – that is, no longer having a valid mission, being economically viable, or lacking trustees or beneficiaries.

Following this transfer, a variety of fortunes awaited the formerly endowed monuments and properties: first of all, monuments that carried obvious historical and aesthetic value – such as major mosques – were recast as cultural heritage of national significance and received protection, repair and restoration through the efforts of the General Directorate of Endowments. Secondly, some properties were transferred to other state ministries. Thirdly, properties and assets of less obvious significance were liquidated to contribute to the struggling Turkish economy. Thus, by 1937, 41 million lira had been generated through the sale of formerly endowed property.[57] Particularly in the years 1929 and 1930, the directorate placed many newspaper advertisements announcing their sale.[58] Due to such sales, some *mütevelli*s ended up becoming proprietors of the assets they had previously administered. In other cases, especially long-term tenants and their offspring who had held the endowment properties by way of double rent (*icareteyn*) were mandated to either purchase the property for 20 per cent of its value or, if they were incapable of doing so, to abandon it.[59] Fourth, a considerable number of formerly endowed properties – especially those with less obvious aesthetic merit, such as mosque dependencies in the form of schools, hospitals, bathhouses and the like – were demolished, as will be discussed below.

As for Istanbul's hamams passing into private hands as a result of the changing legal and institutional framework, their new owners appear to have hardly been concerned with the historic value of their new purchase, and they were also unable to make any profit due to the decreasing number of customers. Thus, many demolished their bathhouses under various pretences in order to make room for more profitable apartment or office buildings, or they turned the now 'useless' baths into warehouses, ateliers or shops for rent.[60] Çemberlitaş Hamamı was lucky enough to escape such a fate, but its three siblings were less fortunate. The Atik Valide Hamamı in Üsküdar was used as a carpenter's workshop and slowly fell into disrepair until restored to a fully functioning bath in 1985. The Büyük Hamam, also in Üsküdar, served as a tobacco warehouse and in 1929 was in extremely ruined condition. Returned to state ownership in 1959, the building was remodelled into a small shopping centre, the Mimar Sinan Çarşısı. The Havuzlu Hamam closed down in the 1920s and has subsequently served as a timber warehouse.

Nationalism greatly affected hamams by way of heritage politics. In the words of architectural historian İpek Türeli:

> The modern conception of heritage is expedient: as a shared value, it strengthens bias among citizens towards their nation or faith, inviting them to realize, together with other citizens, that they are the inheritors of a particular past, and therefore, share a common future. Another aspect of architectural heritage is that it justifies territorial claims.[61]

However, deciding on the content and nature of this heritage often generates much dispute and ambiguous sentiments. A community's relationship to its past, including its material heritage, usually shifts with the establishment of a nation-state, since nation-states generally emerge in opposition to whatever came before – an empire or a colony. The Turkish Republic is no exception, and its relationship to the Ottoman-Islamic past remains laden with tension and ambiguity. In the early Republican period, those periods in Turkey's past which were safely dead and unthreatening to the new order – that is, prehistoric, Classical and Byzantine civilisations – constituted the heritage most useful for the nation's aggrandisement. A case in point is the Hagia Sophia, which was closed as a mosque on 8 December 1934, and re-opened as a museum on 1 February 1935.[62]

Needing national monuments to legitimise Turkey's claim to being a modern nation-state, the government chose to emphasise Hagia Sophia's more distant past as ancient church in a museum context, rather than to acknowledge its uncomfortably recent past as Istanbul's largest sultanic mosque. Not surprisingly, Istanbul's Islamic-Ottoman heritage was downplayed, even though it was undeniably seen as an expression of national artistic genius. In the period between 1923 and 1938, a time when the new Republican government was still consolidating itself, the term 'Ottoman' rarely appeared in the press when referring to Turkey's architectural heritage. Instead, it was replaced by more neutral phrases, such as 'the legacy of our forefathers' and 'our ancient monuments'.[63]

The meaning of architectural heritage also shifted due to the power of capitalism, an economic order intimately related to the invention of the nation-state. While some buildings acquired a national, symbolic value, others that fell outside such a categorisation were reduced to their monetary value and became a commodity for sale. As Kopytoff has argued:

> in every society there are things that are publicly precluded from being commoditized . . . This applies to much of what one thinks of as the symbolic inventory of a society: public lands, monuments, state art collections, the paraphernalia of political power, royal residences, chiefly insignia, ritual objects and so on. Power often asserts itself symbolically precisely by insisting on its right to singularize an object, or a set or class of objects.[64]

The Turkish Republican government, on the one hand, reserved the right to own major monuments deemed to express the national artistic genius, such as major mosques erected by Mimar Sinan;[65] on the other hand, it asserted its civilisational superiority over the preceding empire by allowing and sometimes even encouraging the commoditisation and/or destruction of monuments that were *not* part of the national symbolic inventory. By turning Ottoman imperial hamams – which once had been singularised monuments and part of the empire's symbolic inventory, represented at the World Fairs – and the land that they stood upon into commodities, the Republican government demonstrated a 'thorough' break with the past.

It was not that government officials entirely ignored the value of architectural heritage and the importance of preservation. In 1931, during a visit to Anatolia, Atatürk observed the dilapidated state of Konya's Seljuk monuments and immediately sent a telegram to Ankara in order to speed up restoration work.[66] Such impromptu inititiative from above in response to a specific situation – rather than a carefully drafted and widely implemented general plan of action – was quite symptomatic for the early Republican government's working methods. This episode did lead to an increased awareness of the significance of preserving the built environment among the Kemalist elite, as documented by a large number of newspaper articles on the state of the country's monuments and on repairs to them.[67] Yet a number of problems bedeviled the government organs dealing with urban planning and preservation, rendering them mostly ineffective:[68] in spite of a master plan that was developed by the French urban planner Henri Prost (1874–1959), there was no unified vision resting on widespread consensus, and the absence of the necessary legislative framework caused Prost to complain bitterly.[69] More importantly, money to implement even rudimentary policies in Istanbul was lacking; at that time, most of the state budget assigned to construction went to the new capital, Ankara.[70]

With the foundation of the High Council on Immovable Heritage Items and Monuments (*Gayrımenkul Eski Eserler ve Anıtlar Yüksek Kurulu*) under the Ministry of Education in 1951, as well as the issue of the Regulation for the High Council on Immovable Heritage Items and Monuments (*Gayrımenkul Eski Eserler ve Anıtlar Yüksek Kurulu Talimatnamesi*) the following year, the administrative and legal framework for the preservation of architectural heritage achieved a significant improvement. The council's responsibilities consisted of listing and classifying monuments, devising principles for preservation, and maintaining and restoring historic buildings and sites. With the establishment of the council, the legislature clearly expressed the cultural importance of preservation, and it continued to do so by enacting further laws in the following decades.[71] Still, the ambivalence that had permeated preservation efforts in the late Ottoman period continued to prevail, as evocatively described by Nur Altınyıldız:

> Republican administrations neither undertook extensive repairs of Byzantine and Ottoman monuments nor embarked upon outright demolitions. They perpetuated the dilapidated condition of Istanbul as handed down from the Ottoman Empire, since ruins provided a convenient pretext for treating its architectural heritage with ambivalence. Material vestiges of the Ottoman past were proclaimed as the national patrimony of the emerging Turkish state, supporting its claims over the land. Yet this same heritage was kept at a distance, abandoned in wreckage, since it also represented a disowned past. The seemingly inert neglect and oversight generated its own powerful symbolism of demythification. Decaying Istanbul was the reminder not of the Ottoman age of splendor and magnificence but of its later period of decline, disaster, and darkness.[72]

Moreover, the preservation laws were often quite removed from the practical consideration of politicians who were forced to deal with masses of rural-to-urban migrants streaming into Istanbul. The construction of housing and wide streets suited to automobile traffic took priority, particularly under the tenure of the populist Prime Minister Adnan Menderes (1950–1960) of the Democrat Party. They came at the expense of 7,289 expropriated and demolished buildings.[73]

Menderes showed great personal interest and involvement in the redevelopment of Istanbul, which was now based on a revised version of Prost's master plan, amended in consultation with relevant professionals and government agencies, and on newly enacted legislation.[74] The principles and values underlying the Democrat Party's redevelopment scheme had been formulated in the nineteenth century by those who had mutilated Çemberlitaş Hamamı: it favoured Haussmann's design principles of wide boulevards connecting isolated ancient monuments. Within this urban scheme, neither residential nor small public Ottoman buildings – such as neighbourhood mosques, small *medreses* or baths – were deemed worthy of preservation.[75] Cevat Erder, a trained archaeologist who in 1964 founded the Department of Conservation of Historic Monuments at the Middle East Technical University in Ankara, observed in 1973:

> Ironically, the danger of historic monuments in Turkey, particularly to Seljuq and Ottoman structures, dates from modern times ... with Turkish nationalism and then with the Republic, rejection of the Ottoman heritage became a creed. Monuments such as baths or markets, which had functioned unchanged for centuries, were neglected or replaced with 'superior' modern structures. Entire historic centres within cities were destroyed to make room for new roads and a more modern transportation system.[76]

Hamams were hit particularly hard by the early Republican nationalist attitude towards Ottoman monuments and the urban policies of the 1950s and 1960s. Already in the 1930s, hamams had been destroyed at a rate of three to four per year.[77] This was due to three different factors: first, as symbols of traditional Muslim life of imperial Istanbul, bathhouses were deemed unsuitable for modern city life. The new Republican discourse of modern science claimed that communal bathhouses were not hygienic – an attitude also widely held today.[78] Secondly, as relatively inconspicuous buildings even where imperial foundations are concerned, bathhouses could never attain the same status as the more magnificent mosques codified as national heritage; therefore, they were rarely considered worthy of preservation. A case in point is one of the most controversial proposals of Menderes' redevelopment plans, the extension of the road forming the axis between Sultanahmet and Aksaray. (The portion of that very axis between Sultanahmet and Çemberlitaş had already been widened by the *Islahat-ı Turuk Komisyonu*, resulting in the mutilation of Çemberlitaş

Hamamı, as discussed above.) The first proposal submitted to the council in 1952 included the demolition of the Simkeşhane (Imperial Mint), the Hasanpaşa Han – both dating to the eighteenth century – and the fifteenth-century Beyzazit Hamamı. It was rejected, and a second proposal sparing the hamam reached the council in 1955; debates around the mint and the *han* continued into the latter half of the decade, but in the end demolition was approved.[79]

As this example illustrates, owners and government officials managed to find pretences under which they could demolish even monuments of significance, in line with the legal framework. For example, a bathhouse could be claimed to block the planned route of a new street which from the standpoint of infrastructure was more crucial than an old, 'useless' building. In one case, the Cerrahpaşa Hamamı was destroyed in 1933 under the pretence that the owner had a tax debt of 500 lira.[80] Or government officials could declare an already damaged hamam to be unsalvageable, whether rightfully so or not. Lastly, economic difficulties meant that even for the preservation of major monuments there was little money to spare, let alone for bathhouses.

How were these nationalist and secularist Republican views on bathhouses disseminated? How much resistance was there against the destruction of hamams? If there was any at all, who were these critical voices? Turkish newspapers and magazines constituted a forum where the issue of Ottoman bathhouses came up again and again. Even if the writers of these articles exhibited strong nationalist leanings, the demolition of hamams did provoke a reaction in them. In the following, I will tease out four different themes or rhetoric modes from a number of relevant articles and essays published from the 1930s to the 1970s: auto-ethnography, nationalist pride, nostalgic lament and practical necessity.

The rhetoric mode of auto-ethnography was nothing new; it had already existed in the nineteenth century, especially in the context of Ottoman self-representation at the World Fairs. For the Ottoman elite, displaying their own heritage as exotic, Oriental and a thing of the past according to European ethnographic tropes and methods helped to present the Ottoman Empire as an integral part of European civilisation. This mode of self-representation gained even more currency with the foundation of the republic. The empire was dead, and the new nation-state had to demonstrate that this was indeed so. In a most illustrative example of the auto-ethnographic attitude towards hamams, the historian Ahmet Refik Altınay (1880–1937) penned an article titled 'Istanbul in the Era of the Latticed Balconies and the Veil: The Hamams of Istanbul', meant for a popular readership.[81] Altınay presents an odd collection of historical details – Evliya Çelebi's accounts, the inscription of Çemberlitaş Hamamı, a poem, the transcription of an Ottoman document on the construction of a bath and so forth – and illustrates it not with an Ottoman painting, but with an Orientalist engraving by the British painter Thomas Allom (Figure 6.5).[82] The reclining figures in an unidentified bath's dressing room, smoking and enjoying refreshments, remind the viewer of the Orientalist stereotype of the lazy Muslim very much inclined towards sensual delights. While the title implies that hamams are a thing of the past, of the era when gender segregation still determined the life of Istanbul's women, the pastiche of textual excerpts evokes a travelogue intended to whet the reader's appetite to visit such an exotic place. Altınay omits any reference to functioning hamams in the city; he points towards them as if they were an already dead part of Istanbul's Oriental past, the past of an exotic other.

The auto-ethnographic mode also frames the journalist Kandemir's 1939 article titled 'Old Hamams'.[83] In fact, Kandemir employed an ethnographic method, the interview, in order to investigate the world of historic bathhouses. His informant, Ahmet Taban, had been in the hamam business for seventy years, having worked his way up from apprentice *tellak* to owner of the Aksaray Hamamı. From the first line, Ahmet Taban's utterances set the tone of the article as one of pathos and nostalgia for the good old days: 'The old hamams, my son, alas, neither an old hamam

Figure 6.5 Ahmet Refik Altınay, 'İstanbul Hamamları', *Akşam Gazetesi*, 29 July 1936.

has survived, nor an old hamam bowl . . .'[84] The remainder of the article elaborates on the notion that bathhouses belong to a quickly vanishing past, a notion further supported by the accompanying photographs that imply the writer's modernity and authority (Figure 6.6). Wearing a suit and tie in contrast to Ahmet Taban's collarless traditional clothes, Kandemir keeps his hands in his pockets while the old *hamamcı* shows him precious old towels. Rather than touching the textiles, he gazes at them with scientific-objective interest, as if they were a museum object labelled 'do not touch'.

Authors writing in the auto-ethnographic mode tried to convince their readers that hamams were a thing of the past, but a second, concurrent theme emerges: they held great pride in the achievements of what they defined as 'Turkish' civilisation – and, hence, the Turkish nation. In the early Republican era, historians were encouraged to construct a teleological historical narrative up to the foundation of the republic. Turks had only been one among many different ethnic groups of the Ottoman Empire, but now their ethnic and cultural heritage took centre stage in the so-called Turkish History Thesis, which claimed that all civilisation originated from pre-Islamic Turkic Central Asia.[85] In line with this narrative, writers of both scholarly and popular texts stressed the idea that Turks had brought with them the custom of frequent bathing from Central Asia and introduced it to world civilisation. İbrahim Hakkı Konyalı, a prolific amateur historian (1896–1984), asserted in a 1939 article that '[t]he hamam is the wellspring of all cleanliness, beauty, health and sturdiness. In history, hamams hold such an important position that one can measure the degree of civilisation of a nation [through them]. The Turk owes his much talked-about health, strength, beauty and sturdiness to his cleanliness.'[86] Furthermore, he argues that Turkish baths do not owe anything to Byzantine baths, since their ground plans do not share any similarities and since Turkish baths are of Iranian and Central Asian descent.[87] Thus, he emphasises Turkish over Byzantine heritage, very much in line with the Turkish History Thesis.

This emphasis did not decrease over the decades, as in the 1950s other authors felt obliged to assert the superiority of Turkish over Byzantine baths. Thus, the author of an article published in the *Bulletin of the Turkish Touring and Automobile Association* claimed that 'Turks did not lag behind the Byzantines in terms of hamam construction; they brought into existence more elegant buildings; they made the hamam more useful and practical.'[88] This type of nationalist-chauvinist assertion that elevated the pre-Islamic Turkish heritage over Byzantine and Islamic cultural contributions continued to be published in the 1960s as well. It is worth quoting

N v dedin, ne dediz. Es-
ki hamamlarını evlad,
beylut, ne eski hamam
kaldı, nede tas...
Yetmiş yıldır ha-
mamcılık yapan İstan-
bulun en eski Hamamcısı ak sakallı,
güler yüzlü Ahmet Tahsin bağdaş kurduğu peykede bana biraz daha sokulmak ister gibi tahta çekmecesine kolunu dayayarak, devam etti:

— Artık İstanbul çeşmelerinin ya-
taklan gibi suya hasret çeken, fakat
bir zaman ışıl ışıl pınar başlarına ko-
nan kumrular gibi, kenarlarında gümüş
tasların şakırdadığı kurnaların dili ol-
sada söylese... Şu kuş uçmaz kervan
geçmez hale gelen kapının önüne di-
zilen sıra sıra konak arabalarından içe-
ri kadife, atlas, ipek bohçalar taşına
taşına bilmezdi.

— Konakların hamamları yokmaydu?
— Her evde muhakkak vardı amma,
paşa yemeğe Beykoza, kebap yemeğe
Eyübe, yogurt yemeğe kavağa gidilir-
di. Karın doyurmak başka, yemek yemek başkadır. Evlerdeki hamamlarda
yıkanılır, burada yıkanılmazdı. Eskiden
hamam tiryakiliği vardı. Alıştığı gibi
gününde ve saatinde hamama geleme-
yen, hastaya dönerdi. Biz, kimlerin ne
günü geleceklerini ezbere bilirdik. Bu
meraklılar arasında bele bazıları hamama gelmezler, taşınırlardı. Mesela Ak-
sarayda, şuracıkta bir servet paşa var-
dıkı, her hafta perşembe günleri üç
oğlu, oğlunun arkadaşları, kâhyaları,
agaları ve uşaklarıyle ve bir araba boh-
çalarıyle hamama gittiği zaman, kapıda
adam beklerdi, hani şimdiki iskarça
tramvayların astıkları levhalar gibi, gö-

Yazan

Kandemir

•

hek taşı hasretle sokağa düşenlere:
"Dolmuştur, demeğe mecbur olurduk.
— Hamam parası ne kadardı?
— Yüz para, iki kuruş... Fakat böyle
bir paşa kafilesi geldimi - ki tanrının
günü gelirdi - bir çırpıda yüz, yüzelli
kuruş alırdık.

Hamama kadar gelmeğe üşenenler
komşularına bizden usta, tellâk ister-
ler, ve hıpkı buraya gelmiş gibi yine

hamam parasını gönderirlerdi. En so-
tü günde hamama gelenlerin sayısı
yüzden aşağı düşmezdi.

Ve karşı duvarı baştan başa kap-
lıyan camlı dolapları göstererek
— Bak, dedi, şurada döhen iba de-
gerinde, en ağır ipeklisinden tutta baş-
yağı pamukluşuna kadar tam yüz ta-
kım var. Yirmi beş senedir, bir gün
bile bu bohçaların hepsini açmak nas-
sip olmadı

Saf görünmek istedim
— Hamamlarını çoğaldı çokka?
Alaylı alaylı yüzüme baktı.
— Öyle... Otuz sene evvel İstan-
bulda 160 hamam vardı.

İstanbulun en eski hamamcısı Ahmet Tahsin, bağdaş kurduğu peykede bana biraz daha
sokulmak ister gibi tahta çekmecesine kolunu dayayarak, devam etti.

Figure 6.6 Kandemir, 'Eski Hamamlar', *Yeni Gün* 8, 29 April 1939.

196

at length from one article published in 1967 in the right-wing nationalist popular magazine *Önasya*:

> The cleanest people in the world are the Oğuz [Turks] who lived in the region of Tanrıdağ. These are our forefathers. The Oğuz, although they were long-haired, cut their beards and moustaches and loved to wash often. They were all light-complexioned, pink-cheeked, healthy and beautiful people. They did not look like any of the other Asian peoples. The first people on earth who wore jackets and pants were Turks . . . Turks founded this civilisation in valleys next to springs or on streams, [and] women and men washed themselves a lot. Christians washed themselves very little after they had been baptised and they smelled dirty. Arab tribes were dirty because they could not find water. Islam brought many new rules to ensure that these people are clean. But, the cleanliness of the Turks comes from their own customs before the [arrival of] Islamic regulations.[89]

Uneasy about the Ottoman-Islamic past, the writer exaggerated the Turks' cultural superiority to virtually comedic effect.

Historians and journalists writing about bathhouses, whether in the auto-ethnographic mode or based on the theme of national pride, rarely ever referred to the current state of the hamams, with one notable exception. Ahmet Süheyl Ünver (1898–1986), another amateur historian, prolific writer, painter and surgeon, published numerous short essays on hamams in newpapers and popular magazines, from which a third theme surfaces: nostalgic lament. In an article titled 'The Future of Istanbul's Hamams', Ünver surveys the threatened condition of Istanbul's bathhouses and critiques the derogatory attitude towards these Ottoman monuments so necessary for social hygiene:

> There is no account of the hamams that were demolished in Istanbul over the last twenty-five years. Every year, on average, without any exaggeration at least three or four hamams are being torn down . . . There are many hamams that were destroyed under the pretext of being in the way of road construction. For example, after the Fire of Aksaray the Langa Hamam and the Kızlar Ağası Hamamı were torn down, after the road plans were changed deliberately according to the architectural plans of Monsieur Morsik and the architect Kavafyan. Six years ago, the Cerrahpaşa Hamamı was pulled down because of a tax debt of 500 lira . . . There are many other hamams that were destroyed because of tax debts. The ones that were pulled down because of disagreements among inheritors add up to a large number, too. As can be seen, the future of many other hamams is in danger. Istanbul is becoming more and more disconnected from its most basic needs. In new construction systems, instead of the hamams used during the old times, there are now bathrooms. In fact, poor people who do not have baths in their homes go more frequently

to hamams. This is a basic need and a necessary institution for a city. Perhaps most of the hamams lack modern and hygienic arrangements. However, people have very well been able to wash themselves there without threatening public health. Unfortunately, a sufficient number of modern public baths could not be built, although so many hamams were demolished. Now, Istanbul is more in need of this type of hygienic institutions.

In order to protect the future of our hamams, this type of social institution should be prevented from falling into ordinary people's hands. Most of the hamams that are closed today could be brought into perfect condition with only small repairs and new [building] methods. A law must prevent the destruction of hamams at all costs. In the last twenty years, half of the hamams were pulled down without the intention of rebuilding them. The probability of losing the rest, with the exception of just a few, over the next twenty-five years is not far-fetched.

In fact, only twenty to twenty-five extant hamams are functioning right now according to public and private statistics. More than this number is closed and in ruins. Among the closed ones, the Tahtakale Hamamı and the Beyazıt Hamamı, which are very necessary for the inhabitants of the neighbourhood are being used as warehouses.[90]

Ünver's laments seem to have fallen on deaf ears, since he continued to publish articles of almost identical content over the next five decades, in an attempt to sway the generally derogatory opinion about Istanbul's Ottoman bathhouses without actually using the epithet 'Ottoman'.[91] He was seconded in his laments by the historian Reşat Ekrem Koçu, who in a 1954 article addressed tourism professionals in their association's bulletin.[92] The brief article draws attention to the careless treatment of many valuable architectural masterpieces by turning them into workshops or warehouses, and ends with the plea to enact a law against the demolition and closing down of hamams.

A 1938 newspaper article titled 'Our Hamams are the Healthiest Means of Washing' argues that especially for the urban poor hamams were a much needed amenity, followed by a 1943 call to truck drivers to help transport coal donated to the eighty-seven functioning hamams of Istanbul so that the indigent could wash there for free. The fourth theme thus addresses the continued practical necessity of urban hamams for the lower classes who did not have the resources to either build or buy modern apartments or houses with bathrooms. Using the observations of Ahmet Süheyl Ünver in his capacity as a medical doctor as evidence, the writer argues that at present the lower classes gravely neglect body hygiene, in contrast to thirty years ago when even the poorest who came to the hospital for medical attention were very clean. Ünver, making use of the scientific authority that his profession lent him, called for a reduction of bathing fees in the city. This call was actually heeded: the 1943 notice concerning the coal donated particularly to those bathhouses that had an arrangement with the municipality to wash the poorest for free shows that, probably due to the typhus epidemics that had badly affected Istanbul, officials now acknowledged the crucial significance of hamams for public hygiene.

Yet the connection between hamam visits and the life circumstances of the lower classes that the Republican officials thus established led to the notion that bathhouses were no place for those belonging to the middle or upper classes. Whoever visited the bathhouses now did not do so for enjoyment, but because they did not live in a residence with proper washing facilities. In the Republican era, hamam visits became a marker of low social status. This had not been the case in the Ottoman period, when even high government officials who owned mansions with their own small private hamams occasionally visited public bathhouses.[93] The Republican rhetoric of correlating hamam visits with lower-class identity did much harm to Istanbul's baths, as it deprived them of their most wealthy and most profitable clientele.

Survival

In the face of derogatory attitudes and demolitions, how did Çemberlitaş Hamamı and many other bathhouses of Istanbul survive? Was their situation really so bleak, or were their odds for survival bigger than they seemed at first? Those reformers who espoused a wholesale Europeanisation of every aspect of Ottoman culture would have liked to see hamams disappear entirely (maybe with the exception of a hamam-turned-bathing-culture museum), made redundant by the tubs and showers of modern houses. Yet this was not possible because this 'modern' lifestyle reached only certain segments of society and because tubs, for one, were not suited to the Islamic requirement of full-body ablutions in running water – soaking in stagnant water did not fulfil the canonical requirements. It was only in elite households that one could find bathrooms with tubs and tiles: in the Yıldız Palace of Sultan Abdülhamid II (r. 1876–1909) or in the turn-of-the-century mansion of Ratib Ahmed Paşa, who seemed to have taken a liking to art nouveau furnishings in the latest European fashion.[94]

Owners of less luxurious residences had to make do with an *abdesthane* or *gusülhane*, a small space, the size of a closet, where one could perform small ablutions with water poured from a ewer. The records of the court of the Davud Paşa district in Istanbul describe a mansion in the rather modest neighbourhood of Kasap İlyas in 1845 as:

> A privately owned *konak* with, in the upper floor three rooms, a water-closet [*kenif*], a pantry and a hall, in the middle floor three rooms, a bathroom [*abdesthane*] and water-closet and a hall, in the lower floor a kitchen, a toilet and a storage place for coal plus, in the men's quarters (*selamlık*) a room, a bathroom and a water-closet in the top floor, a room and a bathroom and water-closet in the middle floor, plus stables and a water-well, a garden and garden gates.[95]

Thus, the mansion had toilets on every floor and three bathrooms, one in the private section, two in the men's section. What these facilities for small ablutions looked like in wealthy households of the late nineteenth and early twentieth centuries is described in great detail by Abdülaziz Bey, author of a voluminous work on Ottoman everyday life, customs and traditions:

> If the circumstances allow it, attention should be paid that there is a marble stepping stone in the *abdesthane*, that it is wide and bright, that it is aired out by always leaving the windows open. Attention should be paid that the stone troughs in front of the taps be big and deep so that no water should splatter out, moreover, that the ornamental slab [on the wall behind the trough] be big, that the ornamental relief be [decorated] with flowers and always wiped [well]. Because it counts as bad manners to leave the stone wet, there are two sponges, [and] after being swept clean, it is dried well with the sponges. A round pole of a length of about 1.5 *arşın* is attached to two short iron pieces on the wall next to the stone slab behind the taps. On it, there are hung two towels each with embroidered edges, one for the guests' *abdest* and one to wipe one's hands. Next to the stone trough there is also a deep plate with musk-perfumed soap.[96]

Such a bathroom with marble floor and ornamented stone slabs clearly could be found only in the households of the well-to-do; it provided more than ample washing facilities for small ablutions, but not for a full-body ablution.

Residents of brick houses built in the nineteenth century in the Europeanised district of Pera also had rudimentary washing facilities. Called 'Tanzimat boxes' by Zeynep Enlil for their rectangular layout and appearance, these brick houses typically included a reception hall (*sofa*), two rooms, a kitchen and a toilet/bathroom with a tap with running water (Figure 6.7).[97] The wooden houses of the people of modest means in neighbourhoods not targeted by modernisers had facilities even more rudimentary, and maybe not even an *abdesthane*. So-called *bekar odaları*, dormitory-style rooms (or only beds) rented out to single males, had no facilities at all.[98] And then there were those who did not even have a room to call their own, but who slept in their workplace, in shops, coffee houses

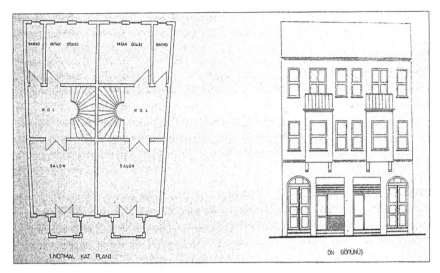

Figure 6.7 Ground plan of 'Tanzimat-box'-type apartment building. *Source*: Enlil, 'Residential Building Traditions', n.d. [2001].

and warehouses – a practice that continues to this day.[99] Thus, hamams remained a physical necessity for the majority of Istanbul's inhabitants, irrespective of the reformers' derogatory attitude and their plans to destroy them. In fact, in the nineteenth century new hamams were constructed in order to respond to the Istanbulites' needs.[100]

Neither did the rapid modernisation of Istanbul's urban fabric in the early Republican period with the introduction of modern houses and apartment buildings deal a final blow to the bathhouses. The well-to-do who could afford to do so generally moved to the new neighbourhoods north of Pera, such as Nişantaşı and Şişli, and left the less privileged behind in *intra muros* Istanbul. In the 1950s, a typical apartment building in the neighbourhood of Laleli, in the old part of the city, exhibited the following arrangement:

A typical building had five stories, with two apartments on each floor. Facing the street would be the entrance, an unassuming lobby, a stairwell in the middle to the upper floors. Apartments were designed around a central hall where the stove would be located (unlike the new part of the city, these buildings had no central heating): towards the street side would be the living room and a 'good' guest-receiving room, and towards the back, with a balcony overlooking the garden, the bedrooms. The kitchen and the bathroom were rudimentary; in the mode of prewar Europe before American plumbing set the standard.[101]

Such washing facilities made an occasional hamam visit indispensable for the physical well-being even of middle-class Istanbulites who lived in apartments built after the turn of the century and in the early Republican period.

Hamams also continued to be focal points of social life. Reformers who aimed to bring Western amenities to Istanbul introduced new sites of sociability, such as theatres (around 1840), public parks (1860s) and cinemas (after 1897). In these new public spaces, men and women broke the norm of gender segregation and socialised as couples. Yet the men and women enjoying themselves together belonged to the elite; for the majority of Istanbulites the hamams kept their value as a site of entertainment and sociability. Indeed, Fanny Davis argues that Ottoman ladies' increased mobility in the nineteenth century led to a greater frequency of hamam visits even among the elite.[102] Nevertheless, alternative sites of sociability in the Eruopean style had greater novelty value, meaning that hamams were not the most fashionable meeting places any more.

The claim that early Republican secularism led to a total re-organisation of Istanbul's urban structure and social life within one or two decades equally needs to be taken with a grain of salt. Relying on sources produced by the elite, historical studies have until recently exaggerated the impact of Kemalist reforms. In reality, however, with the exception of a small ruling elite (who very often were ill at ease with their new lifestyle), the citizens of the newly established Republic continued to live life in the same way as their predecessors had. Symbols of modernity, such as cars, telephones and refrigerators, harmoniously inhabited a traditional Ottoman-Islamic socio-cultural environment. Deeper societal changes occurred only in the 1950s.[103] For the majority of Istanbulites, the hamam continued to be more than a basic necessity for hygiene and physical well-being: it provided a space to socialise and entertain for much of the twentieth century, given that an entertainment industry accessible to all segments of society developed rather late. For example, television did not arrive in Turkey until the 1970s, and recreational shopping did not emerge until the 1980s. In the 1960s and 1970s, many hamam customers came to Çemberlitaş Hamamı for lack of other options for entertainment.[104]

Who exactly were the people who visited Çemberlitaş Hamamı during the first half of the twentieth century and, by doing so, guaranteed its survival? During the First World War – a time when many bathhouses had to close down due to the lack of firewood and henceforth functioned as storage spaces, never to re-open again[105] – Çemberlitaş Hamamı had a rather unpleasant job to perform. It worked as a fumigating station to treat soldiers who had contracted lice, under the supervision of army general Dr Abdülkadir Noyan.[106] This clientele disappeared after the war was over, and the regular bathers returned. The maps that the Central Office of Turkish Insurance Agents commissioned from the cartographer Jacques Pervititch for the evaluation of fire risks give valuable details on the immediate environment of the bathhouse in the years 1923 and 1940 (Figures 6.8, 6.9).[107] Pervititch not only established an address system for the first time, but also paid close attention to building types and materials, and clearly labelled each structure. Around Çemberlitaş Hamamı,

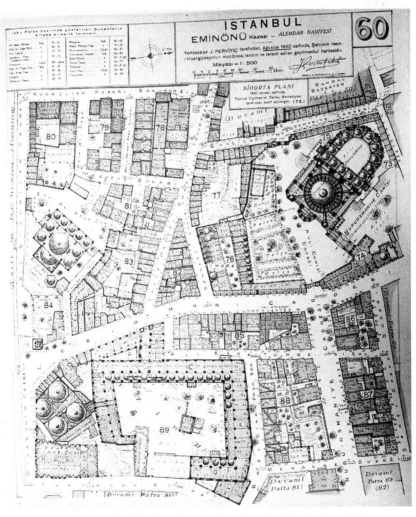

Figure 6.8 Jacques Pervititch, map of the neighbourhood of Çemberlitaş, 1940.
Source: Ersoy, *Jacques Pervititch Sigorta Haritalarında İstanbul*, n.d.

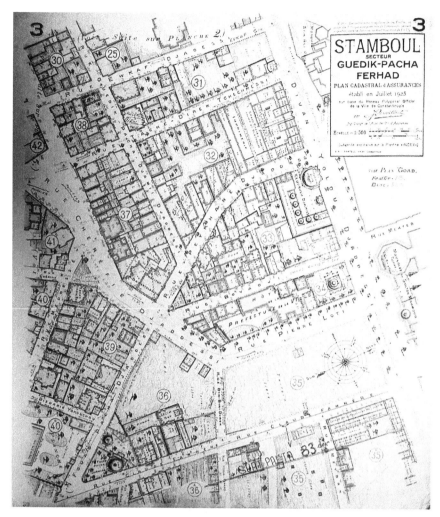

Figure 6.9 Jacques Pervititch, map of the neighbourhood of Çemberlitaş south of the Divanyolu, 1923. *Source*: Ersoy, *Jacques Pervititch Sigorta Haritalarında İstanbul*, n.d.

Pervititch identified most buildings as plain brick structures that housed workshops and shops. There was a factory producing chairs and beds several streets to the west, and two apartment buildings in the more immediate neighbourhood to the north, the Aybel Üzlü Apartmanı, and the Veli-Ata Apartmanı. On the Divan Yolu, to the east, government officials worked in the *Belediye İmar Dairesi* (Municipal Office of Construction). Across the Divan Yolu, there were the municipality building (Hôtel de la Préfecture de Ville), a printing press and the Bacteriological Institute. This area was occupied by residences with small gardens rather than workplaces, consisting of brick structures indicated in pink – the kind of apartment buildings described above. Pervititch identified several residences as *konak*, as mansions belonging to high-ranking persons. On the Rue Claude Farrère, Pervititch inscribed the term 'logements à des pauvres gens' on several wooden and brick buildings – residences for the poor that were unlikely to have bathrooms.

Thus, Çemberlitaş Hamamı in the first half of the twentieth century served as neighbourhood bath to a most varied clientele cutting across most classes of society: store-owners and workers of the shops and ateliers to the north, government officials in the surrounding municipal offices, and middle-class and poor residents living to the south of the Divan Yolu, as well as migrant workers who lived in the shops and warehouses in the commercial areas beyond. Çemberlitaş Hamamı was also among the bath-houses that catered to the poor, supported by the municipality's contribution to their bathing fees in the hope of containing diseases spread through poor body hygiene (such as typhoid).[108] Çemberlitaş Hamamı seems to have survived without too many worries if one considers that even in 1965 the number of visitors still counted between 150 and 200 bathers daily.[109]

In the 1970s, architects in Europe and the United States increasingly found interest in vernacular architecture, and this interest found a sympathetic milieu in Turkey as well. Architects now began to study humbler residential buildings and entire building ensembles within the urban fabric.[110] A 1972 law reflects this shift in interest towards the vernacular, which made it possible to put entire building ensembles under protection and to salvage residential structures in their context.[111] Çemberlitaş Hamamı also profited from this trend. Cemil Gürkök, its owner, instigated large-scale restorations in the years 1972 and 1973, stripping it of haphazard accretions and repairing the damage done by earlier, unprofessional renovations. A plaque at the entrance of the hamam still attests to the restoration that Ahmet Süheyl Ünver, the tireless champion of Istanbul's hamams, highly praised.[112]

By the nineteenth and early twentieth centuries, Çemberlitaş Hamamı had lived to a ripe old age – so old that first the most radical *Tanzimat* reformers and then the most radical early Republican reformers would have liked to declare it dead and turn it into a taxidermied creature that could safely and comfortably be displayed to foreign visitors, as well as to local visitors on an excursion into their own, now foreign past. But Çemberlitaş Hamamı continued to work in spite of the break with its family, the Atik Valide Vakfı, in spite of its mutilation at the hands of the Commission for Road Improvement, regardless of the demeaning task of fumigating soldiers during the First World War, and in spite of the schizophrenic existence that its numerous, often conflicting new identities imposed on it: emblem of a cultural heritage needed for the Ottoman Empire's inclusion in European civilisation, emblem of a 'backward' and 'Oriental' life-style, emblem of the Turkish nation's cultural genius. Like a tough old-timer hardened by experience, it proved to be surprisingly resilient because of its physical necessity and its social value irrespective of new-fangled ideologies.

7

Second Spring

It describes how Çemberlitaş Hamamı has now become a building very much appreciated by foreign visitors, after many painters and authors of the last centuries depicted and praised its joy-giving qualities and enticed foreigners' interests, and how the foreigners think about the hamam; how many people of Istanbul and of the Turkish Republic, after having mostly abandoned visiting this pleasurable place, are again coming to enjoy its blessings, why they do so, and how they think about the hamam; how the managers depict and praise the hamam's qualities for foreign and Turkish visitors alike, and how the attendants think about the hamam; and what the digital age may contribute to its story.

A New Identity III: Tourist Attraction

While in 1841 Çemberlitaş Hamamı provided services to the local inhabitants and generated money for the Atik Valide Vakfı, a phenomenon emerged in Great Britain that in the long run would have a considerable global impact, and also come to shape the hamam's life: tourism. In 1841, Thomas Cook for the first time organised a train excursion, called a 'tour', of a group of 400 or 500 from Leicester to Loughborough and back. In the same year, the first national railway timetable, Bradshaw, appeared, and the first European hotel built as part of a railway station opened in York. Moreover, in the decade between 1830 and 1840, the camera had been invented and the term 'sightseeing' introduced into the English language.[1] The railway and the steamship now made travel a more common pursuit and no longer restricted to the upper classes, who in the nineteenth century undertook recreational trips primarily to resorts along the shores of the Mediterranean. With Thomas Cook's invention of all-inclusive tours, travel became much cheaper and easier in terms of arranging transportation and accommodation. The decline of the aristocracy after the First World War meant that vacation resorts became accessible to anybody who had the necessary disposable income.

The phenomenon of tourism encompasses much more than the mere physical act of traveling to a specific place and back. Tourism is also an act of getting to know an exotic Other, an epistemological performance that finds its origins in a time-period when Europeans set out to explore and colonise new continents. The physical as well as conceptual layouts of the nineteenth-century World Fairs, discussed in Chapter 6, illustrate the premises that equally underpin tourism. Divided literally as well as metaphorically into a centre (Europe and the United States) and the exotic margins (the rest of the world), the comprehensive inventory of civilisations and cultures received a hierarchical ordering. The essence of each civilisation could be grasped by visiting and gazing at the respective pavilion or kiosk that provided representative examples of that civilisation's cultural production and traditions, in the form of buildings, objects and various activities on display. This epistemological performance of nineteenth-century World Fair visitors shaped the behavioural patterns of the tourists of subsequent centuries. Usually traveling from industrialised countries perceived to be situated in the centre, either to other centres or to the exotic margins (but rarely the other way around), tourists have been on the move with the aim to gaze upon, and by extension capture by means of photography, sites, objects and people that they perceive as authentically representative of their destination.[2] Although by now tourists from once 'peripheral' regions seem to have come to dominate certain attractions – if one takes, for example, the high number of East Asian visitors in Vienna, Paris, London and other metropoleis as indication – tourism as a phenomenon still reifies (former) colonial power structures, through both physical movement and the practice of gazing.

The practice of tourism is dependent on a vast body of diverse media that disseminate representations of the destination culture. As cultural theorist Tim Edensor expresses it:

> [s]ymbols, images, signs, phrases and narratives provide the ideas that fuel the commodification and consumption of tourist sites . . . Besides promoting particular tourist locations, such representations are part of a technology of enframing sights and cultures which forms the epistemological apparatus through which tourists see and interpret difference. The culturally located ways of framing sights and arranging narratives is a selective process that usually reproduces the predictable; the already said, written and photographed.[3]

Television programmes, documentary and feature films, travel books and magazines, coffee-table books, brochures, postcards, websites, and Facebook and Instagram posts – all of these invite prospective tourists to visit specific places and sites. What is more, the representations produced and reproduced therein not only instruct tourists *what* to gaze at, but also *how* to do so, by offering various narrative frameworks, such as the sublime, the romantic, the authentic, the timeless, the exotic and the erotic. Touristic practice entails the selection of a specific enframing narrative and then searching out the relevant representations during travel, with the help of guidebooks, brochures, websites and the like. Having located the desired representation, tourists then take possession by means of gazing, whether with the naked eye or through a photographic lens, or by the rapidly vanishing custom of purchasing and sending postcards. Tourist performance thus gives birth to a hermeneutic cycle, as representations fuel a desire to visit and to re-present the same to ever more potential tourists.[4]

As a major source of revenue for Turkey's economy,[5] tourism has inevitably affected attitudes towards cultural heritage, ranging from archaeological sites over historic mosques to museums. When mass tourism with all its attendant practices and performances arrived in Turkey, especially following the Tourism Subvention Act 1982, Çemberlitaş Hamamı quickly acquired an additional identity – that of a tourist attraction. On a more quotidian level, this new identity ensured the continued survival of this and many other bathhouses on Istanbul's historic peninsula, which now largely depend on foreign visitors' rather than local bathers' fees. Employees of Çemberlitaş Hamamı claimed that, without the tourists' interest, bathing culture might very well have died out in the latter decades of the twentieth century.[6] On a symbolic level, the hamam's new identity has, among other meanings, become that of a repository of 'authentic Turkish culture' and a short-hand representation of 'Oriental lifestyle', commodified for and consumed by tourists from around the globe.

The abovementioned hermeneutic cycle of representation constitutes a defining aspect of tourist attractions, which Dean MacCannell has aptly identified as an 'empirical relationship between a tourist, a sight and a marker (a piece of information about a sight [in other words, the textual and pictorial representations that come to form the hermeneutic cycle])'.[7] Therefore, a discussion of the monument's new identity requires a careful excavation and tracing of the themes that most commonly occurred in the interviews and survey I conducted with foreign visitors. With the exception of one 45-year-old female German visitor and self-professed art lover who singled out the Orientalist paintings by Ingres (Figure I.1, above and Figure 7.1) as having shaped her expectations about her hamam visit, the tourists interviewed always reverted to frustratingly general statements of the kind best summarised in the words of a 44-year-old male teacher from New Zealand: 'It is the thing to do while you are in Turkey. They have a famous

Figure 7.1 *Le Bain Turc*, Jean-Auguste-Dominique Ingres, oil on wood, 1852–1859, Musée du Louvre. © RMN-Grand Palais/Art Resource, NY.

reputation.'⁸ Such statements are as telling about the status of hamams within broader touristic representations of Turkey as they are about touristic practices and performances: in MacCannell's words, 'modern international sightseeing possesses its own moral structure, a collective sense that certain sights must be seen'.⁹

When and how, then, did it become *de rigueur* for foreign travellers and tourists to visit bathhouses such as Çemberlitaş Hamamı? And what representations and tropes specifically accompanied them, and continue to do so? Travellers' tales from the sixteenth to the twenty-first century, Orientalist paintings, films, travel magazines and guide books have all contributed to the codification of the hamam visit as integral part of the touristic experience. And in spite of the great variety of media and the diverse geographical and temporal contexts from which these textual and pictorial representations emerged, they often built upon and reinforced each other. The authors of later travel accounts often entered an inter-textual dialogue with earlier ones they had read in preparation for their journey; Orientalist painters read travel accounts; and articles in travel magazines either reproduce Orientalist paintings or include photographs inspired by the latter's iconography. The following pages can lay no claim to offer a comprehensive discussion of bathhouse representations across time and space; however, a selection of texts and images will assist in teasing out a number of tropes that mythologise Çemberlitaş Hamamı and mediate the expectations with which tourists approach it.

The tales of six travellers – both men and women, from the sixteenth to the twentieth centuries – offer such a repeatedly occurring array of themes or tropes: *The Nauigations, Peregrinations and Voyages, Made into Turkie* ... by Nicolas de Nicholay (1517–1583, travelled to the Ottoman Empire in 1551); the *Turkish Letters* by Ogier Ghiselin de Busbecq (1522–1591, as Hapsburg legate stayed in Istanbul for several extended periods in the 1550s and 1560s); *The Turkish Embassy Letters* by Lady Mary Wortley-Montagu (1689–1761, as wife of the British Ambassador to the Porte stayed in the Ottoman Empire from 1717 to 1718); *The City of the Sultan and Domestic Manners of the Turks in 1836* by Julia Pardoe (1806–1862, travelled to Istanbul in 1835); and *Turkish Reflections: A Biography of a Place* by the British author Mary Lee Settle (who lived in Turkey from 1972 to 1974).[10]

The theme of architectural splendour and luxury contributes most to the expectations of today's hamam visitors. With the exception of Settle, all authors praise the magnificence of the bath, the liberal use of marble and other expensive building materials, the high domes and the comfortable sofas to sit upon. In the actual bathing rooms, water flows abundantly from fountains and basins. The dressing room usually features sumptuous textiles, such as rugs, brocaded pillows, silk and velvet spreads and cush-ions. Luxurious are also the different kinds of towels, often fine linen or silk, embroidered and with fringes. The gustatory experience of delicious food and drink – all kinds of sweetmeats, coffee, sherbets and lemonade – match the tactile experience of soft, expensive cloth, and servants are on hand to cater to the bathers' needs. (In the early 1970s, Settle failed to find this type of luxury, as described in the guidebooks she had consulted; its absence and her resulting disappointment point towards the entrenched nature of the trope and the expectations it creates.)

In stark contrast to the praising description of architecture, textiles and refreshments stands the evaluation of the hamam's atmosphere: Lady Mary and Julia Pardoe complained about the hot, sulphurous air and the dense, heavy steam in the hot room.[11] Most European travel writers disliked the high temperatures there and had mixed feelings about the actual bathing procedure, whether they actually partook in it or excused themselves, as did Lady Mary.[12] They perceived the treatment as rough, unaccustomed as they were to scrubbing and massaging, which according to Nicolas de Nicholay made bones crack.[13] Several centuries later, Settle commented: 'It was like being bathed as a small child by an angry mother . . . She grabbed a leg and scrubbed it as if she were taking barnacles off a keel.'[14]

The physical appearance of bathers also constitutes a long-standing theme. The male travellers mentioned here never described male bathers, but some had much to say about the beauty of female ones, even though they would not have been able to observe them. The female travellers, however, did corroborate such imaginative accounts, praising the beauty of Turkish women and emphasising the stunning sight of about 200 partially dressed bathers altogether. Lady Mary likened the female bathers to goddesses: 'There were many amongst them as exactly proportioned as ever any goddess was drawn by the pencil of Guido [Reni] or Titian, and most of their skins shiningly white, only adorned by their beautiful hair divided into many tresses, hanging on their shoulders, braided either with pearl or ribbon, perfectly representing the figures of the Graces.'[15] The female staff received less praise, resulting in the trope of the unsightly, fat, elderly hamam attendant whose appearance had suffered from constant exposure to heat and humidity. Julia Pardoe describes them as 'unsightly objects' with skin the colour of tobacco and the consistency of parchment, and Mary Lee Settle speaks of the masseuse washing her as enormously fat naked old woman.[16] The ugly attendant serves as a contrasting backdrop to elevate the bathing beauties, while also defining the class boundaries between the servant and the one being served.

The accumulation of so many scantily clad bodies allowed travel writers to reflect, and even openly fantasise, about encounters of a homoerotic nature. Nicolas de Nicholay claimed the women used the washing procedure as an excuse to grope and fondle each other.[17] Both Lady Mary and Julia Pardoe vehemently denied de Nicholay's 'feminine wantonness', writing against previous accounts that had claimed such occurrences. Lady Mary's description of the hamam visit was meant not only to inform the reader, but also to serve as criticism of British women's attitudes, Christian notions of womanhood, and the sexual mores and manners of her era.[18]

Interestingly enough, the male travel writers examined here eschewed any remarks on male homoeroticism in the hamam, even though the existence of bathhouse attendants catering to homosexual clients can be proven beyond doubt (see Chapter 4), likely for fear that readers would assume their active engagement. Whether travellers claimed a connection between sexuality and bathing or refuted earlier claims about it, once such a link had been established, it persisted – greatly aided by the fact that in Europe bathhouses often coexisted with brothels.[19] In one interview, one of the managers of Çemberlitaş Hamamı also directly addressed this link when he described having occasionally to handle delicate scenarios: foreign gay bathers sometimes find their expectations of the services offered dashed and 'for obviously made-up reasons' ask to have their bathing fee refunded.[20]

In a sense, hamams have always constituted an epistemological anomaly within Orientalist discourse because their frequent use demonstrated standards of hygiene superior to those of contemporary Europeans. Hence, European authors attempted to counteract this anomaly by condemning hamams as morally decadent spaces.[21] In Billie Melman's words, '[i]n Western imagination, the hamam came to apotheosise the sensual, effeminate Orient. Never actually penetrated by male travelers, the women's public baths were identified as the *loci sensuales* in the erotically charged landscape of the Orient.'[22] For instance, even though denying the occurrence of female homosexuality in the hamam, Pardoe still describes it as 'terrestrial paradise of Eastern women', comparing the scene of women bathing in the hot room to 'the illusory semblance of a phantasmagoria'.[23] Related to the trope of the bathing beauty, another overarching theme thus emerges from the hamam's description across time and space: a 'vision of synaesthetic and sensual indulgence',[24] which was then eagerly picked up and reinforced by nineteenth-century painters.

As the Middle East began to figure ever more prominently in the European imagination following Napoleon's invasion of Egypt and Syria from 1798 and 1802, artists were captivated by Oriental women as evoked in travellers' tales and scholarly accounts. Particularly French painters depicted in a glossy, photographic realism bathing scenes featuring magnificent female nudes, pointing at conceptions of the Orient as effeminate, sensual, exotic and erotic. Foremost among them were Jean-Auguste-Dominique Ingres (1780–1867) and Jean-Léon Gerôme (1824–1904), whose well-known works are continually reproduced in publications on bathhouses, both popular and scholarly, in Turkish and other languages.

Ingres' masterpiece *Le Bain Turc* (1862–1863, Louvre, Figure 7.1) epitomised several decades of his preoccupation with odalisques.[25] Against the barely discernible architectural backdrop and a pool, several groups of nudes are engaged in various activities. In the foreground, a lute player has turned her back to the viewer, and also on a tray containing the remainders of fruit and coffee. On the red sofa, two of the reclining ladies embrace each other intimately, while the full-length figure in the foreground has lazily drifted off in a daydream. Behind the sofa, an African slave carrying a smoking censer and a fair-complexioned, towel-wrapped bather stand against the wall. In the background, one bather sits on the edge of the pool, an African slave plays a drum, a dancer moves with swaying arms, and many more ladies lounge, listen, eat, drink, nap and apply cosmetics. Through the centre walks a bather naked save for a high, yellow headdress with its rear part draping over back and shoulders.

Ingres conjures up an intensely erotic mood through the multitude of female nudes relaxing together and touching each other affectionately. He had never travelled farther south or east than Italy, but based his painting on accounts such as the *Nauigations* of Nicolas de Nicholay. The latter's illustration of a woman going to the hamam in fact served as model for the walking bather with the yellow headdress (Figure 7.2).[26]

Figure 7.2 Women going to the bath, from Nicolas de Nicholay, *The Nauigations, Peregrinations and Voyages, Made into Turkie* . . . *Source*: Bibliothèque nationale de France.

214

More importantly, he had carefully read Lady Mary Wortley-Montagu's account of her bathhouse visits, of which he even copied passages into his sketchbook. Yet his unabashed fascination with the Orient's exotic sensuality led him to disregard her assertions about the absence of 'feminine wantoness'.

Unlike Ingres, Gerôme did actually travel to Anatolia in 1855, and later on visited Egypt, Syria and other regions of the Middle East during several extended journeys, and even learned the Arabic language. A prolific painter of Orientalist subjects – ranging from slave markets to carpet merchants to desert scenes – he also produced many bathing scenes. *The Bath* (completed 1885, Figure I.4, above) exemplifies his treatment of the subject: a nude female bather sitting on a cage-like contraption opposite an enormous, elaborately carved marble basin presents her magnificent backside to the viewer. Her hair is tucked into a knot and thus permits unobstructed view of her luminous back. In stark contrast to her white complexion stands the dark-skinned African slave who scrubs her with a sponge. The bather's tranquillity and her surroundings impart a sense of luxury and sensual indulgence. In the background, towels hanging on a holder are waiting to softly envelop her after the bath. Gerôme has given both the marble floor and the turquoise wall tiles a texture that invites viewers to imagine touching the smooth, heated surfaces. The tiles sporting an inscription and the *muqarna*s pendentives in the corner convey a sense of architectural splendour, albeit an incorrect one, as the whitewashed hamam interiors rarely boast such extravagant decoration.

Because they offer memorable framing devices for specific places and sites, films often constitute effective, even if indirect, sight markers for (potential) tourists. This is also the case with the feature film *Steam: The Turkish Bath* (1997, directed by Ferzan Özpetek), which draws on Orientalist narratives and iconography. The story follows the Italian interior designer Francesco from Rome to Istanbul, where he has inherited an old hamam from his recently deceased aunt. Francesco at first travels to Istanbul with the aim of selling the building quickly and returning to Italy, but he finds himself enchanted by the old bathhouse, the city and the Turkish family who had lived together with his elderly relative. As his stay continues to prolong itself, he decides to keep and renovate the hamam in order to operate it once again as a business. At the same time, he grows closer to the family's adult son Mehmed and discovers that he is gay. They exchange their first kiss in the hot room of the newly renovated bathhouse. Yet Francesco meets a tragic end: the real-estate developer whom Francesco thwarted because of his refusal to sell the hamam so that it could be demolished to make space for a high-rise building hires a killer who stabs him to death.

Özpetek draws on the story-line of the alienated and disenchanted Westerner who travels to the East where he finds his true self in a more 'authentic', sensual and sexually permissive environment.[27] The film poster reflects the conventional plot treatment in its reference to bathing odalisques turning their backs towards the viewer, with Francesco and Mehmed sitting on the göbektaşı in the misty hot room (Figure I.3). Thus, to viewers (and potential tourists) Özpetek presents the hamam as symbol of an 'authentically Oriental' lifestyle and as an intensely erotic space that promises sexual awakening and the pleasures of tenderly budding homo-erotic love. As blockbuster in Turkish cinemas and the country's potential nominee for the 1998 Academy Award for Best Foreign Language Film, *Steam* did much to pique interest among tourists as well as locals and to increase the number of bathers, according to one of Çemberlitaş Hamamı's managers.[28] The film did not make it to the Oscars, since the Turkish Ministry of Culture pulled it from the competition for the nomination, due to its homosexual content.

Orientalist iconography of nude bathers as readily recognisable short-hand also appears in travel magazines, which are geared towards potential tourists actively in seach of new destinations. There, destinations are usually presented within predictable enframing narratives, such as authen-ticity, adventure, exoticism, sensual indulgence, culinary interest and so on. A case in point is Şebnem İşigüzel's 1998 article in the German maga-zine *GEO*, in a special issue covering Turkey.[29] Titled 'Hamam: Washing Day in the Realm of the Senses', it blatantly reproduces the Orientalist narrative of travellers' tales and paintings. Although nude bathing is not welcome in contemporary Turkish baths, several of the photographs illustrating the text display female nudes in the manner of Ingres' and Gerôme's odalisques (Figure 7.3). Both figures and architectural elements float within the soft, enveloping steam. The photographer has framed her scenes in a way that omits any modern addition to the bathhouse – such as plastic signs reminding bathers to wear clogs or prohibiting nudity. A caption promises: 'Between the columns, the Ottoman past seems still alive – and time is captured in the tranquillity.'[30]

A more nuanced article that, at least in some respects, transcends a tired repetition of notions about a timeless Orient appeared in 2000 in the *New York Times Magazine*'s supplement *The Sophisticated Traveler*.[31] Written by the biographer Nancy Milford following a year-long stay in Turkey as Fulbright Fellow, 'Bathed in Tradition', so its title, reflects her own experiences. Some of these, such as her Turkish university colleagues'

Second Spring

Figure 7.3 Şebnem İşigüzel, 'Waschtag im Reich der Sinne', GEO Special: *Türkei*, 1998.

derogatory attitude towards hamams, deny the purported authenticity of hamams in the context of contemporary Turkey. Other experiences, however, are framed in a more conventional Orientalist narrative, bracketed by lengthy quotations from Lady Mary Wortley-Montagu's letters. About her own bath, she writes:

> [The hamam attendant] scrubs me with a rough linen mitt, rinses me, washes my ears, between my toes. She holds my head against her ample breasts, which fall to her waist, her nipples the color of tobacco, while she soaps me down again, and slings a cotton pillowcase fluffy with suds across my back. She pummels me into a state of bliss as I lie on the warm marble bellystone. Shafts of bright light stream into the dark interior of the hamam and I feel as if I were swimming in steam and heat and light.[32]

Thus, Milford takes up two of the conventional themes: the sensual indulgence of the bathing procedure, and the fat old hamam attendant with tobacco-coloured skin – a reference to Pardoe's description? Devoid of naked bathers, the accompanying photograph features two men sitting on a marble bench, wrapped in towels from head to knee, while a small

Figure 7.4 Nancy Milford, 'Bathed in Tradition', *New York Times Magazine Supplement: The Sophisticated Traveler*, 27 February 2000.

medallion depicts a detail of a hamam scene from an old engraving, of a group of women wrapped in *peştemals* from head to toe and wearing high clogs entering the hot room (Figure 7.4).

Once readers of essays such as those in *The Sophisticated Traveler* have decided to follow the call of exotic locales, they are likely to read further information in the most powerful sight marker – that is, the tourist guide books. In John Urry's words:

> the contemporary tourist [is] a modern pilgrim, carrying guidebooks as devotional texts. What matters is what people are told they are seeing. The fame of the object becomes its meaning. There is thus a ceremonial agenda, in which it is established what we should see and sometimes the order in which they should be seen.[33]

Guide books shape tourists' perceptions of their destination by selecting sites, the narrative voice they employ, and the interpretative context into which they inscribe the sites. It is through the prism of the latter two that the following section will examine the *Eyewitness Travel Guide Istanbul*.[34]

On the streets of Istanbul's touristic neighbourhoods in the early 2000s, copies of the *Eyewitness Travel Guide Istanbul* – 'the guides that show you what others only tell you', as the cover page promises – were a frequent sight, tucked into coat pockets and backpacks, and nestled in the hands of foreign visitors trying to orient themselves. In keeping with the promise on the cover page, the book is abundantly illustrated with thumbnail-sized images interspersed throughout the text. The text equally promises to 'set Istanbul in its historical and cultural context',[35] and it does so with cultural sensitivity and in a manner similar to art history textbooks, with the help of colourful architectural drawings and informational text boxes. The topic of Turkish baths receives a full-page treatment with ample illustrations (Figure 7.5). The centre of the page features a schematic drawing that explains the architectural layout of, and thereby indirectly the bathers' movement through, hamams. The author has foregone the addition of Orientalist paintings; rather, the bathers shown are men scrubbing, massaging and reading a newspaper after the bath. Only the illustration titled 'The Body Massage' conveys sensual pleasure and abandon, with a bather sprawled on the *göbektaşı* in front of the hot room's light-dappled marble interior. The brief text claims that 'no trip to Istanbul is complete without an hour or two spent in a Turkish bath (*hamam*), which will leave your whole body feeling rejuvenated'.[36] The imperative tone points to MacCannell's 'moral structure' of tourism, as mentioned above.

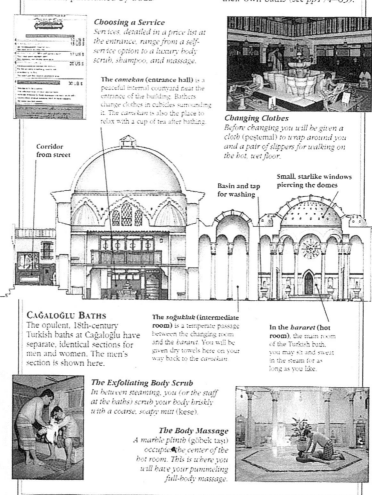

Turkish Baths

No TRIP TO ISTANBUL is complete without an hour or two spent in a Turkish bath *(hamam)*, which will leave your whole body feeling rejuvenated. Turkish baths differ little from the baths of ancient Rome, from which they derive, except there is no pool of cold water to plunge into at the end.

A full service will entail a period of relaxation in the steam-filled hot room, punctuated by bouts of vigorous soaping and massaging. There is no time limit, but allow at least an hour and a half for a leisurely bath. Towels and soap will be provided, but you can take special toiletries with you. Two historic baths located in the old city, Çemberlitaş *(see p81)* and Cağaloğlu (illustrated below), are used to catering to foreign tourists. Some luxury hotels have their own baths *(see pp174–85)*.

Ornate wash basin

Choosing a Service
Services, detailed in a price list at the entrance, range from a self-service option to a luxury body scrub, shampoo, and massage.

The *camekan* (entrance hall) is a peaceful internal courtyard near the entrance of the building. Bathers change clothes in cubicles surrounding it. The *camekan* is also the place to relax with a cup of tea after bathing.

Changing Clothes
Before changing you will be given a cloth (peştemal) *to wrap around you and a pair of slippers for walking on the hot, wet floor.*

Corridor from street

Basin and tap for washing

Small, starlike windows piercing the domes

CAĞALOĞLU BATHS
The opulent, 18th-century Turkish baths at Cağaloğlu have separate, identical sections for men and women. The men's section is shown here.

The *soğukluk* (intermediate room) is a temperate passage between the changing room and the *hararet*. You will be given dry towels here on your way back to the *camekan*.

In the *hararet* (hot room), the main room of the Turkish bath, you may sit and sweat in the steam for as long as you like.

The Exfoliating Body Scrub
In between steaming, you (or the staff at the baths) scrub your body briskly with a coarse, soapy mitt (kese).

The Body Massage
A marble plinth (göbek taşı) *occupies the center of the hot room. This is where you will have your pummeling full-body massage.*

Figure 7.5 Hamams as introduced in the *Eyewitness Travel Guide Istanbul*, 1999. *Source*: DK Publishers.

A small text box about Çemberlitaş Hamamı can be found several pages ahead, next to the description of Constantine's Column in front of its entrance:

> Next to the Constantine's Column, on the corner of Divanyolu Caddesi, stand the Çemberlitaş Baths. This splendid hamam complex was commissioned by Nur Banu, wife of Selim II, and built in 1584 to a plan by the great Sinan. Although the original women's section no longer survives, the baths still have separate facilities for men and women. The staff is used to foreign visitors, so this is a good place for your first experience in a Turkish bath.[37]

While enframing the sight in an objective narrative of splendour and significance as architectural heritage, the text also creates a cultural distance between visitor and sight, implying that a hamam visit will be an experience so exotic that it requires an initiation, much like a mysterious ritual.

In summary, although it may be too reductive to claim that all tourists' perceptions of the hamam converge in a single vantage point, the Orientalist enframing narrative, both textual and pictorial, with its various sub-themes still constitutes a strong determinant. Among these count: architectural splendour, the female bathers' beauty (with its counter-point of the fat, old and/or dark-skinned attendant), luxury and sensual indulgence (with its counter-point of unpleasant heat and rough massage) and homoeroticism. The preceding discussion has aimed to show that some of these tropes, which can be traced back as far as the sixteenth century, and maybe even earlier, still continue to influence the perception of the hamam as a cultural phenomenon at the turn of the twenty-first century. Much like Lady Mary Wortley-Montagu, foreign visitors expect to experience in the bathhouse the sensual Orient, and may be disappointed when it fails to deliver the luxurious indulgence that such a representation promises.[38] The hamam's representations within the hermeneutic cycle of tourism also promises an 'authentic' experience of Turkish culture. It is here that foreign tourists literally come into the most intimate contact with locals and can participate in what they perceive as authentic cultural practice. According to Jonathan Culler:

> [t]he tourist is interested in everything as a sign of itself, an instance of a cultural practice ... All over the world the unsung armies of semioticians, the tourists, are fanning out in search of the signs of Frenchness, typical Italian behavior, exemplary Oriental scenes, typical American thruways, traditional English pubs; and, deaf to the natives' explanations that thruways are the most efficient way to go from one place to another, or that pubs are just convenient places to meet your friends and have a drink, or that gondolas are the natural

way to get around in a city full of canals, tourists persist in regarding these objects and practices as cultural signs.[39]

Thus, tourists see hamams not as places where one simply bathes in the absence of running water in the home and simultaneously socialises, but as signs of Turkishness, regardless of the fact that many locals have never set foot in one, or may even regard it derogatorily, as Milford remarks in her essay 'Bathed in Tradition'. The hermeneutic cycle continues to revolve and reinforce itself around monuments such as Çemberlitaş Hamamı, while the life of most locals moves along a trajectory that no longer intersects with bathhouses.

A New Identity IV: Object of Ottomania

Among the local Turkish visitors, five different groups are discernible based on the frequency of bathhouse visits. The first group entirely shuns hamams, either claiming that they are dirty and unhygienic places where one could catch all sorts of diseases, or harbouring objections to nudity in public, even in a gender-segregated environment. While also never having visited a hamam, the second group feels a sense of embarassment about not being familiar with this emblem of Turkish cultural heritage, with which tourists are better acquainted than they as locals. The third group encompasses individuals who have visited a hamam together with elderly relatives at least once during their childhood, but who have not returned since because they cannot find the appropriate social framework for doing so. The fourth group can be defined as 'internal tourists' – a term coined by Erik Cohen to mean someone who 'travel[s] within the boundaries of one's own country as against travel abroad'.[40] Here, I wish to expand this term to denote a person who physically remains in the same location, yet mentally travels into the past as if it was a foreign country.[41] They frequent the bath for pleasure (*keyif*) or nostalgia (*nostalji*) several times a year, stating that the hamam visit makes them feel connected to their cultural heritage and history. For the fifth and final group, the hamam visit constitutes at least a monthly (if not bi-weekly or even weekly) routine. Members of this group believe that they can get properly clean only from a good rub-down; therefore, washing in the bathhouse makes up a part of their regular regime to maintain physical well-being.

It is especially the internal tourists who are of interest in the present context, because they identify Çemberlitaş Hamamı as a symbol of Ottoman architectural and cultural heritage. A closer look at their motivations and the enframing narratives available to them will shed light on the dynamics of the Ottoman past's popular reception. Internal tourism very much borrows from foreign cultural tourism, which depends on the commodification and consumption of sites, monuments, objects and performances. Much like foreign visitors, internal tourists follow the tips presented in travel and lifestyle magazines, consult guide books and watch relevant feature films, documentaries and television shows. Hence, they perceive their own culture through the epistemological framework inherent in tourism, including its exoticising, Otherising and Orientalising underpinnings. The resulting radical departure from the locals' everyday life creates a considerable social and psychological distance between the host environment and the guest, even if internal tourists may travel only a short bus ride to the site they are visiting.

As observed by Albers and James, 'the media produced by local ethnic groups follow many of the same kinds of conventionalised patterns that have dominated travel discourse in the past …'[42] This is certainly the case with the supplement to a 2002 special issue of *Atlas*, the Turkish version of the similarly very popular *National Geographic*. The eighteen-page booklet, titled 'Tastes, Places: Living History', features on its cover page a photograph of a hamam's misty hot room.[43] In addition to sections with recommendations for museums, restaurants, coffee houses and shops, a major portion of this guide is devoted to hamams, with Çemberlitaş Hamamı listed as one of the six recommended establishments. The accompanying photographs show a bather lying in carefree and sensual abandon underneath the dome of a steamy hot room, while the running taps of an ornamented marble basin suggest the luxury of hot water in unlimited quantities (Figure 7.6).

Another magazine, *Cinetempo*, in December 2002, also included a supplement with an article on hamams, titled 'A New Trend in the City: Hamam'.[44] This article focuses not on historic hamams; rather, it lists Turkish-style baths in various five-star hotels throughout Istanbul and recommends treatments such as 'hamam therapy' with coconut oil and 'hot stone therapy', which were never part of traditional Ottoman bathing culture. The accompanying photograph employs the iconography of Ingres' and Gerôme's bathing odalisques: a half-naked woman sits on the *göbektaşı*, facing a tiled marble basin with taps running (Figure 7.7). She turns her back to the viewer, while combing her wet hair with her fingers. Several colourful, gold-ornamented drinking glasses, a kettle on a tray and two soap containers next to her add a few picturesque set-pieces. Since a visit to the advertised hotel hamams costs between US$20 and US$50 even without a massage, the potential clientele includes only the affluent with both leisure time and sufficient disposable income. Hotel

Figure 7.6 Cover of a travel supplement aimed at Turkish visitors. *Source*: Zihli, *Atlas İstanbul Rehberi*, 2000.

hamams also create a bridge between the first and fourth groups – those who avoid historic bathhouses for hygienic reasons and internal tourists in search of a bathing experience specific to Ottoman-Turkish culture. With the emergence of hotel hamams, the experience is thus tamed and transplanted into a context perceived as 'modern' and 'hygienic'.

The internal tourists following these recommendations to visit specific historic or hotel hamams participate in a phenomenon that has been termed 'Ottomania'. While the founders of the Turkish Republic in the 1920s and 1930s recast the Ottoman past as an archaic Other to the modern state, since the 1980s that same past has been recast yet again. Rejection has given way to nostalgia. In the political arena, where the phenomenon has been called 'neo-Ottomanism', this has meant an emphasis on multiculturalism, tolerance, cosmopolitanism and a neo-imperialist foreign policy that aims to eliminate economic boundaries with countries in the formerly Ottoman space.[45] This political stance first emerged under the right-of-centre, neo-liberal Prime Minister Turgut Özal (1983–1989) and was further reified under the Istanbul mayorship of the Islamist Welfare Party (*Refah Partisi*, RP) of the mid-1990s. It has gained even more currency since 2002, when

224

Figure 7.7 Page of a magazine supplement aimed at Turkish consumers. *Source*: Balcı, 'Şehirde Yeni Moda: Hamam', 2002.

the Islamist Justice and Development Party (*Adalet ve Kalkınma Partisi*, AKP) rose to power.

'Ottomania', then, refers to a nostalgia for the Ottoman past in the cultural arena, in particular the consumption of high as well popular culture – in Potuoğlu-Cook's words, 'a classed and gendered self-Orientalism particular to the post-1980s Turkish free-market economy'.[46] Museums established by wealthy industrialists, such as the Sakıp Sabancı Museum and the Sadberk Hanım Museum of the Koç family, exhibit their collections of Ottoman art objects, while less expensive antiques decorate middle-class homes. Successful TV shows such as *Muhteşem Yüzyıl* (*Magnificent Century*) and many of the novels by the Nobel Prize-winning author Orhan Pamuk are set in the Ottoman past.[47] There has been a considerable increase in popular interest in historical scholarship, catered to by books such as *Bilinmeyen Osmanlı* (*The Unknown Ottoman*) and Ottoman-language courses offered by various institutions outside of universities.[48] Workshops and courses in arts such as marbling paper, miniature painting and calligraphy have mushroomed. Expensive designer shops in up-scale malls sell clothing and decorative objects with Ottoman themes. Gourmet restaurants serve Ottoman cuisine, and urban entertainment includes Anatolian folk dance shows, classical Ottoman music and Sufi electronica concerts. Belly dance has become a 'gentrified' art form acceptable even for urban professional women.[49] In Istanbul's urban space, newly restored architectural monuments glisten, and entire historic neighbourhoods are being renovated to reflect the city's *belle epoque* and have become subject to gentrification,[50] while the architecture of newly constructed gated communities make explicit references to Ottoman vernacular buildings. The meaning attached to the truly manic consumption of all things Ottoman, however, is far from monolithic, as Kasaba and Bozdoğan assert:

> Given that both secular Turks and Islamists look to the Ottoman past, the re-appropriation of Turkey's Ottoman heritage does not, by itself, mark a particular ideological direction. 'Ottoman heritage' is reconstructed by many different groups for various ends, often with different consequences. Islamists celebrate the Islamic glories of the Ottoman Empire and see Islam as the defining element of Ottoman culture, while nationalists take pride in the Turkic origins of the Ottomans . . . And of course, there are others who turn to Ottomania with no deeper motivation than to profit from it by cultivating and catering to this fashion.[51]

As for the readily visible consequences for Istanbul's historic hamams, several bathhouses have been restored and are operating once again, such as the Kılıç Ali Paşa Hamamı, or will soon again be functional, such as the Küçük Mustafa Paşa Hamamı. Several decades ago a kind of monument despised and demolished by the Republican elites, Ottomania has made it now chic to turn them into cafés – such as one coffeeshop on İstiklal Street, where the dressing room's dome now sits inside a modern building and necessitates that café tables be arranged around it – and night clubs – such as the one, aptly named Hammam, in the bathhouse of the Sepetçiler Kasrı (built in 1591, renovated in 1739) on the seashore below the Topkapı Palace.

Internal tourists may visit a hamam to experience what they perceive as a religiously inflected Ottoman tradition, or they may emphasise ethno-nationalist pride in the concept of 'Turkish bath'.[52] Internal tourists partaking in the recently gentrified cultural practice of bathing in a hamam now have a vast array from which to select: expensive bathing packages and therapies at hotel hamams and spas (such as the Sanda Day Spa in the İstinye Park shopping mall),[53] or newly renovated historic buildings in neighbourhoods that range from exclusively local, over tourist-dominated, to gentrified. Çemberlitaş Hamamı is only one among many choices accessible to locals in search of objects of Ottomania.

A New Identity V: The Hamam Managers' and Employees' Perspectives

As discursive spaces, tourist attractions are shaped not only by the narratives with which foreign and domestic or internal tourists approach them, but also by the ways in which local stake-holders – such as entrepreneurs, urban planners and politicians – enframe and commodify them. The argument that local populations are hardly able to withstand or subvert the romanticised imagery imposed upon them by travel agents and other middlemen of tourism, as advanced by Ira Silver, therefore requires a serious re-evaluation, as the case of Çemberlitaş Hamamı will demonstrate.[54] While its business managers do need to contend with the expectations of foreign and domestic/internal tourists desiring an exotic experience with an Oriental Other or an Orientalised Past, they also have at their disposal a number of avenues to shape existing narratives in line with their own vision or offer alternative ones.

One important, and in its global reach, very effective avenue, rather novel for bathhouses in Turkey in the early 2000s, consists of the Cemberlitaş Hamam's website, to be discussed in the following section (Figure 7.8). In addition to its digital presence on the internet, the hamam's management at that time also advertised its services by means of a brochure available at the bathhouse entrance, in tourism offices and hotel receptions in the neighbourhood. The cover features an architectural drawing with a cross-section of the building above the title 'Çemberlitaş Bath: The Original Turkish Bath by Master Architect Sinan' and the print illustration of the Divan Yolu from Julia Pardoe's travelogue (the only known European depiction of the hamam, or rather a part thereof); the text inside provides brief historical information and a description of the bathing procedure, in English, French, German and Spanish (Figure 7.9). The accompanying photographs focus on the building inscription, the dressing rooms in both sections and the men's hot room. Only two photographs illustrate the bathing procedure, and only male bathers populate the scenes. Although the images do advertise the pleasure of bathing, the pictures in their indvidual as well as combined message circumvent the iconography of the female bathing beauty and instead firmly emplace this pleasure within a historically significant architectural context.

In 2003, the management of Çemberlitaş Hamamı added a novel avenue to communicate with its Turkish customers when it launched a campaign to have bathers register as regulars on a list. Registered customers were then sent letters and offered plastic customer cards resembling credit

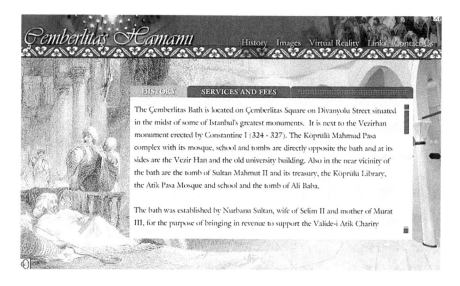

Figure 7.8 Webpages of Çemberlitaş Hamamı in 2004.
Source: www.cemberlitashamami.com.tr, artwork in the public domain.

cards, which would guarantee them bathing fee discounts (Figure 7.10). The letter's text read:

Çemberlitaş Hamamı was built and endowed by Nurbanu Sultan, the wife of Sultan Selim II and mother of Sultan Murat III, in order to generate revenue for the Atik Valide mosque complex in Toptaşı in Üsküdar. According to the *tezkiret'ül-mimarin* [Sinan's autobiographical treatise], it is a work of the architect Sinan. As can be gathered from the inscription, the hamam's construction date is 992/1584.

Çemberlitaş Hamamı was planned as a double hamam [with two units] completely equal to each other and [placed] side by side. The women's dressing room was partly cut off during the widening of the Divanyolu Caddesi (1868). The women's dressing room has been used as storage, rug shop and restaurant, [while] the hot room was used for paper storage. When the hamam was restored in 1972–73, the women's hot room, which had been used as paper storage, was included into the men's section. With the decision of the Committee for the Protection of Cultural and Natural Heritage, dated 13 July 1993 and numbered 4737 Istanbul 1, the hamam's women's section has been returned to its old function and put into sevice; the dressing room has been temporarily constructed out of two corridors. The decision of the abovementioned institution, dated 27 July 2000 and numbered 12065, has given permission to return the women's hot room and dressing room to their original form.

Together with Çemberlitaş Hamamı's restoration project, a sauna, a jacuzzi, a beauty salon, a restaurant and cafeteria, a gym and a section for massages with lotions and special oils will be integrated in a way that does not interefere with the hamam's authentic atmosphere and history.

With the card which we are sending you, you will be able to profit from fee discounts and several other advantages in the hamam and the sections to be added. The card you have in hand now will later be exchanged for a digital card.

Sincerely,
Çemberlitaş Hamamı

The carefully worded letter emphasises the hamam's historic past reaching back to the sixteenth century, its connection to an important (if popularly little known) mosque complex, and its status as the work of an architect who has been cast as national genius. It also refers to the mutilation of the nineteenth century and the restoration efforts of the twentieth century, ensuring that the latter gain the necessary legitimacy through the inclusion of specific legal decisions by the Committee for the Protection of Cultural and Natural Heritage. At the same time, the management presents the planned additions of facilities such as a sauna, jacuzzi, and gym as entirely compatible with the hamam's history and identities. In doing so, the managers imply that the hamam, in spite of its historicity, is not a relic of the past, but that it can play a sustained role for Turkish visitors who perceive themselves as leading a modern lifestyle.

The letterhead, the customer card, and the managers' business cards all displayed a corporate logo that had been recently changed: a dark blue sphere hints at the pierced dome of the hot room, with light rays entering

Figure 7.9 Customer brochure of Çemberlitaş Hamamı. *Source*: Public domain.

Figure 7.10 Customer card for Çemberlitaş Hamamı. *Source*: Courtesy of Çemberlitaş Hamamı's management.

Ruşen BALTACI

Vezirhan Caddesi No.8 Çemberlitaş İstanbul / Türkiye
Tel: (90 212) 522 79 74 · 520 18 50 · 520 15 33   Fax: (90 212) 511 25 35
www.cemberlitasbamami.com.tr   e-mail: contact@cemberlitasbamami.com.tr

Figure 7.11 Business card of Çemberlitaş Hamamı. *Source*: Courtesy of Çemberlitaş Hamamı's management.

(Figures 7.10, 7.11). The sphere's lower edge consists of a silhouette of Istanbul's skyline, with the domes and multiple minarets of two mosques; underneath, 'Çemberlitaş Hamamı' and 'The Turkish Bath' identify the monument. Through both text – not just 'a', but 'the' Turkish Bath – and image – the Istanbul skyline not above, but *below* the expanse of the hamam's dome – the logo's design suggests that Çemberlitaş Hamamı encapsulates the essence of the city's architectural heritage and bathing tradition. The logo also occupies part of the customer card, as it is super-imposed over an old sepia-tone photograph of the Divan Yolu, with the mutilated side of the bathhouse visible.

Rather than falling back on the Orientalist iconography of bathing beau-ties or the trope of sensual indulgence, this choice of imagery privileges the theme of the hamam's great architectural value in its historic context over any exotic or erotic content. This choice paralleled the message projected to the foreign customers by means of the printed brochure (and the website to be discussed below), and it also would have appealed to the type of Turkish customers whom the managers hoped to attract. That attracting Turkish customers was of great commercial significance found expression not only in the efforts to gather, monitor and maintain a base of regulars, but also in the words of one interviewee: one of the managers openly stated that a great number of local visitors enhanced the hamam's value and popularity also among foreign tourists, because they usually like to patronise establishments that Turks themselves prefer, due to the 'local colour' that they impart.[55]

In stark contrast to the management's narrative centred on architectural heritage as a site for the traditional bathing procedure stand the narra-tives of the employees who come into closest contact with the bathers, with further distinctions observable between male and female attend-ants. Between October 2001 and February 2003, seven female attendants worked at Çemberlitaş Hamamı. None of them had had much schooling beyond primary education, and most of them worked outside the home out of necessity rather than by choice. In some cases, they even supported their nuclear family with their income, because the husband was unemployed. It thus came as no surprise that in the countless casual conversations and semi-structured interviews I conducted with them in the women's dress-ing room, the two most often recurring themes consisted of family and economic hardship. The latter was intricately linked to repetitive discus-sions about the number of customers and the reasons behind the dwindling number of foreign visitors, especially in the immediate aftermath of 9/11.

While the attendants had a vague idea about Çemberlitaş Hamamı's his-toric value, none of them attached great significance to it. The 56-year-old Gülşen, who at that point had worked there for twelve years, responded to the question 'You know that this is a historical hamam; is this a special place for you, or just a workplace?' with the following statement: 'Well, for me the hamam is work, earning money.'[56] Since the women were com-puter illiterate and without access to the internet, they first learned about

Çemberlitaş Hamamı's website when, together with other source material I had gathered, I brought printouts to the women's section and asked about their opinion. All of them agreed that the website was 'a wonderful thing', because it would bring more customers and hence more income through bathing and massage fees. All of them also emphatically talked about the importance of providing good service and achieving customer satisfaction, whether among local or foreign visitors, so that they would return and bring friends, too. Underlining that they liked to have local and foreign visitors alike, they also admitted that their lack of foreign-language skills sometimes made dealing with tourists more difficult – a difficulty that the management attempted to remove by hiring an English-speaking female employee to assist with communication, and by explaining the bathing procedure on the website and in the printed brochure ahead of time.

Due to the gendered nature of the hamam, my contact with the male attendants was much more limited; they elected to have the longest-serving *tellak* represent them in an extended interview.[57] The 30-year-old Sefer, originally from Tokat, had worked at Çemberlitaş Hamamı for fourteen years and showed great enthusiasm about several aspects of his profession. Taking pride in his skills as a masseur, which he had honed over a total of sixteen years on the job, he talked at length about the physiological effects of bathing and receiving a massage in a traditional bathhouse. For him, the hamam was 'an addiction, like cigarettes; once you have tried it, you can't leave it'. Upon my question as to whether the hamam's historic value was important to him, he emphatically nodded: 'Of course, of course.' In order to be able to draw a meaningful comparison to Gülşen's perspective, I followed up: 'So it is not just a place to earn money?' Sefer elaborated: 'Well, the special thing about it is this. It is historic, and it is beautiful. For example, the domes are high. Because of that, one doesn't feel uncomfortable from the heat inside. Because of that, there is no better place to relax than this [hamam], I think.' Sefer repeatedly stated that he thought Çemberlitaş Hamamı to be the best of all bathhouses in Istanbul, articulating a link between the bathing experience and the built environment where it takes place, in a way that Gülşen did not. The difference between local and foreign customers featured in his answers only indirectly, when he stated that Turkish visitors were more familiar with the hamam's customs and traditions and therefore more likely to appreciate the *tellak*'s massage, whether symbolically or financially, in the form of tips. Sefer's perspective was broader than Gülşen's in that it encompassed the hamam not only as a source of income and pride in the quality of services they offered, but also great pride about working in a historic hamam that through its architectural qualities enhanced the bathers' experiences.

A New Identity VI: The Digital Age

The end of my research in 2004 coincided with a time period when the internet became much more widely accessible and a stronger everyday presence in Turkey. It also coincided with a moment a few short years before the rise of the smart phone with its drastic consequences for communications, information-gathering, knowledge-sharing, the presentation of heritage sites and tourist attractions, as well as the presentation of tourists' and visitors' selves in relation to the sites they visit. This moment therefore presents a convenient break in the history of Çemberlitaş Hamamı's reception, which will serve as a kind of endpoint to its life story as it is told here, but not before touching upon one of the earlier versions of the hamam's website as an emblem of its newest, online identity. Furthermore, the following paragraphs will speculate on the potentialities and pitfalls of digital media, as applied in the cultural heritage sector and as they may shape the monument's fate in the foreseeable future.[58]

Through the 2003/4 version of Çemberlitaş Hamamı's website, the management attempted to impart a carefully constructed vision of the establishment's identity, in images as well as in Turkish, English and Spanish text.[59] A simple, monochromatic title page centred on the words 'Çemberlitaş Hamamı: The Turkish Historical Bath' invites visitors to click on the desired language, redirecting them to the website proper while the download icon of a schematic *kurna* is slowly being filled from two taps. The background image merges an excerpt from Thomas Allom's engraving of a male bather wrapped in towels, reclining and smoking a long-stemmed pipe, with a digital reconstruction of Çemberlitaş Hamamı's men's hot room (Figure 7.8, above). The upper border between the background image and the headline (including the links to further pages) consists of a *çintemani* design, a reference to imperial Ottoman visual culture that is easily recognisable to Turkish website visitors.[60] The page titled 'History' contained a brief essay on the monument's architectural features by Onur Yalçın and Ali Dereli, the architects responsible for the most recent restoration. The page titled 'Images' allowed website visitors to browse through a total of thirty-four pictures, ranging in content from historic photographs of the hamam's exterior (four), digital images projecting the planned appearance post-renovation (fifteen), photographs of the current interior without human protagonists (two), photographs of male bathers washing against a dramatically illuminated background (twelve), and one single photograph of a female bather viewed from the back through a blurry lens, framed by the door of one of the hot room's marble dividing walls. The page titled 'Virtual Reality' allowed users to enter the 360-degree view of both men's and women's dressing and hot rooms, in their projected post-renovation state. Through their decisions surrounding the website's content, the managers without a doubt emphasised Çemberlitaş Hamamı's identity as a historic monument of great architectural value and their contributions to the preservation of Ottoman cultural heritage. Yet narratives of the hamam as a place of 'Oriental delights' and exotic as much as erotic pleasure – so crucial for its identity as tourist attraction – needed to be reckoned with as well. This is achieved by giving some limited space to Thomas Allom's engraving in the Orientalist tradition as background image. The iconography of the female bathing beauty received only a small, abashed nod in a single, hazy photograph that evokes the bathing odalisques of Ingres and Gerôme; instead, male bathers resting on the *göbektaşı*, being slathered with soap foam or receiving a massage promise the sensory pleasure of washing in the hamam.

Much like Çemberlitaş Hamamı was once part of an extensive network of monuments and locations linked through Nurbanu Sultan's endowment, so it is now linked to many other sites on the worldwide web – such as Google, Wikipedia, YouTube and TripAdvisor. The instant availability of information, as well as the capability to easily compare the information retrieved, thanks to the smart phones of potential visitors standing outside the bathhouse means that decision-making processes about whether to enter this or another hamam have changed. Rather than allowing the monument itself to draw them in, many visitors now experience it in mediated form, even while standing on the sidewalk in front of it, as they quickly research its history, the services offered, the fee, and the evaluations and comments that previous visitors have left, for example, on TripAdvisor or on www.hamamlar.com, a Turkish site dedicated exclusively to information on bathhouses and user-provided recommendations and opinions. Evaluation mechanisms of this kind make it even more crucial for the hamam management to not only operate the establishment in the best possible way, but also to carefully construct and manage their online identity and presentation so as to gain a competitive advantage over other bathhouses.

Both tourism and cultural heritage sectors have been greatly transformed with the now ubiquitous use of digital media content – which I take to mean any audio, photo, video or text content that has been encoded in order to make it machine-readable and to transfer it over networks consisting of computers and hand-held digital devices, in such a way that groups of users can interact with the content and each other. The above-mentioned online self-presentation and knowledge-sharing is merely one facet; according to Kalay's more general definition, in the heritage sector, 'digital media are used to create cultural content through scanning, modeling and archiving; to manage the content through powerful search engines and database management tools; and to disseminate the content through the world wide web to audiences who otherwise might never be able to access it'.[61] Archaeologists, art historians, architects and urban planners are now able to use laser scanning to capture monuments and sites, to create 3D models and reconstruct buildings and even entire cities in digital format, for purposes of analysis, interpretation and preservation. Virtual reality models allow users to move, in real time, through a digital environment; in the case of *Pure Land: Augmented Reality Edition*, the virtual reality model has replaced the actual monument, since the exhibited Cave 220 in Dunhuang, China, is no longer accessible due to issues of conservation.[62] In cases where computer-generated images can be viewed in situ, so as to combine real-time and virtual experiences, we speak of 'augmented reality'; this has been beautifully employed at Cluny where the third church of the Abbey – dating to the twelfth century, but destroyed during the French Revolution – has been digitally 'reborn', so that visitors today can compare past and present states with the help of terminals.[63] Other uses of information and communications technology at cultural heritage sites include mobile device-based guides, virtual museums, and digital archives and databases, as they are now also part of the websites of major museums around the world.

How had digital media already shaped the life-story of Çemberlitaş Hamamı by 2004, and what else is to be expected? What potential does the digital age hold for this monument, and what dangers can be detected? As can be gathered from the description of the hamam's website, the section titled 'Virtual Reality' shared the 3D model generated for the purposes of restoration with a larger public, thus demonstrating the preparations for and processes of such an undertaking. The emphasis on science – specifically, computer science, civil engineering and mathematics – that this 3D model imparts legitimised the work of the architects and communicated the care and attention that the hamam management bestows on the monument. While at present I am not aware of any actively working tour-guide mobile applications that allow foreign and/or local cell phone users easy access to interpretative guidance to the history of Çemberlitaş Hamamı and its neighbourhood, such digital media content could certainly be of great advantage, if done well. For instance, the use of on-site digital media content in the form of augmented reality at a cultural heritage site has been proven to result in an enhanced sense of place and greater place attachment; in a case study conducted in Taiwan, participants using a mobile augmented reality application strongly felt that the site thus contextualised was unique and therefore worthy of preservation, in contrast to participants who visited the site without using such technology.[64] The creation of better informed and hence also more interested resident stake-holders in Istanbul would most certainly benefit the preservation and maintenance of its architectural and urban heritage, especially beyond the most obvious examples on the beaten tourist path.

For scholars, the use of augmented or virtual reality in the quest to reconstruct historic monuments, sites and even entire cities has become quite commonplace, and major problematic issues – such as the misleading aesthetisation of models, dealing with missing data, reconciling contradictory evidence and presenting convergent interpretations – have been discussed and mostly resolved.[65] In fact, digital media offer many opportunities to tell narratives not in the generally linear mode determined by the parameters of scholarly publications, but organised and linked in non-linear ways, such as tree structures and arrays of categories.[66] In more concrete terms, an expansive virtual reality model of Çemberlitaş Hamamı may allow the user to move through the building, click on a decorative element such as the epigraphic panels in the men's hot room and be presented at once with several text boxes of the transcription, the translation and more than one interpretation of the text's meaning, potentially even contradictory ones. Clicking on an architectural element such as the *göbektaşı* could lead the user to a text box explaining its function as well as an overlaid image of the older version as it was recorded by Glück in the early twentieth century. On a larger scale, a virtual reality model of the hamam and its neighbourhood may allow users to move backward and forward in time, while removing and adding subtractions and accretions to the monument – such as the cut-off corner and the shops enveloping it – as well as the surrounding buildings – such as the Vezir Han. The ability to visualise the dynamic nature of the monument and its environment's history and to render obvious various linkages are likely to garner new research questions; for lay users, the more nuanced understanding derived from such a visualisation may lead not only to an enhanced sense of place, as mentioned above, but also to a greater awareness of how different pieces of evidence – sometimes in alignment, sometimes in contradiction – contribute to the making of a historical narrative.[67]

Yet a technology-based engagement with a monument such as Çemberlitaş Hamamı is also fraught with several problems. First among these ranks a practical concern, especially from the viewpoint of the hamam's management: that of expense and profitability. While augmented reality has been touted as providing enormous opportunities for a relatively small investment, as creating new value through a richer and memorable experience, and as giving a competitive advantage to the relevant heritage site,[68] there also exists evidence as to the opposite: statistical data collected for the National Awareness, Attitudes and Usage Study (NAAU) about the benefits of online resources and mobile applications provided by cultural institutions seems to indicate that it is not the availability of apps – which only a very small percentage of visitors (about 5 per cent) uses on site – that makes for a satisfactory visitor experience, but human interaction.[69] Most online knowledge-gathering is still done on the world wide web, and before rather than during the visit. Based on these data, Çemberlitaş Hamamı's management should focus on maintaining and improving their web presence – which may still very well include a virtual reality model – and the quality of the human interactions within the bathhouse, rather than commissioning any mobile applications. It is the social nature of the hamam visit, and not the digital simulacrum of its architectural container, that will continue to form the most important facet of Çemberlitaş Hamamı's identity and attraction.

Related to this very point is the second problem – that is, an exaggerated focus on the digital media tools rather than the 'real thing' and the authentic experience. As Bernadette Flynn expresses it aptly:

> [i]n this era of digital technology and connectivity, access to heritage is increasingly mediated through the consumption of signs, electronic images, and simulacra. In virtual heritage, an algorithmically accurate large-scale 3D model of a cathedral or castle is taken as the hallmark of authenticity. However, the reduction of the monument or artifact to visual stimulation disrupts its connection to material evidence and thus to history. What is lost is the aura of the well-crafted object or the exquisitely designed monument that resonates with the memory trace of previous civilizations.[70]

Tourists standing in front of monuments or museum displays, but completely engrossed in their smartphones, either skimming through information or posting hastily snapped selfies documenting their visit, rather than carefully looking at what they have travelled to see, have become a familiar sight. However, especially a hamam cannot be properly understood and contextualised by virtually navigating through a digital reconstruction, no matter how masterfully done; rather, one must walk through the dressing and washing rooms while feeling the changes in temperature and the humidity, touching the warm marble, and experiencing the scratchy scrubbing glove on one's bare skin.

Another point, connected to the issue of authenticity, consists in the fact that few end-users of digital media content are aware of how their own perceptual apparatus and the aesthetics of virtual 3D models and the like shape what they see. Their 'period eye' diverges greatly from that of a seventeenth-century Istanbulite, for instance.[71] Before the more widespread embrace of 'Western' mathematical science in the nineteenth century, Ottoman notions of space did not rest on the Cartesian coordinate system that underlies computer-generated 3D modelling, as the visual modes in which architectural, urban and geographical space were depicted in Ottoman paintings clearly demonstrates.[72] Art historians have long reflected on the culturally conditioned nature of the way we see, and setting out from their vantage point, one may discover creative ways to employ virtual reality – such as integrating Ottoman maps and miniatures – so as to create also among a lay audience an awareness of historical visual modes, an awareness that scratches at the privileged position of a 'scientifically objective', computer-generated image.

As one of the three hamams of Istanbul most frequented by tourists,[73] Çemberlitaş Hamamı has not only continued to work vigorously beyond the life span that the early Republican reforming elites would have envisioned for it, but it has even experienced a second spring through the addition of a new identity – that of tourist attraction. Where it was once part of a family network of empire-wide reach due to the economic links created by Nurbanu Sultan's endowment, it has now become inscribed into an even more expansive capitalist network, one of global reach, whether physically or online. In the world of post-industrial capitalism, Istanbul has begun to compete on a 'global market of cityhood',[74] and for the purposes of this competition cultural heritage needs to be displayed and promoted as a marketable commodity.[75] Based on a century-old, but endlessly reified, Orientalist narrative with its various sub-themes of architectural magnificence, sensual indulgence and eroticism, foreign tourists seek to purchase the experience of the 'authentic' cultural practice of bathing in a hamam. Needless to say, like in centuries past, profit continues to be of paramount importance to operate Çemberlitaş Hamamı as a viable business, for managers as well as employees, and the global tourism market has added a welcome clientele (and profit). Global tourism has also created the need to manage expectations resulting from Orientalist narratives and to maintain a balance between foreign and local visitors by equally catering to the latter. As the hamam has become instrumental in tourism development, conversely tourism has become instrumental in its heritagisation.[76] Tourism's role in the promotion of heritage becomes even more evident when contrasting the current status of Çemberlitaş Hamamı with that of the Atik Valide Mosque Complex: tucked away in the hills behind Üsküdar and therefore far away from the tourism circuit, the complex has been marginalised and received very little attention until a recent renovation made especially the dependencies once more accessible and presentable. Thus, within the context of globalisation, one of the many entangled and mutually constitutive identities of Çemberlitaş Hamamı has become, for internal tourists and Turkish consumers of Ottomania, 'a diacritical mark of their ethnic or cultural identity, a vehicle of self-representation before an external public'.[77]

Epilogue

Unlike the life story of an Ottoman poet who constituted the subject of an entry in a biographical dictionary, or the life story of other Istanbul hamams which were demolished in the course of early Republican urban planning schemes, that of Çemberlitaş Hamamı does not terminate with a clear-cut ending defined by the disappearance of its physical existence. (Moreover, given its online presence and the possibilities that the digital age affords through 3D modeling, virtual reconstruction and the like, even its physical disappearance would not result in its complete demise.) Its life story, as it has been told here, ends not with death, but rather arbitrarily around 2004 with the completion of my research. A dozen years – eventful for Turkey, Istanbul and Çemberlitaş Hamamı, to say the least – have passed since then.

Following international high-profile events such as the success of Nuri Bilge Ceylan's film *Distant* at the 2003 Cannes Film Festival and Orhan Pamuk's Nobel Prize for literature in 2006, Istanbul rose to even greater prominence as tourist destination. For 2010, the city was chosen as the European Capital of Culture, resulting in a flurry of renovation and restoration work of Ottoman monuments, as well as a great variety of other cultural and artistic undertakings.[1] In the same year, the *New York Times* ranked Istanbul in nineteenth place among 'The 31 Places to Go in 2010', so the title of the article.[2] By then, the ever increasing influx of tourists had also begun to include a visibly greater percentage of visitors from the Middle East, so that many shops and restaurants in tourist-dominated areas now boast signs proclaiming that their staff speak Arabic.[3] Under the AKP government, the promotion of Turkey's cultural heritage, especially of the Ottoman past, has attained unprecedented heights; for instance, in 2003 Miniatürk, a theme park featuring the 1/25-scaled miniature models of significant architectural monuments began to receive visitors and immediately became a great success.[4] The Panorama 1453 Historical Museum, established in 2009 and an equally popular success, celebrates the Ottoman conquest of Constantinople in a heroic narrative presented in the form of dioramas.[5] Yet events such as the Gezi Park Protests in 2013, which aimed to protect one of Istanbul's increasingly rare green spaces against demolition and the reconstruction of the Ottoman Taksim Artillery Barracks disguising a shopping mall in its place, have also demonstrated the socially constructed and highly contested nature of heritage.[6] Where and how Ottoman heritage is best remembered or forgotten are by no means straightforward or clear-cut decisions, since they involve many different power relations and numerous stake-holders with divergent visions of past, present and future.

As for hamams, many more hotels have started to feature 'Turkish baths', such as the Sanda Day Spa in the up-scale İstinye Park shopping mall in 2007 (Figure E.1). Çemberlitaş Hamamı itself was restored in 2006 by the architects Halil Onur and Ali Dereli, so that its women's dressing room became fully functional again after it had for many years been occupied by the restaurant Cennet, serving Anatolian fare mostly to tourists. The Kılıç Ali Paşa Hamamı, another of Mimar Sinan's bath-houses, in the now fashionable café- and gallery-studded neighbourhood of Tophane, started to offer its services in 2013 (Figure E.2), and the

Figure E.1 Hamam in the Sanda Day Spa, İstinye Park shopping mall, Istanbul, 2007.
Source: Author's photograph.

Figure E.2 State of preservation and restoration of the Kılıç Ali Paşa Hamamı, 1578–1581, Istanbul. *Source*: Courtesy of Cafer Bozkurt Mimarlık.

restoration of the Küçük Mustafa Paşa Hamam was nearing completion at the time of this writing (Figure E.3). The Turkish Hamam Culture Museum in the bathhouse of Bayezid II – established in the late fifteenth century, it was the workplace of the infamous Patrona Halil in the eighteenth century, but has now passed into the ownership of Istanbul University – celebrated its opening in May 2015 and has quietly started to showcase to the public the objects that Ottoman bathers would have taken with them (Figure E.4).[7] Outside of Turkey, in Europe, new cousins are born to Çemberlitaş Hamamı. For example, the bath-restaurant *Aux Gazelles* in Vienna's city centre opened its doors in 2003 (Figures E.5, E.6), its owner conceptualising it as a multi-cultural meeting point for different groups, including locals and the many ethnic minorities from Islamic countries who reside in Austria's capital.

As it happens since Çemberlitaş Hamamı's birth in 1583 with each social, economic and cultural transformation, albeit at a now much more rapid pace, the monument continues to experience small and large shifts in its meanings, to the same extent that local and foreign bathers, managers and employees continue to attach new narratives emerging

Figure E.3 Site visit to the restoration of the Küçük Mustafa Paşa Hamamı, 1477, Istanbul, February 2016. *Source*: Author's photograph.

from the abovementioned developments and events – and, therefore, new identities – to it. (Even the scholarly narrative told here is likely to shape the hamam's fate, in ways and to an extent that cannot be foreseen at this juncture, and it is hoped that more scholars will take up aspects of the monument's history that remained outside the present work's scope, such as the story of its latest renovation.) One may argue, then, that Çemberlitaş Hamamı suffers from an excess of identities, a split personality of sorts, which will continue to grow and split endlessly for as long as it exists.

But rather than pathologising such richness of meaning, we may consider it an asset and antidote to essentialising approaches that exclusively focus on the limited temporal and spatial context of a monument's making and intend to fix it within inflexible categories. Architectural historians have made large strides in this direction, as evidenced in the conceptual framework that undergirds the collection of essays in *Architecture and Tourism: Perception, Performance and Place*. In D. Medina Lasansky's words:

Figure E.4 Turkish Hamam Culture Museum in the bathhouse of Bayezid II, Istanbul. *Source*: Author's photograph.

buildings and spaces [can be] understood as a set of activities, products and attitudes that complement and complete both the design and meaning of specific sites. Architecture [can be] thought of as a process of reception, representation, use, spectacularisation and commodification as meaning is mediated by the rhetorical strategies of diverse media and performance.[8]

Ottoman historians have only recently begun to feel more comfortable with dismantling fixed categories, accepting the multiplicity and constructed nature of meaning, and embracing notions of multiple or hybrid identities. But, as Cemal Kafadar asserts:

[i]n our rethinking of history writing through essentializing national, religious and state-based categories . . . we can benefit from deeper excavation of premodern conceptualizations of identity as embodied in the notion of Rumi-ness, among others, and better understand the vicissitudes of selfhood in the plural environments that we study.[9]

It remains to hope that the preceding pages have indeed been able to offer not only the life story of Çemberlitaş Hamamı in all its richness and depth, but also to convey a sense of its Rumi-ness – that is, an identity loosely

Figure E.5 Tea room in the bath-restaurant *Aux Gazelles*, Vienna, 2003.
Source: Author's photograph.

Figure E.6 Hot room of *Aux Gazelles*, Vienna, 2003. *Source*: Author's photograph.

attached to a region (Anatolia) and wide open to cultural appropriations (such as that of Roman-ness by Turkish-speaking Muslims in the late Middle Ages and the early Ottoman Empire) – which can constitute a most useful way of thinking for future investigations into the history of monuments and objects in the Lands of Rum, as well as beyond.

Appendix: Endowment Deed of the Atik Valide Vakfı (VGM, D. 1766)

The *valide sultan* wanted to join the blessings of the transitory world with the blessings and the joys of the eternal afterworld, because a wise person would not tie his hopes to the uncertain possessions of the world only. With this in mind, the abovementioned *valide* opened her generous hand to everybody and wanted to bestow a gift that is always open to the entire public, in order to do good deeds and to escape the sufferings of the terrible day [Day of Last Judgement], when not possessions and children, but only embracing Allah with a clean heart will be beneficial. Accordingly, she allotted from her unencumbered possessions and properties those parts that will be mentioned in detail in this deed of trust. In genuine and sincere determination, devoid of hypocrisy and deceit, with only the purest of intentions, she ordered the construction of many great and magnificent edifices of charity. The following are among these.

1. A high and stately sacred mosque containing all kinds of beauty and architectural embellishment, built in Yeni Mahalle in Üsküdar.
2. Because she assigns much value and importance to the reputation of science and education, and in order to elevate and ennoble the scholars among the people, she built a *medrese* [theological school] adjacent to the north of the abovementioned mosque's courtyard. This *medrese*, whose buildings and location are exalted, consists of nineteen rooms. She allotted fifteen of these rooms as residence to students who want to acquire science and education and to sages who want to shape their beings with virtue and beauty, two [of the rooms] to the *muid* [tutor] employed [there], and the largest one as classroom for the *müderris* [teacher], and also one of the rooms as residence to the *bevvab* [doorman] whose duty it is to lock and unlock the door of the *medrese*. The abovementioned *vakıf* endowed this *medrese* to all people of intelligence and seekers of wisdom, who will gain complete insight by making use of primary and secondary sciences, and who will deal with natural and religious sciences.

3. Also in the vicinity of the abovementioned mosque, a *mekteb* [primary school], which the founder, upon Allah's will, has bequeathed to all Muslim children for the learning and understanding of the Qur'an.

4. Also across from the abovementioned mosque a *darülkurra* [seminary for the study of Qur'an recital], which the founder bestowed on all Muslims who desire to study the science of properly reciting the Qur'an.

5. Also across from the abovementioned mosque and in the vicinity of the *darülkurra*, a *darülhadis* [seminary for the study of the traditions and sayings of the Prophet], which the founder bequeathed to those students and scholars who want to study *hadis* [traditions of the Prophet] and *tefsir* [exegesis of the Qur'an].

6. An *imaret* [soup kitchen] which the founder built in the vicinity of the *darülhadis*, containing a beautiful kitchen, a clean refectory, two *han*s [inns for travellers], rooms known as *tabhane* [refectory] for the lodging and feeding of visitors, a storage room, a wood storage, and other necessary service facilities, for the poor and wretched, for travellers and guest, and for the pious residents.

7. A *rıbat*, known as *hankah* [monastery], consisting of a few beautifully domed spacious cells which the founder built in the vicinity of the abovementioned mosque for the residence of dervishes who respect the religious law.

8. A *darüşşifa* [hospital] consisting of high and beautiful rooms and cells, which the founder built next to the *imaret* and bequeathed to all types of patients for their treatment and medication. Because all of these buildings are well-known in the area, there is no need to describe and explain them.

9. A pleasant *mescid* [small mosque] which the founder built in the town of Lapseki in order to encourage learned people and to attain the rewards of the other world, as promised by the Prophet.

10. A beautiful *mekteb* which the founder built, upon Allah's will, in the vicinity of the *mescid*, for the teaching of the Holy Qur'an to the children of the poor and any [other] indigent children.

Concerning the *imaret* built next to the abovementioned *mescid*: this *imaret* consists of rooms called a *matbah* [kitchen] and a *tabhane*, rich in blessings and food, a peerless refectory and a *han*, a toilet, a wood storage and other necessary facilities; and its door is open to everyone. The abovementioned founder endowed this *imaret* to the poor and wretched and to the crowds of the weak and needy. Thereafter, the *valide sultan* – who is of great repute and honour and who knows about every kind of benefaction and kindness – in the wish that the abovementioned charities shall survive forever and that no harm or damage shall come upon them, with good intention and strong determination endowed to the business affairs of the abovementioned charities many properties – villages, rental properties, farms; in short, all kinds of *vakıf* which are legally owned and rented out.

The endowed properties are the following:

1. An entire *han* consisting of twenty-two double-storied rooms in the Yeni Mahalle in Üsküdar.
2. Adjacent to the abovementioned *han* fourteen shops, bordered on three sides by the street and on one side by the property of Mehmed the Barber and [that] of Ayni, daughter of Mustafa.
3. Also, two adjacent hamams, one for men, the other for women and heated by a furnace, in the abovementioned neighbourhood.
4. One small house and three shops bordered on three sides by the street and on one side by a slaughterhouse where sheep are slaughtered.
5. All of the sixteen shops opposite the abovementioned hamam, bordered on two sides by the street and on one side by the mill built for the abovementioned *imaret* and on the other side by the *menzil* [mansion, halting place, station] called caravansaray; in one of the shops, sheep heads and trotters are cooked.
6. An entire house built for the production of candles, called *şem'hane*.
7. Also, seventeen shops, each consisting of a *hücre* [room] and a yard in the back, bordered on three sides by the street and on one side by the garden of Mustafa the Barber.
8. Also, an entire workshop reserved for the slaughter of cattle, together with twenty-nine shops; in the back of each there is a *hücre*, bordered by the street on three sides and on one side by the *menzil* called the *debbağhane* [tannery], where hides are tanned.
9. Also, all of the six houses which were built for tanning hides and which are bordered on several sides by *hücres* reserved as rented living quarters for families, by the street on one side, and the above-mentioned shops on the other sides.

The following shall be known: the imperial rescript and decree orders that only the tanners who rent the abovementioned houses can purchase, for a price known among the tanners, the hides of the sheep, goats and cows [from the slaughterhouses mentioned in the list below] and that no other butchers apart from these shall purchase them. [These slaughterhouses are the following:] the slaughterhouse located at one of the gates of Istanbul, known as the Çatladı Kapu, where the sheep for the imperial kitchen are slaughtered; and the slaughterhouse in the Yeni Mahalle in Üsküdar; and the shop of Süleyman the Butcher, son of Cafer, located in the neighbourhood of Karaköy in Galata; and the shop of the reputable and honourable Mehmed Ağa in the abovementioned neighbourhood of Karaköy; and again the abovementioned Mehmed Ağa's shop on one of Istanbul's quays, the Emin İskele; and the shop of the abovementioned Süleyman the Butcher, son of Cafer, located close to the bridge in Üsküdar; and the shop in Kasımpaşa, which is one of the shops of the *vakıf* of the late Süruri; and [the slaughterhouses] in the villages in the dependencies of Galata, [that is] Yenihisar, Tarabya, Sarıyer, and Büyükdere; and [the slaughterhouses] in the villages in the dependencies of Üsküdar, called Beykoz, Yoros, Kanlıca, İstavros, and Çengâr.

Thereafter, the abovementioned founder gave one share of the abovementioned hides to the renters of the tanneries in one of the prosperous neighbourhoods in Üsküdar, which is part of the *vakıf* of the abovementioned Mehmed Ağa, because of [his] kindness and generosity. This share is three-tenths; the hides are all collected and divided into ten shares and seven of these shares shall be taken by the renters of the tanneries of the *vakıf* of the exalted founder; the remaining three shares will be taken first of all by the renters of the tanneries of the *vakıf* of the abovementioned Mehmed Ağa. Then, the exalted founder required that this distribution will eternally continue in a formal manner and that no one shall breach it.

10. Also, a big stable with sixteen cells built as residences for people with families, bordered on two sides by the street, and on one side by the *menzil* called the *debbağhane*, and on the other side by the *vakıf* of Mehmed Ağa.
11. Again, a slaughterhouse in the abovementioned neighbourhood, bordered on two sides by the street, on the third side by the furnace of the abovementioned hamam, and on the fourth side by the caravansaray.
12. Again, two *hücre*s in their entirety in the abovementioned neighbourhood, reserved as residence for married couples, bordered on the first side by the road, on the second side by the estate of the founder, on the third side by the *vakıf* of Hayrettin Çavuş, [and] on the fourth side by the property of a person called Hacı Reis.
13. Located in Istanbul in the vicinity of Dikilitaş, two hamams adjacent to each other, one for women, the other for men – there is no need to describe and define it, because its connection to the founder is well known among noble and lowly people – together with all of the neighbouring nine shops.

14. Sixty-five one-storied and double-storied *hücre*s, bordered on three sides by the street and on the fourth side by the *vakıf*s of Ahmet Paşa and Sinan Paşa and the property of Defterdar Mehmed Çelebi.

   . . . and the rent of the four shops' plot with a width and length of twenty *zira*, which has been annexed to the hamam's plot, shall be 1,440 *dirhem* yearly.

   And also the annual rent of the one shop's plot, with a width and length of five *zira*, which is taken together with the rent from the abovementioned Ahmet Paşa's *vakıf* and which is attached to this field.

15. Located in the vicinity of the Aya Kapu in the neighbourhood of the Gül Cami, a single hamam – there is no need to describe it, because its connection to the founder is well known.

16. Four single-storied and three double-storied *oda*s [rooms], consisting of a well and two toilets and bordered on three sides by the street and by the *vakıf* [property] of the abovementioned founder in the vicinity of the abovementioned hamam.

17. A shop called *serhane* [where sheep heads and trotters are cooked], bordered on three sides by the street, next to the abovementioned houses.

18. Opposite the abovementioned hamam, a shop with a room on the top floor, bordered on two sides by the street and the property of Rüstem the Barber.

19. Next to the abovementioned hamam's furnace, four *hücre*s.

20. In the vicinity of the hamam at one of Istanbul's fortified gates, the Yeni Kapu, two adjacent *hücre*s, the boundaries of which are known by the neighbours.

21. Outside the Yeni Kapu, a shop with two *hücre*s on top of it, bordered on three sides by the street and on one side by the fortification wall.

22. Opposite the abovementioned shop, the plots of two shops, paying to the Ayasofya's *vakıf* a yearly rent of 25 *dirhem* and including two *hücre*s on the top floor, bordered on two sides by the street and on one side by the fortification wall.

23. Outside one of Istanbul's gates, the Aya Kapu, two shops in their entirety – one of them a slaughterhouse, the other a candle-maker's workshop – the plots of which pay to Ayasofya's *vakıf* a yearly rent of 360 *dirhem*, bordered on two sides by the street and the *zımmi* [non-Muslim community] of Barose and the sea.

24. In one of Istanbul's neighbourhoods, the neighbourhood of . . ., twenty-seven *hücre*s built as living quarters for married couples and bordered on two sides by the street and on one side by the property

of Ayşe, daughter of Davud, and on the other side by the properties of Gazanfer, son of Abdullah, and Mehmed, son of Abdullah, and Hüseyin, son of Abdullah, and Nasuh, son of Abdullah, and the property of Piyade Mehmed.

25. In the dependency of Skopje in the vicinity of the villages of Çeltikçi and Galhova, an entire farm purchased from Üveys Bey, consisting of: one interior courtyard; and in this courtyard two single-storied *oda*s and one double-storied *oda* and two *oda*s with earthen floor; and one exterior courtyard; and in this courtyard facing one another two *oda*s with earthen floor, a bread oven, a camel stable, and next to the oven and stable one *hücre*; and three granaries; and two *oda*s, one of them for livestock, the other for hay; and one garden with four mills in it; and the river supplying water for the mills; and one *oda* overlooking the mills on the river and the garden; and two other gardens; a vineyard; two kitchens; and five pastures yielding 230 cartloads of hay annually; and a field of 40 *kıt'a* where a total of 1,000 *kile* of grain are sown every year; and a forest where cattle graze; and a grove; and all other movable property necessary and important for running the farm.

26. In the dependency of Yoros in the village of Orhanlü, a farm together with its cattle, which was bought from Defterdar İbrahim and which is bordered by the street going to Sarı Pınar starting from the pasture of Mehmed and Ali, then [by the borderline] going from the pasture of Çeltik to Karakirlis, then from there to Kayalu Dere, then from this valley to Koz Pınarı, then from there to the flank of the Alemdağı, then from there to Çoban Pınarı, then from there to the pasture of Ağdacı, then from there to the abovementioned Mehmed Ali's pasture; [it] consists of eight *oda*s; and one granary; and some pastures which altogether yield about 150 cartloads of hay; and fields which are sown with about 600 *kile* of grain; and one mill; and three springs; and other movable property for running the farm.

27. A melon field and a pasture, bordered on one side by the street and on one side by the woods and on one side by the back of the exalted founder's mill and on the other side by the Çoban Pınarı.

28. A *menzil*, consisting of three wooden *oda*s and one courtyard, bordered on two sides by the street and the other two sides by the abovementioned founder's farm (these are all in the village of Orhanlü).

29. Located in the dependency of Silivri in the vicinity of Kabakçı Köyü, a farm together with its slaves and cattle, which was purchased from the *tevkici* [scribe specialising in drawing the imperial signature] Feridun Bey and which consists of an exterior courtyard including

seven *hücre*s; one bread oven; three granaries; and a wooden *hücre* with an awning in front of it; a stable with a length of fifty *arşun*; and another stable made of wood with a length of thirty *arşun*; and a straw rick with a length of forty *arşun*; and another stable in the village of Çıbıklı with a length of fifty *arşun*; and a hamam with a pool in its centre; two mills; and a vineyard of three *kıt'a*; and three gardens; and a field of eighty *kıt'a*, which is sown with 120 *müdd* of grain, the *müdd* being the obvious and well-known [weight unit]; and a pasture of six *kıt'a*, which yields in itself about 100 cartloads of hay; and various movable property necessary for running farms.

30. Located in the district of Yoros, a farm which was bought from Defterdar Mustafa, together with its slaves and cattle and diverse movable property customary for farms, consisting of one *oda* with earthen floor; one granary; two double-storied *oda*s; a stable with four *hücre*s; one kitchen; one bread oven; one mill; two springs; one woodland; one melon field; and a few pastures and fields; all of this [is] bordered on two sides by the farm of the abovementioned founder and on one side by the Alemdağı, on the other side by the village of Samandra and the farm of the butcher's son.

31. Located on the flank of the Alemdağı and connected to the district of Yoros, a farm was made part of the *vakıf*, together with the movable property used on farms, which was bought from Hasan Paşa and which consists of two facing *oda*s with earthen floor and in between them an interior courtyard including a hall; and an exterior courtyard with a big granary in it; a big stable; four *hücre*s; a kitchen; another stable; a well; and a vineyard in the size of one and a half *cerip*. [The farm is] bordered on one side by the farm of Cafer Çelebi, and on two sides by the street and on one side by the abovementioned Alemdağı; its fields and pastures are bordered by İnehan to the south, by Cafer Çelebi's fields to the east, to the west by the water channel leading to the *zaviye* [dervish convent] named Sarı Kadı [Sarı Gazi] Tekkesi, to the north by the fields of the late Cafer Çelebi and the boundary of the abovementioned Alemdağı.

32. Located in the village af Samandra in the vicinity of the Alemdağı in the dependency of Üsküdar, a farm together with its cattle and various movable property necessary and important for running a farm; [and with the following parts:] two *oda*s with earthen floor with a hall in front of them; three *hücre*s; a cow stable; a mule stable; a straw rick; a horse stable; two *oda*s with earthen floor close to the abovementioned horse stable; a hall; a kitchen; a granary; a big stable accommodating thirty mules; two melon fields, the borders of which are well known

among the people; a field known by the name of Karapınar, which can be sown with twenty *kile* of wheat, and a field known as Haydar field and to be sown with twenty *kile* of wheat; a pasture with well-known borders, which yields approximately twenty cartloads of hay; and another pasture located in the vicinity of the empty field called Köy Yeri, which yields about thirty wagonloads of hay. [The farm] was bought from Şemsi Paşa and is bordered to the east by a street called Nal Döken, to the south by the big tree in the place called Köy Deresi, to the west by the place called Karlice Kırkderesi at Aydos Mountain, then [drawing] a line from this place, ending at the abovementioned street.

33. Located in the place called Çavuş Kuyu in the dependency of the *has* [royal domain] of Istanbul, a vineyard bordered by the Katip Aydın vineyard and the Bali Çavuş vineyard and on two sides by the public road.

34. Located among the vineyards of Konstantiniyye in the dependency of the *has* of Istanbul, an entire *menzil*, consisting of three *oda*s with earthen floor and a trellis and a stable and a well and a vineyard. [It is] bordered on two sides by the property of the exalted founder and on the other two sides by the public road.

35. In the vicinity of the abovementioned *menzil*, an entire field, bordered on three sides by the property of the exalted founder and on the other side by the public road.

36. Located in the vicinity of the place called Çavuş Kuyusu in the dependency of Istanbul, an entire vineyard, lengthwise [measuring] twenty *zira* and bordered on the fourth side by the pasture of Faik Ağa.

37. Located outside one of the gates of Istanbul, the Topkapu, a vineyard, bordered on two sides by the Armenian vineyard, on the third side by the field belonging to the son of Niksarlı, on the other side by the public road.

38. Outside the abovementioned Topkapu, a field and a pasture, the borders of which are well known to the neighbours.

39. Located in one of the neighbourhoods of Istanbul, the neighbourhood of Samanviran, an entire *menzil*, consisting of two *oda*s with earthen floor; three double-storied *oda*s; a hall; a stable; a well; a courtyard; and a toilet. [It is] bordered on two sides by the public road and the private road, and [it is also] bordered by the *vakıf* of Şahin and the property of Sarraf Ramazan.

40. Located in the vicinity of the central gate of the castle of Rodos, an entire *menzil* on a plot of land [measuring] lengthwise 105 and in width twenty-one *zira*, bordered on one side by the interior wall of

the castle, on the second side by the public road close to the wall of Hamamcı Yunus' house and on one side by the endowments of Kasımpaşa and Halil Bey and the *vakıf* of the Tireliler Mosque and on the other side by the shops endowed to the Blessed Mosque and the public road.

41. Located in the vicinity of the houses next to the old hamam in the abovementioned castle, an entire empty field in the width of forty-one *zira*.

42. Located in one of the neighbourhoods of Bursa, in the neighbourhood of Atpazarı, a bread oven, the boundaries of which are well known to the neighbours.

43. Next to the Reyhan Çarşısı in Bursa, a bread oven, the boundaries of which are well known to the neighbours.

44. Located in one of the neighbourhoods of Bursa, in Maksim, a bread oven, the boundaries of which are well known to the neighbours.

45. Located in one of the neighbourhoods of Üsküdar, in Yeni Mahalle, in front of the shops and houses where the Copts live, an empty field where a horse market is held. The imperial rescript and decree orders that in the town of Üsküdar the horse market shall be held only there and that nowhere else shall a horse be bought or sold and that the tax income taken per horse on this market shall be given to the *mütevelli* of the abovementioned *vakıf* and appropriated by the *vakıf*.

46. The *cizye* [head tax] of the Jews and Christians and Copts living in the abovementioned Yeni Mahalle. Whether these *millets* [non-Christian communities] take up residence in the abovementioned neighbourhood or not, the *mütevelli* of the abovementioned *vakıf* takes according to the deed of trust the *cizye* [head tax] of those who are considered permanent residents, [also] with a period of residence of less than six months; and nobody shall obstruct this. (The imperial rescript and decree orders that the abovementioned *mütevelli* shall add to the possessions of the *vakıf* the public and private treasury and the possessions of the missing and the disappeared and other canonically lawful tithes and customary taxes, and what is taken as *badıhava* tax [occasional tax] because of crime and murder and any other reason; and that the abovementioned *vakıf* shall spend it; and nobody shall obstruct this.)

1. An amount of the produce – to be determined in the future – from the pasture where the horses of the sultan stay in summer and which is known as Başyatak and Kafir Adası, located in İpsala, in the *kaza* [township] of İpsala of Sultan Murad Han, son of Selim Han, is also

a part of the *vakıf*'s whole. The imperial rescript and decree orders that the sheep of the butcher appointed to the *imaret* shall spend the winter and be fed in that season on the abovementioned pasture and places; and that no one else's sheep shall spend the winter there; and that the sheep shall stay there in summer as well as in winter; and that the abovementioned butcher shall give to the *vakıf* 12,000 *dirhem* from the fee for the abovementioned pasture; and that the *mütevelli* of the abovementioned *vakıf* shall take this sum; and that he shall spend it for the business of the *imaret*. As the order and imperial decree necessary for the execution of this order says, no tax for the right to passage shall be taken from the amount [of sheep] appointed for being slaughtered in the *imaret* every day, when the *imaret*'s butcher leads the sheep between Istanbul and Üsküdar over the Golden Horn. With the abovementioned amount of thirty sheep per day, the sum – from which tax shall not be taken – totals 10,620 sheep in a year.

2. The sheep and the income accrued from their milk and their lambs and their wool, which have been endowed together with the above-mentioned farms, shall be spent for the places where the various [amounts of] income of the abovementioned *vakıf* are expended.

The exalted Sultan Murad Han, son of Sultan Selim Han, appoints the locations mentioned below as pasture and shelter for the abovementioned sheep:

3. One of the places mentioned above is the sheep meadow located in the dependencies of Üsküdar, in the vicinity of the *karye* [village] of Azarlar in the *nahiye* [district] of Taşköprü.
4. And one is the meadow of Çekudlen.
5. And one is the meadow in the *karye* of Haveşlu.
6. And one is the meadow located in Gürgenpınar and Divane Bellük.
7. And one is the meadow and pasture located in the *karye* of Çınık and Doğanlu and Ördeklü in the dependencies of Üsküdar. These are entirely part of the dependencies of Üsküdar.
8. And one is the meadow known by the name Kayırca.
9. And one is the meadow of Suvad, located in the vicinity of Akçakenise.
10. And one is the meadow located in the vicinity of Yenice.
11. And one is the meadow and pasture located on the Suvad and in the vicinity of the *karye* named Ordakan.
12. And the meadows and pastures located in the valley known under the name Eğirmen Deresi.
13. And the Büyükdere meadow located in the place called Nebi Hoca.

These are all part of the dependencies of the *kaza* of Şile and Kandıra.

The imperial rescript and decree orders that the abovementioned sheep shall find shelter in the mentioned places and that they shall be fed there and that they shall not be disturbed; nobody shall interfere in this matter. The sheep owners who have kept and sheltered their sheep there for a long time shall not be intruded upon.

14. The entire [income] of the famous *karye* known by the name of the *has* of Yeni Il located in the prosperous *vilayet* [province] of Anatolia.
15. The [income of the] *karye* of Yeniköy and Çoğoba located in the *kaza* of Yanbolu.
16. The [income of the] *karye* of Bozacı and Hamza Virani and Çukoba and Domuzli, called Nevahi and located in the *kaza* of Çömlek.
17. The [income of the] *karye* called Ayvalu and Arizlu and Çavuşlu and Modası and Sekban, located in the *kaza* of Zağraeskisi.
18. The [income of the] *karye* called Tilki Köyü and Yeniköy in the *kaza* of Karinabad.
19. The [income of the] villages called Doşova and Akdere in the *kaza* of Şumlu.
20. The [income of the] *karye* located in the *kaza* of Yenipazar and Eskiköy and Kanlova. (Translator's note: This is from another copy under the numbers 61, 62, 64, 65, 66.)
21. The entire [income] of the two *karye*s called Kadıoğlu and Husunlu in the *kaza* of Rodoscuk, located in the *vilayet* of Rumeli. All of these districts become property [of the *vakıf*], as they are handed over into the possession of the founder by the glorious Sultan Murad Han, son of the Sultan. The boundaries of the districts, which are called Yeni Il Hasları and the borders of which are mentioned explicitly in the *hudutname* [book of borders], begin in the place called Kezbili in the north of the Tecir Dağı, go to the well-known neighbourhood of Tennurcik and from there to the back of the mountain and to the *han* called Tacimuhtaç and from there end in the place called Bağlutaş. And it continues from there to the *gedik* [leasehold] of Tozaklu and from there to the pass of Çaltık and from there down to the bridge and from there to Kızıltaş and from there to Sultanpınarı and, going from there along the way, it joins the road. And from there [the boundary goes] to the narrow path in the east and to the cemetery of Harun and from there to the public road, from there to the tomb of Harun, from there to the place called Kızıkbeli, from there to the *gedik* of İğde, from there to the place called Yoroklu Ziyareti, and from there to the place called Muymulce Gediği, and from there to Aktaş, and

from there to the place called Sinbili, and from there to the marked border of the place called Başviran Gediği, and from there to the well-known place called Sarı Bayrak Tepesi, and from there to the narrow path, and from there to the marked border, and from there to the road passing there and the top of the meadow, and from there to the road and the marked border, and from there to the place called Selo Meşhedi, and from there to the road called Göç Yolu and to Yumru Taş, and from there to the Taş Kömesi adjacent to the field of Hasan Çavuş, and from there to the narrow path and the place called Döke, and from there it joins the place called Çiğdemli Tepe. And from there to the place called Namazgah, and from there to the well-known place called Eski Meşhedi, and from there to the place called Otuz Müdalk, and from there to the place called Kızılhisar, and from there to the place called Kızılca Ziyaret, and from there to the place called Lori Yuvası, and from there to the river, and from there to the river that flows to Yeni İl, and from there to the place where the river of the Nakıl Pınarı joins the abovementioned [river], and from there to the well-known farmhouse located on the flank of the mountain called Yoyaria and to the place called Tülice Tepe, and from there to the back of the mountain and to the well-known neighbourhood called Ağçehan Gediği, and from there to the abovementioned mountain and to the well-known stone called Yüklük Kaya, and from there to the summer camping ground called Aykarçari, and from there to the place called Çatel Ziyaret, and from there to the Kandilli pasture, and from there to the well-known neighbourhood called Kırkpınar İni, and from there to the place called Karacaviran Tepesi, and from there to the well-known neighbourhood called Siyor Gölü, and from there to the well-known neighbourhood called Kuzukulağı Gediği, and from there to the place known as Özbey Virani Arazisi, and from there it continues and ends at the courtyard road which touches the well-known summer campground called Çorak Çayırı. And from there to the place called Çikan Viran, and from there to the narrow path going to the place called Sekiz Avşari Yurdu, and from there to the well-known place called Ağcecik Mağarası, and from there to the yellow path, and from there to the neighbourhood known as Küçük Karadoruk Gediği, and from there to Yelliburun, and from there to Kuşkayası, and from there to the public road and the place called Kafile Geçidi, and from there to Karaağıl, and from there to the neighbourhood called Domanece, and from there to Nasır Kuyusu, and from there to the well-known neighbourhood called Yelken, and from there to the well-known place called Çorum Beleni, and from there to the place called Küriceova, and from there to Çiçeklu, and from there to Neşriye Pınarı, and from there to the neighbourhood called Güldede, and from there to the public road and to Hankara, and from there to the neighbourhood called Boran Gediği, and from there to the tree called Yoğun Ağaç, and from there to the Kethüda Pınarı, and from there to the neighbourhood called Sarı Şeyh Viranı, and from there to the place called Kızılçölek, and from there to Taşlu Geçid, and from there to the neighbourhood called Kazyuvası, and from there to the Tatoğlu Bridge, going along the river, and from there to the endowed mill opposite the ruin located in the vicinity of Kazımak, and from there to the well-known neighbourhood called Ferde Tepesi, and from there to Merkezoğlu, and from there to Arslan Tarlası, and from there to the public road going to the town of Sivas, and from there to the cemetery in the north of the well-known neighbourhood called Karaziyaret Tepesi, and from there to the neighbourhood called Bağlama, and from there to Dikili Taş, and it passes from there and to the neighbourhood called Küçük Bayındır, and from there to the well-known neighbourhood called Güzeloğlan Meşhedi, and from there to the place called Çardak Sırtı, and from there to the public road and to the place called Arap Beyi, and from there to Tunus Buğaşı, and from there to the valley of Karakoyunlu, and from there to Tar Viranı, and from there to Dikik Kaya, and from there to Eşte Yayla, and from there to Kızıl Gedik, and from there to Ağcelu Viranı, and from there to the end of the Pekmez Deresi, and from there to Kurmazucesi, and from there to Battal Üyüğü, and from there to Değirmen Ocağı, and from there to Tavukkaçan, and from there to the mountain called Çakalköy, and from there to the neighbourhood called Alaçorağa, and from there to Habil Pınarı, and from there to the public road going from Sivas to Aleppo, and from there to Tecer Dağı, the backside of the mountain, and [the border] ends at the well-known place called Gezbeli which is the beginning of the border. Concerning the borders of the fields located in the vicinity of Saruçin Ali and İnli Viranı and and Tatlucık and İskender Viranı and the abovementioned *karye*: it first starts in the south of the place known as Körcepınar and [goes] to Ademkayası, and from there to the beginning of the valley called Kurt Deresi, and from there to the well-known neighbourhood called Ağcepur, and from there to the beginning of the valley called Düğün Deresi, and from there to the Alim Pınarı located in the west part of the valley known as Keçilu Deresi, and from there to the place called Tatlucık Sınırı, and from there to the place where the road splits, and from there to the Alim Pınarı, and from there to Kızıltepe where the

Akdağ and Kızıltepe are located, and from there to the well-known neighbourhood called Kızılparmaklar, and from there to the well-known mountain called Aktepe, and from there to the well-known neighbourhood called Ziyaret Üyüğü, and from there to the known neighbourhood called Kızılkıran, and from there to Porsuk Deresi, and from there to the well-known neighbourhood called Elma Ağacı, and from there to the place known as Suluçukur, and from there to the well-known mountain called Sağce Tepe, and from there it ends, passing Körcepınar, which is located at the beginning of the border. There is no need to describe and define [the borders], because the borders and markers of the abovementioned *vakıf* properties are entirely known among the neighbours and the people. There is no need to define and describe them, because the borders and boundaries have been described and surveyed in the pages of a valid *defter*, called *hudutname*, in an exact and excellent manner by a very accurate scribe who brings the secret out into the open and uncovers the hidden.

The exalted founder has endowed the previous and current *vakıf* properties in their entirety with a safe and sound *vakıf* and with inexorable and evident dedication in mortmain to pious use, together with all that is possibly necessary, which have been written down or not written down, with the borders and dependencies and appendages and roads and principles that have been mentioned or not mentioned.

The exalted founder set the [following] condition: a *mütevelli* shall be appointed, who looks after the business affairs of the entire *vakıf* properties and guards the important affairs of the charity, such as constant repair and renovation, the accumulation of income, the receiving and paying [of money], the giving and receiving of debt and the distribution [of charity] in a proper manner and in the best method. He shall be strong and of pure thoughts, smart, mature, reliable; characterised by [his will to] protect and by trustworthiness; well known for his ability and piety; serious in doing his service; he shall properly perform his assigned duties; pay the [*vakıf*'s] debt; take rent from every single one the *vakıf*'s renters; lend mortgages in return for rent income in a proper way, [that is] canonically lawful, without negligence and carelessness, [and] act according to the shari'a; the salary of the *mütevelli* shall be 100 *dirhem* daily; and the *mütevelli* shall have a *katip* [scribe] who is trustworthy and of good judgement; acquainted with scientific calculation; skilled in the methods of keeping books and secretarial tasks; and he shall write down everything that needs to be recorded – little or much – in a *defter* without negligence; and this scribe's daily salary shall be 20 *dirhem*.

Likewise, the exalted founder set the condition that there shall be appointed someone who is suitable and skilful in [dealing with] business affairs – be they the abovementioned charity or the renters – and capable of performing these tasks and this appointment.

1. A *cabi* [tax collector] shall be appointed to work in the town of Üsküdar; he shall be very honest and trustworthy with the rent income obtained once a month; a quite devout and faultless *katip* [scribe]; and these [two] shall be given five *dirhem* daily.
2. An independent *cabi* and a scribe shall be appointed to collect the income from the farms in Üsküdar and Yoros and deliver it to the *mütevelli*.
3. Two very honest *cabis* and two scribes shall be appointed to collect the income of the villages in the district of Yanbolu.
4. She set the condition that a trustworthy *cabi* and a trustworthy scribe shall be appointed to collect the income from the villages in the district of Rodoscuk and deliver it to the *mütevelli*; these [two] shall each receive five *dirhem* daily.
5. The abovementioned founder set the condition that a *mütevelli* shall be appointed to collect the rent and other income from the villages known as Yeni İl, be it much or little, to take and safe-keep it and to bring and deliver it to the actual *mütevelli*. He shall be intelligent and reliable, sound in judgement, and at the same time trustworthy, distinguished among his predecessors, superior over his peers; he shall be given a daily salary of 30 *dirhem*; and this *mütevelli* shall have a private scribe who is very trustworthy and reliable, fair and persistent; in short, endowed with the qualities detailed above; and this scribe shall receive 15 *dirhem*; and two more very honest scribes shall be appointed to deal with the business affairs of the abovementioned villages, and they each shall receive five *dirhem*.
6. The abovementioned founder set the condition that the *vakıf*'s entire matters and business affairs shall be under the orders and the judgement of the exalted Darüssaade Ağası Mehmed Ağa, who is very trustworthy and of great virtue and merit. The business and management and the *vakıf*'s matters of the shari'a shall be in his hands – by whatever means that will please him – as well as the progress of the customary business transactions of the *cariyes* [female harem slaves], and the tasks of breaking and changing the [*vakıf*'s] condition, the hiring and firing of the employees of the charity; he shall receive 40 *dirhem* daily, as long as he is alive; then, the [next] official called Darüssaade Ağası shall be given the [task of] supervision; and if the person called Lakıa Kapu Ağası were more expert and suitable, the supervision shall be delegated

to him. The business of the *vakıf* shall be directed in the manner written down above.

Concerning the charitable places: based on the wish that the charitable places shall be in good order, the abovementioned founder set the condition that persons who are capable of fulfilling their true purpose in the most proper and beautiful way, [as] originally intended by the founder, as described in detail below, shall be hired.

The exalted founder set the condition that one person shall be appointed to the Holy Mosque which possesses all kinds of beauty and charm; [the person] shall be acquainted with rhetoric and literature; very smart and with brilliant ideas; knowledgeable in sciences and literature; capable of composing the *hutbe* [Friday sermon] and the sermon; acquainted with the concepts of the sermons that he shall deliver and with the meanings of the exalted words that he shall include in these sermons and [with the meanings] of the *sunna* and the literature on speeches; he shall follow the path of the experts of wisdom; be capable of reading the Holy Qur'an with an Arabic accent according to custom, with composure and artfulness; be acquainted with the conditions and principles of prayer; at prayer times, he shall make [the worshippers] hurry to the performance [of prayer]; he shall beware of incidents that may cause people to hate and feel aversion when following a leader; he shall be pious, righteous and exhibit good behaviour; on Fridays and holidays, he shall read the *hutbe* in the manner customary in the city; and he shall receive 20 *dirhem* daily.

The abovementioned founder [set the condition that] to this mosque shall be appointed two *imam*s who have the following qualities and qualifications: they shall show respect and care for the commands of religion to the highest degree; they shall lead people in the obligatory five prayers and other recommended prayers; and they shall perform the duty of an *imam* alternately in a way so that each shall do the tasks assigned to him; they shall both be knowledgeable about the proper and improper ways of prayer; they shall desire the soul's righteousness and redemption; they shall pray in observance of the general rules of prostration and bow in worship with perfect humility and peace of mind; they shall keep to praying on time; they shall obey the entire *sunna* and the canonically laudable parts of prayer; they shall be pious, act according to the shari'a, [and] be rightous [and] chaste; they shall avoid obvious and hidden mistakes when reciting the Holy Qur'an in a proper and accepted manner; they shall know where to pause and where to stop [when reciting the Qur'an]; they themselves shall possess righteousness and a beautiful voice; they shall abstain from actions that would cause people to hate them; they shall be among those people who, because they themselves lead a clean life, set an example for others to follow; and they shall awake desire and ardour in everybody because of their qualities as *imams*; and each shall be given a [daily] salary of ten *dirhem*.

And [the founder] set the condition that, from among the pious, eight persons shall be appointed as *müezzin*s for prayer times. They shall read the *ezan* [call to prayer] at all prayer times and announce the arrival of prayer time to men and women, to all Muslims; they shall read the *ezan* as soon as the time comes, with a loud and beautiful voice, obeying the rules and traditions of the call to prayer; they shall call out when the congregation is ready; they shall read the call to prayer on the minaret in a state of superior ritual purity, alternating four every day; and their [daily] salary shall be five *dirhem* each.

And she set the condition that to this mosque five persons shall be appointed from among those endowed with a beautiful mindset; they shall be known for their asceticism; they shall obey God; refrain from [the desire to attain] status and carnal passion; know the improper and the proper conditions of prayer; their souls shall search for righteousness and happiness. Every one of these five persons shall pray twenty-five *rekat* [prayer cycles] in the abovementioned mosque with contentment and pious reverence in their heart during the prostrations; they shall donate the benefit [of the prayers] to the soul of the exalted founder; and the [daily] salary of each of them shall be four *dirhem*.

And she set the condition that to this mosque shall be appointed ten persons from among the *hafız* [Qur'an reciters] who are known for their excellent virtue and who have extensive skill and capacity in reading the Qur'an with a beautiful voice. These persons shall gather every Friday in the abovementioned mosque shortly before noon; every one of them shall read from the Holy Qur'an with a soul-caressing and beautiful voice in a way that shall awake pleasure in the listener, closely following the traditions and rules of chanting and reciting; they shall read more blessed verses; one of them shall be the leader, called *ser mahfil*; and his [daily] salary shall be six, that of the others three *dirhem*.

And she set the condition that to the abovementioned mosque shall be appointed one person who has a beautiful and pleasurable voice that will give cheer to the heart of the listener. After the Qur'an reciters have read the Holy Qur'an in the Holy Mosque on Friday, this person shall read the verses of the *nuut-i nebeviyye* [eulogy and praise on the Prophet], Peace be upon Him; and his [daily] salary shall be five *dirhem*.

The abovementioned founder set the condition that a *muarrif* shall be appointed to this mosque. This *muarrif* shall read in the manner known everywhere and to everybody the parts consisting of the *ilahi* [praise of God] and the *salatü selami resuli* [prayer of the Greeting to the Prophet]; he shall recite a eulogy for the magnificent sultan; he shall pray for the exalted founder who has performed pious deeds, and for other Muslims; and his [daily] salary shall be five *dirhem*.

The abovementioned founder set the condition that four *kayyum* shall be appointed to this mosque. These shall, in an alternating manner, wait upon the mosque; open its door; lock it; sweep it; spread and collect the carpets; and night and day perform other necessary tasks in the known manner and tradition; and their [daily] salary shall be five *dirhem* each.

And the founder set the condition that to this mosque shall be appointed thirty men who are ascetic and pious, and who shall be occupied with tasks that show the road to salvation and righteousness. Ten of them shall pray in this mosque with the use of a *tesbih* [rosary] after the morning prayer, ten of them after the noon prayer, ten of them after the afternoon prayer; and every one shall recite the word of oneness [the *şehade*: There is no God but God, and Muhammad is his Prophet] one thousand times; they shall donate the benefit [of their prayers] to the soul of the exalted founder. The [daily] salary of each of them shall be two *dirhem*; from among [a group of] ten of these thirty persons one shall be the leader; and the [daily] salary that he receives shall be three *dirhem*.

And she set the condition that ninety persons shall be appointed. They shall each read parts of the Holy Qur'an, thirty after the morning prayer, thirty after the noon prayer and thirty after the afternoon prayer; at every one of these three times, the Qur'an shall have been read completely; the benefit of each reading shall be donated to the soul of the exalted founder; and their [daily] salary shall be two *dirhem*.

And in addition to these ninety persons, six persons shall be appointed to read the Holy Qur'an every day. Five of these six persons shall donate the benefit of five parts of the Qur'an to the soul of the last of the prophets, God may grant him perfection, and [the benefit] of one [of these six parts] to the soul of the Honourable Ayşe, sacred wife of our Prophet, mother of the believers, as well as to the respected wife, the Honourable Fatima, God may grant her contentment; the [daily] salary of each shall be two *dirhem*.

The abovementioned founder set the condition to appoint a pious person to keep the Holy Qur'an [copies]. This person shall bring and open the Qur'an chest to the readers of the Holy Qur'an; he shall distribute them; collect them after reading and put them into the chest; and while the reciters are reading the Holy Qur'an, he shall also be occupied with the customarily known prayers; and his [daily] salary shall be three *dirhem*.

The abovementioned founder set the condition that there shall be appointed among those thirty persons one leader, called *ser mahfil*, who shall read the Qur'an, and his [daily] salary shall be one *dirhem* more than that of the others.

And she set the condition that one *buhurcu* shall be appointed. This person shall produce beautifully smelling smoke and perfume this mosque on Fridays and at other holy times, as is tradition in other mosques; and his [daily] salary shall be eight *dirhem*.

And she set the condition that to the abovementioned mosque there shall be appointed a *muvakkit*, who knows the art of time-keeping, in order to tell the *müezzins* the prayer times with signs in the customary manner; and his [daily] salary shall be seven *dirhem*.

The abovementioned founder set the condition to appoint to this mosque two persons to alternately safekeep the Qur'an copies endowed and placed there in order to be read, as is customary among *musahif-i hafiz* [librarians]; and the [daily] salary of each of them shall be four *dirhem*.

The abovementioned founder set the condition that one person shall be appointed to recite the [Qur'an] verses starting with 'amenerresul' [Q. 2:285–286] to its end after the Friday prayer and to donate the benefit [of the verses] to the soul of the exalted founder; and his [daily] salary shall be two *dirhem*.

The abovementioned founder set the condition that one person shall be appointed to recite ten verses from the Holy Qur'an in an excellent manner and with reverence and a beautiful voice; and his [daily] salary shall be two *dirhem*.

The abovementioned founder set the condition that one person shall be appointed to recite in a very beautiful voice that gives joy and cheerfulness to the soul of the listener sura 'Yasin', which is called the heart of the Qur'an, and which has reached us in the book narrated by our Prophet, after morning prayer is completed; and his [daily] salary shall be two *dirhem*.

The abovementioned founder set the condition that one person shall be appointed to read sura 'al-Mülk', to save the [regular] reciters from exhaustion, after the pious Muslims have finished the night prayer; and his [daily] salary shall be two *dirhem*.

The abovementioned founder set the condition that one person shall be appointed to recite sura 'Al 'Imran', which will complete the recitations, after the afternoon prayer is finished, [and] which will bring great recompense and reward in the afterworld; and his [daily] salary shall be two *dirhem*.

The abovementioned founder set the condition that from among the pious a very trustworthy person shall be appointed as *murakib* [supervisor]. This person shall supervise and control whether the employees correctly perform their tasks and whether they complete the duties and obligations with which they have been entrusted. If one of the employees does not fulfil his duties without a valid excuse, [the supervisor] shall warn the *mütevelli* by noting a point, and when the *mütevelli* hands out the salaries to the employees at the beginning of the month, he shall cut the *kıstelyevm*, the salary of that day; if this employee insists on making negligence and idleness a habit and once again lapses after the warning and the cancellation of the salary, the *mütevelli* shall dismiss him and appoint in his place a person who shows seriousness in his work, who completes the duties of the job given to him, and who never permits idleness and negligence in his job, so that his salary is lawfully earned; and the [daily] salary of this *murakib* shall be three *dirhem*.

The abovementioned founder set the condition that a *perdeci* shall be appointed in order to safekeep the curtains in the customary ways, who hangs them in winter, who fixes them if they need repairs; and his [daily] salary shall be three *dirhem*.

Concerning the *medrese*: she set the condition that one person shall be appointed as teacher to the abovementioned *medrese*; he shall be endowed with superior virtue and highest excellence, [and] known among his peers for his science and knowledge; he shall be distinguished in the speculative and practical sciences; he shall be superior to his peers in the fundamental and secondary sciences; he shall be capable of dealing seriously with complicated and difficult problems; he shall have virtues, habits and moral qualitites that endear him to everybody; he shall be occupied with expounding to others and contributing to science; he shall demonstrate great seriousness in the matter of teaching science to those who desire to benefit [from his learning]; he shall spend all of his time with the acquisition of excellence; he shall be inclined towards spreading and inculcating knowledge, in the true meaning of the word, to the experts of learning; he shall be entirely occupied with lecturing and giving lessons; and his daily salary shall be 60 *dirhem*.

And [she set the condition that] sixteen students from among those who are capable and desiring of the acquisition of knowledge, who are currently studying in the *medrese* and reading the customary books, shall reside [there]; and from among [these sixteen] a *muid* [tutor] shall be appointed; he shall be the best in knowledge and virtue, the one most inclined to remove ignorance and acquire learning; and this student shall not stop giving lessons in this way without any rightful excuse; and the salary of the *muid* shall be five, the salary of the others two *dirhem*. And one *bevvab* [doorman] shall be there in order to see after the task of opening the *medrese*'s door and locking it firmly at night; and his salary shall be two *dirhem*; and one *süpürgeci* [sweeper] shall be appointed in order to sweep the *medrese* and look after cleaning tasks; and his salary shall be two *dirhem*.

Concerning the *darülhadis*: the abovementioned founder, who is endowed with munificence and generosity and many virtues and perfections, set the condition that to this *darülhadis* shall be appointed a person who is pious, wise, free of all shame and blemishes; he shall be very God-fearing; lead a clean life; and abstain from committing any sins; he shall combine theoretical as well as practical knowledge in one single person; he shall be without laziness; occupied with the acquisition of the knowledge of God; and very diligent in the matter of enlightening the spirit with any kind of science; he shall have acquired the habit of constant study; he shall devote his life to the benefits of teaching and lecturing; and he shall turn his attention to all the necessary elements of worship and submission; he shall teach there to the students who have the desire to save their souls from blemishes and embellish themselves with virtue; [he shall teach] the *sunna* [traditions of the Prophet], the *tefsir* [exegesis of the Qur'an] and other sciences, without fail in his duty; and his daily salary shall be 40 *dirhem*. And she set the condition that twelve students shall live in the cells of the *darülhadis*; that they shall desire to receive instruction in all kinds of sciences and to protect their souls from all blemishes; that they receive knowledge from the abovementioned teacher; they shall listen carefully to his blessed words and lectures; and their salaries shall be two *dirhem* each.

Concerning the *darülkurra*: the abovementioned founder set the condition that a *şeyhülkurra* shall be appointed. This *şeyhülkurra* shall have knowledge of the Arabic language; be an expert in the arts of literature and skilled in teaching the recitation styles; he shall recite the Qur'an properly; he shall be peerless in chanting; he shall make the students study and be of benefit to them; he shall be most glorious in knowing the whole Qur'an by heart; he shall recite properly and well; he shall have mastered the opinions and traditions of the authorities on recitation; he shall be able to chant and read according to the traditions of the biggest reciters; he shall be one of the people whose knowledge about the tradition is passed from mouth to mouth; he shall be distinguished among the exceptionally famous; he shall distinguish between the secret and the introduced, between improper and proper pronunciation, between negligence and perfection, between *revim* [technical term of Qur'an recital] and *işmam* [giving a consonant a slight vowel sound]; he shall know the articulation and qualities of the letters; he shall have [the ability of] reciting and [know] the nuances of recital; he shall be acquainted with the details of the sciences; he shall have received the knowledge of recital from the big *şeyhs*; and he shall have received his knowledge from the highest authority of recital; he shall have listened; learned and taught a lot; he shall have been trained by combining theory and practice in his person; he shall be serious and wearing the cloak of dignity; he shall be wearing the cloak of modesty which is a sign and principle of good and excellent people; he shall be perceived as skilful and worthy of respect by young and old; he shall be able to explain and lecture on the acclaimed books that have been written about the ten reciting styles of the ten authorities of reciters.

These ten authorities are the following: Şeyh İmami Sünni; Nafi bin Ebi Naimilmedeni; İmam Kebir Abdullah ibni Kesir; Amir bin Elulah, who comes first in teaching; İmami Fazıl Mahir Abdullah ibni Amir; İmai Asım bin Ebinnueud, who is very devout and God-fearing; İmami Necip Hamza bin Habib; İmami Ebulhasen Aliyyilkisai, whose Arabic is strong and who is powerful in the science of recital; İmam Yakub Hadrami, who is very clever; İmam Ebu Cafer Ka'ka', who is well-versed in the art of recital; and the great İmam Half bin Hişam. These ten persons are experts of the science of recital; they are trustworthy; they are imams and [intellectual] defenders [of Islam]. Each one of them has transmitters and a path of tradition. The *şeyhülkurra* to be appointed to this *darülhadis* shall teach the ten styles of recital; lecture and give speeches; reinvigorate these ten styles by means of his writings; and teach the rules. And he shall teach İmami Şatibi's eulogy and its interpretation written by İmam Caberi and the *mukaddeme* [introduction], the books of İmam Cezri, and other respected and advanced rule books written on this topic; and the daily salary of this *şeyhülkurra* shall be 30 *dirhem*.

And she set the condition that ten persons shall be appointed to the *darülkurra* from among the Qur'an reciters who are serious and diligent; who read well; who have the capability to select those who are intelligent by nature; who harbour the desire to benefit [from learning]; who are talented; they shall benefit continuously from the knowledge of the abovementioned *şeyh*; they shall learn from him; they shall recite what they have learned and let him listen [to it]; every single one of them shall be occupied with a special reading style and *rivayet* [style of reading the Qur'an, as handed down from master to pupil]; and all of them shall stand ready in the abovementioned *darülkurra* four times per week in the manner of tradition everywhere; they shall study the Holy Qur'an with the abovementioned *şeyh* with great accomplishment; they shall learn the theory and practice of reciting; they shall master the relevant rules, both secret and evident; they shall be occupied with studying the respected works that are classified as dealing with the science of reciting; they shall spend all their efforts on memorising, studying and comprehending [recitation], abstaining from any evil behaviour; and the [daily] salary of each of them shall be two *dirhem*.

Concerning the *mekteb*: the abovementioned founder set the condition to appoint a *muallim* [teacher] to the *mekteb*. This teacher shall be an expert in reading and reciting; he shall be a Muslim who is diligent and serious in teaching the Holy Qur'an; he shall teach Muslim children; he shall instill in them the commands of the Qur'an; he shall commit to their memories, as much as he can, the words and conditions of prayer; to the children he shall open the wings of kindness; he shall look at them as if they were his own children, without making a distinction among them in teaching and leading them on the path; he shall respect the rules of teaching and education and work hard in order to heighten their judgement as much as possible; and he shall be given a daily salary of eight *dirhem*.

The abovementioned founder set the condition that one trustworthy and pious person shall be appointed to the *mekteb* as *kalfa* [teacher's assistant]. This *kalfa* shall repeat the children's lessons; he shall follow the best method of explaining; he shall protect the children from evil behaviour while the teacher is not present; he shall apply a method that guides to the biggest success in teaching and preserving polite manners and that is most appropriate; and his [daily] salary shall be three *dirhem*.

Concerning the *ribat* called *hankah*: the abovementioned founder set the condition of appointing to the *hankah* a *şeyh* who is pious, God-fearing, open-hearted and clean, diligent in worship, serious in his submission and very pious; conforming to canonical law; content with few worldly possessions; accepting his fate; adorned with very high moral quality; free from disgraceful conduct; he shall have conversed with famous *şeyhs*; he shall serve the important saints; he shall be a preacher who is kind towards everybody; he shall bring everybody onto the right path; he shall combine in his person theoretical and practical knowledge; he shall protect his soul from mistakes and idleness; he shall always follow the path of orthodoxy; he shall have the means of asceticism entirely in his hand; in all situations, he shall be cautious not to give in to carnal passion; he shall have experienced a revelation and spiritual communion with God; he shall always have his soul under control. This *şeyh* shall show the path to the disciples who live in the cells of the *hankah*, who have turned their faces away from bad ways and are on the path to salvation, who are determined to follow the path, who follow the quality of piety; he shall preach and give advice to the congregation of Muslims in the Holy Mosque on blessed days and nights; he shall teach them the things that will be of use to them in this world and the Hereafter; and his [daily] salary shall be 25 *dirhem*. And the thirty-two poor [dervishes] who live in the abovementioned cells and are occupied with worship shall be given two *dirhem* each.

And she set the condition that one person shall be appointed to open and lock the door of the *hankah*, to sweep and to look after cleaning tasks; and he shall be given a [daily] salary of two *dirhem*.

Concerning the *darüşşifa*: the abovementioned founder set the condition that two doctors with the following qualities shall be appointed: they shall have knowledge of the science of medicine; they shall be skilled in the science of anatomy; they shall be deserving of honour and respect; they shall have strengthened their knowledge through experience and practice; they shall have repeated and strengthened the rules and fundamentals of their arts by seeing many unhealthful conditions; they shall know all the secrets and details of medicine and science; they shall have filled their hearts with medical science up to their mouths; they shall have knowledge and erudition about the [various] states of health; while they administer medicine, they shall show gentleness and kindness; they shall have had much experience in the preparation of medicines; they shall be knowledgeable about the state of health of the patients and about the suitability of the medicines; in this way, they shall combine theoretical and practical knowledge in one person; they shall not deem it proper to remain helpless and idle; they shall take every precaution in the matter of patient treatment; they shall never use hard words when seeing patients; they shall treat all patients with kindness and politeness, as if they were their nearest family and relatives; they shall encounter their patients with gentleness and with respect towards their condition, by taking them under the shadow of their compassion; each of these two doctors shall observe the condition of every patient; they shall care about and pay attention to the condition and dignity of the suffering and the poor; they shall examine pulse and temperature and other signs; they shall always ask after the condition of the patients; they shall use all possible facilities in treating [patients]; if the condition of the patient makes it necessary that the doctor visits again, they shall immediately run to the patient. That is, the doctors are obliged to follow these written rules and specific fundamentals. They shall not break any of these rules; and they shall never neglect heeding them; if they do so, the money they receive shall be unlawful, and they shall always be subjected to torment in the afterworld; one of these two doctors shall be given as [daily] salary 20 *dirhem*, the other 15 *dirhem*.

The abovementioned founder set the condition that two *göz mütehassısıs* [ophthalmologists] shall be appointed to the hospital. The two eye specialists shall be very knowledgeable about eye treatment; they shall be skilful in diagnosing things that will cause disease to the eye or blindness; they shall be familiar with the prescription of treatment; they shall have won fame among their peers for good treatment and much experience; one of them shall be given as [daily] salary five, the other four *dirhem*.

The abovementioned founder set the condition that two *cerrah*s [surgeons] shall be appointed to this hospital. They shall know so much about the bodily effects and conditions that they will be experts in this art [of surgery], so that the wounded will benefit from their treatment, just as the body benefits from the spirit; they shall be skilled in preparing salves for wounds and other medicines; they shall be kind and gentle; they shall work hard to rightfully execute the services rendered [in the hospital], in return for the money that they should be able to receive without being subjected to any blame or reproach; one of them shall be given as daily salary five, the other four *dirhem*.

The abovementioned founder set the condition that a *vekilharc* [steward] shall be appointed to this hospital. This *vekilharc* shall never commit treachery; he shall be endowed with the qualities of trustworthiness and integrity, buy the things the patients need, as required, and while executing purchases, try to buy cheap; he shall be diligent and ambitious in his duty, [that is] the execution of the necessary service; and he shall be given a [daily] salary of three *dirhem*.

She set the condition that a *katip* [scribe] shall be appointed to the hospital, who shall be skilled in the art of writing and in book-keeping; who shall be capable of answering immediately if a question arises; who shall write down the things that the *vekilharc* has bought for the hospital; who shall register the incoming and outgoing [items] in the present *defter*; and he shall be given a [daily] salary of three *dirhem*.

The abovementioned founder set the condition that four more men shall be employed in the hospital. These shall look after the patients' affairs and well-being, after the tasks necessary for the patients; they shall always respect their condition; they shall always keep them under their supervision and attention; they shall not leave them alone for a single moment during the day; they shall be occupied with serving them without being disgusted or procrastinating; they shall serve the patients also at night faultlessly and without negligence, taking turns, two [working] one night, and two the other night; and the [daily] salary of each shall be three *dirhem*.

And she set the condition that two *eczacı*s [pharmacists] shall be appointed to the hospital. They shall have excellent capability to prepare and improve the required medicine and *macun* [medicated preparation of sugar] and potions; and the [daily] salary of each shall be three *dirhem*.

And she set the condition that two male *aşçıs* [cooks] shall be appointed. They shall cook dishes beneficial to the patients, in such a way that a skilful and smart doctor can trust and rely on them; they shall pay particular attention that the food is cooked well, so that it stimulates the patients' appetite; and the [daily] salary of each shall be three *dirhem*.

And the founder set the condition that two male *çamaşırçıs* [laundrymen] shall be appointed to this hospital. These shall wash the patients' laundry, such as bedding, covers, dirt, spills and stains, and they shall clean any dirt in close proximity to the patients; and the [daily] salary of each of them shall be three *dirhem*.

And two persons shall be appointed to the hospital to crush and grind the medicine [ingredients]; and their [daily] salary shall be two *dirhem*. And one *ferraş* shall be appointed to sweep those places that have to be swept and to perform cleaning tasks; and his [daily] salary shall be one *dirhem*. And one *külhancı* [furnace attendant] shall be appointed to heat the hamam for the patients and to massage them there and to look after other tasks related to the hamam; and his [daily] salary shall be two *dirhem*; and a carrier of pots, called a *kasekeş*, shall be appointed to the hospital to carry around the vessels whenever necessary in the customary way; and his [daily] salary shall be one *dirhem*. And two persons shall be appointed to look after the bottles and similar belongings of the patients and to see to it that nothing remains behind during the day; at night, they shall take turns; and their [daily] salary shall be three *dirhem* each. And one *kilarcı* [clerk of the pantry] shall be appointed in order to look after storage-related tasks, such as safekeeping the hospital storage and putting things there and bringing things to be taken out, and to record the amount [of things] kept in storage, summarily as well as in detail; and he shall be given four *dirhem* [daily]. And she set the condition that one person shall be appointed as *imam* to perform an *imam*'s tasks for the most important prayers of worship in the place assigned to the hospital employees and the convalescing patients for prayer; and his [daily] salary shall be four *dirhem*; and also to the hospital one *müezzin* shall be appointed to read the call to prayer at prayer times and to bid the people to the most highly esteemed aspects of worship; and his [daily] salary shall be two *dirhem*.

Concerning the *imaret*: the abovementioned founder set the condition that one person shall be appointed to look after the cooking in the *imaret* and to offer the food cooked according to the conditions announced in this *vakıfname* to the entitled guests, employees, and the poor; to keep the cooks, bakers and other *imaret* employees under his control and supervision, and to prevent any treachery or negligence in the execution of the services rendered; the person shall be pious and righteous and modest; he shall not be greedy, but content; he shall be soft-spoken and very easy-going and shy away from breaking people's hearts, he shall not be irritable, but have a big heart; and he shall pay to himself a [daily] salary of 15 *dirhem*.

The abovementioned founder set the [following] condition: a trustworthy, pious person who does not cheat and embezzle shall be appointed as *vekilharc* [steward]; he shall work hard when it comes to buying food and other necessities for the *imaret* and [when it comes to] acting in a religiously lawful manner so as to accomplish the required tasks and to protect the *imaret*'s interests; and he shall completely abstain from [cheating] and avoid treachery; and his [daily] salary shall be five *dirhem*. And one person from among those knowledgeable experts skilled in writing and calculation shall be appointed to the office of scribe to the *vekilharc*; he shall faultlessly and perfectly write down the requisites and necessities bought for the *imaret*, whether a lot or little; and his [daily] salary shall be five *dirhem*. And one person shall be appointed as *kilarcı* [clerk of the pantry]; a person who shall be endowed with trustworthiness and piety, who, thanks to his good memory, shall know the people going in and coming out of the *imaret*'s storage, and who shall not embezzle the items put in storage; and his [daily] salary shall be six *dirhem*. And one person shall be appointed *mühürcü* [keeper of seals], a person who is serious in his service, who is reliable and does not cheat in his task of sealing the storage door when it is opened and closed, night or day; and his salary shall be two *dirhem*. And one strong person who is hard-working even when he gets tired [shall be hired] to chop firewood; and his [daily] salary shall be one *dirhem*. And one reliable person shall be appointed to safekeep the firewood; he shall take out the required amount of firewood every day; and his [daily] salary shall be two *dirhem*. And two strong men shall be appointed to thresh the wheat and separate the husks, in short, to improve the wheat [so that it is] without blemishes; and the [daily] salary of each shall be two *dirhem*. And one man shall be appointed to keep the bran in storage; and his salary shall be one *dirhem*. And six male *ekmekçi*s [bakers] – who have the excellent ability to make appetising, delicious bread, who are expert and without fault in their art – shall be appointed; and the [daily] salary of one of them, as their *reis* [leader], shall be five *dirhem*, and the others' shall be four *dirhem* each. And six *aşçı*s [cooks] shall be appointed; cooks who are expert at and skilful in cooking, who know very well how to cook every kind of appetising food and to prepare the most delicious dishes, whose clothes are spotlessly clean; and one of them shall be their *reis*, and he shall be given six *dirhem*; and each of the others shall be given five *dirhem* [daily]. And four men shall be appointed *nakib* [warden]; two of them shall look after the meat, and the other two after the bread; and the [daily] salary of each shall be three *dirhem*. And two men shall be appointed as *kaseşuy* to wash the pots in which the food is cooked and the dishes from which it is eaten; and their [daily] salary shall be four *dirhem* each. And four men shall be appointed *kase taşıyı* [waiters] to carry the pots from the tables to the washing place after each meal; and the [daily] salary of each shall be one *dirhem*. And four men shall be appointed in order to pick over the rice, to clean it of impurities, and to separate the good from the bad; and the [daily] salary of each shall be one *dirhem*. And two male *hamal*s [porters] shall be appointed, one of whom shall carry meat and the other flour; they shall be respectful in carrying out big and small tasks; and the [daily] salary of each shall be two *dirhem*. And one trustworthy man shall be appointed, someone who is endowed with the right qualities and capabilities for the task of safekeeping the wheat and flour storage; and his [daily] salary shall be four *dirhem*. And one smart person shall be appointed as scribe to the storage; a scribe who writes down the income and expenses of the storage without delay and who always keeps to the rightful side, who has knowledge of the art of calculation and is a most excellent accountant, who does not even miss the tiniest thing; and his [daily] salary shall be five *dirhem*. And one man shall be appointed to distribute the barley to the guests' animals without cutting too much and without wasting anything; he shall be very accurate, not suffer from the disease of treachery, and be capable of safekeeping the barley storage without fault; and his [daily] salary shall be two *dirhem*. And two *ferraş* [janitors] shall be appointed from among the men to sweep the toilets mornings and evenings with a broom; and the [daily] salary of each shall be two *dirhem*. And two *ibrikçi*s shall be appointed to fill the ewers [with water] for those who want to take ablution before prayer; and the [daily] salary of each shall be two *dirhem*. And two male *ahurcı*s [stablehands] shall be appointed to wait on the stables and sweep them and look after important business; and the [daily] salary of each shall be two *dirhem*. And two men shall be appointed to collect the garbage gathered in the *imaret* and clean the *imaret* of waste and other impurities and throw the garbage onto ash heaps; and the [daily] salary of each shall be two *dirhem*s. And three male *bevvab*s [doormen] shall be appointed to open and lock the *imaret*'s gate and prevent crowding and disorder and ensure order while food is distributed to the poor and the orphans; and their [daily] salary shall be two *dirhem* each. And four male *ferraş* [janitors] shall be appointed to sweep the cells called *tabhane* [refectory] and give food to the guests residing there and see to other services rendered to [the guests]; and the [daily] salary of each shall be four *dirhem*. And two men shall be appointed to light the guests' candles; and their [daily] salaries shall be four *dirhem* each. And two *ferraş* shall be appointed to sweep the *imaret* and look after cleaning tasks and perform other known necessary tasks; and the [daily] salary of each shall be four *dirhem*. One *kurşuncu* shall be appointed to repair the lead covering of the domes, roofs and other places belonging to the *vakıf*; and his [daily] salary shall be four *dirhem*. And a *mani-i nukkuş* shall be appointed to prevent miserable people from drawing inappropriate scribbles on the walls and remove graffiti drawn on the walls; and his [daily] salary shall be two *dirhem*. And two *merem-metçis* [repairmen] shall be appointed to repair the mosque that the exalted founder endowed, the rooms of the *medrese*, the *imaret* and other [build-ings]; and the [daily] salary of each will be three *dirhem*.

The abovementioned founder [set the condition that] seven persons from among those who are knowledgeable about water and the affairs and states of the waterways shall be appointed; they shall recognise leaks in the waterways and repair them. Each person's area of work shall be assigned in the following way: one of them shall look after the waterways bringing water to the pool of the exalted founder's Holy Mosque in the town of Üsküdar, the *medrese*, the *imaret*, the hospital, and the hamam, as well as the waterways going to the neighbourhood of Sarıkadı [Sarı Gazi] in the vicinity of the town [of Üsküdar]. Two of them shall be responsible for looking after the waterways leading to the hamam of the exalted founder in the vicinity of Dikilitaş and to the hamam in the vicinity of Ayakapı; one of them shall look after the waterways in various places outside of Istanbul, such as Akyar and Kum Lağımı and Ali Paşa Çayırı and Güzelcehisar and Ayvalık, and after the waterways connected to that leading to the mosque of the late martyr Sultan Bayazid Han; the other shall look after the mentioned waterways located inside Istanbul; and each of the *su yolcu*s [waterway engineers] shall have a *çırak* [apprentice]; and these shall help [the engineers] in their work without fault. One of the waterway engineers will be the others' *reis* [supervisor], called *bölükbaşı* [head of the unit], and he will supervise them.

If one of them for a task assigned to him needs the help of another who is [actually] assigned to another task, this person shall immediately help him first performing the task as necessary; the *reis* shall work together with the others when repairing and improving the waterways; he shall bring together all of them and undertake these tasks together with them; and he shall not allow laziness or negligence. When they see a disruption, they shall immediately go there and repair and renovate it, so that a bigger damage shall not result from delay and negligence. The daily salary of the *reis* shall be ten *dirhem*, that of the other *usta*s [masters] five, and that of the apprentices two *dirhem*.

The abovementioned founder set the condition that four *çırağcıs* shall be appointed to light the lamps and candles of the Holy Mosque; and the daily salary of each shall be four *dirhem*. And four male *ferraşulharem* shall be appointed to sweep the sanctuary of the Holy Mosque and perform the cleaning; and the [daily] salary of each shall be four *dirhem*. And a trustworthy person shall be appointed as *hafızıkütüp* [librarian] to safe-keep the books endowed for the teacher of the abovementioned *medrese* and for the *şeyh* of the abovementioned *darülhadis*; he shall not hand them out to anybody else, whoever they may be, except for the above-mentioned teacher and *şeyh*; and his [daily] salary shall be three *dirhem*. And one *bevvab* [doorman] shall be appointed to close and lock the door of the *darülkurra* and *darülhadis* in the usual manner; and his [daily] salary shall be one *dirhem*. And one person who is capable of writing in beautiful script and is expert in the art of writing shall be appointed as *hüsnühat muallimi* [writing teacher] to teach writing to the children in the abovementioned *mekteb*; and his [daily] salary shall be two *dirhem*. And a *bevvab* [doorman] shall be appointed to the *mekteb* to open and lock the door of the abovementioned *mekteb* and to sweep and clean it; and his [daily] salary shall be two *dirhem*.

Concerning the mosque in the town of Lapseki: the abovementioned founder set the condition that one person who is pious, devout and reli-gious, who knows the shari'a and the fundamentals, requirements and traditions of prayer shall be appointed to the mosque as *imam*, under the condition that he shall recite sura 'al-Mülk' after the night prayer; and his [daily] salary shall be five *dirhem*. And a pious person who knows about the canonical [prayer] times and has the mentioned praiseworthy quali-ties shall be appointed to the mosque as *müezzin*; and his [daily] salary shall be two *dirhem*. And ten persons shall be appointed from among the reciters of the Holy Qur'an; each one shall read a part of the Holy Qur'an and donate the benefit [of the recital] to the soul of the abovementioned founder; and the [daily] salary of each shall be two *dirhem*. And one pious person shall be appointed to recite in this mosque sura 'al-Fath' after the noon prayer with a beautiful voice; he shall donate the benefit [of the verse] to the soul of Yazıcıoğlu who is buried in the town of Gallipoli; and his [daily] salary shall be two *dirhem*. And the abovementioned *müezzin* shall recite sura 'Al 'Imran' in the mosque after the afternoon prayer; and one person shall be appointed to the Blessed Mosque to perform the sweeping and care-taking tasks; and his [daily] salary shall be two *dirhem*.

The abovementioned founder set the condition that a pious person shall be appointed as *muallim* to the abovementioned *mekteb* to teach Muslim children and give lessons in the Holy Qur'an; and his [daily] salary shall be three *dirhem*. Likewise, a *kalfa* [assistant] shall be appointed to the teacher; he shall repeat the children's lessons; and his [daily] salary shall be two *dirhem*.

Concerning the *imaret* in the town of Lapseki: the abovementioned founder set the condition that a person who is pious, devout, trustworthy, righteous, clean, religious, abstinent and content, trusting in God and knowledgeable in the shari'a, not greedy, courteous and who welcomes the arriving guests according to custom, who performs the task of offering food and feasting those coming and going, shall be appointed to the *imaret* as *şeyh*; and his [daily] salary shall be eight *dirhem*. Then, the abovementioned founder set the condition that Mehmed Dede bin [father's name illegible] shall be *şeyh* of the *imaret* for life; and his [daily] salary shall be twenty *dirhem*. And one person shall be appointed as scribe to the storage of this *imaret*; this person shall write down the income and expenses of the storage; he shall avoid registering too much or too little coming in or going out; and his [daily] salary shall be three *dirhem*. And a *kilarcı* shall be appointed, someone who is endowed with the quality of righteousness and the will to protect and who shall safekeep the storage; and his [daily] salary shall be two *dirhem*. And a *vekilharc* [steward] shall be appointed to buy the best and most appropriate of the items needed for the *imaret*; and his [daily] salary shall be three *dirhem*. And one cook shall be appointed to this *imaret*, someone who is expert and skilful in his art, who is serious in his job; and his [daily] salary shall be three *dirhem*. And a *çanakçı* [potter] shall be appointed to the *imaret* to do his usual task; and his [daily] salary shall be two *dirhem*. And two more persons shall be appointed to the *imaret*, one of them to perform the threshing of the wheat and picking out the husks, the other to maintain and repair the waterways; and the [daily] salary of each of them shall be two *dirhem*. And one person who is righteous and permanently performing his job well, shall be appointed as *ferraş* and *hancı* to the *han* in the vicinity of the *imaret*; and his [daily] salary shall be two *dirhem*. And one person shall be appointed to repair and maintain the *vakıf* property here all the time without allowing negligence or delay; and his [daily] salary shall be two *dirhem*.

Concerning the *rıbat* which is known under the name *hankah* and which is adjacent to the *imaret*: the abovementioned founder set the condition that a *şeyh* endowed with the following qualities shall be appointed: this *şeyh* shall be learned and devout, and his life shall be clean; he shall be very pious; he shall act according to the statutes of canonical law; he shall abstain from what is sinful and be religious; he shall be a preacher who is kind towards the people; he shall urge people to follow the path of orthodoxy and spirituality; he shall be able to teach disciples and those who wish to follow the right way of orthodoxy and are endowed with the qualities of piety and devotion, and those devotees who follow the profession of the experts in determination and caution and who dwell in the cells of the *hankah*; and his [daily] salary shall be twelve *dirhem* under the condition that he read aloud sura 'Ya Sin' from the Holy Qur'an every day after the morning prayer and donates the benefit [of the sura] to the soul of the abovementioned founder; and the [daily] salary of each of the ten poor Sufi dervishes who live in the abovementioned cells and are occupied with worshipping shall be one *dirhem*; and it shall be a condition for the dervishes who are able to do so to recite in the appropriate manner the abovementioned parts of the Qur'an. And one righteous person who is afraid of the tortures of hell and the pains of the next world shall be appointed *cabi*; he shall distribute the salaries to the employees in the abovementioned town; he shall complete whatever remains undone of the *imaret*'s business affairs; he shall inform the *mütevelli* about those who show negligence in the performance of their tasks; he shall thus supervise the *vakıf* in this town; and his [daily] salary shall be five *dirhem*.

The abovementioned founder set the condition that, from the income of the abovementioned *vakıf*, 200 *dirhem* shall be spent [daily] on the ingredients necessary for the medicine, potions, *macun* and [dietary] foods, and other items; these shall not be skimped with if they are necessary for the well-being of the patients in the abovementioned hospital; the remainders of the potions and the *macun* shall be given to others [from outside the hospital] who want them, because every day – except for Fridays – two doctors shall give potions and *macun* to those who request them, as long as they are convinced that they want those [medications] urged by necessity, for treatment.

The abovementioned founder set the condition that twice a year clothes shall be given to thirty poor and needy children from among those who study the Holy Qur'an in the abovementioned *mekteb*, in accordance with their [economic] condition, as it is publicly known, once on the day when the *mevlid* of the Prophet is recited in [the month of] Rebiülevvel, the other time once during [the month of] Holy Ramadan.

The abovementioned founder set the following conditions:

1. On *bayram* days, clothes, turbans and shoes in the worth of 1,500 *dirhem* shall be bought and given to the poor and needy among the Muslim orphans, with the wish to accumulate good deeds from God.
2. From the profit of the *vakıf*, every day for life eight *dirhem* shall be given to the founder's freed slave called Laleruh; after her death, this [amount] shall be given to no one and stay in the *vakıf*['s coffers].

3. To the widows and poor and needy from among the freed slaves of the founder and the late Sultan Selim Han, son of Sultan Süleyman Han, every day two *dirhem* and food cooked in the *imaret* shall be given, one [meal] in the morning, the other in the evening. If one of them passes away, the salary given to her shall be discontinued and stay in the *vakıf*['s coffers].

4. She set the condition that, from the profit of the *vakıf*, every day for life thirty *dirhem* shall be given to Belkis Hatun, daughter of Abdullah.

Then, the founder set the following conditions:

1. In the *imaret*, every day food shall be cooked twice, except for the Holy Month of Ramadan, because in the days of Ramadan dishes assigned only to the fast shall be cooked. She set the condition that on the other days two meals shall be cooked, one of them rice soup for breakfast, the other wheat soup for dinner. The *bayram* days are exceptional in that, on those days, for the morning very nice and delicious dishes shall be prepared. Thursdays are exceptional in that, on those days, for the morning wheat soup shall be cooked, and for the evening a few different kinds of delicious dishes, as they are customary in other *imarets*.

2. Every day 260 *okka* of very fat mutton shall be cooked, half of it in the morning, half of it in the evening.

3. For the wheat soup, every day 6 *kile* of pure wheat and for rice soup every day – with the exception of Friday nights, the days of the month of Ramadan, and holidays – 7 *kile* of pure rice shall be used.

4. For [the kind of] bread called *fodula* and cooked in the *imaret*, 25 *kile* of flour shall be used every day.

5. For *dane* and *zerde*, which shall be cooked on Friday nights and in the month of Ramadan and on holidays, 20 *kile* of rice shall be used. For the guests who come to the *imaret*, enough food for 56 tables shall be prepared every day, and for the food called *dane* in Turkish, 3.5 *kile* of rice shall be used.

6. For the guests on Friday nights, in the month of Ramadan and on the two holidays, 56.5 *kile* of rice shall be used for the two kinds of food called *zerde* and *ekşiaş* in Turkish; 37 *kile* of those shall be for *zerde*, 19.5 for *ekşiaş*.

7. Every year, 9,730 *kıyye* of pure oil and 141 *kıyye* of honey without wax [shall be purchased]; of these, 3,068 *kıyye* shall quickly be given as breakfast to guests the moment they arrive; the remaining portion shall be used in the food cooked in the *imaret*.

8. And [the founder] set the condition that [the following] shall be used: every year 12,085 *dirhem* of pepper; 5,090 *dirhem* of

mastic; 2,067 *dirhem* of saffron; and for the dish called *zerba* in Turkish 2,430 *kıyye* of starch; 405 *kıyye* of dried apricots; 810 *kıyye* of [the kind of] dried plums called *amaskene*; 810 *kıyye* of almonds; 3,561 *kıyye* of red raisins; and for *ekşiaş* 488 *kıyye* of black raisins; for *ekşiaş* 93 *okka* and 300 *dirhem* of fruit leather; and again for *ekşiaş* 1,500 *dirhem* of mint; and for all the dishes cooked in the *imaret*, every day 1 *kile* of salt, 1 *kile* of chickpeas, and 10 *kıyye* of onions shall be used; and for the *ekşiaş*, every year 84 *kıyye* of cumin; and 2,671 *yük* of wood, the *yük* calculated based on *çeki*; every year 411 *kıyye* of olive oil to be burnt in the lamps in the rooms and kitchen that are reserved as residence for guests of the *hankah*; candles bought with the amount of 900 *dirhem*, for the perusal of the cooks and bakers; for the rice soup, every year parsley bought with the amount of 1,080 *dirhem*; and 100 jugs of pickles for pickled grapes prepared with grape juice and mustard shall be used; and every year 2,400 *kıyye* of pumpkins; 1,600 *kıyye* of sour grapes; and 1,600 *kıyye* of thick yoghurt shall be used.

The abovementioned founder also set these conditions:

1. Of the food cooked in the *imaret*, two full meals shall be given every day – one in the morning, the other in the evening – to every one of the students in the *medrese*, to the *muid*, the *bevvab* and the *ferraş*. This meal consists of one ladle of soup or some other stew, a piece of meat weighing 50 *dirhem*, and a piece of bread weighing 200 *dirhem*.
2. Every one of the students of the *darülkurra* and *darülhadis* and all the *bevvab*s and the *ferraş* shall be given two full meals every day; and every one of the *imaret* employees shall be given two full meals every day; every one of the *hatip* and the two *imam*s and the eight *müezzin*s, the leader of the *huffaz*, the *muarrif*s, the *na'than* who reads the *nuut-i nebeviyye* [eulogy of the Prophet], the *hafız-ı kütüp*, the *kayyum*s and the *ferraş* and the *serrac* who light the candles and lamps in the Holy Mosque, the *buhurcu*, the *muvakkit*, the keeper of Qur'an copies, the *noktacı* who notes it down when any negligence occurs in the work of those appointed, the teacher of the *mekteb*, his assistant, and the *ferraş* shall be given two full meals every day.
3. To the dervishes who live in the *hankah* two full meals shall be given every day; to the children who learn the Holy Qur'an in the *mekteb* fifteen full meals shall be given twice daily; and the rest of the food shall be distributed to the needy, the poor and the residents.

The abovementioned founder also set these conditions:

1. [The founder] set the condition that in the *imaret* in the town of Lapseki, every day – except for Fridays and other Holy Nights – food shall be cooked twice and that one day rice soup shall be cooked, the other day wheat soup. On Friday nights and nights of the Holy Month of Ramadan, in addition to the food called *dane pirinç* and the food usually served in *imarets*, another delicious dish shall be added, for example, *zerde* on the first, *zerba* on the second, and *ekşiaş* on the third night.

Concerning the food to be added to *dane*:

1. The abovementioned founder set the condition that [the following ingredients] shall be used: for the [purchase of the] oil for these [dishes], every day four *dirhem*; every day 15 *dirhem* shall be assigned to [the purchase of] ingredients such as rice and honey, and for the soup to be cooked every day, wheat shall be bought for the amount of ten *dirhem*, rice for the amount of seven *dirhem*, bread for the amount of 20 *dirhem*, meat for the amount of 20 *dirhem*, salt for the amount of three *dirhem*, and onions and other necessary ingredients. Every day firewood shall be bought for the amount of ten *dirhem*; every day there shall be spent two *dirhem* for the rush mats and candles in the mosque, the *mekteb*, and the *hankah*, and two *dirhem* for parsley and other necessary [ingredients].

2. She set the condition that one of the abovementioned dishes shall be served in addition to *dane*, which will be cooked on the *Berat Kandili* [night of the fourteenth to fifteenth day of the month of Şaban, a blessed night] and *Regaip Kandili* [night of the first Thursday to Friday of the month of Recep, a holy night] and on holidays; and this food shall be distributed to the poor [dervishes] living in the cells of the *hankah*, to the residents and arriving travelers, and the poor among the town inhabitants, especially poor elderly women [widows or women who never married] and other elderly persons.

The abovementioned founder set the following conditions:

1. Every year at the time of the reading of the Holy Mevlid of the Prophet two kinds of dishes, called *dane* and *zerde* among the people, shall be cooked; they shall be given to all the poor and needy who are expecting these dishes. For these two dishes 100 *kıyye* of meat and 30 *kile* of rice shall be used; for the first, *dane*, 20 *kile* [of rice] and for the second, *zerde*, 10 *kile* shall be used; 150 *kıyye* of oil, 120 *kıyye* of honey, 3/8 *kile* of chickpeas, 175 *dirhem* of pepper, 33 *kıyye* of onions, 25 *dirhem* of saffron, 15 *dirhem* of mastic, bread bought with 200 *dirhem*, and

1,500 *dirhem* shall be purchased. Among the nine *hafiz* who will read the Holy Qur'an with a beautiful voice 500 *dirhem* shall be distributed, and to each of the three persons who read the Holy Mevlid with a beautiful voice shall be given 500 *dirhem*; 700 *dirhem* shall be appointed for each of the seven persons who will read the *nuut-i nebeviyye*, Peace be upon the Prophet, and 100 *dirhem* for other exalted eulogies.

The abovementioned founder assigned fifteen tables to feasting the persons representing the *müderris*, the *hatip*, the *imam*s who will be present at the first assembly of the reading of the Holy Mevlid, and for every one of the banquet tables [she ordered] sixteen kinds of delicious dishes and three kinds of sweet drinks; she appointed two tables to the *medrese*, two to the *hankah*, one to the *darülhadis*, one each for the *darülkurra* and the *darüşşifa*, another one for the *mevlidhan* [chanter of the nativity poem] and the other readers, one for the employees of the Holy Mosque, one for the employees of the *vakıf*, consisting of the *mütevelli*, scribe and *cabi*, and one table for the persons serving at the banquet. She assigned for the sherbet served at the Holy Mevlid 54 *kıyye* of sugar, 84 *kıyye* of honey, 4 *kıyye* of *kandinebat* [special sugar consumed at Mevlid], 60 *kıyye* of rose water, 15 *dirhem* for the purchase of aloe wood, and 20 *dirhem* for the purchase of incense.

The abovementioned founder set the condition that every year 35 *müdd* of wheat from the produce of the villages of Yeni İl shall be given to sixteen poor persons; and 2 *müdd* shall be appointed to Şabana (father's name not legible), 2 to Ebulhudaye Keza, 2 to Şeyh Mahmud Beyluniye, 2 to Abdülgaffer bin (father's name not legible), and 2 *müdd* each to Mevlana Muhiddin, Seyyid Cemal, Ahmed Halife, Şeyh Mahmud Maliki and Ama İbrahim, and to the children of Nasır, Hacı Hamza, Daimülhayr, and Musa 1 *müdd* each; 3 *müdd* to Derviş Mahmud, 5 *müdd* to the *zaviye* of Ali Babaoğlu Ahi Mehmed, and 5 *müdd* to the *hatip* of the mosque located in Yeni İl. In case one of these persons passes away, the assigned amount shall be distributed to a poor wise person by the decree of the sultan, whenever a dearth of food rations occurs and in case of necessity.

The abovementioned founder set the condition that exactly 200 gold dinar of standard weight shall be given to two persons endowed with the following qualities: they shall be trustworthy and God-fearing, known for their asceticism and religiosity, and completely acquainted with the rites of the pilgrimage; they shall be expert in the flawless performance of the duties of pilgrimage; they shall have performed the pilgrimage once or several times before; and this sum shall be given under the condition that they shall not hold any other duties and appointments, so that they shall not abandon their jobs when they receive their salaries; they shall not commit a fraud, such as appointing a deputy [to go on pilgrimage in their stead], in order to receive the money [themselves]; those who do such [bad] deeds will be far from the abovementioned required praiseworthy qualities; consequently, they shall follow the rules, regulations, and traditions of the pilgrimage; they shall not break any laws; these two persons shall be selected from among the people having all the abovementioned qualities in order to perform the pilgrimage in the name of the founder within [the framework of] the abovementioned rules [and] with perfect humility and complete peace of mind.

The abovementioned founder set the condition that during her life alterations and changes to the records, increases and decreases, the hiring and firing of the charity's employees and salaried people, the employment and dismissal of whomever she wants, the expenditure and administration of this *vakıf* according to her wishes shall be in her own hands. After her death, a person of merit and who is qualified as *mütevelli* shall be appointed from among the people who are known for the desired qualities and the right moral values to the post of *mütevelli* of the *vakıf*, whoever that may be, with the approval of the incumbent sultan. This *mütevelli*, whom the sultan appoints, shall not break the rules and limitations that the founder has set; he shall perform his duties within the [parameters of the] regulations; he shall break not a single one of these [regulations]; he shall not be willing to show any negligence or tolerance of mistakes in the duties of the salaried employees; the duty of the *mütevelli* shall be performed in the same way as other, similar matters and tasks; every single one of these tasks shall be handed over to those who are the perfect persons for the job and of excellent capacity.

In this *vakıfname*, which concerns the actual establishment of the *vakıf*, the arrangement of the conditions and the reasons for expenses, the items written summarily as well as in detail are determined fully in the *meclis-i şer'i* [court of canon law] and in the entire written copy. The son of the *valide sultan* and founder, Sultan Murad, represents [her] in the decisions and establishment and registration of the *vakıf*, and in other affairs concerning this matter, and Mehmed Ağa bin Abdurrahman, who has been determined as his agent, states and swears in this copy [of the *vakıfname*] that the *valide sultan* endowed all the abovementioned places, with all of her acts of dedication being valid and respected in the correct situation. Every single one of them she delivered separately a long time ago into the hands of the respective recipients, and many great people prayed the daily and the Friday prayers in the abovementioned Friday mosque and in the small mosque; in the house of knowledge, teaching and studying has taken place for quite some time now. In the *imaret* and the *han*, many poor and pious among the Muslims have been offered food.

However, the founder, the *valide sultan*, passed away without registering this *vakıf* and without adding the decree of a judge; her inheritance has been passed on to her son, Sultan Murad Han. Because the decree was not added to the requirements of the *vakıf*, the abovementioned villages, rental properties and other various incomes in their entirety passed into the possession of Sultan Murad Han; he also dedicated [to the *vakıf*] all of these properties, according to the abovementioned regulations and rules, in a manner canonically valid and according to the explicit and visible [conditions of] dedication, for the [benefit of the] soul of the founder; and after this written *vakıf* record had been delivered in the legally valid manner to Ali bin Mustafa from among the grand and important people, whom the *mütevelli* appointed, and after it was received in the same way, Sultan Murad Han appointed his *vekil* [deputy] to the post, wanting to withdraw from this *vakıf* and returning it to his property as it had existed before. When he asked for withdrawal from this *vakıf* and for returning [the *vakıf* property] in the name of the client, the *mütevelli* rose to dispute the claim and bring [the matter] to trial. They were heard in court in the presence of a judge who signed the upper part of the *vakfiye* [document]; the judge also carefully and attentively considered the state and origin of this dispute, and he found a strongly convincing document and clear proof in the hands of the *mütevelli*. Relying on the votes of the authorities who agreed on the requirements of the *vakıf*, he decreed with a canonically valid document the correctness and requirements of this *vakıf*, and with this document copy, each one of the *vakıf* properties became a required endowment property, and they did so for eternity. Consequently, no caliph, sultan, vizier, müfti, judge, teacher, governor, commander, minor or grand personage, who believes in God and accepts the Prophet, shall have the right and authority to change or diminish [the *vakıf*], transfer it to another place or annul, overturn, destroy, or abandon it, and change it, or cause it to be forgotten. If someone dares to break the conditions of this *vakıf* or one of the laws and records, or if someone cancels or changes it with malicious intent, he will commit a significant unlawful act and take upon himself a big sin. This *vakfiye* was written, confirmed in front of witnesses, and decreed at the beginning of the month of Rebiülsani [Rebiülahir] of the year 990.

Notes

Preface

1. Adapted from Esra Akın and Howard Crane's translation of the preface of the *Biographical Memoir of Construction* (*Tezkîretü'l-Bünyân*), one of the five versions of an autobiography dictated to the author by the chief architect Sinan. Mimar Sinan, *Sinan's Autobiographies*, p. 114.

Introduction

1. A small selection of literary accounts of the hamam includes: Nicolas de Nicholay, *The Nauigations, Peregrinations and Voyages, Made into Turkie*, originally published in 1585; Ogier Ghiselin de Busbecq, *Turkish Letters*, first published in 1588; Lady Mary Wortley-Montagu, *The Turkish Embassy Letters*, written between 1717 and 1718; Julia Pardoe, *The City of the Sultan and Domestic Manners of the Turks in 1836*; and Mary Lee Settle, *Turkish Reflections*. For a more extensive list of travel writers and their works, see Stéphane Yérasimos, *Les voyageurs dans l'empire Ottoman (XIVe–XVIe siècles)*.

2. Written survey conducted in February 2003. Such statements very much confirm Dean MacCannell's claim that 'modern international sightseeing possesses its own moral structure, a collective sense that certain sights must be seen.' Dean MacCannell, *The Tourist*, p. 41.

3. For the following section, see Nina Ergin, 'Introduction', *Bathing Culture of Anatolian Civilizations*, p. 2.

4. Hans Wehr, *Dictionary of Modern Written Arabic*, pp. 237–8.

5. Muslim ibn al-Hajjaj al-Qushayri, *Sahih Muslim*, Book 2, No. 556.

6. Stephen Blake, 'Hamams in Mughal India and Safavid Iran'.

7. For the claim that Seljuk Anatolian baths provided only hot water, see Yılmaz Önge, *Anadolu'da XII.–XIII. Yüzyıl Türk Hamamları*.

8. See, for example, Françoise de Bonneville, *Book of the Bath*; Maud Tyckaert, *Hammams*; Orhan Yılmazkaya, *A Light onto a Tradition and Culture: Turkish Baths*. Coffe-table books that include chapters on hamams, but are not exclusively devoted to bathing, are: Philippa Scott, *Turkish*

Delights; Alev Lytle-Croutier, *Harem*. At the same time, however, bathing and hygiene within Europe, the United States and elsewhere have become the subject of an increasing amount of scholarly work, showing that scholars also now investigate less 'exotic' bathing practices and related cultural norms. For much earlier studies, see Edward Schafer, 'The Development of Bathing Customs in Ancient and Medieval China'; David Glassberg, 'The Design of Reform'; Richard Bushman and Claudia Bushman, 'The Early History of Cleanliness in America'; Thierry Terret, 'Hygienization'; Suellen Hoy, *Chasing Dirt*. For more recent work, see Sally Sheard, 'Profit is a Dirty Word'; Claire Parker, 'Improving the Condition of the People'; special issue of *Médiévales* 43 (2002) on 'Le bain: espaces et pratiques'; Teresa Breathnach, 'For Health and Pleasure'; Lee Butler, 'Washing Off the Dust'; Douglas Biow, *The Culture of Cleanliness in Renaissance Italy*; Melissa Mandell, 'The Public Bath Association of Philadelphia'; Virginia Smith, *Clean*; Georges Vigarello, *Concepts of Cleanliness*; Kathleen Brown, *Foul Bodies*; Bas van Bavel, 'Economic Origins of Cleanliness in the Dutch Golden Age'; Steven Zdatny, 'The French Hygiene Offensive of the 1950s'; D. Max Moerman, 'The Buddha and the Bathwater'. For studies that focus specifically on the built environment related to bathing, see Marilyn T. Williams, *Washing the 'Great Unwashed'*; Joanna Marschner and Joanne Marschner, 'Baths and Bathing at the Early Georgian Court'; Jill Caskey, 'Steam and Sanitas in the Domestic Realm'; Stephanie Hanke, 'Bathing "all'antica"'; Andrea Renner, 'The Nation that Bathes Together'; Alisno Hoagland, 'Introducing the Bathroom'.

9. The most recent monographic publications include several surveys on Anatolian hamams: Canan Çakmak, *Tire Hamamları*; Osman Eravşar, *Tokat Tarihi Su Yapıları (Hamamlar)*; and Harun Ürer, *İzmir Hamamları*. For an article approaching a monographic survey of hamams in Hungary, see Balasz Sudar, 'Baths in Ottoman Hungary'. Between 20 April and 31 July 2006, an exhibition on bathing traditions and barbers in the Ottoman Empire took place in the Topkapı Palace. The accompanying catalogue is: Emine Bilirgen et al., *Hamam: Osmanlı'da Yıkanma Geleneği ve Berberlik Zanaatı*. Between 7 November 2009 and 7 March 2010, the exhibition 'Eski Hamam, Eski Tas' ('Old Hamam, Old Bowl', a Turkish proverb meaning 'same old story') took place in the Tofaş Art Gallery, located in the renovated Umurbey Hamam in Bursa. The exhibition catalogue is entitled *Eski Hamam, Eski Tas*. In December of 2007, the Research Center for Anatolian Civilizations, Koç University, Istanbul, organised the two-day symposium 'Baths and Bathing Culture of Anatolian Civilizations: Architecture, History and Imagination'. This was followed in April 2009 by the comparative symposium 'Fürdö Hamam Sauna', which examined the bathing traditions and buildings of Hungarians, Turks and Finns. The presented papers of the former have been published in an edited volume: Ergin (ed.), *Bathing Culture of Anatolian Civilizations*. For an overview of

the state of Turkish scholarship on baths and an example of the favoured method of formal analysis, as well as a list of relevant MA and PhD theses, see Alidost Ertuğrul, 'Hamam Yapıları ve Literatürü'.

10. See at: http://turkhamamkulturu.istanbul.edu.tr. For a catalogue to the museum's collection, see *II. Bayezid Türk Hamam Kültürü Müzesi/Bayezid II Turkish Bathhouse Culture Museum*.

11. A very useful guide to the extensive literature on Roman baths has been published in Hubertus Manderscheid, *Bibliographie zum römischen Badewesen*; Hubertus Manderscheid, *Ancient Baths and Bathing*. For some of the most important studies on Roman baths, see Fikret Yegül, *Baths and Bathing in Classical Antiquity*; Fikret Yegül, *Bathing in the Roman World*; Garrett Fagan, *Bathing in Public in the Roman World*; Janet DeLaine et al. (eds), *Roman Baths and Bathing*.

12. Edmond Pauty, *Les hammams du Caire*; Michel Écochard and Claude LeCoeur, *Les Bains de Damas*; Martin Dow, *The Islamic Baths of Palestine*. On the hamams of Cairo and Jerusalem, see also these more recent articles: Nicholas Warner, 'Taking the Plunge: The Development and Use of the Cairene Bathhouse', and Martin Dow, 'The Hammams of Ottoman Jerusalem'.

13. On Spain, see Catherine Asher, 'The Public Baths of Medieval Spain'; on Hungary, see Sudar, 'Baths in Ottoman Hungary'; on Greece, see Eleni Kanetaki, 'Ottoman Baths in Greece'.

14. Heinz Grotzfeld, *Das Bad im arabischen Mittelalter*.

15. André Raymond, 'Les bains publics au Caire à la fin du XVIIIe siècle'; André Raymond, 'La localisation des bains publics au Caire au quinzième siècle d'après les hitats de Maqrizi'; André Raymond, 'La localisation des bagnes à Tunis aux XVIIe et XVIIIe siècles'.

16. Mohammed Hocine Benkheira, 'Hammam, nudité et ordre moral dans l'Islam medieval', 2007.

17. The bibliography at the end of Janine Sourdel-Thomine's substantial entry on 'hammam' in the *Encyclopedia of Islam* (*EI2*, 2nd edn) presents a good overview of the early French scholarship on this topic.

18. Oleg Grabar et al., *City in the Desert*; Oleg Grabar, *The Formation of Islamic Art*.

19. Robert Hamilton, *Walid and His Friends*.

20. Garth Fowden, *Qusayr Amra*.

21. Lara Tohme, 'Out of Antiquity'; Lara Tohme, 'Between Balneum and Hamam'.

22. See at: http://hammams.org. Of a more historical nature is the project 'Balnéorient', which has existed since 2006, offering a framework for researchers to trace the different aspects of bathing culture of the Near East from Antiquity to the present day. Sponsored by the Agence nationale de la recherche, France, it organises annual colloquia and makes the project participants accessible online. See at: http://balneorient.hypotheses.org.

23. Magda Sibley (ed.), *Special Issue on Traditional Public Baths – Hammams – in the Mediterranean = International Journal of Architectural Research* 2 (2008).

24. See, for example, the bibliographies appended to the following encyclopedia entries on Islamic baths: Andrew Petersen, *Dictionary of Islamic Architecture*; Jonathan Bloom and Sheila Blair, *Grove Encyclopedia on Islamic Art and Architecture*.

25. Renata Holod and Hassan-Uddin Khan, *The Mosque and the Modern World*.

26. Heinrich Glück, *Probleme des Wölbungsbaues*. The larger study never materialised.

27. For instance, Glück insists that the reason for so little change in the hamams' architectural form over the centuries is the atemporal and conservative nature of Oriental art (*Probleme des Wölbungsbaues*, p. 55). He also claims that in Oriental society there is no place for the individual creative artist and that, as a result, Ottoman art is only minor art when compared with true (European) art (pp. 58–9).

28. Karl Klinghardt, *Türkische Bäder*.

29. See particularly Önge, *Anadolu'da XII.–XIII. Yüzyıl Türk Hamamları*. For a study along similar conceptual lines, but on early Ottoman hamams and focusing exclusively on the technical aspect of constructing transition zones in the domes, see Seda Say, *Kubbeye Doğru*.

30. Semavi Eyice, 'İznik'te "Büyük Hamam" ve Osmanlı Hamamları Hakkında bir Deneme'. This paradigmatic typology of six different ground plans is based on the layout of the hot room: type A with a four-*iwan* ground plan with four niches; type B with a star-shaped ground plan; type C has a square ground plan with surrounding rooms; type D has a plan with domed bays and is quite rare; type E consists of a rectangle with two adjoining niches; and type F has a square warm room, a hot room and a niche of the same size. The validity of this scheme has rarely been questioned, but rather enforced by the fact that it appears in numerous Turkish publications on baths. See, for example, Ertuğrul, 'Hamam Yapıları ve Literatürü', and Elif Şehitoğlu, *Historic Hammams of Bursa*. Ayşıl Tükel Yavuz is one of the few to have questioned this typology, 'which gives the impression that the design of the building starts with the *sıcaklık*, and the rest of the spaces are attached to fill in the remaining space within the exterior wall'. See Tükel Yavuz, 'Baths of Anatolian Seljuk Caravanserais', n. 96.

31. Semavi Eyice, 'İstanbul'un Ortadan Kalkan Bazı Tarihi Eserleri'.

32. Mehmet Haskan, *İstanbul Hamamları*.

33. Suraiya Faroqhi, *Subjects of the Sultan*. Faroqhi mentions public baths only briefly in reference to women's social life, implying that hamams played a less significant role in men's social life. Her source in describing the goings-on in the bathhouse is not an Ottoman document, but Lady Mary Wortley-Montagu's travel account (see n. 2, above). See also Ekrem Işın, *Everyday Life in Istanbul*. One article in this collection of essays treats

the hamam as social space, but only in the form of a series of anecdotes extracted from primary sources.

34. Cengiz Kırlı, 'Struggle over Space'; Cengiz Kırlı, 'Coffeehouses: Public Opinion'; Cengiz Kırlı, *Sultan ve Kamuoy*; Cengiz Kırlı, 'Coffeehouses: Leisure and Sociability in Ottoman Istanbul'.

35. Suraiya Faroqhi and Christoph Neumann (eds), *The Illuminated Table, The Prosperous House*; Suraiya Faroqhi and Christoph Neumann (eds), *Ottoman Costumes*; Suraiya Faroqhi (ed.), *Animals and People in the Ottoman Empire*. For a more recent study of Ottoman material culture, see Suraiya Faroqhi, *A Cultural History of the Ottomans*.

36. Amy Singer, *Constructing Ottoman Beneficence*, p. 44.

37. Cf. Ergin, 'Introduction', *Bathing Culture of Anatolian Civilizations*, p. 5.

38. Cf. ibid., p. 6.

39. The endowment deed is preserved in at least three versions in the Archives of the General Directorate of Endowments in Ankara: Defter Nos 121, 1426 and 1427 contain versions in Arabic; D. 1766, pp. 136–70, contains a twentieth-century Turkish translation of the original, which I have used here. Different versions existed for different purposes: one copy was kept in the palace archive, while another must have stayed with the endowment administrator for use as reference in his day-to-day dealings. Also, in the first stages of organising the properties and stipulations, changes could have occurred, necessitating further, amended versions of the document. The different endowment deeds are also discussed and analysed in Pınar Kayaalp-Aktan, 'Atik Valide Mosque Complex'.

40. These decrees are preserved in summary fashion in the Prime Ministry's Ottoman Archives in Istanbul, in the form of bound registers. Mühimme, 48/269/765, 48/341/1000, 48/357/1047, 60/106/261, 64/141/368. The latter is also published in Ahmet Refik Altınay, *Onuncu Asr-ı Hicride İstanbul Hayatı*, p. 32.

41. The accounting books are preserved in the Topkapı Palace Library (TSK), the Topkapı Palace Archives (TSA) and in the section Maliyeden Müdevver (MAD) in the Prime Ministry's Ottoman Archives (BOA). TSK, E.H. 3064. TSA, D. 9912, D. 1901, D. 1781. BOA, MAD 5827, 3002, 987, 7434, 15742, 5247 (published in Said Öztürk, *Osmanlı Arşiv Belgelerinde Siyakat Yazısı*, pp. 236–9), 5886, 5273, 1672, 2263, 2105; EV.HMH. VLSA, 6/102, 6/104.

42. TSK, Revan Odası 1934; published in Mübahat Kütükoğlu, *Osmanlı'da Narh Müessesi ve 1640 Tarihli Narh Defteri*.

43. TSA, E. 246/61, E. 246/62; BOA, EV.HMH.VLSA, 6/102, 6/104.

44. BOA, Kamil Kepeci Müteferrik Defterleri 7437.

45. Published in Ahmet Refik Altınay, *Onikinci Asr-ı Hicri'de İstanbul Hayatı*, p. 217.

46. BOA, D.HMH.VLSA, 282/27, 282/30, 290/117, 291/78, 292/101; TSA, E. 246/291.

47. These proceedings have been published in transcribed form in Osman Ergin, *Mecelle-i Umûr-ı Belediyye*. The nineteenth-century newspaper in question here is the official gazette, the *Takvîm-i Vekâyi*.

48. The newspaper and magazine articles in chronological order are the following: Refik, 'İstanbul Hamamları'; Ahmet Süheyl Ünver, 'Hamamlarımız en Sıhhi Yıkanma Vasıtasıdır'; Ünver, 'İstanbul Hamamlarının İstikbali'; Ünver, 'Türk Hamamları'; Ünver, 'İstanbul Hamamları'; Ünver, 'İstanbul Hamamları, Hali ve İstikbali'; Ünver, 'Tarihi bir Hamam Halka Açıldı: Çemberlitaş Hamamı'; İbrahim Konyalı, 'Bizans ve Osmanlı Hamamları'; Kandemir, 'Eski Hamamlar'; Anonymous, 'Hamamlar'; S. Demiren, 'Bizans Hamamları'; Reşad Koçu, 'Çarşı Hamamlarımız'; E. B. Şapolyo, 'Türk Hamamları'; Metin And, '16. Yüzyılda Temizlik ve Hamamlar'.

49. I have limited myself to the following Turkish articles: *Hürriyet Tarih*, 4 December 2002; Zeynep Balcı, 'Şehirde Yeni Moda: Hamam'; Tülay Zihli, *Atlas İstanbul Rehberi*. Articles from English- and German-language magazines include Şebnem İşigüzel, 'Waschtag im Reich der Sinne'; Nancy Milford, 'Bathed in Tradition in Istanbul'.

50. *Steam* (1997, directed by Ferzan Özpetek); *The Accidental Spy* (2001, directed by Teddy Chan). Furthermore, during my fieldwork, several television documentaries were filmed there or were prepared to be filmed: a travel magazine on the Discovery Channel; a documentary on baths around the world for a US channel; and a documentary on hamams for the German–French channel ARTE.

51. See, for example, at: www.cemberlitashamami.com.tr; www.suleymaniye-hamami.com; www.galatasarayhamami.com; www.cagalogluhamami.com.

52. Fieldwork at Çemberlitaş Hamamı was carried out between November 2001 and February 2003, with the help of a Dissertation Fellowship Grant from the MacArthur Interdisciplinary Program on Global Change, Sustainability and Justice and a William W. Stout Fellowship Grant, both from the University of Minnesota.

53. Çemberlitaş Hamamı is depicted on a seventeenth-century map of the water conduits of Köprülü Mehmed Paşa's charitable endowment. Süleymaniye Library, Köprülü Su Yolu Haritası.

54. A partial, if somewhat improbable, view of Çemberlitaş Hamamı is visible in the engraving showing Constantine's Column in Pardoe, *City of the Sultan*. I am grateful to Halil Onur for bringing this image to my attention. There is one anonymous nineteenth-century photograph preserved in the Istanbul University Library; another, similar, photograph is reproduced in the Ottoman newspaper *Servet-i Fünun*, 6 June 1890.

55. Although I tried to include in this project the *kadı sicilleri* (judges' records documenting court cases ranging from inheritance distribution over real estate transactions to murder), I have not been able to find any references to Çemberlitaş Hamamı in the entries I read. It is likely that, among the

approximately ten thousand entries where one could potentially find mention of it, some new information will emerge; however, after several weeks of fruitless searching I decided to base this biography on the already available material and hope that another researcher will have more luck in locating the hamam in the judges' records.

56. Hayden White, 'Historical Text as Literary Artifact', p. 231.
57. Aslı Niyazioğlu, 'Lives of a Sixteenth-Century Ottoman Sheikh', p. 608. A similar point is made by Aksan, 'The Question of Writing Premodern Biographies of the Middle East', p. 193.
58. One of the foremost examples is the great Arab scholar Ibn Khaldun (1332–1406), who proposed the theory that no society can remain permanently at a high level of development, since decay always follows maturity. Ibn Khaldun, *Muqaddimah*. A famous example of a historical study following in Ibn Khaldun's footsteps and predicated on the model of rise, golden age and decline is Edward Gibbon's *Decline and Fall of the Roman Empire*, originally published between 1776 and 1788.
59. For a recent translation of the work, see Giorgio Vasari, *Vite*.
60. For further discussion of the genre, see James Stewart-Robinson, 'The Tezkere Genre in Islam'; Tarif Khalidi, *Arabic Historical Thought in the Classical Period*, pp. 44–8; Judith Tucker, 'Biography as History'; Jawid Mojaddedi, *The Biographical Tradition in Sufism*.
61. For a survey of Ottoman literature that carries biographical elements, see Abdülkadir Özcan, 'Osmanlı Tarih Edebiyatında Biyografi Türünün Ortaya Çıkışı ve Gelişmesi'.
62. On the latter, see Hatice Aynur and Aslı Niyazioğlu, *Aşık Çelebi ve Şairler Tezkeresi Üzerine Yazılar*.
63. See, for example, the dynastic history titled *Târîh-i Âl-i Osman* by Süleyman the Magnificent's court historiographer Ârifi, in five volumes. The second volume is dedicated solely to the life of Osman, the founder of the dynasty, and the fifth volume to Süleyman the Magnificent, covering the events under his rule up to 1555.
64. For a published version of this work, see Mustafa Âli, *Mustafa Âli's Künhül-Ahbar*. For an evaluation of Âli's innovative use of biography, see Cornell Fleischer, *Bureaucrat and Intellectual in the Ottoman Empire*, pp. 245–6.
65. See, for example, Vahidi's *Menakıb-i Hoca-i Cihan ve Netice-i Can*.
66. The most famous travel book, the seventeenth-century *Seyahatname* by Evliya Çelebi, contains so much interspersed information on the author's patron that the patron's life has become the subject of a book-length biography: Robert Dankoff, *The Intimate Life of an Ottoman Statesman*.
67. The life and adventures of an Ottoman prisoner of war in the Hapsburg Empire are recounted by himself in Osman Ağa, *Kendi Kalemiyle Temeşvarlı Osman Ağa*. A German translation of the work also exists: Osman Ağa, *Der Gefangene der Giauren*. Another captivity narrative is that of a sailor

abducted by pirates in the Mediterranean: Halil Sahillioğlu, 'Akdeniz'da Korsanlara Esir Düşen Abdi Çelebi'nin Mektubu'.

68. For studies on examples of this genre, see Cemal Kafadar, 'Self and Others'; Cemal Kafadar, 'Mütereddit bir Mutasavvıf'; Cemal Kafadar, *Kim Var İmiş Biz Yoğ İken*; Derin Terzioğlu, 'Man in the Image of God in the Image of the Times'.

69. See, for example, Cafer Çelebi, *Risâle-i Mi'mâriyye*. For a discussion of the treatises on the life and works of the architect Sinan, see below.

70. A number of sultans have been the subject of biographies in Turkish, published by the Ministry of Culture and Tourism and several university presses. See, for example, Yılmaz Öztuna, *Kanuni Sultan Süleyman*; Ahmet Uğur, *Yavuz Sultan Selim*. However, these focus primarily on sultans who had major military and political achievements and do not constitute a concerted effort to systematically cover the dynasty. For a scholarly biography written in French, see André Clot, *Soliman le Magnifique*. In English, see Franz Babinger, *Mehmed the Conqueror*. The original German version was published in 1953. For the recent biography of Hürrem Sultan, see Leslie Peirce, *Empress of the East*. For biographies on Ottoman palace officials, see Theoharis Stavrides, *Sultan of Vezirs*; Jane Hathaway, *Beshir Agha*. While Fleischer's study of the historian Mustafa Âli (see n. 64, above, *Bureaucrat and Intellectual in the Ottoman Empire*) and Colin Imber's study of Süleyman the Magnificent's grand mufti Ebussuud also qualify as biographies, they both focus on the intellectual life of their subjects. Imber, *Ebu's-Suud*.

71. Derin Terzioğlu, 'Tarihi İnsanlı Yazmak'.

72. For an extended discussion of the issue of individuality in the context of the Ottoman Empire, see Rhoads Murphey, 'Forms of Differentiation and Expression of Individuality in Ottoman Society'.

73. For a discussion of Sinan's autobiographies and their value for creating a portrait of him as a human being and as craftsman, see Gülru Necipoğlu, *Age of Sinan*, pp. 127–47. See also Mimar Sinan, *Sinan's Autobiographies*.

74. Ibid.

75. James Stewart-Robinson, 'Ottoman Biographies of Poets'.

76. Dwight Reynolds, *Interpreting the Self*, p. 247. A linear and chronologically coherent narrative, divided into chapters that correspond to major developments and shifts in the subject's life, only appeared as a widespread feature of Middle Eastern auto/biography with the introduction of the genre of the novel.

77. Igor Kopytoff, 'Cultural Biography of Things', pp. 66–7.

78. Chris Gosden and Yvonne Marshall, 'Cultural Biography of Objects', p. 169.

79. Ian Hodder, *Entangled*.

80. Jody Joy, 'Reinvigorating Object Biography', pp. 540–1. This essay – together with Anthony Harding's 'Introduction: Biographies of

Things' – provides a useful overview over the relevant literature, in much greater depth than what can be offered here.

81. Richard Davis, *Lives of Indian Images*.
82. Paul Stephenson, *The Serpent Column*.
83. Vildan Serdaroğlu, 'When Literature and Architecture Meet', pp. 273–4.
84. Agah Levend, *Türk Edebiyatında Şehr-Engizler*, p. 77. The Turkish original, as transcribed by Levend, reads: *Ne denlu varise hurrem maâbid/ mubârek kubbeler âlî mesâcid/ kaunundur şeh-i pîrûz-bahtı/ olupdur minber anun tâc u tahtı* (added emphasis).
85. Süleyman Saadettin Efendi [known as Müstakimzade], *Tuhfe-i Hattâtîn*, p. 78. The original reads: *az cümle re'îsi'l-cevâmi' olan Ayasofya-yı kebire*.
86. I first came across the Ottoman literary use of this metaphor in Gülru Necipoğlu, 'Life of an Imperial Monument', pp. 201–2. Necipoğlu quotes these authors, but in her discussion of the adaptive reuse of the Hagia Sophia in the Ottoman period she does not fully develop the potential of the biographic approach. In her article, the concept of a life story functions as a thread along which the author organises stories about the Hagia Sophia's perception.
87. The original reads: *Yatar hammâm gibi gözlerin göke diktib Zâtî/ derûnı nâr-i hecr ile yanar mânend-i tûn olmi?* Zati, *Zati Divanı*, ghazal 602/5. As translated in Vildanoğlu, 'When Literature and Architecture Meet', p. 282.
88. Reynolds, *Interpreting the Self*; Michael Mascuch, *Origins of the Individualist Self*, p. 14. For recent contributions, see Olcay Akyıldız, Halim Kara and Börte Sagaster (eds), *Autobiographical Themes in Turkish Literature*; Ralf Elger and Yavuz Köse (eds), *Many Ways of Speaking About the Self*; and the chapters by Astrid Meier, Aslı Niyazioğlu and Nelly Hanna in Ruggiu (ed.), *Uses of First-Person Writings*.
89. Meropi Anastassiadou and Bernard Heyberger (eds), *Figures anonymes, figures d'élite*.
90. Maurits van den Boogert, 'Resurrecting *Homo Ottomanicus*', p. 18.
91. Christine Isom-Verhaaren and Kent Schull (eds), *Living in the Ottoman Realm*.
92. Murphey, 'Forms of Individuality', p. 135. Other studies that point to the importance of relations to others in the formation of Ottoman individuality include: Kafadar, 'Self and Others'; Steve Tamari, 'Biography, Autobiography, and Identity in Early Modern Damascus'.
93. On identity formation in relation to groups in Europe, see Nathalie Davis, 'Boundaries and the Sense of Self in Sixteenth-Century France'; Carol Walker Bynum, 'Did the Twelfth Century Discover the Individual?'. On the idea of autonomy as myth, see Paul Eakin, *How Our Lives Become Stories*, pp. 43–68.
94. See Isom-Verhaaren and Schull (eds), *Living in the Ottoman Realm*, pp. 2–3.
95. See Christine Isom-Verhaaren, 'Constructing Ottoman Identity in the Reigns of Mehmed II and Bayezid II'.

96. On the complex interplay between physical space, ethnicity and language, considering the rather unstable term 'Rum(î)' as a designation for Anatolia and the Balkans, see Cemal Kafadar, 'A Rome of One's Own'. On the term 'Rumî' and its meanings, see also Salih Özbaran, 'In Search of Another Identity'.

97. On the construction of a specific Sunni religious identity, see Derin Terzioğlu, 'How to Conceptualize Ottoman Sunnitization'; Nabil al-Tikriti, 'Ibn-i Kemal's Confessionalism and the Construction of an Ottoman Islam'.

98. For an example of occupational identity, see Charles Wilkins, 'Ibrahim ibn Khidr al-Qaramani'.

99. On the identity of Turcophone seamen, see Christine Isom-Verhaaren, 'Was there Room in Rum for Corsairs?'

100. On the way in which Ottoman literati were pivotal in crystallising a Turkic identity for the Ottoman dynasty, see Murat Cem Mengüç, 'Interpreting Ottoman Identity with the Historian Neşri'; on the importance of ethnic origin among the Ottoman elite, see Metin Kunt, 'Ethnic-Regional (*cins*) Solidarity in the Seventeenth-Century Ottoman Establishment'.

101. Reynolds, *Interpreting the Self*, p. 243.

102. This argument forms the backbone of Necipoğlu's *Age of Sinan*.

103. Personal communication with D. Fairchild Ruggles, Historians of Islamic Art Majlis, University of Seattle, Washington, 21 February 2004.

104. Blair and Bloom, in a state-of-the-field article, observe the absence of monographs examining works of art over a sustained period of time, giving as a most surprising example the Dome of the Rock: 'Despite all the glossy publications and interpretative articles, we still do not have a single serious work containing plans, sections, inscriptions, and interpretations of the Dome of the Rock from its construction in 692 to its emergence as the symbol of Palestinian nationhood in the twenty-first century'; Sheila Blair and Jonathan Bloom, 'The Mirage of Islamic Art', pp. 162–3.

105. One of the seminal works investigating the cosmos of an 'ordinary' historical person is Carlo Ginzburg, *The Cheese and the Worms*. Middle Eastern historians have now also begun to critically engage with historical records left, not by the elite, but by commoners: Dana Sajdi, *Barber of Damascus*.

Chapter 1

1. For a fictional treatment about Nurbanu's life story based on thorough historical background research, see Katherine Nouri Hughes, *The Mapmaker's Daughter*.

2. Susan Skilliter, 'Letters of the Venetian "Sultana" Nurbanu'; Leslie Peirce, *Imperial Harem*.

3. Ibid., p. 515; Benjamin Arbel, 'Nurbanu (c. 1530–1583)', p. 247.

4. This version has been suggested by Arbel in 'Nurbanu (c. 1530–1583)'.

5. Kayaalp-Aktan, 'Atik Valide Mosque Complex', p. 42, n. 99.
6. This was not an isolated instance of fabricated ties between a European power and the women of the Ottoman harem. See Christine Isom-Verhaaren, 'Royal French Women in the Ottoman Sultan's Harem'.
7. The ten extant letters written by Nurbanu between 1578 and 1583 to several ambassadors and to the Doge of Venice have been published in Skilliter, 'Letters of the Venetian "Sultana" Nurbanu'.
8. It is possible that she gave birth to a fifth child, a daughter named Fatma, in 1559. A. D. Alderson, *Structure of the Ottoman Dynasty*, table XXXI.
9. On the endowment, see Mustafa Cezar, *Typical Commercial Buildings of the Ottoman Classical Period*, p. 287. For a detailed description of Selim's mosque complex, see Necipoğlu, *Age of Sinan*, pp. 234–8.
10. Peirce, *Imperial Harem*, p. 53.
11. Skilliter, 'Letters of the Venetian "Sultana" Nurbanu', p. 51.
12. For a document on the procurement of marble and other building materials, dated to 20 February 1571, see Refik, *Onuncu Asr-ı Hicride İstanbul Hayatı*, p. 34.
13. On Hürrem Sultan's patronage specifically, see Necipoğlu, *Age of Sinan*, pp. 268–92; Peirce, *Empress of the East*, pp. 176–94. On female architectural patronage in the Ottoman Empire in general, see Ülkü Bates, 'Women as Patrons of Architecture in Turkey'; Ülkü Bates, 'Architectural Patronage of Ottoman Women'; Leslie Peirce, 'Gender and Sexual Propriety in Ottoman Royal Women's Patronage'; Lucienne Thys-Şenocak, 'The Yeni Valide Mosque Complex of Eminönü'; Lucienne Thys-Şenocak, *Ottoman Women Builders*; Isom-Verhaaren, 'Mihrimah Sultan'; Kayaalp-Aktan, 'Atik Valide Mosque Complex'. See also Peirce, *Imperial Harem*; Singer, *Constructing Ottoman Beneficence*.
14. Peirce, *Imperial Harem*, p. 62.
15. For an Ottoman account of the circumstances of Murad's succession to the throne, see Mustafa Selânikî, *Târîh-i Selânikî*, p. 98. For a more detailed summary based on Selânikî and other sources, see Kayaalp-Aktan, 'Atik Valide Mosque Complex', pp. 53–4.
16. Peirce, *Imperial Harem*, p. 188.
17. Ibid., p. 126.
18. Ibid., p. 126. BOA, MAD 422, 487.
19. For the names of the persons who were part of her faction, see Kayaalp-Aktan, 'Atik Valide Mosque Complex', pp. 55–6. For the names and positions of the court officials who married her daughters, see also Alderson, *Structure of the Ottoman Dynasty*, table XXXI.
20. On the mosque complex in Lapseki, see TSK, E.H. 3064; VGM, D. 1766, pp. 137, 162, 166. On the mosque in Sarıgazi, see Ayvansarayî, *Garden of the Mosques*, p. 549.
21. For the pulpit, see Ayvansarayî, *Garden of the Mosques*, p. 44. On the manuscripts, see Nimet Bayraktar, 'Üsküdar Kütüphaneleri', p. 49. Upon

the dissolution of the mosque's endowment, these manuscripts were transferred to the Museum of Turkish and Islamic Art, the Süleymaniye Library and the Hacı Selim Ağa Library in Üsküdar.

22. Peirce, *Imperial Harem*, p. 192.
23. Selânikî, *Târîh-i Selânikî*, pp. 140–1.
24. Ibid., p. 141.
25. Skilliter, 'Letters of the Venetian "Sultana" Nurbanu', p. 525.
26. For these sources and their content, see Necipoğlu, *Age of Sinan*, p. 281; Kayaalp-Aktan, 'Atik Valide Mosque Complex', p. 81.
27. Peirce, *Imperial Harem*, p. 210.
28. Necipoğlu, *Age of Sinan*, pp. 129–31.
29. On statements indicating Sinan's quandary, see Necipoğlu, *Age of Sinan*, pp. 133–4. All dates and facts concerning Sinan's life and career are taken from the same publication, chapter 4.
30. This number is based on the *Tezkiretü'l-Bünyân* (Necipoğlu, *Age of Sinan*, p. 135). In an earlier study of Sinan's corpus, Kuran has calculated the number of Sinan's buildings as 477, based on the five different versions of his autobiography, which all give different numbers. Aptullah Kuran, *Sinan*, p. 29.
31. For the evaluation of this version's reliability, see Kuran, *Sinan*, p. 34.
32. There exists an imperial decree dated AH 16 Safer 992/28 February 1584 appointing Sedefkâr Mehmed Ağa. See Ernst Egli, *Sinan*, p. 42.
33. Cafer Çelebi, *Risâle-i Mi'mâriyye*.
34. As translated by Fleischer, *Bureaucrat and Intellectual in the Ottoman Empire*, p. 254.
35. Isom-Verhaaren, 'Constructing Ottoman Identity', p. 112.
36. On this genre, see Bağcı, 'From Adam to Mehmed III'.
37. Necipoğlu, 'Word and Image', p. 45.
38. Yegül, *Baths and Bathing in Classical Antiquity*, p. 29.
39. Ibid., pp. 6–29.
40. Albrecht Berger, *Das Bad in der Byzantinischen Zeit*, p. 35.
41. For a detailed discussion of the continuation of Greek bathing tradition in the Roman period, the similarities and dissimilarities between Greek and Roman bathing culture, and elements of bath architecture, see Janet DeLaine, 'Some Observations on the Transition from Greek to Roman Baths'. See also Yegül, *Bathing in the Roman World*, pp. 41–5. For a study that evaluates the six most influential approaches to the problem of the Roman public bath's origin and development from Greek predecessors, see Garrett Fagan, 'Genesis of the Roman Public Bath'.
42. Yegül, *Baths and Bathing in Classical Antiquity*, p. 61; Yegül, *Bathing in the Roman World*, pp. 52–4.
43. For a succinct overview and discussion of imperial thermae, see Yegül, *Bathing in the Roman World*, pp. 101–32.
44. On the origins and development of the hypocaust system, see Yegül, *Bathing in the Roman World*, pp. 81–90.

45. On recommendations for medicinal bathing in the Roman world, see Garrett Fagan, 'Bathing for Health with Celsus and Pliny the Elder'.
46. Fagan, *Bathing in Public in the Roman World*, pp. 38–9.
47. DeLaine, 'Introduction', *Roman Baths and Bathing*, p. 12.
48. Ibid., p. 13.
49. For a discussion of these bath-gymnasium complexes, see Yegül, *Bathing in the Roman World*, pp. 154–80. For a succinct overview of the Byzantine baths of Constantinople based on a combination of archaeological and literary evidence, see Fikret Yegül, 'Baths of Constantinople'.
50. The highly symmetrical complexes of Sardis, Milet and Ephesus, consisting of a row of rectangular barrel-vaulted halls and low colonnades arranged around a courtyard, were no longer built after the fourth century. By then, social and intellectual aspects of bathing were emphasised over the physical. The bath-gymnasium complexes have very little in common with the Islamic baths that appeared in the twelfth and thirteenth centuries in Asia Minor, and provide no link between Romano-Byzantine and Islamic bathing culture. The view that the architectural characteristics of the Ottoman hamams of Istanbul have not been modelled after the Byzantine baths of Constantinople, even if bathing culture in general must have left an impression on the early Ottomans before the conquest of the city, is also held by Berger, *Das Bad in der Byzantinischen Zeit*, p. 95, and Yegül, *Baths and Bathing in Classical Antiquity*, p. 350. Berger mentions that the Greek Orthodox Patriarch Athanasios I (in office 1289–1293 and 1303–1309) allowed Turks to use his church's bath (*Das Bad in der Byzantinischen Zeit*, p. 69).
51. Dow, *The Islamic Baths of Palestine*, p. 34. This view has been challenged based on the evidence of more recent archaeological research by Fournet, 'Ancient Baths of Southern Syria'. I thank the author for providing me with an off-print ahead of the publication of the proceedings.
52. For a sophisticated discussion of interactions between Muslims and Christians along the Islamic-Byzantine frontier, based on archaeological and geomorphological data as well as textual sources, see A. Asa Eger, *Islamic-Byzantine Frontier*.
53. Leah di Segni, 'Greek Inscriptions of Hammat Gader', pp. 237–40, no. 54.
54. For details on the site, see Grabar et al., *City in the Desert*; K. A. C. Creswell, *Short Account of Early Muslim Architecture*, p. 164.
55. Fournet, 'Ancient Baths of Southern Syria', n.p.
56. Ibid.
57. On Khirbat al-Mafjar, see Hamilton, *Walid and His Friends*. For the argument that Umayyad baths had a primarily secular function and provided meeting points in the desert, where tribal representatives could get together with their new leaders, see Tohme, 'Between Balneum and Hamam'.
58. Yegül, *Baths and Bathing in Classical Antiquity*, pp. 339, 341; Yegül, *Bathing in the Roman World*, p. 210.

59. For an extended discussion of the rooms' function, see Grabar et al., *City in the Desert*, pp. 90–7.
60. Yegül, *Bathing in the Roman World*, pp. 207–10; Yegül, *Baths and Bathing in Classical Antiquity*, pp. 326, 329, 346–9; Yegül, 'The Roman Baths at Isthmia in their Mediterranean Context'.
61. Creswell dates the bathhouse to after the city's completion on the basis of archaeological evidence, but posits that its similarity to Umayyad baths makes a much later date unlikely. Creswell, *Short Account of Early Muslim Architecture*, p. 258.
62. Philipp Hitti, *History of the Arabs*, p. 338.
63. Two baths were located close to the mosque of al-Mutawakkil, one in the Balkuwara Palace, one in the circular basin and one in the Dar al-'Amma. On the first three, see Thomas Leisten, *Excavation of Samarra*. On the bath in the circular basin, see Hafiz Husayn al-Hayani, 'al-Birka al-Da'iriyya Dakhil Qasr al-Khalifa, Samarra'.
64. Alasdair Northedge, 'Interpretation of the Palace of the Caliph at Samarra'.
65. I am indebted to Alasdair Northedge for pointing out this bath to me and for providing me with a ground plan.
66. Michael Morony, *Iraq after the Muslim Conquest*, pp. 266–8.
67. The few existing baths receive only cursory mention in survey texts or constitute isolated case studies which do not allow any general conclusions. For two case studies, see David Whitehouse, 'Excavations at Siraf: Fourth Interim Report'; David Whitehouse, 'Excavations at Siraf: Fifth Interim Report'; Galina Asanova and Martin Dow, 'Sarrafan Baths in Bukhara'.
68. Kai Ka'us ibn Iskandar, *Mirror for Princes*, p. 79.
69. On the region of southern Turkey and northern Syria as a crossroads of bathing cultures in the Roman period, see Fikret Yegül, 'Cilicia at the Crossroads'; Fikret Yegül, 'Baths and Bathing in Roman Antioch'. For a recent study of Antioch in the late Roman and early Islamic periods, see A. Asa Eger, '(Re)Mapping Medieval Antioch'. Especially Antioch's bath C, an imperial establishment renovated around the mid-fourth century, includes a domed octagonal hall with niches, which seems to presage Ottoman centralised hot rooms. Yegül, *Bathing in the Roman World*, fig. 88.
70. For the Turkish version, see Kai Ka'us ibn Iskandar, *Book of Advice*.
71. Önge, *Anadolu'da XII.–XIII. Yüzyıl Türk Hamamları*. For an opposing view, see Howard Crane, 'Anatolian Saljuq Architecture and Its Links to Saljuq Iran', pp. 266–7.
72. Ahmet Süheyl Ünver, 'Anadolu Selçuklarında Sağlık Hizmetleri'.
73. For an extensive survey of such baths, see Tükel Yavuz, 'Baths of Seljuk Anatolian Carvansarais'.
74. Önge, *Anadolu'da XII.–XIII. Yüzyıl Türk Hamamları*, p. 95. Two concrete examples of an Ottoman choice of site based on the availability of water and spolia are the Eski Kaplıca in Bursa, erected by Sultan Murad I (r. 1362–1389) over the remains of a sixth-century thermal bath, and the

Haseki Hamam in Istanbul (1553), commissioned by the wife of Sultan Süleyman the Magnificent (r. 1520–1566) and built over the remains of the Byzantine Zeuxippos bath, once the most magnificent *thermae* of Constantinople.

75. For more details and further specific cases of such transitions, see Zeki Atçeken, *Konya'da Selçuklu Yapılarının Osmanlı Devrinde Bakımı ve Kullanılması*.
76. On the baths of Bursa, see Şehitoğlu, *Historic Hammams of Bursa*; see also Çiğdem Kafesçioğlu, *Constantinopolis/Istanbul*, p. 104.
77. This number is based on the list of Ottoman monuments published in Ekrem Hakkı Ayverdi, *İlk 250 Senenin Osmanlı Mimârisi*.
78. Yegül, *Baths and Bathing in Classical Antiquity*, p. 324; Yegül, *Bathing in the Roman World*, pp. 200–6; Berger, *Das Bad in der Byzantinischen Zeit*, pp. 56–71. For a more extended discussion of hamams in post-conquest Istanbul, see Kafesçioğlu, *Constantinopolis/Istanbul*, pp. 103–9, 182.
79. For a ground plan based on its state in the early nineteenth century, see Richard Pullan and Charles Texier, *L'architecture byzantine*. On the urban context of the Çukur Hamamı, see Kafesçioğlu, *Constantinopolis/Istanbul*, p. 82.
80. Kafesçioğlu, *Constantinopolis/Istanbul*, p. 108.
81. For a discussion of Mahmut Paşa's patronage as a whole, see ibid., pp. 109–19.
82. Ibid., p. 117.

Chapter 2

1. It is not the purpose of this chapter to give an extensive account of Nurbanu's endowment, but rather a background for the construction of Çemberlitaş Hamamı. For such an account, see Kayaalp-Aktan, 'Atik Valide Mosque Complex'.
2. For a discussion of the origins and history of Islamic pious charitable endowments, see Amy Singer, *Charity in Islamic Societies*. A concise introduction can be found in Ahmed Dallal, 'The Islamic Instituiton of Waqf'. For a discussion of the relevant historiography, including an extensive bibliography, see Miriam Hoexter, 'Waqf Studies in the Twentieth Century'.
3. On the importance of food to promote imperial power, see Ergin, Neumann and Singer (eds), *Feeding People, Feeding Power*.
4. Halil İnalcık, 'Istanbul'. Endowments could have such diverse functions as providing dowrys for orphaned girls, the repair of roads and walkways, support for tax payments and the feeding of animals.
5. Gabriel Baer, 'Women and Waqf', p. 10.
6. For the full text, see the Appendix.
7. Cf. Singer, *Constructing Ottoman Beneficence*, p. 164.
8. For 1632, see BOA, MAD 3002. For 1644/5, see BOA, MAD 987.

9. VGM, D. 1766, p. 136 (author's translation).

10. For an in-depth analysis of the founder's motivations as expressed in the deed of trust, see Pınar Kayaalp-Aktan, 'The Atik Valide's Endowment Deed'.

11. Aşık Mehmed, *Menâzırü'l-'Avâlim*, TSK, E.H. 1446, fols. 394r–v. As quoted in Necipoğlu, *Age of Sinan*, p. 292.

12. The decree has been published in transcription in Refik, *Onuncu Asr-ı Hicride İstanbul Hayatı*, p. 34.

13. For a detailed history of the building progress based on these archival records, see Necipoğlu, *Age of Sinan*, pp. 284–5.

14. On the Friday preacher's appointment, see Ayvansarayî, *Garden of the Mosques*, p. 117.

15. Elsewhere I have argued that this addition may not necessarily have been due to Nurbanu's increased status as she became the sultan's mother rather than his spouse, but to the mosque interior's unsatisfactory acoustic characteristics. Nina Ergin, 'Soundscape of Sixteenth-Century Istanbul Mosques', pp. 216–17.

16. Kuran, *Sinan*, p. 181. Godfrey Goodwin, *Ottoman Architecture*, p. 289. The earliest document using the name 'Atik Valide' that I have encountered is an accounting book: BOA, MAD 2263.

17. For more detail on Qur'an recital in the mosque, see Ergin, 'Soundscape of Sixteenth-Century Istanbul Mosques'. On the interplay between the recited and the epigraphic text, see Nina Ergin, 'Multi-Sensorial Message of the Divine and the Personal'.

18. On the deployment of incense in mosques, see Nina Ergin, 'Fragrance of the Divine'.

19. VGM, D. 1766, p. 153.

20. VGM, D. 1766, p. 155.

21. VGM, D. 1766, p. 164.

22. Baha Tanman, 'Atik Valide Külliyesi', p. 408.

23. For the argument that Ottoman women could make a space distinctly their own by endowing Qur'an recitations, see Nina Ergin, 'Ottoman Royal Women's Spaces'.

24. For a discussion of the sensory dimensions of Ottoman hospital architecture, especially as it contributed to the patients' well-being, see Nina Ergin, 'Healing by Design?'

25. VGM, D.1766, p. 156.

26. VGM, D. 1766, p. 166.

27. VGM, D. 1766, p. 160.

28. Evliya Çelebi, *Seyahatname*, p. 234.

29. For the historical significance of *zerde* and a sixteenth-century recipe of this dish, see Stefanos Yérasimos, *Sultan Sofraları*, p. 142.

30. For a more detailed discussion of the political significance of food distribution at mosques, see Ergin, '"And in the Soup Kitchen Food Shall be Cooked Twice Every Day"'.

31. The convent belonged to the Halvetiyye order until 1670/1, when it was taken over by the Karabaşiyye branch. After 1685, the Nuriyye branch took over the convent, to be replaced by the Şabaniyye in 1713. Tanman, 'Atik Valide Külliyesi', pp. 71–2.

32. VGM, D. 1766, p. 163.

33. Kazım Çeçen, *Üsküdar Suları*, pp. 44–8.

34. VGM, D. 1766, p. 161.

35. For a discussion of the distribution of eighteenth-century Istanbul's bath-houses across the urban space, with the help of GIS-generated maps, see Ergin, with Özarslan, 'Mapping Istanbul's Hamams', especially maps 4.1 and 4.2. For a discussion of bathhouse locations in fifteenth-century Cairo, see Raymond, 'La localisation des bains publics au Caire'. For another study that takes location together with strategic water use in consideration, see Ingrid Hehmeyer, 'Mosque, Bath, and Garden'.

36. The author himself concedes that his assigning different occupational groups to specific hamams is a humorous undertaking; nevertheless, even jokes contain a kernel of truth, and in this case Evliya likely reproduces popular notions about who visited which bathhouse in the city. Evliya Çelebi, *Seyahatname*, pp. 158–9.

37. VGM, D. 1766, p. 138.

38. Mimar Sinan, *Sinan's Autobiographies*, p. 73. The other treatises mention only one hamam related to the patronage of the *valide sultan* in Üsküdar.

39. BOA, Mühimme 26/264/111.

40. On the repairs, see TSA, E. 246/479 and E. 246/529. On its use as carpenter's shop, see Haskan, *İstanbul Hamamları*, pp. 284–5.

41. For more information on the renovation, see Ergun Taneri and Adnan Kazmaoğlu, 'Atik Valide Hamamı Yeniden Kullanım Projesi'.

42. 1583 is also the date proposed in Haskan, *İstanbul Hamamları*, p. 77.

43. Ayvansarayî, *Garden of the Mosques*, p. 489.

44. For more detail on the Büyük Hamam's history during the twentieth century, see Haskan, *İstanbul Hamamları*, pp. 77–8; İbrahim Hakkı Konyalı, *Abideleri ve Kitabeleriyle Üsküdar Tarihi*, pp. 446, 450; Baha Tanman, 'Mimar Sinan Hamamı', p. 468; Behçet Ünsal, 'Sinan'ın Son Bir Eseri Üsküdar Büyük Hamamın Aslı Şekline Dönüşümü'.

45. VGM, D. 1766, p. 139.

46. On the new city gate, see the imperial decree dated 24 March 1582: BOA, Mühimme 48/20/76.

47. Mimar Sinan, *Sinan's Autobiographies*, pp. 53, 73, 99.

48. Ayvansarayî, *Mecmua-i Tevarih*, p. 374 (author's translation).

49. On the hamam's history during the twentieth century, see Haskan, *İstanbul Hamamları*, p. 178.

50. For the text of the sale advert, see Banu Sezgin, 'İstanbul'daki Günümüz Ulaşmış Mimar Sinan Eserleri', p. 479. Another MA thesis at the same institution consists of a renovation proposal for the Havuzlu Hamam, includ-

ing restitution plans: İmre Eren Özbek, 'Fatih İlçesinde Ayakapı Hamamı Restorasyon Projesi'. Unfortunately, the owner has shown no interest in the proposed project.

Chapter 3

1. Maurice Cerasi, *Istanbul Divan Yolu*, p. 13. For the sake of convenience and brevity, I will use the name 'Divan Yolu' also for periods before the eighteenth century.
2. In his typically aphoristic manner, Ayvansarayi wrote about the mosque: 'The Dikilitaş Mosque near the Valide Hamam. Its builder was Fenarizade Ahmed Paşa.' Ayvansarayî, *Garden of the Mosques*, p. 129.
3. Cerasi, *Istanbul Divan Yolu*, pp. 93–7. On the theatrical and experiential quality of Ottoman architectural space in general, see Jale Erzen, 'Aesthetics and Aisthesis in Ottoman Art and Architecture'; on the gaze as a component of architectural design, see Kafesçioğlu, *Constantinopolis/Istanbul*, p. 104; Thys-Şenocak, 'The Yeni Valide Mosque Complex of Eminönü'; and Gülru Necipoğlu, 'Framing the Gaze in Ottoman, Safavid and Mughal Palaces'.
4. On processions, see Cerasi, *Istanbul Divan Yolu*, pp. 47–56, 119–21.
5. On the patronage of the different paşas, see ibid., pp. 57–62.
6. Ibid., pp. 87–8. See also Ergin, 'Mapping Istanbul's Hamams', pp. 116–17.
7. Yılmaz Önge, 'Eski Türk Hamamlarında Aydınlatma', p. 126.
8. Other examples are the Haseki Hamamı in Istanbul (1553), the Sokollu Hamamı in Edirne (1568/9) and the Sokollu Hamamı in Lüleburgaz (about 1570). Yılmaz Önge, 'Sinan'ın İnşa Ettiği Hamamlar', p. 256; Yılmaz Önge, 'Anadolu Türk Hamamları Hakkında Genel Bilgiler', vol. 1, p. 408.
9. The original reads: *Bi-hamdillah bugün Sultan Murad'ın . . . / bu hammam-ı sefa-fer 'acib ca-yı latif oldu / Cihan durdukça eyler namını merhumenin ihya / havası hoş binası dilkeş önü nazif oldu/ görüb itmamını Sa'i-i Da'i dedi tarihin / yapıldı valide sultan hammamı şerif oldu/ 992.*
10. BOA, D.HMH.VLSA, 282/77.
11. The Ottoman text reads: *habbeza hammam açub sefa / ab-ı ruh ol hevası dilküşa / mermer nakşını vird çün her zaman / mevc-i derya-yı melahatten nişan / sofalar menziline ehl-i sefa / camlar ayine-i 'alem-nüma / ca-be-ca o avizeler her takdan / oldı lebrizine afakda / o mermerden direklerdir meğer / ya tolar bir nice serr-i simin / bir dem içre ehl-i dünya-yı hemin / nola anlarsa suyun halvet-nişin . . . hakidir kafur hayy-ı ab-ı gülab / ca-be-ca o taslar simin habab / nola ger dönse hazineye daima / koynuna 'üryan girer her dilruba / Sa'i-ya rica-yı tarih-i niku güftmüş huld-ı berrin o hammam 992.* The lines omitted here will be discussed in Chapter 5. I am indebted to Hilal Kazan for her help with the poem's transcription and to Behice Tezçakar for her assistance in translating the verses.
12. VGM, D. 1766, p. 139.
13. BOA, Mühimme, 48/269/766; Mühimme 48/357/1047.

14. The original text reads: *Dikilitaş önünde bina etdirecek hammam* (added emphasis).
15. The original text reads: *bina eylediği mübaşer eylediği hammam* (added emphasis).
16. For a discussion of the city's intricate relationship to water across time, see Paul Magdalino and Nina Ergin (eds), *Istanbul and Water*.
17. BOA, Mühimme 48/269/766.
18. For the conversion of Ottoman liquid measures, see Ünal Öziş and Yalçın Arısoy, 'Water Conveyance Systems of the Great Architect Sinan'.
19. BOA, Mühimme 48/357/1047.
20. Kazım Çeçen, *İstanbul'un Osmanlı Dönemi Suyolları*.
21. BOA, Mühimme 60/106/261.
22. BOA, Mühimme 64/141/368. Transcription published in Refik, *Onuncu Asr-ı Hicride İstanbul Hayatı*, p. 49.
23. For a detailed case study of how water management and development created alliances and contradictions among social networks, see Deniz Karakaş, 'Water Resources Management and Development in Ottoman Istanbul'.
24. BOA, Mühimme 48/341/1000.
25. The remaining sections in this chapter have previously been published in a similar version in Nina Ergin, 'Bathing Business in Istanbul'.
26. For bathhouse furnishings, see Raymond, 'Les bains publics au Caire à la fin du XVIIIe siècle', p. 142.
27. The terminology has changed over the centuries. The term *natır* used to refer to a male bathhouse servant who in the hierarchy stood below the *tellak*, but still had his own guild. Today, it is only used for a female bath-house attendant.
28. For a list of bathhouse employees, see Mustafa Uzun and Nurettin Albayrak, 'Hamam: Kültür ve Edebiyat'. For a brief discussion of bath workers in medieval Baghdad, see Muhammad 'Abdul Jabbar Beg, 'Workers in the Hammamat'.
29. See Ergin, 'Bathing Business in Istanbul', p. 148, n. 6.
30. On migrant workers in hamams, see Nina Ergin, 'Albanian Tellâk Connection'.
31. Robert Olson, 'The Esnaf and the Patrona Halil Rebellion in 1730', p. 335. For a book-length analysis of the revolt, see Münir Aktepe, *Patrona İsyanı (1730)*. Published primary sources on the event include Faik Reşit Unat, *1730 Patrona İhtilali Hakkında bir Eser*; Destari Salih, *Destari Salih Tarihi*.
32. This decree has been published in transcription in Koçu, 'Dellak'. I have not been able to locate the original in the archives.
33. This shift from a primarily Albanian to a primarily Anatolian workforce becomes visible when comparing three different registers of hamam employ-ees. In a register dating to 1735, the workforce in the *extra muros* hamams was still almost exclusively Albanian. İstanbul Belediye Kütüphanesi, Muallim Cevdet Tasnifi, *İstanbul Hamamcı Esnafı ve Tellaklarının İsimlerini Havi*

Defter; I am indebted to Ahmet Yaşar for providing me with digital images of this source. In a second register dating to 1752, their regions of origin began to show more variation, with Anatolians and Istanbulites slowly but surely making inroads into this professional group. BOA, Kamil Kepeci Müteferrik Defterleri 7437. See Ergin, 'Albanian Tellâk Connection', tables IV and V. An even later register recording Istanbul's *esnaf* working in the settlements along the Golden Horn and the Bosphorus, dated by Kırlı to the turn of the nineteenth century, records hamam workers as hailing almost exclusively from the eastern Anatolian town of Sivas. BOA, Başmuhasebe-DBŞM 42648; see Cengiz Kırlı, 'Profile of the Labor Force', p. 137.

34. BOA, Kamil Kepeci Müteferrik Defterleri 7437; Ergin, 'Albanian Tellâk Connection.'
35. See Ergin, 'Albanian Tellâk Connection', table III.
36. For an overview of the staff size of Istanbul's hamams, see ibid., table II.
37. On this migration dynamics, see ibid., pp. 247–54.
38. TSK, H. 1344. Many of the illustrations are published in Nurhan Atasoy, *1582 Surname-i Hümayun*. See also Gisela Prochazka-Eisl, *Surname-i Hümayun*. For an interpretation of the event in light of Bakhtin's theory of the carnivalesque, see Derin Terzioğlu, 'Imperial Circumcision Festival of 1582'.
39. See Atasoy, *1582 Surname-i Hümayun*, p. 89.
40. Evliya Çelebi, *Seyahatname*, p. 329.The original reads: *Islâmbol'un dörd mevleviyyet yerinde yüz elli bir hammâm olduğu bâlâda imâretler evsâfında tahrir olunmuşdur. Ammâ bu esnâf alayında yüz elli bir hammâmcılar cümle pür-silâh ubûr ederler, ankâ ve muta'azzım sâlih kimesnelerdir . . . Bu hammâmcılar cümlesi küheylân atlara süvâr olup huddâmları arabalar üzre keçeden hammâmlar edüp münevver câmlar ile müzeyyen edüp, 'Gele Vefâ hammâmına cânım, gire Hacı Kadın hammâmına hânım, göre Çinili hammâmı cânım' deyü nîlgûn fûtaya sarmış bedeni uryânın diberân-ı uryân dellâklar böyle nidâ ederek hammâmlarıyla bile ubûr ederler.*
41. Evliya Çelebi, *Seyahatname*, p. 329. The original reads: *Neferât cümle 2000 . . . Bu dellâklar cümle uryân olup ibrîşim peştemâller ile dilberânları kâküllerin perişân edüp ellerinde fütûnî kîse ve bellerinde seng-i mûs ve mümessek sâbûn ile birbirlerinde kîse ve sâbûn sürerek güzer ederler.* The number of 2,000 *tellak*s working in Istanbul is a reasonable estimate and not one of Evliya's usual exaggerations, since the abovementioned register dating to 1752 mentions a total of 2,400 *tellaks* and *natırs* employed in Istanbul, Üsküdar and Eyüp.
42. Evliya Çelebi, *Seyahatname*, p. 329.
43. See Atasoy, *1582 Surname-i Hümayun*, pp. 78–9.
44. See Eunjong Yi, *Guild Dynamics*; Onur Yıldırım, 'Ottoman Guilds', p. 77. Suraiya Faroqhi has worked extensively on guilds. See, for example, Suraiya Faroqhi, *Towns and Townsmen of Ottoman Anatolia*; Suraiya Faroqhi, *Bread from the Lion's Mouth*; Suraiya Faroqhi and Randi Deguilhem, *Crafts and*

Craftsmen of the Middle East. See also Fatmagül Demirel, *Osmanlı'dan Cumhuriyet'e Esnaf ve Ticaret.*

45. BOA, Mühimme 69/152/302.
46. This *nizamname* excerpt has been published in transcription in Koçu, 'Dellak'. I was not able to find the original (author's translation).
47. Kütükoğlu, *Osmanlılar'da Narh Müessesi*, pp. 260–1 (author's translation).
48. On these duties of the *muhtesib* as laid out in foundational medieval Islamic texts, see Roy Mottahedeh and Kristen Stilt, 'Public and Private', p. 737.
49. Grotzfeld, *Das Bad im arabischen Mittelalter*, pp. 12–13; Robert Mantran, *Istanbul dans la seconde moitié du XVIIe siècle*, p. 504.
50. For a concise introduction to the concept of *gedik*, see Yıldırım, 'Ottoman Guilds', pp. 89–93.
51. Yi, *Guild Dynamics.*
52. Ibid., ch. 3.
53. The notion of *gedik* with its attendant rights and obligations changed over time according to the economic needs of both the guild and the state. For a discussion of these changes, see Engin Akarlı, 'Gedik'.
54. On the Elçi Han, see Semavi Eyice, 'Elçi Han'.
55. On this and other *han*s, see Ceyhan Güran, *Türk Hanların Gelişimi ve İstanbul Hanları Mimarisi*. On their architectural as well as social dimensions, see Işık Tamdoğan-Abel, 'Les *han*, ou l'étranger dans la ville ottomane'; Mathilde Pinon-Demirçivi, 'Le Grand Bazar d'Istanbul et ses environs'.
56. Goodwin, *Ottoman Architecture*, p. 361.
57. Kütükoğlu, *Osmanlılar'da Narh Müessesi*, pp. 260–2.
58. See Şevket Pamuk, *İstanbul ve Diğer Kentlerde 500 Yıllık Fiyatlar ve Ücretler*, p. 193.
59. BOA, MAD 3002, pp. 44–5.
60. Ibid.
61. See Suraiya Faroqhi, 'Crisis and Change, 1590–1699'.
62. TSA, E. 246/291. For a more detailed discussion of the document, see Chapter 5 below.
63. For the *inan* type, see Haim Gerber, 'Muslim Law of Partnership in Ottoman Court Records', pp. 113–14; Murat Çizakça, *Comparative Evolution of Business Partnerships*, pp. 79–82. On *vücuh*, see ibid.. pp. 82–3.
64. TSA, E. 246/421–25.
65. Yi, *Guild Dynamics*, ch. 3. For their presence in the eighteenth century, see Donald Quataert, 'Janissaries, Artisans, and the Question of Ottoman Decline', pp. 197–203.
66. Serkan Delice, 'The Janissaries and their Bedfellows', p. 125.
67. BOA, D.HMH.VLSA 282/27, 290/117. For more information on the renovations financed by her, see Chapter 5, below.
68. There is an ever-growing literature on Ottoman women's economic status. In many cases, these studies are based on judges' records (*kadı sicilleri*)

in which the legal details of economic transactions of all kinds, as well as disputes over property were recorded. See, for example, Ronald Jennings, 'Women in Early 17th Century Ottoman Judicial Records'; Yvonne Seng, 'Invisible Women'; Margaret Meriwether, *Kin Who Count*; Fariba Zarinebaf-Shahr, 'Role of Women in the Urban Economy of Istanbul'; Suraiya Faroqhi, *Stories of Ottoman Men and Women*; Peirce, *Imperial Harem*; Leslie Peirce, *Morality Tales*; Madeline Zilfi, *Women in the Ottoman Empire*; Irvin C. Schick and Amila Buturovic, *Women in the Ottoman Balkans*; Duygu Köksal and Anastasia Falierou, *A Social History of Late Ottoman Women*.

Chapter 4

1. For an in-depth study on ritual purity, see Marion Katz, *Body of Text*. For an earlier influential work based on anthropological theory, see Kevin Reinhardt, 'Impurity/No Danger'.
2. *Sahih Muslim*, Book 2, No. 475. See also Book 2, No. 476.
3. *Sahih Muslim*, Book 2, Nos 495, 496. Trimming the beard, cutting the nails, shaving the pubes and plucking the armpits should be done at least once every forty days. *Sahih Muslim*, Book 2, No. 497.
4. The Islamic law and practice of ritual purity and its underlying concepts were neither uniform nor undisputed, especially in the first *hijri* centuries. For a masterful study that analyses their emergence and codification within textual sources, see Katz, *Body of Text*.
5. *The Holy Qur'an*, p. 247. On this sura, its variant readings and exegesis, see John Burton, 'The Qur'an and the Islamic Practice of Wudu''.
6. There are countless traditions explaining how the ablution is to be performed, by describing Muhammad's manner of ablution as a model. See, for example, *Sahih Muslim*, Book 2, Nos 436, 437, 453; *Sahih al-Bukhari*, vol. 1, Book 4, Nos 142, 161, 185, 186, 190, 191, 196. For a study of the symbolic content of the smaller ablution, see Marion Katz, 'Study of Islamic Ritual'.
7. *Sahih al-Bukhari*, vol. 1, Book 5, No. 266. There are many *hadith* with almost identical text in the same volume and book, under the numbers 257, 259, 273, 275, 279.
8. *Sahih Muslim*, Book 2, No. 556.
9. Of the four rites of Sunni Islam, the Shafi'i, Hanefi and Hanbali rites hold the view that water that has touched a person's body has been used and, therefore, is unclean and no longer suitable for ritual purification. K. K. Mohammed, 'Hammams (Baths) in Medieval India', p. 43.
10. Sura 5:6. *Holy Qur'an*, pp. 247–8. A portion of Sura 4:43 has virtually the same wording.
11. *Sahih Muslim*, Book 4, No. 1839; *Sahih al-Bukhari*, vol. 3, Book 34, No. 330. The event is related in more detail in a twelfth-century *hadith* collection belonging to the Maliki rite: *Mishkat al-Masabih*, vol. 1, p. 109.

12. According to Haskan, this hamam is mentioned in the endowment deed of Sultan Mehmed II. See Haskan, *İstanbul Hamamları*, p. 288. For its location, see Kafesçioğlu, *Constantinopolis/Istanbul*, p. 102, fig. 71.

13. The Turkish text reads: *Natırları peştemalları temiz tutub Müslüman ile gayrimüslim futalarını karıştırmıyalar. Berberler dahi gayri müslimleri tıraş eyledikleri ustura ile müslüman tıraş etmiyeler.* This document is quoted in Ünver, 'İstanbul Yedinci Tepe Hamamları'na dair bazı notlar'. According to Ünver, the original is to be found in documents Nos 75 and 78 of the *Kanuname maa Kanunname-i Celalzade*, TSK, H. 2894.

14. On debates about the notion that non-Muslims may be inherently impure – one that the Sunni consensus in fact did not espouse – see Katz, *Body of Text*, pp. 149–64.

15. Kütükoğlu, *Osmanlılar'da Narh Müessesi*, p. 261 (author's translation).

16. The movement also gained supporters at court through the preachers and spiritual advisers of several important court members. See Madeline Zilfi, 'Kadizadelis'; Marc Baer, 'Great Fire of 1660'.

17. *Sahih Muslim*, Book 3, Nos 663, 664, 665, 666; *Sahih al-Bukhari*, vol. 1, Book 5, No. 279.

18. *Sahih Muslim*, Book 3, Nos 667, 668.

19. *Mishkat al-Masabih*, vol. 1, p. 90.

20. So far, no comprehensive study has been undertaken on the issue of bathing as outlined in *fiqh*. A useful introduction and summary of relevant sources can be found in M. Kamil Yaşaroğlu, 'Hamam: Fıkıh', pp. 433–4. For a lengthy study concerning the issue of nudity in the hamam, based on legal sources, see Benkheira, 'Hammam, nudité et ordre moral dans l'Islam medieval', 2008.

21. For a discussion of the body and modesty in Islamic civilisation, see Fuad Khuri, *Body in Islamic Culture*, pp. 35–48.

22. James Redhouse, *Turkish and English Lexicon*, p. 1327.

23. Wortley-Montagu, *Turkish Embassy Letters*, p. 59. The famous bathhouse passage and the way in which Lady Mary reported what she saw there has been the subject of much literary criticism and dense theorising. See, for example, Srinivas Aravamudan, 'Lady Mary Wortly Montagu in the Hammam'; Arthur Weitzman, 'Voyeurism and Aesthetics in the Turkish Bath'.

24. See Elyse Semerdjian, 'Naked Anxiety'; Elyse Semerdjian, 'Sexing the Hammam'.

25. For a description of such a visit, see Kandemir, 'Eski Hamamlar', p. 15; Abdülaziz Bey, *Osmanlı Âdet, Merasim ve Tabirleri*, pp. 299–301. The latter publication is based on a manuscript in several volumes, titled *Âdât ve Merasim-i Kadime, Tabirât ve Muamelât-ı Kavmiye-i Osmaniye*, in which Abdülaziz ibn Cemaleddin (1850–1918) wrote down his observations on the everyday life of his time; in some instances, he researched and added material going back as far as the sixteenth century.

26. 'Abdarra'uf bin Tag al-'Arifin al-Munawi, *Kitab an-nuzah al-bahiya az-zahiya fi ahkam al-hammam aş-şariya at-tıbbiya*, c. 1600, Ms. Or. Wetzstein 1505, Preußischer Kulturbesitz; as quoted in Grotzfeld, *Das Bad im arabisch-islamischen Mittelalter*, p. 85 (author's translation).
27. For a discussion of the concept of leisure in the Ottoman world, see Sariyannis, 'Time, Work and Pleasure'.
28. Kırlı, 'Struggle over Space'; Kırlı, 'Coffeehouses'; Çaksu, 'Janissary Coffeehouses in Late Eighteenth-Century Istanbul'; Mikhail, 'The Heart's Desire'. For an article discussing coffee houses, baths, taverns and gardens as public space, see Tülay Artan, 'Forms and Forums of Expression'. See also James Grehan, 'Smoking and "Early Modern" Sociability'.
29. Wortley-Montagu, *Turkish Embassy Letters*, p. 59.
30. Mantran, *Istanbul dans la seconde moitié du XVIIe siècle*, p. 161.
31. Kırlı, 'Struggle over Space', pp. 187–8.
32. Cabi Ömer Efendi, *Cabi Tarihi*, vol. 1, p. 392.
33. Haluk Akbay, 'Çemberlitaş Hamamı Baskını Vak'ası', pp. 3819–20.
34. The original reads: *Eyü saatte olsunlar, Hüda onları ve bezm-i dini anların şerrinden mahfuz buyursun.* This prayer addresses *jinns*, supernatural beings of flame or vapour who supposedly meet in ruins, cemeteries, at the foot of big trees and particularly in dark places where dirty water overflows, such as bathhouses and latrines. If a person disturbs the *jinn* they may play harmless tricks on that person, or in more serious cases inflict illness. Ottomans even hesitated to pronounce the word *jinn* so as not to disturb them and replaced it by the first part of the phrase above, *eyü saatte olsunlar*, meaning: 'beings who, I hope, are in good humour and well-disposed towards us'. Pertev N. Boratav, 'Djinn'.
35. Abdülaziz Bey, *Osmanlı Âdet, Merasim ve Tabirleri*, pp. 24–5.
36. For the life stages of an Ottoman and the importance of marriage within the life cycle, see Peirce, 'Seniority, Sexuality and Social Order'.
37. A. Boudhiba, 'Le Hammam', p. 11.
38. Evliya Çelebi, *Seyahatname*, p. 158 (author's translation).
39. The ethnographer Marjo Buitelaar in her study of Moroccan baths in the 1990s made the observation that less wealthy women used the hamam visit as an opportunity to form patron–client relationships with the wealthier ones. Marjo Buitelaar, 'Public Baths as Private Places'. It is likely that Ottomans used the hamam visit in a similar way. For a similar argument concerning the Şengül Hamamı in contemporary Ankara, see Elif Ekin Akşit, 'Women's Quarters in the Historical Hammam'; Elif Ekin Akşit, 'Kadınların Hamamı ve Dönüşümü'.
40. In a 1939 interview, the *hamamcı* Ahmet Taban, one of the oldest and most experienced in Istanbul at the time, described the way in which he and his colleagues in other hamams would recognise a customer's status: 'A person who just put on new clothes an hour ago cannot show off to the *hamamcı*. We understand a man's class from his walk, his manner of sitting, his

way of looking, and his talk. And accordingly, we give him a towel set.'
Kandemir, 'Eski Hamamlar', p. 14 (author's translation).

41. For an excellent survey of hamam textiles that also includes references to archival evidence, see Hülya Tezcan, 'Osmanlı Hamam Tekstilinin Tarihçesi'.

42. For more examples of different hamam kit items, see the excellent reproductions in the exhibition catalogues *Eski Hamam, Eski Tası* and *Âb-ı Hayat*. For a study on various materials used for cosmetic procedures in medieval Islamic bathhouses, see Fanny Bessard, 'Pratiques sanitaires, produits d'hygiène et de soin dans les bains médiévaux'.

43. İrfan Orga, *Portrait of a Turkish Family*, p. 17.

44. Kafesçioğlu, *Constantinopolis/Istanbul*, p. 108.

45. For the legalistic definition of *muhaddere* and its implications, see Leslie Peirce, '"The Law Shall not Languish"'.

46. Fanny Davis, *Ottoman Lady*, pp. 131–3; see also Faroqhi, *Subjects of the Sultan*, pp. 106–7.

47. The original reads: *Mes'ele: Hamama ve kurâya giden Hind muhaddere olur mu? Elcevap: Olur, ırz ü vakarla ve hadem ü haşem ile giderse.* Mehmet Düzdağ, *Şeyülislam Ebussuud Efendi Fetvaları*, p. 55 (No. 154, see also No. 155).

48. Ibid., p. 54 (Nos. 146, 147).

49. On this aspect of Roman bathing, see Fagan, *Bathing in Public in the Roman World*, pp. 35–6. For the Byzantine period, see Claudine Dauphin, 'Brothels, Baths and Babes', pp. 62–4.

50. On *jinn*s in bathhouses, see Geert Jan van Gelder, 'The *Hammam*'. For a more extended discussion of and bibliography on these creatures, see Boratav, 'Djinn'. The belief that ghosts and demons lived in bathhouses, in places where polluted water collected, can be traced back to pre-Islamic times, to the Roman Near East. See Zena Kamash, 'What Lies Beneath?'

51. For a more extended discussion of the paradoxical nature of the hamam as an Islamic institution, see van Gelder, 'The *Hammam*'.

52. Grotzfeld, *Das Bad im arabisch-islamischen Mittelalter*, p. 95.

53. For a modern example, see Moris Farhi, 'Lentils in Paradise'.

54. Dror Ze'evi, *Producing Desire*, p. 112. For the meaning of the hamam in medieval dream interpretation in the Arab world, see van Gelder, 'The *Hammam*', p. 19.

55. Halil İnalcık, 'Osmanlı İdare, Sosyal ve Ekonomik Tarihiyle İlgili Belgeler', p. 49. Translation from Walter Andrews and Mehmet Kalpaklı, *Age of Beloveds*, p. 285.

56. See Marinos Sariyannis, 'Prostitution in Ottoman Istanbul'.

57. Gelibolulu Mustafa Ali, *Gelibolulu Mustafa Ali ve Meva'idu'n-nefa'is fi kava'idi'l mecalis*, p. 293.

58. Evliya Çelebi, *Seyahatname*, p. 137.

59. Murat Bardakçı has published this manuscript in a book for a popular audience, without any scholarly apparatus. He claims to have an early

twentieth-century copy in his possession after acquiring it at an auction, but refuses to share it with the wider community of historians. Murat Bardakçı, *Osmanlı'da Seks*. For the English translation of extended passages from the manuscript text and a thorough discussion in reference to masculinity, see Delice, 'The Janissaries and their Bedfellows', pp. 124–32.

60. Hayati Develi, *XVIII. YY İstanbul'a Dair Risale-i Garibe*. The untitled and undated text is found in a compendium in the Nuruosmaniye Library, No. 4925, fols. 48b–76a. For references to prostitution in hamams, see pp. 22, 31 and 36.

61. Mü'minzâde Seyyid Ahmed Hasîb Efendi, *Ravzatü'l-Kübarâ: Tahlil ve Metin*, p. 26.

62. See Delice, 'The Janissaries and Their Bedfellows'. His discussion is based on archival documents such as BOA, MAD 2483/1122.

63. Jan Schmidt, 'Sünbülzade Vehbi's *Şevk-Engiz*', p. 22.

64. An excerpt of this document has been published in Koçu, 'Dellak', pp. 4367–8.

65. For a study treating the contemporary period in detail, especially concerning the way in which gay men interact with hamams' architectural spaces, see Burkay Pasin, 'A Critical Reading of the Ottoman-Turkish Hamam as a Queered Space'.

66. The biographical information given here is based on Selim Kuru, 'Sixteenth-Century Scholar', pp. 1–30.

67. G. M. Meredith-Owens, *Meşa'irü üş-şu'ara or Tezkere of 'Aşık Çelebi*, fols. 294b (ll. 17)–295a (line 1). Translation by Andrews and Kalpaklı, *Age of Beloveds*, p. 284.

68. Kuru, 'Sixteenth-Century Scholar', p. 242.

69. Ibid., p. 248.

70. Ibid., pp. 269–72.

71. Ibid., p. 202.

72. Ibid., p. 249.

73. Ibid.

74. For an in-depth study of a late eighteenth-century example of such coarse, if humourous poetry referencing hamams as sites of hetero- and homoerotic pleasure, see Schmidt, 'Sünbülzade Vehbi's *Şevk-Engiz*'.

75. For divan poetry, see, for example, Asaf Çelebi, *Divan Şiirinde İstanbul*, p. 19. For a translation of this specific poem, see below, pp. 150–1. For etiquette books, see, for example, Gelibolulu Mustafa Ali, *Cami'u'l-buhûr der mecâlis-i sûr*, p. 210. For biographical dictionaries, see, for example, Kınalızade Hasan Çelebi, *Tezkiretü'ş-Şuarâ*, vol. 2, pp. 883, 984.

76. Güven Kaya, 'Türk Edebiyatında Hammâmiyeler'. For the classification of themes, see pp. 446–55. For the place of this genre within erotic literature in general, see Schick, 'Representation of Gender and Sexuality in Ottoman and Turkish Erotic Literature'. On erotic hamam poetry in the Arabic language, see van Gelder, 'The *Hammam*', pp. 15–20.

77. Fuzûlî, *Fuzûlî Divanı*, p. 494 (author's translation).

78. Emine Fetvacı, 'Love in the Album of Ahmed I'.

79. TSK, B. 408, fol. 18a.

80. Fetvacı, 'Love in the Album of Ahmed I', pp. 39–40.

81. For a comprehensive introduction to the genre and a catalogue of known plays including their full text, see Cevdet Kudret, *Karagöz*. For a play titled 'Hamam' revolving around a drug-induced dream that takes place in a bathhouse, see vol. 3, pp. 1197–1202.

82. See *Çifte Hamamlar Oyunu Yahut Karagöz'ün Dayak Yemesi* (*The Play in the Double Hamam, or Karagöz Gets a Beating*) in Muhittin Sevilen, *Karagöz*, pp. 92–112.

83. To give an example of such a real-life occurrence, in seventeenth-century Kayseri a *hamamcı* was brought to court for, among other things, his negligence in patching a hole between the sections. See Patricia Khleif, '"There Goes the Neighborhood!"', p. 133.

84. Enderuni Fazıl Hüseyin, *Zenanname*, 1793, Istanbul University Library, T. 5502.

85. Ibid.

86. This discussion of Ottoman medical traditions is based on Miri Shefer-Mossensohn, *Ottoman Medicine*, pp. 21–45.

87. On the transmission of Galen's Theory, see Istvan Ormos, 'Theory of Humours in Islam'. On Galenic medicine (including specific recommendations for medicinal bathing) as transmitted in the medieval Islamic world by an eminent scholar serving the sultan in Cairo in the late twelfth century, see Gerrit Bos, 'Maimonides on the Preservation of Health'.

88. Avicenna, *Canon of Medicine*, p. 196.

89. Ibid.. p. 308.

90. Ibid.. p. 305.

91. Ibid., p. 197.

92. The following adverse effects are listed in Avicenna, *Canon of Medicine*, pp. 197, 308.

93. Ibid., p. 195.

94. Ibid.

95. Seyyid Muhammed el-Hüseynî el-Edirnevî et-Tabib Emir Çelebi, *Unmuzecü't-Tıb*, Süleymaniye Library, Mihrişah Sultan, 0000342, fols. 19–20.

96. VGM, D. 1766, p. 158.

97. For these tasks expected of the *tellak* in the Süleymaniye's hospital, see VGM, D. 608/23, p. 231.

98. Shefer-Mossensohn, *Ottoman Medicine*, p. 189. Bathing was also prescribed to cure insanity, thought to result from an excess of dry humours that could be cured by being brought back to balance through moisture. Ibid., p. 83.

99. This point has been made by Osman Ergin, *Türk Şehirlerinde İmaret Sistemi*, p. 42; Işın, *Everyday Life in Istanbul*, pp. 268–9. Cleanliness among *imaret*

workers is also emphasised in the endowment deed of the Atik Valide Vakfı; see VGM, D. 1766, p. 159.

100. Solomon Schweigger, *Neue Reyssbeschreibung*, pp. 112, 114.

101. Shefer-Mossensohn claims that the Istanbul University Library manuscript copy of Sabuncuoğlu's famous treatise *Cerahiyyetü'l-Haniyye* (*The Surgical Operation of the Khan*), written during the reign of Mehmed II (r. 1444–1446, 1451–1481), includes miniatures that show surgeons operating on patients in hamams. Shefer-Mossensohn, *Ottoman Medicine*, p. 52. See also Gönül Güreşsever, 'Kitab al-Cerrahiyet al-Hâniye'. Although in my opinion the miniatures themselves do not include enough visual information to justify such a claim based solely on the images, I believe it is very likely that surgeons used hamams as treatment facilities, especially since those outside the imperial hospital system did not have clinics of their own.

102. See Carla Makhlouf Obermeyer, 'Pluralism and Pragmatism', p. 185.

103. See Shefer-Mossensohn, *Ottoman Medicine*, p. 83.

104. Zeki Karagülle, 'Health Effects of Hamams'.

105. Interview with Sefer Yüce, 9 February 2003.

106. For an extensive discussion of this transformation process, see Kafesçioğlu, *Constantinopolis/Istanbul*.

107. Kritovoulos, *History of Mehmed the Conqueror*, p. 105.

108. Ibid., p. 140.

109. Evliya Çelebi, *Seyahatname*, p. 65.

110. For a ground plan, see Pullan and Texier, *L'architecture byzantine*.

111. Ekrem Ayverdi, *Osmanlı Mimarisinde Fatih Devri 855–886 (1451–1481)*, vol. 4, pp. 590–611; Tahsin Öz, *Fatih Mehmet II Vakfiyeleri*.

112. See Kafesçioğlu, *Constantinopolis/Istanbul*, pp. 106–7.

113. See ibid., p. 108. At present, there do not seem to exist any sources indicating that fifteenth-century Ottomans thought about non-Muslims as 'impure', an issue addressed above and discussed in Katz, *Body of Text*, pp. 149–64.

114. Kafesçioğlu, *Constantinopolis/Istanbul*, p. 182.

115. Özer Ergenç, 'Osmanlı Şehrindeki 'Mahalle'nin İşlev ve Nitelikleri Üzerinde', p. 72.

116. For a detailed account of the workings of a *mahalle*, see the case study in Cem Behar, *A Neighborhood in Ottoman Istanbul*. On social relations within neighbourhoods, as envisioned in a variety of prescriptive texts, see also Işık Tamdoğan-Abel, 'Les relations de voisinage d'après les livres de morale ottomans'.

117. İnalcık, 'Istanbul'; for a detailed study of the residential fabric of Istanbul, see also Stéphane Yérasimos, 'Dwellings in Sixteenth-Century Istanbul'.

118. This is how, for example, the Venetian bailo Marcantonio Barbaro described sixteenth-century Istanbul. See Minna Rozen and Benjamin Arbel, 'Great Fire in the Metropolis', p. 155.

119. Ayvansarayî, *Garden of the Mosques*.

120. de Nicholay, *Nauigations*, pp. 58a–60a; Reinhold Lubenau, *Beschreibung der Reisen*, vol. 1, pp. 169–72; Hans Dernschwam, *Hans Dernschwam's Tagebuch*, p. 136; Schweigger, *Neue Reyssbeschreibung*, p. 116; Busbecq, *Turkish Letters*, p. 82.

121. Çelebi, *Divan Şiirinde İstanbul*, pp. 18–19 (author's translation). I am indebted to Hilal Kazan and Sooyong Kim for help with several problematic passages. This poem has also been published in Kaya, 'Türk Edebiyatında Hammâmiyeler', and in that version contains additional verses. However, I have chosen Çelebi's transcription, since Kaya's contains several misreadings.

122. Robert Dankoff, *An Ottoman Mentality*, pp. 50, 69.

123. Evliya Çelebi, *Seyahatname*, pp. 158–60; see also Yüksel Yoldaş-Demircanlı, *İstanbul Mimarisi için Kaynak Olarak Evliya Çelebi Seyahatnamesi*, pp. 376–428. Considering his tendency to exaggerate, one has to receive these numbers with caution, especially since the numbers given in another passage account to 156 hamams, with 95 *intra* and 65 *extra muros* (p. 252). The number of 156 is more likely to be accurate, since Mehmet Haskan in his survey arrives at a number close to that. Haskan, *Istanbul Hamamları*. The inspection register dated to 1752 lists a total of 177 hamams in that year. Ergin, 'Mapping Istanbul's Hamams', table 4.1. For a comparison of the different numbers of hamams given by travel writers and Ottoman authors, see Ebru Boyar and Kate Fleet, *Social History of Ottoman Istanbul*, p. 250.

124. Eric Dursteler, *Venetians in Constantinople*.

125. Ibid., p. 20.

126. Isom-Verhaaren and Schull, *Living in the Ottoman Realm*, p. 5.

127. See, for example, Elisabeth Zacharidou, 'Co-existence and Religion'; Gilles Veinstein, *Syncrétismes et hérésies dans l'Orient seldjoukide et ottoman*.

Chapter 5

1. Refik, *Onikinci Asr-ı Hicri'de İstanbul Hayatı*, p. 216. The whereabouts of the original document are not mentioned in this publication.

2. TSA, D. 1901. The heading under which repairs can be found is *'ani'l-meremmat*.

3. For the rest of the poem's text, see Chapter 3.

4. The original reads: *ferşi san ayineden billur/kurnalar dürr kâseler fağfurdan/ böyle bir ca-yı sefa-efza mı var/su gibi ahbab seyrine akar/goncagül-i hat-midir cam meğer/lalelerdir anda zerrin lüleler.*

5. The original reads: *terakkub haline geçmişdi ser-i rahında ey yar/sana müjden efendi himmet-i vala-yı Selim geldi 1184.*

6. The original reads: *kilmağa dellağı pakiza traş/andırır abdal-veş dünya ne baş.*

7. I am most grateful to Christoph Neumann and Behice Tezçakar for their help in translating the poem and formulating this scenario.

8. BOA, D.HMH.VLSA, 282/27.
9. BOA, D.HMH.VLSA, 282/30.
10. Cf. Karakaş, 'Water Resources Management and Development in Ottoman Istanbul'; Deniz Karakaş, 'Clay Pipes, Marble Surfaces'.
11. BOA, D.HMH.VLSA, 290/117.
12. BOA, D.HMH.VLSA, 291/78.
13. The original reads: *hamâm-ı mezbûr ezmîneden berü tamir olmadığından ekser mahali harab ve beherhal tamire muhtac olduğundan.*
14. BOA, D.HMH.VLSA, 292/101.
15. TSA, E. 246/291. Some of the details of this business partnership have already been discussed in Chapter 3. The case of the procrastinated repairs will be discussed in greater detail later in this chapter.
16. For a description of such a fire, see Rozen and Arbel, 'Great Fire in the Metropolis'.
17. Lubenau, *Beschreibung der Reisen*, vol. 2, pp. 14–15 (author's translation).
18. Mustafa Naima, *Tarih-i Naima*, vol. 5, p. 258.
19. See Chapter 3, Table 3.1, above.
20. Mustafa Cezar, 'Osmanlı Devrinde İstanbul Yapılarında Tahribat Yapan Yangınlar', p. 338.
21. TSK, H. 1565, p. 287. See also Cezar, 'Osmanlı Devrinde İstanbul Yapılarında Tahribat Yapan Yangınlar', p. 338 (author's translation).
22. See Chapter 3, Table 3.1, above.
23. For a contemporary account of the Greatest Fire, see Derviş Efendi-zade Derviş Mustafa Efendi, *1782 Yılı Yangınları.*
24. Orhan Sakin, *Tarihsel Kaynaklarıyla İstanbul Depremleri*, pp. 32–7; N. N. Ambraseys and C. F. Finkel, *Seismicity of Turkey*; N. N. Ambraseys, *Earthquakes in the Eastern Mediterranean and the Middle East*. For a survey of narrative sources on earthquakes, fires and epidemics, see Ürekli, 'Osmanlı Döneminde İstanbul'da Meydana Gelen Âfetlere İlişkin Literatür'.
25. Mehmed Raşid, *Tarih*, vol. 5, p. 161. As quoted and translated in Ambraseys and Finkel, *Seismicity of Turkey*, p. 106.
26. Ambraseys and Finkel, *Seismicity of Turkey*, pp. 126, 129; Ambraseys, *Earthquakes in the Eastern Mediterranean*, pp. 577–9; Sakin, *Tarihsel Kaynaklarıyla İstanbul Depremleri*, p. 73.
27. Ambraseys and Finkel, *Seismicity of Turkey*, pp. 137–9, 143; Ambraseys, *Earthquakes in the Eastern Mediterranean*, pp. 590–3. For an admirably thorough exposition of the repair work that this earthquake necessitated, based on a wealth of archival sources, see Deniz Mazlum, *1766 İstanbul Depremi.*
28. Ambraseys and Finkel, *Seismicity of Turkey*, pp. 138–9; Ambraseys, *Earthquakes in the Eastern Mediterranean*, pp. 595–6. For a detailed discussion of the work on the Atik Ali Paşa Mosque, so extensive that Mazlum calls it a 'restoration' rather than repair, see Mazlum, *1766 İstanbul Depremi*, pp. 164–91.

29. Because repairs to hamams following the earthquake were delegated to the owners and *mütevellis*, while the guild of imperial architects were pre-occupied with the many damaged mosques (see Mazlum, *1766 İstanbul Depremi*, pp. 42–6, table 2), archival documentation is likely to be limited. See ibid., p. 35.

30. BOA, YEE, 11/14/126/C. For a transcription, see Sakin, *Tarihsel Kaynaklarıyla İstanbul Depremleri*, pp. 123–30.

31. Feriha Öztin, *10 Temmuz 1894 İstanbul Deprem Raporu*. See also Ambraseys, *Earthquakes in the Eastern Mediterranean*, pp. 774–9. For a paper that presents a survey of the damaged monuments, see C. F. Finkel and N. N. Ambraseys, 'The Marmara Sea Earthquake of 10 July 1894'.

32. Öztin, *10 Temmuz 1894 İstanbul Deprem Raporu*, pp. 98, 100–2.

33. Sakin, *Tarihsel Kaynaklarıyla İstanbul Depremleri*, p. 139.

34. Author's personal conversation with female bathhouse attendant who related one such incident, February 2003.

35. The original reads: *şiddet-i rüzgar ve doluda*. TSA, E. 246/291.

36. BOA, D.HMH.VLSA, 282/27.

37. In answering these questions, I have made use of the following literature: Emre Madran, 'Restorer Artisans in the Ottoman Empire'; Halil Kunter, 'Türk Vakıfları ve Vakfiyeleri'; Muzaffer Erdoğan, 'Osmanlı Mimari Tarihinin Arşiv Kaynakları'. For the following background information on renovation procedures, see Nina Ergin, 'Taking Care of the Atik Valide Imaret'.

38. The definition of *meremmetçi* is not clear-cut. Some repairmen might have specialised in masonry or other branches of construction, while others worked as jacks-of-all-trades. For instance, the endowment deed of Haseki Sultan's *imaret* in Jerusalem specifies that a person knowledgable in the skills of carpentry, masonry and stone-cutting should be hired. S. H. Stephan, 'Endowment Deed of Khasseki Sultan', p. 191, n. 1. The endowment of Mehmed the Conqueror even included workmen specialising in the repair of hamams. Madran, 'Restorer Artisans in the Ottoman Empire', p. 354. Repairs to bathhouses required special knowledge and skill, for instance, in the mixing and application of hydraulic mortar. See Mazlum, *1766 İstanbul Depremi*, p. 68.

39. VGM, D. 1766, pp. 160–1.

40. VGM, D. 1766, p. 160.

41. Ibid. I am indebted to Machiel Kiel for pointing out this strategy with regard to maintenance.

42. For a discussion of double rent, see Chapter 6, below.

43. See, for example, TSA, D. 1901.

44. See Chapter 3, above. TSA, E. 246/291.

45. The original reads: *şimdi vaktimiz değil*.

46. For a discussion of conflict management both in and outside of court, see Boğaç Ergene, 'Pursuing Justice in an Islamic Context'.

47. Lowenthal, *The Past is a Foreign Country*, p. 59.
48. Ibid., pp. 391–5.
49. Zeynep Çelik, 'Istanbul: Urban Preservation as Theme Park', p. 85.
50. Michael Meinecke, 'Probleme der Denkmalpflege und Altstadtsanierung', p. 56 (author's translation).

Chapter 6

1. This is not to mean that there was an overall 'decline'. For a study that challenges the decline thesis and masterfully summarises the relevant historiography, see Dana Sajdi, 'Decline, its Discontents and Ottoman Cultural History'.
2. R. J. Barnes, *Introduction to Religious Foundations*, pp. 69–70. In spite of its new name, the administration of endowments remained under the supervision of the chief eunuch of the harem (*darüssaade ağası*) until 1826, when Mahmud II (r. 1826–1839) undertook a reorganisation of the ministry.
3. Barnes, *Introduction to Religious Foundations*, p. 55.
4. On the dating of this practice, see Klaus Kreiser, 'Icareteyn'.
5. For an extended discussion of this mechanism in a different setting, see Miriam Hoexter, 'Adaptation to Changing Circumstances'. For a monographic study based on legal rulings and court records, see Süleyman Kaya, *Osmanlı Hukukunda İcareteyn*.
6. Barnes, *Introduction to Religious Foundations*, p. 53.
7. BOA, D.HMH.VLSA, 282/27.
8. TSA, E. 246/291. The original reads: *ta'mir ve termim masarifi mallarından ber-'alel-vakıf mu'accelelerine mahsuben mutassarufları ta'mir ve termim etmek şurut-ı vakf-ı müşarun-ileyhadan olub.*
9. TSA, E. 246/421–5.
10. The terms 'modernisation', 'modernising' and 'Europeanisation' or 'Westernisation' are problematic, because they imply a binary dichotomy between 'backward' and 'modern', between West and East. However, in the later Ottoman Empire 'modernisation' was one of the rallying points in public discourse, and the Ottoman elites widely used the term. Therefore, I will continue to use the term as well. Fatma Göçek, *Rise of the Bourgeoisie, Demise of Empire*; Kemal Karpat, 'Transformation of the Ottoman State, 1789–1908'; Şerif Mardin, 'Super Westernization'.
11. On the last point, see Zeynep Çelik, *Remaking of Istanbul*, p. 32. For more detailed accounts of the *Tanzimat* period, see Donald Quataert, *Ottoman Empire, 1700–1922*; Suraiya Faroqhi, *Cambridge History of Turkey, vol. 3: The Later Ottoman Empire, 1603–1839*.
12. On the formation, activities and mentality of the municipal council working in Pera as the experimental district to lead the way towards Europeanising the entire city, see Steven Rosenthal, 'Foreigners and Municipal Reform in Istanbul'.

13. Çelik, *Remaking of Istanbul*, p. 49.
14. Murat Gül, *Emergence of Modern Istanbul*, p. 28. The document in question has been published in Ergin, *Mecelle-i Umûr-ı Belediyye*, vol. 3, pp. 1240–3. For a summary translation, see Gül, *Emergence of Modern Istanbul*, pp. 28–9.
15. See, for example, Zeynep Çelik, 'Bouvard's Boulevards'.
16. These regulations included the *Ebniye Nizamnamesi* (Buildings Regulation) of 1848, the *Sokaklara Dair Nizamnamesi* (Regulation Concerning Streets) of 1858, and the *Turuk ve Ebniye Nizamnamesi* (Streets and Buildings Regulation) of 1863. For more detailed information on these and other regulations, see Rosenthal, 'Foreigners and Municipal Reform'; Çelik, *Remaking of Istanbul*; Gül, *Emergence of Modern Istanbul*, pp. 40–71.
17. In the first year of its existence, the commission built 3,500 *arşın* of sewers and 100,000 *arşın* of streets and repaired 60,000 *arşın* of sidewalks. Mustafa Cezar, *Osmanlı Başkenti İstanbul*, p. 321. On the commission's history and activities, see Rosenthal, 'Foreigners and Municipal Reform'; Gül, *Emergence of Modern Istanbul*, pp. 49–50.
18. Gül, *Emergence of Modern Istanbul*, p. 50.
19. For a catalogue of the monuments along the Divan Yolu, including annotations about changes they received, see Cerasi, *Istanbul Divan Yolu*, pp. 135–44.
20. Nur Altınyıldız, 'Architectural Heritage of Istanbul', p. 285.
21. Cengiz Can, 'Barborini, vol. 2, p. 54; Cengiz Can and Paolo Ghirardelli, 'Giovanni Battista Barborini à Istanbul'.
22. Glück, *Probleme des Wölbungsbaues*, p. 136.
23. Haskan, *İstanbul Hamamları*, p. 101.
24. The contrast between demolition and presentation as important cultural heritage has been analysed in Nina Ergin, 'Between East and West'.
25. Haussmann even visited Istanbul for two months in 1873, upon the invitation of the Ottoman viceroy of Egypt, İsmail Paşa. Gül, *Emergence of Modern Istanbul*, p. 52.
26. Altınyıldız, 'Architectural Heritage of Istanbul', p. 285.
27. Many of the arguments about the Ottoman reaction to and partial appropriation of the European historical narrative have been made in Wendy Shaw, *Possessor and Possessed*. There also existed a counter-narrative to the elevation of Byzantine heritage as a linking point to European civilisation, due to the problematic relationship with Greece. For the framing of the Byzantine Empire as the 'worst state' due to corruption, lawlessness and excess, in contrast to the morally upstanding early Ottomans, see Michael Ursinus, 'Der schlechteste Staat'.
28. Shaw, *Possessor and Possessed*, p. 68.
29. In another instance, the mayor Cemil Paşa, who would have happily demolished the Haseki Hamamı, was even forced to resign for 'abusing Islamic monuments'. Altınyıldız, 'Architectural Heritage of Istanbul', p. 285.

30. Ergin, *Mecelle-i Umûr-ı Belediyye*, vol. 2, p. 955. See also Gül, *Emergence of Modern Istanbul*, p. 51. For a study that also addresses the removal of a cemetery in another part of the city, see Mehmet Kentel, 'Assembling "Cosmopolitanism"'.

31. Altınyıldız, 'Architectural Heritage of Istanbul', p. 287.

32. The paragon of this phenomenon was the famous Jermyn Street Hammam that the political radical and Turcophile David Urquhart built in London in 1862, with the utilitarian aim to offer adequate washing facilities to the working classes. Thereby, he hoped to rectify the social rift between the classes in terms of bodily hygiene and, by implication, also morals. An extended discussion of the Turkish bath movement exceeds the scope of this study, and has already been presented in Nebahat Avcıoğlu, 'The Turkish Bath in the West', and Nebahat Avcıoğlu, *Turquerie and the Politics of Representation*, pp. 189–252. Suffice it to say here that, due to 'its origin in utilitarianism, philanthropy and candid politics', the Turkish bath movement 'rejects a straightforward Orientalist interpretation' (Avcıoğlu, 'Turkish Bath in the West', p. 267). On various aspects of the Victorian bath, see also Breathnach, 'For Health and Pleasure'; John Potvin, 'Vapour and Steam'. The Victorian era was not the first time that Ottoman bathing culture made an appearance west of the empire. For a brief discussion of Italian Renaissance baths that borrowed from Ottoman hamam architecture, see Hanke, 'Bathing "all'antica"'.

33. Zeynep Çelik, *Displaying the Orient*, p. 60.

34. For more information on Parvillée, see Béatrice St. Laurent, 'Léon Parvillée'; Miyuki Aoki, 'Leon Parvillée'. On the Ottomans' quest to define their architectural past and inscribe it into modern historiography, as well as Parvillée's role in it, see Ahmet Ersoy, 'Architecture and the Search for Ottoman Origins'.

35. Çelik, *Displaying the Orient*, p. 63. For a detailed account of the Ottoman section at 1873 World Fair in Vienna, see Ahmet Ersoy, *Architecture and the Late Ottoman Historical Imaginary*, pp. 29–90.

36. Çelik, *Displaying the Orient*, p. 2.

37. Mary Loise Pratt, *Imperial Eyes*.

38. See Çelik, *Displaying the Orient*, p. 136.

39. Ersoy, *Architecture and the Late Ottoman Historical Imaginary*, p. 4.

40. Ibid., p. 81.

41. See Avcıoğlu, 'Turkish Bath in the West'; Avcıoğlu, *Turquerie and the Politics of Representation*, pp. 189–252.

42. For a similar argument about the Ottoman Revival style of architecture implying the death of the classical style, see Altınyıldız, 'Architectural Heritage of Istanbul', p. 286.

43. For literature on this topic, see n. 8 in the Introduction.

44. One example of such an invented tradition meant to give cohesiveness to group identity is the distinct Highland culture of Scotland, including the

tartan-patterned kilt and the bagpipe. The Scottish Highlanders did not form a distinct group before the late seventeenth century, although since the nineteenth century they have claimed that their regional culture was of greater antiquity. Hugh Trevor-Roper, 'Invention of Tradition'.

45. For detailed histories of the establishment of the Turkish Republic, see Bernard Lewis, *Emergence of Modern Turkey*; Erik Zürcher, *Turkey: A Modern History*.
46. Ünver, 'Türk Hamamı', p. 92.
47. Secularism in Turkey does not mean a constitutional separation of religious and political affairs; rather, the state keeps strict control over religious matters. See Niyazi Berkes, *Development of Secularism in Turkey*, pp. 479–506.
48. An increased mobility of women has also affected twentieth-century Moroccan bathhouses in the same way. Buitelaar, 'Public Baths as Private Places', p. 119.
49. For more photographs of young Istanbulites bathing together, see Üster, *Once Upon A Time*; Evren, *İstanbul'un Deniz Hamamları ve Plajları*.
50. For an in-depth discussion of residential architecture in the Republican period, for the upper to the working classes, see Sibel Bozdoğan and Esra Akcan, *Turkey: Modern Architectures in History*, pp. 80–103, 138–69. For these and a variety of other topics related to urban life, on the occasion of the Republic's seventy-fifth anniversary, see *75 Yılda Değişen Kent ve Mimarlık*.
51. Klinghardt, *Bäder Konstantinopels*, p. 1 (author's translation).
52. Ibid., p. 16.
53. Gizem Zencirci, 'From Property to Civil Society', p. 536.
54. Engin Işın and Alexandre Lefèbvre, 'The Gift of Law', p. 13.
55. Altınyıldız, 'Architectural Heritage of Istanbul', p. 287.
56. On the work of Mimar Kemalettin, see Sibel Bozdoğan, *Modernism and Nation-Building*, pp. 16–55.
57. *Cumhuriyetten Önce ve Sonra Vakıflar*, p. 9.
58. See Can Binan, 'Treatment of the Ottoman Architectural Legacy in the Early Republican Press', p. 380.
59. Zencirci, 'From Property to Civil Society', p. 538. On this law, see also Reşad Koçu, 'Bilicareteyn Tasarruf', pp. 2777–8.
60. On the destruction of Istanbul's hamams in the twentieth century, see Eyice, 'İstanbul'un Ortadan Kalkan Bazı Tarihi Eserleri'; Semavi Eyice, 'Hamam', p. 426; as well as Ahmet Süheyl Ünver's essays discussed below.
61. İpek Türeli, 'Heritagisation of the "Ottoman/Turkish House" in the 1970s', p. 4.
62. In contrast, the Justice and Development Party (*Adalet ve Kalkınma Partisi*, AKP) has spearheaded efforts to turn this declared Monument of World Heritage once more into a mosque, and in May 2014 a prayer service was held, sparking widespread criticism especially abroad. See, for example,

'Muslim group prays in front of Hagia Sophia', *Hürriyet Daily News*, 31 May 2014, at: http://www.hurriyetdailynews.com/muslim-group-prays-in-front-of-hagia-sophia-.aspx?pageID=238&nID=67225&NewsCatID=338; Owen Matthews, 'As Turkey Turns from West, Istanbul's Most Iconic Building is Claimed for Islam', *Newsweek*, 3 June 2015, at: http://europe.newsweek.com/turkey-turns-west-islanbuls-most-iconic-building-claimed-islam-328102?rm=eu.

63. Binan, 'Treatment of the Ottoman Architectural Legacy in the Early Republican Press', p. 380.
64. Kopytoff, 'Cultural Biography of Things', p. 73.
65. On the process by which Mimar Sinan was constructed as national treasure, see Gülru Necipoğlu, 'Creation of a National Genius'.
66. Binan, 'Treatment of the Ottoman Architectural Legacy in the Early Republican Press', p. 378.
67. Ibid., p. 380.
68. For a detailed and masterful account of the way in which Istanbul was reshaped, or at least envisioned to be reshaped, between 1933 and 1950, see Gül, *Emergence of Modern Istanbul*, pp. 92–126.
69. On Henri Prost, who had been invited in 1936 by Atatürk himself based on his previous work in Morocco, see Gül, *Emergence of Modern Istanbul*, pp. 92–126. See also the exhibition catalogue *From the Imperial Capital to the Republican Modern City: Henri Prost's Planning of Istanbul (1936–1951)*.
70. On the 'rivalry' between Istanbul and Ankara, see Gül, *Emergence of Modern Istanbul*, pp. 84–91.
71. Doğan Kuban, *Istanbul, An Urban History*, pp. 440–3.
72. Altınyıldız, 'Architectural Heritage of Istanbul', p. 293.
73. For the number of demolished buildings, see Kuban, *Istanbul, An Urban History*, p. 431; Altınyıldız, 'Architectural Heritage of Istanbul', p. 295; Gül, *Emergence of Modern Istanbul*, p. 153.
74. For a summary reappraisal of Menderes' role in Istanbul's transformation, often portrayed as single-handedly responsible to the destruction of the city's architectural heritage, see Gül, *Emergence of Modern Istanbul*, pp. 172–8.
75. On residential architecture as cultural heritage, see Carel Bertram, *Imagining the Turkish House*; Türeli, 'Heritagisation of the "Ottoman/Turkish House" in the 1970s'.
76. Cevat Erder, 'Care of Historic Monuments and Sites in Turkey', p. 280.
77. Ünver, 'İstanbul Hamamların İstikbalı', p. 537.
78. About half of my Turkish interviewees who had never visited a hamam held this paradoxical attitude and gave it as reason why they would not want to visit. As follow-up question, I asked whether they would swim in a swimming pool, and the answer was always positive, even though communal soaking in chlorinated water can hardly be more hygienic than washing with running water in a hamam.

79. See Gül, *Emergence of Modern Istanbul*, pp. 153, 170.
80. Ünver, 'İstanbul Hamamların İstikbalı', p. 538.
81. Refik, 'İstanbul Hamamları'. In 1919, Ahmet Refik Altınay became professor of history at the Darülfünun, the forerunner of Istanbul University. He wrote for both scholarly and popular audiences. After the end of the First World War and before the proclamation of the Republic, he was one of the leading members of the liberal *Hürriyet ve İtilaf* party (Freedom and Reconciliation Party).
82. On Thomas Allom, see Wendy Shaw, 'Between the Picturesque and the Sublime'.
83. Kandemir, 'Eski Hamamlar', pp. 14–15.
84. Ibid., p. 14. The original reads: *Eski hamamlar mı evlad, heyhat, ne eski hamam kaldı, ne de tas* . . . Taban plays here with the Turkish proverb *eski hamam, eski tas* (old hamam, old hamam bowl), meaning 'same old story'.
85. For a primary source text, see Afet İnan et al., *Türk Tarihinin Ana Hatları*. For a concise discussion of its content and practical application, see Soner Çağaptay, 'Race, Assimilation and Kemalism'. For a sophisticated analysis of how even the Hittites came to be constructed as Turkish, see Can Erimtan, 'Hittites, Ottomans and Turks'.
86. Konyalı, 'Bizans ve Osmanlı Hamamları', p. 14.
87. On the 'Turkishness' of Ottoman architecture, see Sibel Bozdoğan, 'Reading Ottoman Architecture through Modernist Lenses', p. 202.
88. Be-Se, 'Bizans Hamamları', p. 13.
89. Şapolyo, 'Türk Hamamları', p. 10. Enver Şapolyo (1900–1972) was a graduate of the Faculty of Letters at Istanbul University, and taught history in different high schools while also writing articles for the popular press. An ardent nationalist, he actively supported the Ankara government in its struggle to establish the Turkish Republic.
90. Ünver, 'İstanbul Hamamların İstikbalı', pp. 537–8 (author's translation).
91. Ünver, 'Türk Hamamları'; Ünver, 'İstanbul Hamamları'; Ünver, 'İstanbul Hamamları, Hali ve İstikbali'.
92. Koçu, 'Çarşı Hamamlarımız', p. 12.
93. Abdülaziz Bey, *Osmanlı Adet, Merasim ve Tabirleri*, pp. 299–301.
94. For images of the bathrooms of various Istanbul mansions, see Diana Barillari, *Istanbul 1900*.
95. İstanbul Müftülüğü Şer'iye Sicilleri Arşivi, Davud Paşa Mahkemesi, 8/110, p. 2a. As quoted and translated in Behar, *A Neighborhood in Ottoman Istanbul*, p. 149.
96. Abdülaziz Bey, *Osmanlı Adet, Merasim ve Tabirleri*, p. 170 (author's translation).
97. Zeynep Enlil, 'Residential Building Traditions and the Urban Culture of Istanbul in the Nineteenth Century', p. 307.
98. For a study on *bekar odaları* and the element of moral disorder they introduced into the urban space, see Hamadeh, 'Mean Streets'.

99. Behar, *A Neighborhood in Ottoman Istanbul*, pp. 149–50.
100. See Semavi Eyice, 'İstanbul Tarihi Eserler: Hamamlar', p. 103. As of yet, these nineteenth-century hamams have not been subject to study.
101. Çağlar Keyder, 'A Tale of Two Neighborhoods', pp. 173–4.
102. Davis, *Ottoman Lady*, p. 133.
103. Kemal Karpat, *Ottoman Past and Today's Turkey*, p. 27.
104. Personal communication with Ruşen Baltacı, 5 February 2003.
105. Glück, who conducted his research in Istanbul in the years 1916 and 1917, records this sad state of Istanbul's hamams. Glück, *Probleme des Wölbungsbaues*, pp. 8–9.
106. Ünver, 'Tarihi bir Hamam Halka Açıldı: Çemberlitaş Hamamı'.
107. These maps have been published in Ersoy et al., *Jacques Pervititch Sigorta Haritalarında İstanbul*. Pervititch prepared the map surveying the neighbourhood south of the Divan Yolu in 1923, and the map surveying the neighbourhood to the north in 1940. For the scant biographical information available about the cartographer, see Sabancıoğlu, 'Jacques Pervititch and his Insurance Maps of Istanbul'.
108. Ünver, 'Türk Hamamı', pp. 89, 92.
109. Akbay, 'Çenberlitaş Hamamı', p. 3819.
110. See Türeli, 'Heritagisation of the "Ottoman/Turkish House" in the 1970s'; Bertram, *Imagining the Turkish House*; Bozdoğan and Akcan, *Turkey: Modern Architectures in History*, pp. 96–103.
111. Kuban, *Istanbul, An Urban History*, p. 441; Türeli, 'Heritagisation of the "Ottoman/Turkish House" in the 1979s'.
112. Ünver, 'Tarihi bir Hamam Halka Açıldı: Çemberlitaş Hamamı'.

Chapter 7

1. For these events constituting the emergence of tourism, see John Urry and Scott Lash, *Economies of Signs and Spaces*, p. 261.
2. For a more detailed genealogical history of the tourist gaze, see Judith Adler, 'Origins of Sightseeing'.
3. Tim Edensor, *Tourists at the Taj*, p. 13.
4. On this hermeneutic cycle, see Patricia Albers and William James, 'Travel Photography', p. 136.
5. In 1985, revenue from tourism was US$770 million, in 1992, it was US$3.6 billion. See Öykü Potuoğlu-Cook, 'Beyond the Glitter', p. 637.
6. This claim repeatedly occurred in the interviews conducted with the managers and employees of Çemberlitaş Hamamı, November 2001–February 2003.
7. MacCannell, *The Tourist*, p. 41.
8. Interview with 45-year-old female tourist from Germany, 10 December 2001; interview with 44-year-old male tourist from New Zealand, 9 February 2002.

9. MacCannell, *The Tourist*, p. 42.
10. de Nicholay, *Nauigations*, pp. 58a–60a; de Busbecq, *Turkish Letters*, pp. 119–20; Wortley-Montagu, *Turkish Embassy Letters*, pp. 58–60; Pardoe, *City of the Sultan*, vol. 1, pp. 129–37; Settle, *Turkish Reflections*, pp. 48–9.
11. 'There were four fountains of cold water in this room, falling first into marble basins, and then running on the floor in little channels made for that purpose, which carried the streams into the next room, something less than this, with the same sort of marble sofas, but so hot with steams of sulphur proceeding from the baths joining to it, 'twas impossible to stay there with one's clothes on.' Wortley-Montagu, *Turkish Embassy Letters*, p. 58. 'For the first few moments, I was bewildered; the heavy, dense sulphureous vapour that filled the place, and almost suffocated me . . .', Pardoe, *City of the Sultan*, p. 133.
12. 'I excused myself with some difficulty, they being however all so earnest in persuading me, I was a last forced to open my shirt, and show them my stays [her corset], which satisfied them very well, for I saw they believed I was so locked up in that machine, that it was not in my own power to open it, which contrivance they attributed to my husband . . .'. Wortley-Montagu, *Turkish Embassy Letters*, pp. 59–60.
13. ' . . . the seruants which there are in greate number, require you to lay yourselfe along the flat voppon your bellie, & then one of these great lubbers after they haue well pulled and stretched your armes as well before as behinde in such sort that he wyll make your bones too cracke, and well rubbed the sooles of your feete, mounteth vpon your backe, and so with his feet slydeth vp and downe vpon you, and vpon your raynes, as if he woulde brouse them in peeces, and then againe maketh you to turne on your backe pulling and remouing your ioyentes as before is said . . . .'. de Nicholay, *Nauigations*, p. 58b.
14. Settle, *Turkish Reflections*, p. 48.
15. Wortley-Montagu, *Turkish Embassy Letters*, p. 59.
16. 'These bathing-women of whom I saw several as I traversed the great hall, are the most unsightly objects that can be imagined; from constantly living in a sulphureous atmosphere, their skins have become of the colour of tobacco, and of the consistency of parchment; many among them were elderly women, but not one of them was wrinkled; they had, apparently, become aged like frosted apples; the skin had tightened over the muscles, and produced what to me at least was a hideous feature of old age.' Pardoe, *City of the Sultan*, p. 135. 'At one of the basins an enormously fat naked old woman, with arms of iron, was sitting washing her underwear. She was the attendant, a eunuch figure, pendulous and mighty.' Settle, *Turkish Reflections*, p. 48.
17. ' . . . it cometh to passé that amongst the women of Leuan, ther is very great amity proceeding only through the frequentation & resort to bathes:

yea & sometimes become to fervently in loue the one of the other as if it were with men, in such sort that perceiuing some maiden or woman of excellent beauty they will not ceasse vntil they haue found means to bath with them, & to handle & gope them euery where at their pleasures, so ful they are of luxuriousness & feminine wantonness; euen as in times past wer the Tribades, of the number wherof was Sapho the Lesbian which transferred the loue wherewith the pursued a 100 women or maidens vpon her only friend Phaon.' de Nicholay, *Nauigations*, p. 60a.

18. See Billie Melman, *Women's Orients*, p. 92.
19. Patrick Connor, 'On the Bath', p. 38.
20. Interview with Ruşen Baltacı, 1 February 2002.
21. Connor, 'On the Bath', pp. 34–5.
22. Melman, *Women's Orients*, p. 89.
23. Pardoe, *City of the Sultan*, pp. 130, 134.
24. Connor, 'On the Bath', p. 34.
25. Uwe Fleckner, *Jean-Auguste-Dominique Ingres*, pp. 48–55.
26. For a detailed list and discussion of the many works that served as Ingres' inspiration, see Fleckner, *Jean-Auguste-Dominique Ingres*, pp. 35–47.
27. For a more detailed analysis of both plot and visual elements, as well as a positive critique, see Joseph Boone, *Homoerotics of Orientalism*, pp. 152–61.
28. Interview with Ruşen Baltacı, 3 February 2002.
29. İşigüzel, 'Waschtag im Reich der Sinne'.
30. Ibid., p. 86.
31. Milford, 'Bathed in Tradition in Istanbul'.
32. Ibid., p. 73.
33. John Urry, *Tourist Gaze*, p. 129.
34. Nick Inman, *Eyewitness Travel Guide Istanbul*. The book has been translated into many different languages, including German, French and Turkish.
35. Ibid., p. 6.
36. Ibid., p. 67.
37. Ibid., p. 81.
38. On 15 December 2001, the hamam attendants relayed to me an incident that had occurred in the first week of that month: a female foreign tourist left indignantly after having waited on the *göbektaşı* in the hot room for ten minutes. She dressed herself and asked to have her fees refunded because she had not received any services. Such a story tells not only about the communication difficulties between the attendants and foreign visitors, but also about the latter harbouring unrealistic expectations based on an Orientalist imaginary of boundless luxury and indulgent service at the hands of attendants immediately and exclusively focusing on the individual bather's every need and desire.
39. Jonathan Culler, 'Semiotics of Tourism', pp. 127–8.
40. Erik Cohen, 'Who is a Tourist?' p. 538.

41. I borrow this phrase from Lowenthal, *The Past is a Foreign Country*.
42. Albers and James, 'Travel Photography', p. 154.
43. Zihli, *Atlas İstanbul Rehberi*.
44. Balcı, 'Şehirde Yeni Moda: Hamam', p. 16.
45. On neo-Ottomanism, see Yılmaz Çolak, 'Ottomanism vs. Kemalism'; Nora Fisher Onar, 'Echoes of a Universalism Lost'; M. Hakan Yavuz, 'Turkish Identity and Foreign Policy in Flux'.
46. Potuoğlu-Cook, 'Beyond the Glitter', p. 634.
47. On the reception of this TV show, see, for example, Murat Ergin and Yağmur Karakaya, 'Neo-Ottomanism and Ottomania'.
48. Ahmet Akgündüz and Said Öztürk, *Bilinmeyen Osmanlı*.
49. 'Belly dance, historically a morally and economically suspect profession, has entered local elite social space through the heightened recycling of Ottoman goods, buildings, discourses, and performance practices for tourist and local consumption.' Potuoğlu-Cook, 'Beyond the Glitter', p. 634.
50. On the case of Soğukçeşme Street next to the Topkapı Palace, heavily restored as an ensemble to offer an environment and view conforming to nineteenth-century Orientalist engravings, see Çelik, 'Istanbul: Urban Preservation as Theme Park'. On Pera/Beyoğlu especially in the 1990s, see Ayfer Bartu, 'Who Owns the Old Quarters?'; Ayfer Bartu, 'Rethinking Heritage Politics in a Global Context'. On the once Jewish- and Armenian-dominated, but now gentrified and largely homogenised neighbourhood of Kuzguncuk, see Amy Mills, *Streets of Memory*. On the social inequalities caused by urban renewal projects and the rise of gated communities, see Ayfer Bartu-Candan and Biray Kolluoğlu, 'Emerging Spaces of Neoliberalism'.
51. Reşat Kasaba and Sibel Bozdoğan, 'Turkey at a Crossroads', p. 14.
52. Bathing as a practice to feel connected to one's national heritage is not unique to Turkey; in Japan, traditional inns with hot springs (*onsen*) appeal to harried white-collar workers who visit them as 'nostalgic repositories of "pure" Japaneseness'. Nelson Graburn, 'The Past in the Present in Japan'.
53. On the hamam of the Sanda Day Spa, see Ergin, 'Between East and West'.
54. Ira Silver, 'Marketing Authenticity in Third World Countries', p. 310. A parallel argument about nineteenth-century Ottomans being defenceless objects of Orientalism has been masterfully dismantled by Ahmet Ersoy, who has examined the way in which they wittily played with Orientalist imagery and expectations in order to fashion a self-identity that served various political, economic, and cultural ends. Ersoy, *Architecture and the Late Ottoman Historical Imaginary*.
55. Interview with Ruşen Baltacı, 1 February 2002.
56. Interview with Gülşen, 1 February 2002.
57. Interview with Sefer, 9 February 2002.
58. I am greatly indebted to Lauren Davis, who guided me through the literature on the topic of digital cultural heritage.

59. See at: www.cemberlitashamami.com.tr. The website has undergone several changes since then. Of course, Çemberlitaş Hamamı is not the only bathhouse presenting itself to the public by digital means; a comparison of the online presence of different establishments shall be left to future study.

60. For a discussion of the origin of the *çintemani* pattern, see Jaroslav Folda, 'An Icon of the Crucifixion and the Nativity at Sinai'. On the mechanisms and meanings of pattern distribution in the Ottoman Empire, see Gülru Necipoğlu, 'Kanun for the State'. On its widespread usage today, see Tülay Gülümser, 'Contemporary Usage of Turkish Traditional Motifs in Product Designs'.

61. Yehuda Kalay, 'Introduction: Preserving Cultural Heritage through Digital Media', p. 1.

62. On the project and exhibition, see at: http://alive.scm.cityu.edu.hk/projects/alive/pure-land-ii-2012.

63. Jérémie Landrieu et al., 'Digital Rebirth'.

64. Yu-Lien Chang et al., 'Apply an Augmented Reality in a Mobile Guidance'.

65. Diane Favro, 'In the Eyes of the Beholder'.

66. Rodrigo Paraizo and Jose Ripper Kos, 'Urban Heritage Representations in Hyperdocuments'.

67. Many digital media projects at heritage sites also allow lay users to contribute their own narratives, whether as amateur historian or as evaluator of the visiting experience. While the possibility of contributing certainly encourages interaction and engagement, not all narratives contributed will be of equal value. A careful monitoring is necessary, as stake-holders can use such mechanisms to advance a specific political agenda, for example. Given the fraught nature of Ottoman heritage in Istanbul, as discussed in Chapters 6, 7 and the Epilogue, it is likely that volunteer contributions may exhibit extreme political inclinations and even include inflammatory material.

68. Frances Tscheu and Dimitrios Buhalis, 'Augmented Reality at Cultural Heritage Sites'.

69. Colleen Dilen, 'Are Mobile Apps Worth it for Cultural Organizations?'

70. Bernadette Flynn, 'The Morphology of Space in Virtual Heritage', pp. 349–50.

71. Michael Baxandall, *Painting and Experience in Fifteenth-Century Italy*, particularly pp. 29–108.

72. For a recent study that investigates various modes of rendering architectural, urban and geographical space at the Holy Sites of Mecca and Medina, see Sabiha Göloğlu, 'Depicting the Holy: Representations of Mecca, Medina, and Jerusalem in the Late Ottoman Empire'.

73. The other two are the Çağaloğlu Hamamı and the Galatasaray Hamamı.

74. Potuoğlu-Cook, 'Beyond the Glitter', p. 653.

75. See Ayşe Öncü, 'Narratives of Istanbul's Ottoman Heritage'; Ayşe Öncü, 'Politics of Istanbul's Ottoman Heritage in the Era of Globalism'; Deniz Göktürk et al. (eds), *Orienting Istanbul*.

76. See Girard, 'What Heritage Tells Us About the Turkish State and Society'.
77. Erik Cohen, 'Authenticity and Commoditization in Tourism', p. 383.

Epilogue

1. For a thorough discussion of Istanbul at the turn to the twenty-first century, see Göktürk et al. (eds), *Orienting Istanbul*.
2. See at: http://www.nytimes.com/2010/01/10/travel/10places.html?pagewan ted=all&_r=0.
3. At the time of research, there were still only few Arab tourists, and I did not encounter any in Çemberlitaş Hamamı. However, given their current strong presence, a study surveying Middle Eastern visitors' attitudes towards the Ottoman heritage of Istanbul would constitute a most interesting and valuable contribution.
4. Öncü, 'Narratives of Istanbul's Ottoman Heritage'; Öncü, 'Politics of Istanbul's Ottoman Heritage'; İpek Türeli, 'Modeling Citizenship in Turkey's Miniature Park'. The park also includes a miniature of Mimar Sinan's Haseki Hamam.
5. See Radha Dalal, 'Placing the Spectator on the Scene of Conquest'.
6. For an analysis of the Gezi Park protests, see Efe Can Gürcan and Efe Peker, *Challenging Neoliberalism at Turkey's Gezi Park*; İdil Işıl Gül, *Gezi Park Olayları*. For a succinct history of the heritage politics that led up to the protests, see Ersoy, *Architecture and the Late Ottoman Historical Imaginary*, pp. 246–51.
7. The museum's website can be found at: http://turkhamamkulturu.istanbul. edu.tr.
8. D. Medina Lasansky, 'Introduction', *Architecture and Tourism*, p. 3.
9. Kafadar, 'A Rome of One's Own', p. 21.

References

Abbreviations

DBİA   *Dünden Bugüne İstanbul Ansiklopedisi*, İstanbul: Kültür Bakanlığı & Tarih Vakfı, 1994.

EI2   *Encyclopedia of Islam*, 2nd edn, Leipzig, Leiden: Brill, 1960–.

İA   *İslam Ansiklopedisi*, İstanbul: Milli Eğitim Basımevi, 1993.

İstA   *İstanbul Ansiklopedisi*, Koçu, Reşad Ekrem (ed.), İstanbul: İstanbul Ansiklopedisi ve Neşriyat Kollektif Şirketi, 1965.

TDVİA   *Türkiye Diyanet Vakfı İslam Ansiklopedisi*, İstanbul: Türkiye Diyanet Vakfı, 1997.

Documentary Sources

Topkapı Palace Library (Topkapı Saray Kütüphanesi, TSK)
     B. 408.
     E.H. 1446, 3064.
     H. 1344, 1565, 2894.
     Revan Odası 1934.
Topkapı Palace Archives (Topkapı Saray Arşivi, TSA)
     D. 1901, 1781, 9912.
     E. 246/61–62, 246/291, 246/421–425, 246/479, 246/529.
Prime Ministry's Ottoman Archives (Başbakanlık Osmanlı Arşivi, BOA)
     Başmuhasebe-DBŞM 42648.
     D.HMH.VLSA, 282/27, 282/30, 282/77, 290/117, 291/78, 292/101.
     EV.HMH.VLSA, 6/102, 6/104.
     Kamil Kepeci Müteferrik Defterleri 7437.
     MAD 422, 487, 987, 1672, 2105, 2263, 3002, 5247, 5273, 5827, 5886, 7434, 15742.
     Mühimme 26/264/111, 48/20/76, 48/269/766, 48/341/1000, 48/357/1047, 60/106/261, 64/141/368, 69/152/302.
     YEE, 11/14/126/C.
İstanbul Belediye Kütüphanesi
     Muallim Cevdet Tasnifi, *İstanbul Hamamcı Esnafı ve Tellaklarının İsimlerini Havi Defter.*

General Directorate of Endowments, Ankara (Vakıflar Genel Müdürlüğü, VGM)
D. 121, 608/23, 1426, 1427, 1766.

Published Sources

Âb-ı Hayat: Geçmişten Günümüze İstanbul'da Su ve Su Kültürü (Istanbul: Kültür ve Turizm Bakanlığı Kültür Varlıkları ve Müzeler Genel Müdürlüğü, Adell, 2010).

Abdülaziz Bey, *Osmanlı Âdet, Merasim ve Tabirleri*, ed. Kazım Arısan and Duygu Arısan Günay (Istanbul: Tarih Vakfı Yurt Yayınları, 1995).

Abu Muhammad al-Husayn ibn Mas'ud ibn Muhammad al-Farra' al-Baghawi, *Mishkat al-Masabih*, trans. James Robson (Lahore: Muhammad Ashraf, 1975).

Adler, Judith, 'Origins of Sightseeing', *Annals of Tourism Research* 16 (1989): 7–29.

Akarlı, Engin, 'Gedik: A Bundle of Rights and Obligations for Istanbul Artisans and Traders, 1750–1840', in Alain Pottage and Martha Mundy (eds), *Law, Anthropology, and the Constitution of the Social: Making Persons and Things* (Cambridge: Cambridge University Press, 2004), pp. 166–200.

Akbay, Haluk, 'Çenberlitaş Hamamı', *İstA*.

Akbay, Haluk, 'Çemberlitaş Hamamı Baskını Vak'ası', *İstA*.

Akgündüz, Ahmet and Said Öztürk, *Bilinmeyen Osmanlı* (İstanbul: Osmanlı Araştırmaları Vakfı, 1999).

Aksan, Virginia, 'The Question of Writing Premodern Biographies of the Middle East', in Mary Ann Fay (ed.), *Auto/Biography and the Construction of Identity and Community in the Middle East* (New York: Palgrave, 2002), pp. 191–200.

Akşit, Elif Ekin, 'Kadınların Hamamı ve Dönüşümü', in Ayten Alkan (ed.), *Cins Cins Mekan* (Istanbul: Varlık Yayınları, 2009), pp. 136–67.

Akşit, Elif Ekin, 'The Women's Quarters in the Historical Hammam', *Gender, Place & Culture* 18 (2011): 277–93.

Aktepe, Münir, *Patrona İsyanı (1730)* (Istanbul: Edebiyat Fakültesi, 1958).

Akyıldız, Olcay, Halim Kara and Börte Sagaster (eds), *Autobiographical Themes in Turkish Literature: Theoretical and Comparative Perspectives* (Würzburg: Ergon, 2007).

Albers, Patricia and William James, 'Travel Photography: A Methodological Approach', *Annals of Tourism Research* 15 (1988): 134–58.

Alderson, A. D., *The Structure of the Ottoman Dynasty* (Oxford: Clarendon Press, 1965).

Altınyıldız, Nur, 'The Architectural Heritage of Istanbul and the Ideology of Preservation', *Muqarnas* 23 (2007): 281–306.

Ambraseys, N. N., *Earthquakes in the Eastern Mediterranean and the Middle East: A Multidisciplinary Study of Seismity up to 1900* (Cambridge: Cambridge University Press, 2009).

Ambraseys, N. N. and C. F. Finkel, *The Seismicity of Turkey and Adjacent Areas: A Historical Review, 1500–1800* (Istanbul: Eren Yayınevi, 1995).

References

Anastassiadou, Meropi and Bernard Heyberger (eds), *Figures anonymes, figures d'élite: Pour une anatomie de l'homo ottomanicus* (Istanbul: ISIS, 1999).

And, Metin, '16. Yüzyılda Temizlik ve Hamamlar', *Hayat Tarihi Mecmuası* 10 (1969): 14–18.

Andrews, Walter and Mehmet Kalpaklı, *The Age of Beloveds: Love and the Beloved in Early Modern Ottoman and European Culture and Society* (Durham, NC: Duke University Press, 2005).

Aoki, Miyuki, 'Leon Parvillée: Osmanlı Modernleşmesinin Eşiğinde bir Fransız Sanatçı', PhD dissertation, Istanbul Technical University, 2002.

Aravamudan, Srinivas, 'Lady Mary Wortly Montagu in the Hammam: Masquerade, Womanliness, and Levantinization', *ELH* 62 (1995): 69–104.

Arbel, Benjamin, 'Nurbanu (c. 1530–1583): A Venetian Sultana?' *Turcica* 24 (1992): 241–59.

Artan, Tülay, 'Forms and Forums of Expression: Istanbul and Beyond, 1600–1800', in Christine Woodhead (ed.), *The Ottoman World* (London: Routledge, 2011), pp. 378–406.

Asanova, Galina and Martin Dow, 'The Sarrafan Baths in Bukhara', *Iran* 39 (2001): 187–205.

Asher, Catherine, 'The Public Baths of Medieval Spain: An Architectural Study', in M. J. Chiatt and K. L. Reyerson (eds), *The Medieval Mediterranean: Cross-Cultural Contacts* (St. Cloud, MN: North Star Press, 1988), pp. 25–34.

Atasoy, Nurhan, *1582 Surname-i Hümayun: An Imperial Celebration* (Istanbul: Koçbank, 1997).

Atçeken, Zeki, *Konya'da Selçuklu Yapılarının Osmanlı Devrinde Bakımı ve Kullanılması* (Ankara: Türk Tarih Kurumu, 1998).

Avcıoğlu, Nebahat, *Turquerie and the Politics of Representation, 1728–1876* (Farnham: Ashgate, 2011).

Avcıoğlu, Nebahat, 'The Turkish Bath in the West', in Nina Ergin (ed.), *Bathing Culture of Anatolian Civilizations: Architecture, History and Imagination* (Louvain: Peeters, 2011), pp. 267–304.

Avicenna, *The General Principles of Avicenna's Canon of Medicine*, trans. Mazhar Shah (Karachi: Naveed Clinic, 1966).

Aynur, Hatice and Aslı Niyazioğlu (eds), *Aşık Çelebi ve Şairler Tezkeresi Üzerine Yazılar* (Istanbul: Koç Üniversitesi Yayınları, 2011).

Ayvansarayî, *The Garden of the Mosques: Hafız Hüseyin Ayvansarayi's Guide to the Muslim Monuments of Istanbul*, trans. and ed. Howard Crane (Leiden: Brill, 2000).

Ayverdi, Ekrem Hakkı, *Osmanlı Mimarisinin İlk Devri: Ertuğrul, Osman, Orhan Gaaziler Hüdavendigar ve Yıldırım Bayezıd 630–805 (1230–1402): İstanbul Mimari Çağının Menşesi* (Istanbul: Fetih Cemiyeti, 1966).

Ayverdi, Ekrem Hakkı, *İlk 250 Senenin Osmanlı Mimârisi* (Istanbul: Baha Matbaası, 1976).

Ayverdi, Ekrem Hakkı, *Osmanlı Mimarisinde Fatih Devri 855–886 (1451–1481)* (Istanbul: Istanbul Fetih Cemiyeti, 1989).

Babinger, Franz, *Mehmed the Conqueror and His Time* (Princeton, NJ: Princeton University Press, 1978).

Baer, Gabriel, 'Women and Waqf: An Analysis of the Istanbul *Tahrir* of 1546', *Asian and African Studies* 17 (1983): 9–27.

Baer, Marc, 'The Great Fire of 1660 and the Islamization of Christian and Jewish Space in Istanbul', *International Journal of Middle East Studies* 36 (2004): 159–81.

Bağcı, Serpil, 'From Adam to Mehmed III: Silsilenâme', in *The Sultan's Portrait: Picturing the House of Osman* (Istanbul: İşbank, 2000), pp. 188–201.

Balcı, Zeynep, 'Şehirde Yeni Moda: Hamam', *Cinetempo*, 12–18 December 2002, p. 16.

Bardakçı, Murat, *Osmanlı'da Seks: Sarayda Gece Dersleri* (Istanbul: Gür Yayınları, 1993).

Barillari, Diana, *Istanbul 1900: Art Nouveau Architecture and Interiors* (New York: Rizzoli, 1996).

Barnes, R. J., *An Introduction to the Religious Foundations in the Ottoman Empire* (Leiden: Brill, 1987).

Bartu, Ayfer, 'Who Owns the Old Quarters? Rewriting Histories in a Global Era', in Çağlar Keyder (ed.), *Istanbul between the Global and the Local* (Lanham, MD: Rowman & Littlefield, 1999), pp. 31–44.

Bartu, Ayfer, 'Rethinking Heritage Politics in a Global Context: A View from Istanbul', in Nezar AlSayyad (ed.), *Hybrid Urbanism: On the Identity Discourse and the Built Environment* (Westport, CT: Praeger, 2001), pp. 131–55.

Bartu-Candan, Ayfer and Biray Kolluoğlu, 'Emerging Spaces of Neoliberalism: A Gated Town and a Public Housing Project in İstanbul', *New Perspectives on Turkey* 39 (2008): 5–46.

Bates, Ülkü, 'Women as Patrons of Architecture in Turkey', in Lois Beck and Nikki Keddie (eds), *Women in the Muslim World* (Cambridge, MA: Harvard University Press, 1978), pp. 245–60.

Bates, Ülkü, 'The Architectural Patronage of Ottoman Women', *Asian Art* 6 (1993): 50–65.

van Bavel, Bas, 'The Economic Origins of Cleanliness in the Dutch Golden Age', *Past & Present* 205 (2009): 41–69.

Baxandall, Michael, *Painting and Experience in Fifteenth-Century Italy* (Oxford: Oxford University Press, 1974).

Bayraktar, Nimet, 'Üsküdar Kütüphaneleri', *Vakıflar Dergisi* 16 (1982): 45–59.

Beg, Muhammad 'Abdul Jabbar, 'Workers in the Hammamat in the Arab Orient in the Early Middle Ages (8th to 11th Centuries A.D.)', *Rivista degli Studi Orientali* 47 (1972): 77–80.

Behar, Cem, *A Neighborhood in Ottoman Istanbul: Fruit Vendors and Civil Servants in the Kasap İlyas Mahalle* (Albany, NY: SUNY Press, 2003).

Benkheira, Mohammed Hocine, 'Hammam, nudité et ordre moral dans l'Islam médiéval', *Revue de l'Histoire des Religions* 224 (2007): 319–71.

References

Benkheira, Mohammed Hocine, 'Hammam, nudité et ordre moral dans l'Islam médiéval', *Revue de l'Histoire des Religions* 225 (2008): 75–128.

Berger, Albrecht, *Das Bad in der Byzantinischen Zeit* (Munich: Institut für Byzantinistik und Neugriechische Philologie, 1982).

Berkes, Niyazi, *The Development of Secularism in Turkey* (New York: Routledge, 1998).

Bertram, Carel, *Imagining the Turkish House: Collective Visions of Home* (Austin, TX: University of Texas Press, 2008).

Be-Se, 'Bizans Hamamları', *TTOK Belleten* 110 (1951): 13.

Bessard, Fanny, 'Pratiques sanitaires, produits d'hygiène et de soin dans les bains médiévaux (VIIIe–IXe siècles)', *Bulletin d'Etudes Orientales* 57 (2006/7): 111–25.

Bilirgen, Emine, Feza Çakmut, Selma Delibaş and Deniz Esemenli, *Hamam: Osmanlı'da Yıkanma Geleneği ve Berberlik Zanaatı* (Istanbul: Topkapı Sarayı Müzesi, 2006).

Binan, Can, 'The Treatment of the Ottoman Architectural Legacy in the Early Republican Press', in Nur Akın, Afife Batur and Selçuk Batur (eds), *Seven Centuries of Ottoman Architecture: A Supra-National Heritage* (Istanbul: YEM Yayın, n.d. [2001]), pp. 377–81.

Biow, Douglas, *The Culture of Cleanliness in Renaissance Italy* (Ithaca, NY: Cornell University Press, 2006).

Blair, Sheila and Jonathan Bloom, 'The Mirage of Islamic Art: Reflections on the Study of an Unwieldy Field', *The Art Bulletin* 85 (2003): 152–84.

Blake, Stephen, 'Hamams in Mughal India and Safavid Iran', in Nina Ergin (ed.), *Bathing Culture of Anatolian Civilizations: Architecture, History and Imagination* (Louvain: Peeters, 2011), pp. 257–66.

Bloom, Jonathan and Sheila Blair, *Grove Encyclopedia on Islamic Art and Architecture* (Oxford: Oxford University Press, 2009).

de Bonneville, Françoise, *The Book of the Bath* (New York: Rizzoli, 1998).

van den Boogert, Maurits, 'Resurrecting *Homo Ottomanicus*: The Constants and Variables of Ottoman Identity', *Osmanlı Araştırmaları/Journal of Ottoman Studies* 44 (2014): 9–20.

Boone, Joseph, *The Homoerotics of Orientalism* (New York: Columbia University Press, 2014).

Boratav, Pertev N., 'Djinn: In Turkish Folklore', *EI2*.

Bos, Gerrit, 'Maimonides on the Preservation of Health', *Journal of the Royal Asiatic Society* 4 (1994): 213–35.

Boudhiba, A., 'Le Hammam: contribution a une psychanalyse de l'Islam', *Revue tunesienne des sciences sociales* 1 (1964): 7–14.

Boyar, Ebru and Kate Fleet, *A Social History of Ottoman Istanbul* (Cambridge: Cambridge University Press, 2010).

Bozdoğan, Sibel, *Modernism and Nation-Building: Turkish Architectural Culture in the Early Republic* (Seattle, WA: University of Washington Press, 2001).

Bozdoğan, Sibel, 'Reading Ottoman Architecture through Modernist Lenses: Nationalist Historiography and the "New Architecture" in the Early Republic', *Muqarnas* 24 (2007): 199–221.

Bozdoğan, Sibel and Esra Akcan, *Turkey: Modern Architectures in History* (London: Reaktion, 2012).

Breathnach, Teresa, 'For Health and Pleasure: The Turkish Bath in Victorian Ireland', *Victorian Literature and Culture* 32 (2004): 159–75.

Brown, Kathleen, *Foul Bodies: Cleanliness in Early America* (New Haven, CT: Yale University Press, 2009).

Buitelaar, Marjo, 'Public Baths as Private Places', in Karin Ask and Marjit Tomsland (eds), *Women and Islamization: Contemporary Dimensions of Discourse on Gender Relations* (Oxford: Berg, 1998), pp. 103–23.

Burton, John, 'The Qur'an and the Islamic Practice of Wudu'', *Bulletin of the School of Oriental and African Studies* 51 (1988): 21–58.

de Busbecq, Ogier Ghiselin, *Turkish Letters* (London: Sickle Moon Books, 2001).

Bushman, Richard, and Claudia Bushman, 'The Early History of Cleanliness in America', *Journal of American History* 74 (1988): 1213–38.

Butler, Lee, '"Washing Off the Dust": Baths and Bathing in Late Medieval Japan', *Monumenta Nipponica* 60 (2005): 1–41.

Bynum, Carol Walker, *Jesus as Mother: Studies in the Spirituality of the High Middle Ages* (Berkeley, CA: University of California Press, 1982).

Cabi Ömer Efendi, *Cabi Tarihi (Tarih-i Sultan Selim-i Salis ve Mahmud-ı Sani – Tahlil ve Tenkidli Metin)*, ed. Mehmet Beyhan (Ankara: Türk Tarih Kurumu, 2003).

Cafer Çelebi, *Risâle-i Mi'mâriyye: An Early Seventeenth-Century Ottoman Treatise on Architecture*, trans. and ed. Howard Crane (Leiden: Brill, 1987).

Çağaptay, Soner, 'Race, Assimilation and Kemalism: Turkish Nationalism and the Minorities in the 1930s', *Middle Eastern Studies* 40 (2004): 86–101.

Çakmak, Canan, *Tire Hamamları* (Ankara: Kültür Bakanlığı, 2002).

Çaksu, Ali, 'Janissary Coffeehouses in Late Eighteenth-Century Istanbul', in Dana Sajdi (ed.), *Ottoman Tulips, Ottoman Coffee: Leisure and Lifestyle in the Eighteenth Century* (London: I. B. Tauris, 2007), pp. 117–32.

Can, Cengiz, 'Barborini, Giovanni Battista', *DBİA*.

Can, Cengiz and Paolo Ghirardelli, 'Giovanni Battista Barborini à Istanbul', *Observatoire Urbain d'Istanbul* 8 (1995): 2–7.

Cantay, Tanju, 'Mimar Sinan'ın Az Tanınan Bir Eseri: Ayakapı Hamamı', *Taç Vakfı Dergisi* 2 (1987): 18–21.

Caskey, Jill, 'Steam and Sanitas in the Domestic Realm: Baths and Bathing in Southern Italy in the Middle Ages', *Journal of the Society of Architectural Historians* 58 (1999): 170–95.

Çeçen, Kazım, *Üsküdar Suları* (Istanbul: İstanbul Büyükşehir Belediyesi, 1991).

Çeçen, Kazım, *İstanbul'un Osmanlı Dönemi Suyolları* (Istanbul: Renk Ajans, 2000).

Çelebi, Asaf Halet, *Divan Şiirinde İstanbul* (Istanbul: Halk Basımevi, 1953).

References

Çelik, Zeynep, 'Bouvard's Boulevards: Beaux-Arts Planning in Istanbul', *Journal of the Society of Architectural Historians* 43 (1984): 341–55.

Çelik, Zeynep, *The Remaking of Istanbul* (Berkeley, CA: University of California Press, 1986).

Çelik, Zeynep, *Displaying the Orient: Architecture of Islam at Nineteenth-Century World's Fairs* (Berkeley, CA: University of California Press, 1992).

Çelik, Zeynep, 'Istanbul: Urban Preservation as Theme Park: The Case of Soğukçeşme Street', in Zeynep Çelik, Diane Favro and Richard Ingersoll (eds), *Streets: Critical Perspectives on Public Space* (Berkeley, CA: University of California Press, 1994), pp. 83–94.

Cerasi, Maurice, *The Istanbul Divan Yolu: A Case Study in Ottoman Urbanity and Architecture* (Würzburg: Ergon, 2006).

Cezar, Mustafa, 'Osmanlı Devrinde İstanbul Yapılarında Tahribat Yapan Yangınlar ve Tabii Afetler', *Türk Sanatı Tarihi Araştırma ve İncelemeleri* 1 (1963): 327–414.

Cezar, Mustafa, *Typical Commercial Buildings of the Ottoman Classical Period and the Ottoman Construction System* (Istanbul: Türkiye İş Bankası, 1983).

Cezar, Mustafa, *Osmanlı Başkenti İstanbul* (Istanbul: Erol Kerim Aksoy Kültür, Eğitim, Spor ve Sağlık Vakfı, 2002).

Chang, Yu-Lien, Huei-Tse Hou, Chao-Yang Pan, Yao-Ting Sung and Kuo-En Chang, 'Apply an Augmented Reality in a Mobile Guidance to Increase Sense of Place for Heritage Places', *Education Technology & Society* 18 (2015): 166–78.

Çizakça, Murat, *A Comparative Evolution of Business Partnerships* (Leiden: Brill, 1996).

Cichocki, Nina, 'Continuity and Change in Turkish Bathing Culture in Istanbul: The Life Story of the Çemberlitaş Hamam', *Turkish Studies* 6 (2005): 93–112.

Clot, André, *Soliman le Magnifique* (Paris: Fayard, 1983).

Cohen, Erik, 'Who is a Tourist? A Conceptual Clarification', *Sociological Review* 22 (1974): 527–55.

Cohen, Erik, 'Authenticity and Commoditization in Tourism', *Annals of Tourism Research* 15 (1988): 371–86.

Çolak, Yılmaz, 'Ottomanism vs. Kemalism: Collective Memory and Cultural Pluralism in 1990s Turkey', *Middle Eastern Studies* 42 (2006): 587–602.

Connor, Patrick, 'On the Bath: Western Experiences of the Hamam', *Renaissance & Modern Studies* 31 (1987): 34–42.

Crane, Howard, 'Anatolian Saljuq Architecture and Its Links to Saljuq Iran', in Robert Hillenbrand (ed.), *The Art of the Saljuqs in Iran and Anatolia* (Costa Mesa, CA: Mazda, 1994).

Creswell, K. A. C., *A Short Account of Early Muslim Architecture*, rev. and suppl. James Allan (Aldershot: Scolar Press, 1989).

Culler, Jonathan, 'Semiotics of Tourism', *American Journal of Semiotics* 1 (1981): 127–40.

Cumhuriyetten Önce ve Sonra Vakıflar (Istanbul: Cumhuriyet Matbaası, 1937).

Dalal, Radha, 'Placing the Spectator on the Scene of Conquest: Istanbul's 1453 Panorama History Museum', paper presented at *The Bodhi Tree and the Orchid: A Symposium in Honor of Fredrick and Catherine Asher*, University of Chicago, February 2014.

Dallal, Ahmed, 'The Islamic Instituiton of Waqf: A Historical Overview', in Stephen Heynemann (ed.), *Islam and Social Policy* (Nashville, TN: Vanderbilt University Press, 2004), pp. 13–43.

Dankoff, Robert, *The Intimate Life of an Ottoman Statesman: Melek Ahmed Pasha (1588–1662) as Portrayed in Evliya Çelebi's Book of Travels* (Albany, NY: SUNY Press, 1991).

Dankoff, Robert, *An Ottoman Mentality: The World of Evliya Çelebi* (Leiden: Brill, 2004).

Dauphin, Claudine, 'Brothels, Baths and Babes: Prostitution in the Byzantine Holy Land', *Classics Ireland* 3 (1996): 47–72.

Davis, Fanny, *The Ottoman Lady: A Social History from 1718 to 1918* (Westport, CT: Greenwood, 1986).

Davis, Nathalie Zemon, 'Boundaries and the Sense of Self in Sixteenth-Century France', in Thomas Heller, Morton Sosna and David Wellbery (eds), *Reconstructing Individualism: Autonomy, Individuality, and the Self in Western Thought* (Stanford, CA: Stanford University Press, 1986), pp. 53–63.

Davis, Richard, *Lives of Indian Images* (Princeton, NJ: Princeton University Press, 1997).

DeLaine, Janet, 'Some Observations on the Transition from Greek to Roman Baths in Hellenistic Italy', *Meditarch* 2 (1989): 111–25.

DeLaine, Janet et al. (eds), *Roman Baths and Bathing: Proceedings of the First International Conference on Roman Baths held at Bath, England, 30 March–4 April 1992* (Portsmouth: Journal of Roman Archaeology, 1999).

Delice, Serkan, 'The Janissaries and their Bedfellows: Masculinity and Male Friendship in Eighteenth-Century Ottoman Istanbul', in Gul Ozyegin (ed.), *Gender and Sexuality in Muslim Cultures* (Farnham: Ashgate, 2015), pp. 115–37.

Demirel, Fatmagül (ed.), *Osmanlı'dan Cumhuriyet'e Esnaf ve Ticaret* (Istanbul: Tarih Vakfı Yurt Yayınları, 2012).

Demiren, S., 'Bizans Hamamları', *TTOK Belleten* 110 (1951): 13.

Dernschwam, Hans, *Hans Dernschwam's Tagebuch einer Reise nach Konstantinopel und Kleinasien (1553/55)*, ed. Franz Babinger (Berlin: Verlag von Dunckner & Humblot, 1986).

Derviş Efendi-zade Derviş Mustafa Efendi, *1782 Yılı Yangınları [Harik Risalesi 1196]*, ed. Hüsamettin Aksu (Istanbul: İletişim, 1994).

Destari Salih, *Destari Salih Tarihi: Patrona Halil Ayaklanması Hakkında bir Kaynak*, trans. and ed. Bekir Sıtkı Baykal (Ankara: Ankara Üniversitesi Dil ve Tarih-Çoğrafya Fakültesi, 1962).

Develi, Hayati (ed.), *XVIII. YY İstanbul'a Dair Risale-i Garibe* (Istanbul: Kitabevi, 2001).

References

Dilen, Colleen, 'Are Mobile Apps Worth it for Cultural Organizations?', available at: https://www.colleendilen.com/2017/04/05/are-mobile-apps-worth-it-for-cultural-organizations-data.

Dow, Martin, *The Islamic Baths of Palestine* (Oxford: Oxford University Press, 1996).

Dow, Martin, 'The Hammams of Ottoman Jerusalem', in Sylvia Auld and Robert Hillenbrand (eds), *Ottoman Jerusalem, the Living City: 1517–1917* (London: Altajir World of Islam Trust, 2000).

Dursteler, Eric, *Venetians in Constantinople: Nation, Identity and Coexistence in the Early Modern Mediterranean* (Baltimore, MD: Johns Hopkins University Press, 2006).

Düzdağ, Mehmet Ertuğrul, *Şeyülislam Ebussuud Efendi Fetvaları Işığında 16. Asır Türk Hayatı* (Istanbul: Enderun Kitabevi, 1972).

Eakin, Paul, *How Our Lives Become Stories* (Ithaca, NY: Cornell University Press, 1999).

Écochard, Michel and Claude LeCoeur, *Les Bains de Damas: Monographies Architecturales* (Beirut: Institut Français de Damas, 1942).

Edensor, Tim, *Tourists at the Taj: Performance and Meaning at a Symbolic Site* (London: Routledge, 1998).

Eger, A. Asa, '(Re)Mapping Medieval Antioch: Urban Transformations from the Early Islamic to the Middle Byzantine Periods', *Dumbarton Oaks Papers* 67 (2013): 95–134.

Eger, A. Asa, *The Islamic-Byzantine Frontier: Interactions and Exchange Among Muslim and Christian Communities* (London: I. B. Tauris, 2015).

Egli, Ernst, *Sinan: Der Baumeister Osmanischer Glanzzeit* (Zurich: Verlag für Architektur, 1954).

Eldem, Sedad Hakkı, *Türk Evi Plan Tipleri*, 2nd edn (Istanbul: İTÜ Mimarlık Fakültesi Baskı Atölyesi, 1968).

Elger, Ralf, and Yavuz Köse (eds), *Many Ways of Speaking About the Self: Middle Eastern Ego-Documents in Arabic, Persian and Turkish (14th–20th Century)* (Wiesbaden: Harrassowitz, 2010).

Enderuni Fazıl Hüseyin, *Zenanname*, 1793, Istanbul University Library, T. 5502.

Enlil, Zeynep, 'Continuity and Change in İstanbul's Nineteenth Century Neighborhoods: From Traditional House to Apartment House', PhD dissertation, University of Washington, 1994.

Enlil, Zeynep, 'Residential Building Traditions and the Urban Culture of Istanbul in the Nineteenth Century', in Nur Akın, Afife and Selçuk Batur (eds), *Seven Centuries of Ottoman Architecture: A Supra-National Heritage* (Istanbul: YEM Yayın, n.d. [2001]), pp. 306–15.

Eravşar, Osman, *Tokat Tarihi Su Yapıları (Hamamlar)* (Konya: Arkeoloji ve Sanat Yayınları, 2004).

Erder, Cevat, 'The Care of Historic Monuments and Sites in Turkey', in L. C. Brown (ed.), *From Medina to Metropolis: Heritage and Change in the Near Eastern City* (Princeton, NJ: Darwin Press, 1973), pp. 277–88.

Erdoğan, Muzaffer, 'Osmanlı Mimari Tarihinin Arşiv Kaynakları', *Tarih Dergisi* 5/6 (1951/2): 95–122.

Ergenç, Özer, 'Osmanlı Şehrindeki 'Mahalle'nin İşlev ve Nitelikleri Üzerinde', *Osmanlı Araştırmaları* 4 (1989): 69–78.

Ergene, Boğaç, 'Pursuing Justice in an Islamic Context: Dispute Resolution in Ottoman Courts of Law', *Political and Legal Anthropological Review* 27 (2004): 51–71.

Ergin, Murat and Yağmur Karakaya, 'Neo-Ottomanism and Ottomania: Multiple Representations of the Past and Popular Culture', *New Perspectives on Turkey* 56 (2017): 33–59.

Ergin, Nina, 'Taking Care of the Atik Valide Imaret', in Nina Ergin, Christoph K. Neumann and Amy Singer (eds), *Feeding People, Feeding Power: Imarets in the Ottoman Empire* (Istanbul: Eren, 2007), pp. 151–67.

Ergin, Nina, 'The Soundscape of Sixteenth-Century Istanbul Mosques: Architecture and Qur'an Recital', *Journal of the Society of Architectural Historians* 67(2) (2008): 204–21.

Ergin Nina (ed.), *Bathing Culture of Anatolian Civilizations: Architecture, History and Imagination* (Louvain: Peeters, 2010).

Ergin, Nina, 'Between East and West: Modernity, Identity, and the Turkish Bath', *Trondheim Studies on East European Cultures & Societies* 29 (2010).

Ergin, Nina, 'Bathing Business in Istanbul: A Case Study of the Çemberlitaş Hamamı in the Seventeenth and Eighteenth Centuries', in Nina Ergin (ed.), *Bathing Culture of Anatolian Civilizations: Architecture, History and Imagination* (Louvain: Peeters, 2011), pp. 142–67.

Ergin, Nina, 'The Albanian Tellâk Connection: Labor Migration to the Hamams of Eighteenth-Century Istanbul, based on the 1752 İstanbul Hamâmları Defteri', *Turcica* 43 (2011 [2012]): 231–56.

Ergin, Nina, 'A Multi-Sensorial Message of the Divine and the Personal: Qur'anic Inscriptions and Recitation in Sixteenth-Century Ottoman Mosques', in Mohammad Gharipouri and Irvin C. Schick (eds), *Calligraphy and Architecture in the Muslim World* (Edinburgh: Edinburgh University Press, 2013), pp. 105–18.

Ergin, Nina, 'The Fragrance of the Divine: Ottoman Incense Burners and their Context', *The Art Bulletin* 96(1) (2014): 70–97.

Ergin, Nina, 'Ottoman Royal Women's Spaces: The Acoustic Dimension', *Journal of Women's History* 26(1) (2014): 89–111.

Ergin, Nina, 'Healing by Design? An Experiential Approach to Early Modern Ottoman Hospital Architecture', *Turkish Historical Review* 6(1) (2015): 1–37.

Ergin, Nina, with contributions by Yasemin Özarslan, 'Mapping Istanbul's Hamams of 1752 and Their Employees', in Suraiya Faroqhi (ed.), *Bread from the Lion's Mouth: Artisans Struggling for a Livelihood in Ottoman Cities* (New York, Oxford: Berghahn, 2015), pp. 108–35.

Ergin, Nina, '"And in the Soup Kitchen Food Shall be Cooked Twice Every Day": Gustatory Aspects of Ottoman Mosque Complexes', in Rebecca Brown

References

and Deborah Hutton (eds), *Rethinking Place in South Asian and Islamic Art, 1500–Present* (New York: Routledge, 2016), pp. 17–37.

Ergin, Nina, Christoph K. Neumann and Amy Singer (eds), *Feeding People, Feeding Power: Imarets in the Ottoman Empire* (Istanbul: Eren, 2007).

Ergin, Osman Nuri, *Türk Şehirlerinde İmaret Sistemi* (Istanbul: Cumhuriyet Matbaası, 1939).

Ergin, Osman Nuri, *Mecelle-i Umûr-ı Belediyye* (Istanbul: Büyükşehir Belediyesi Kültür İşleri Daire Başkanlığı Yayınları, 1995).

Erimtan, Can, 'Hittites, Ottomans and Turks: Ağaoğlu Ahmed Bey and the Construction of Turkish Nationhood in Anatolia', *Anatolian Studies* 58 (2008): 141–71.

Ersoy, Ahmet, 'Architecture and the Search for Ottoman Origins in the Tanzimat Period', *Muqarnas* 24 (2007): 79–102.

Ersoy, Ahmet, *Architecture and the Late Ottoman Historical Imaginary: Reconfiguring the Architectural Past in a Modernizing Empire* (Farnham: Ashgate, 2015).

Ersoy, Seden, et al. (eds), *Jacques Pervititch Sigorta Haritalarında İstanbul, Istanbul in the Insurance Maps of Jacques Pervititch* (Istanbul: Tarih Vakfı, n.d.).

Ertuğrul, Alidost, 'Hamam Yapıları ve Literatürü', *Türkiye Araştırmaları Literatür Dergisi* 7 (2009): 241–66.

Erzen, Jale, 'Aesthetics and Aisthesis in Ottoman Art and Architecture', *Journal of Islamic Studies* 2 (1992): 1–24.

Eski Hamam, Eski Tas (Istanbul: Yapı Kredi Kültür Sanat Yayıncılığı, Tofaş Sanat Galerisi, 2009).

Evliya Çelebi, *Evliya Çelebi Seyahatnamesi: Topkapı Sarayı Kütüphanesi Bağdat 304 Numaralı Yazmanın Transkripsyonu, 1. Kitap*, ed. Robert Dankoff, Seyit Ali Kahraman and Yücel Dağlı (Istanbul: Yapı Kredi Yayınları, 2006).

Evren, Burçak, *İstanbul'un Deniz Hamamları ve Plajları* (Istanbul: İnkılap Kitabevi, 2000).

Eyice, Semavi, 'İznik'te "Büyük Hamam" ve Osmanlı Hamamları Hakkında bir Deneme', *Tarih Dergisi* 11 (1960): 99–120.

Eyice, Semavi, 'Elçi Han', *Tarih Dergisi* 24 (1970): 93–129.

Eyice, Semavi, 'İstanbul'un Ortadan Kalkan Bazı Tarihi Eserleri', *Tarih Dergisi* 27 (1973): 133–78.

Eyice, Semavi, 'İstanbul Tarihi Eserler: Hamamlar', *İA*.

Eyice, Semavi, 'Hamam', *TDVİA*.

Fagan, Garrett, *Bathing in Public in the Roman World* (Ann Arbor, MI: University of Michigan, 1999).

Fagan, Garrett, 'The Genesis of the Roman Public Bath: Recent Approaches and Future Directions', *American Journal of Archaeology* 105 (2001): 403–26.

Fagan, Garrett, 'Bathing for Health with Celsus and Pliny the Elder', *Classical Quarterly* 56 (2006): 190–207.

Farhi, Moris, 'Lentils in Paradise', in Mai Ghoussoub and Emma Sinclair-Webb (eds), *Imagined Masculinities: Male Identity and Culture in the Modern Middle East* (London: Saqi, 2000), pp. 251–62.

Faroqhi, Suraiya, *Towns and Townsmen of Ottoman Anatolia: Trade, Crafts and Food Production in an Urban Setting* (Cambridge: Cambridge University Press, 1984).

Faroqhi, Suraiya, 'Crisis and Change, 1590–1699', in Halil İnalcık and Donald Quataert (eds), *An Economic and Social History of the Ottoman Empire, 1300–1914* (Cambridge: Cambridge University Press, 1994), pp. 411–530.

Faroqhi, Suraiya, *Subjects of the Sultan: Culture and Daily Life in the Ottoman Empire* (London: I. B. Tauris, 2000).

Faroqhi, Suraiya, *Stories of Ottoman Men and Women: Establishing Status, Establishing Control* (Istanbul: Eren, 2002).

Faroqhi, Suraiya (ed.), *The Cambridge History of Turkey, vol. 3: The Later Ottoman Empire, 1603–1839* (Cambridge: Cambridge University Press, 2006).

Faroqhi, Suraiya (ed.), *Animals and People in the Ottoman Empire* (Istanbul: Eren, 2010).

Faroqhi, Suraiya (ed.), *Bread from the Lion's Mouth: Artisans Struggling for a Livelihood in Ottoman Cities* (New York, Oxford: Berghahn, 2015).

Faroqhi, Suraiya, *A Cultural History of the Ottomans: The Imperial Elite and its Artifacts* (London: I. B. Tauris, 2016).

Faroqhi, Suraiya and Christoph Neumann (eds), *The Illuminated Table, The Prosperous House: Food and Shelter in Ottoman Material Culture* (Würzburg: Ergon, 2003).

Faroqhi, Suraiya, and Christoph Neumann (eds), *Ottoman Costumes: From Textile to Identity* (Istanbul: Eren, 2004).

Faroqhi, Suraiya and Randi Deguilhem (eds), *Crafts and Craftsmen of the Middle East: Fashioning the Individual in the Muslim Mediterranean* (London: I. B. Tauris, 2005).

Favro, Diane, 'In the Eyes of the Beholder: Virtual Reality Re-Creations and Academia', *Journal of the Roman Archaeology Supplement Series* 61 (2006): 321–34.

Fay, Mary Ann (ed.), *Auto/Biography and the Construction of Identity and Community in the Middle East* (New York: Palgrave, 2002).

Fetvacı, Emine, 'Love in the Album of Ahmed I', in Mehmet Kalpaklı (ed.), *Festschrift in Honor of Walter G. Andrews = Journal of Turkish Studies* 34 (2010): 37–51.

Finkel, C. F. and N. N. Ambraseys, 'The Marmara Sea Earthquake of 10 July 1894 and its Effect of Historic Buildings', *Anatolia Moderna/Yeni Anadolu* 7 (1997): 49–57.

Fleckner, Uwe, *Jean-Auguste-Dominique Ingres, Das türkische Bad: Ein Klassizist auf dem Weg zur Moderne* (Frankfurt: Fischer, 1996).

Fleischer, Cornell, *Bureaucrat and Intellectual in the Ottoman Empire: The Historian Mustafa Âli (1541–1600)* (Princeton, NJ: Princeton University Press, 1986).

References

Flynn, Bernadette, 'The Morphology of Space in Virtual Heritage', in Fiona Cameron and Sarah Kenderdine (eds), *Theorizing Digital Cultural Heritage: A Critical Discourse* (Cambridge, MA: MIT Press, 2007), pp. 349–68.

Folda, Jaroslav, 'An Icon of the Crucifixion and the Nativity at Sinai: Investigating the Pictorial Language of its Ornamental Vocabulary: Chrysography, Pearl-Dot Haloes, and Çintemani', in Iris Shagrir, Ronnie Ellenblum and Jonathan Riley-Smith (eds), *In Laudem Hierosolymitani: Studies in Crusades and Medieval Culture in Honour of Benjamin Z. Kedar* (Aldershot: Ashgate, 2007), pp. 163–79.

Fournet, Thibaud, 'The Ancient Baths of Southern Syria in their Near Eastern Context', *International Frontinus-Symposium on Technical and Cultural History of Ancient Thermal Springs*, Aachen, 18–22 March 2009.

Fowden, Garth, *Qusayr Amra: Art and the Umayyad Elite in Late Antique Syria* (Berkeley, CA: University of California Press, 2004).

From the Imperial Capital to the Republican Modern City: Henri Prost's Planning of Istanbul (1936–1951) (Istanbul: Istanbul Research Institute, 2010).

Fuzûlî, *Fuzûlî Divanı*, ed. Ali Nihat Tarlan (Ankara: Akçağ Yayınları, 1998).

van Gelder, Geert Jan, 'The *Hammam*: A Space between Heaven and Hell', *Quaderni di Studi Arabi* 3 (2008): 9–24.

Gelibolulu Mustafa Ali, *Cami'u'l-buhûr der mecâlis-i sûr*, ed. Ali Öztekin (Ankara: Türk Tarih Kurumu, 1996).

Gelibolulu Mustafa Ali, *Gelibolulu Mustafa Ali ve Meva'idu'n-nefa'is fi kava'idi'l mecalis* (Ankara: Türk Tarih Kurumu, 1997).

Gerber, Haim, 'The Muslim Law of Partnership in Ottoman Court Records', *Studia Islamica* 53 (1981): 109–19.

Ginzburg, Carlo, *The Cheese and the Worms: The Cosmos of a Sixteenth-Century Miller* (New York: Penguin, 1982).

Girard, Muriel, 'What Heritage Tells Us About the Turkish State and Society', *European Journal of Turkish Studies* 19 (2014): 1–21.

Glassberg, David. 'The Design of Reform: The Public Bath Movement in America', *American Studies* 20 (1979): 5–21.

Glück, Heinrich, *Probleme des Wölbungsbaues: Die Bäder Konstantinopels* (Vienna: Halm & Goldmann, 1921).

Gosden, Chris and Yvonne Marshall, 'The Cultural Biography of Objects', *World Archaeology* 31 (1999): 169–78.

Göçek, Fatma Müge, *Rise of the Bourgeoisie, Demise of Empire: Ottoman Westernization and Social Change* (New York: Oxford University Press, 1996).

Göktürk, Deniz, Levent Soysal and İpek Türeli (eds), *Orienting Istanbul: Cultural Capital of Europe?* (London: Routledge, 2010).

Göloğlu, Sabiha, 'Depicting the Holy: Representations of Mecca, Medina, and Jerusalem in the Late Ottoman Empire', PhD dissertation, Koç University, 2018.

Goodwin, Godfrey, *A History of Ottoman Architecture* (London: Thames & Hudson, 1971).

Grabar, Oleg, *The Formation of Islamic Art* (New Haven, CT: Yale University Press, 1973).

Grabar, Oleg et al., *City in the Desert: Qasr al-Hayr East, An Account of the Excavations Carried out at Qasr al-Hayr East on Behalf of the Kelsey Museum of Archaeology at the University of Michigan with the help of Harvard University and the Oriental Institute, the University of Chicago, Harvard Middle Eastern Monographs* XXIII/XXIV (Cambridge, MA: Harvard University Press, 1978).

Graburn, Nelson, 'The Past in the Present in Japan: Nostalgia and Neo-Traditionalism in Contemporary Japanese Domestic Tourism', in Richard Butler and Douglas Pearce (eds), *Change in Tourism: People, Place, Processes* (London: Routledge, 1995), pp. 31–70.

Grehan, James, 'Smoking and "Early Modern" Sociability: The Great Tobacco Debate in the Ottoman Middle East (Seventeenth to Eighteenth Centuries)', *American Historical Review* 111 (2006): 1352–77.

Grotzfeld, Heinz, *Das Bad im arabischen Mittelalter: Eine kulturgeschichtliche Studie* (Wiesbaden: Otto Harrassowitz, 1970).

Gül, İdil Işıl (ed.), *Gezi Park Olayları: İnsan Hakları Hukuku ve Siyasi Söylem Işığında bir İnceleme* (Istanbul: İstanbul Bilgi Üniversitesi, 2013).

Gül, Murat, *The Emergence of Modern Istanbul: Transformation and Modernisation of a City* (London: I. B. Tauris, 2012).

Gülümser, Tülay, 'Contemporary Usage of Turkish Traditional Motifs in Product Designs', *İdil Dergisi* 1 (2012): 218–30.

Güran, Ceyhan, *Türk Hanların Gelişimi ve İstanbul Hanları Mimarisi* (Ankara: Vakıflar Genel Müdürlüğü Yayınları, 1976).

Gürcan, Efe Can and Efe Peker, *Challenging Neoliberalism at Turkey's Gezi Park: From Private Discontent to Collective Class Action* (New York: Palgrave Macmillan, 2015).

Güreşsever, Gönül, 'Kitab al-Cerrahiyet al-Hâniye (İstanbul Tıp Tarihi Enstitüsü Nüshası) Minyatürleri', in *I. Milletlerarası Türkoloji Kongresi: Tebliğler* (Istanbul: [n.p.], 1979), vol. 3, pp. 771–94.

Hafız Hüseyin Ayvansarayî, *Mecmua-i Tevarih*, ed. Fahri Devir and Vahid Çabuk (Istanbul: İstanbul Edebiyat Fakültesi Yayınları, 1985).

Hamadeh, Shirineh, 'Mean Streets: Space and Moral Order in Early Modern Istanbul', *Turcica* 44 (2012/13): 249–77.

'Hamamlar', *Akşam Gazetesi*, 15 June 1943, p. 3.

Hamilton, Robert, *Walid and His Friends: An Umayyad Tragedy* (Oxford: Oxford University Press, 1988).

Hanke, Stephanie, 'Bathing "all'antica": Bathrooms in Genoese Villas and Palaces in the Sixteenth Century', *Renaissance Studies* 20 (2006): 674–700.

Harding, Anthony, 'Introduction: Biographies of Things', *Distant Worlds Journal* 1 (2016): 5–10.

Haskan, Mehmet, *İstanbul Hamamları* (Istanbul: TTOK, 1995).

Hathaway, Jane, *Beshir Agha: Chief Eunuch of the Ottoman Imperial Harem* (London: Oneworld, 2006).

References

al-Hayani, Hafiz Husayn, 'al-Birka al-Da'iriyya Dakhil Qasr al-Khalifa, Samarra: Tanqib wa Siyana', *Sumer* 48 (1996): 89–103.

Hehmeyer, Ingrid, 'Mosque, Bath, and Garden: Symbiosis in the Urban Landscape of San'a, Yemen', *Proceedings of the Seminar for Arabian Studies* 28 (1998): 105–15.

Hitti, Philipp, *History of the Arabs from the Earliest Times to the Present* (New York: St. Martin's Press, 1970).

Hoagland, Alison, 'Introducing the Bathroom: Space and Change in Working-Class Houses', *Buildings & Landscapes: Journal of the Vernacular Architecture Forum* 18 (2011): 15–42.

Hodder, Ian, *Entangled: An Archaeology of Relationships between Humans and Things* (Oxford: Wiley-Blackwell, 2013).

Hoexter, Miriam, 'Adaptation to Changing Circumstances: Perpetual Leases and Exchange Transactions in Waqf Property in Ottoman Algiers', *Islamic Law and Society* 4 (1997): 319–33.

Hoexter, Miriam, 'Waqf Studies in the Twentieth Century: The State of the Art', *Journal of the Economic and Social History of the Orient* 41 (1998): 474–95.

Holod, Renata and Hassan-Uddin Khan, *The Mosque and the Modern World* (London: Thames & Hudson, 1997).

Hoy, Suellen, *Chasing Dirt: The American Pursuit of Cleanliness* (New York: Oxford University Press, 1995).

Hughes, Katherine Nouri, *The Mapmaker's Daughter* (Encino: Delphinium Books, 2017).

Hürriyet Tarih, 4 December 2002.

Ibn Khaldun, *The Muqaddimah: An Introduction to History*, trans. Franz Rosenthal (Princeton, NJ: Princeton University Press, 1989).

Imber, Colin, *Ebu's-Suud: The Islamic Legal Tradition* (Edinburgh: Edinburgh University Press, 1997).

İnalcık, Halil, 'Istanbul', *EI2*.

İnalcık, Halil, 'Osmanlı İdare, Sosyal ve Ekonomik Tarihiyle İlgili Belgeler: Bursa Kadı Siçillerinden Seçmeler', *Belgeler* 10 (1980/1): 23–167.

İnan, Afet et al., *Türk Tarihinin Ana Hatları* (Istanbul: Devlet Matbaası, 1930).

Inman, Nick (ed.), *Eyewitness Travel Guide Istanbul*, rev. edn (New York: DK, 1999).

İşigüzel, Şebnem, 'Waschtag im Reich der Sinne', *GEO Special: Türkei* (1998): 84–9.

Işın, Ekrem, *Everyday Life in Istanbul: Social Historical Essays on People, Culture and Spatial Relations* (Istanbul: Yapı Kredi Yayınları, 2001).

Işın, Engin and Alexandre Lefèbvre, 'The Gift of Law', *European Journal of Social Theory* 8 (2005): 15–23.

Isom-Verhaaren, Christine, 'Royal French Women in the Ottoman Sultan's Harem: The Political Uses of Fabricated Accounts from the Sixteenth to the Twenty-First Century', *Journal of World History* 17 (2006): 159–96.

Isom-Verhaaren, Christine, 'Constructing Ottoman Identity in the Reigns of Mehmed II and Bayezid II', *Journal of the Ottoman and Turkish Studies Association* 1 (2014): 111–28.

Isom-Verhaaren, Christine, 'Was there Room in Rum for Corsairs? Who Was an Ottoman in the Naval Forces of the Ottoman Empire in the 15th and 16th Centuries?' *Osmanlı Araştırmaları/Journal of Ottoman Studies* 44 (2014): 235–64.

Isom-Verhaaren, Christine, 'Mihrimah Sultan: A Princess Constructs Ottoman Dynastic Identity', in Christine Isom-Verhaaren and Kent Schull (eds), *Living in the Ottoman Realm: Empire and Identity, 13th to 20th Centuries* (Bloomington, IN: Indiana University Press, 2016), pp. 150–65.

Isom-Verhaaren, Christine and Kent Schull (eds), *Living in the Ottoman Realm: Empire and Identity, 13th to 20th Centuries* (Bloomington, IN: Indiana University Press, 2016).

Jennings, Ronald, 'Women in Early 17th Century Ottoman Judicial Records: The Sharia Court of Anatolian Kayseri', *Journal of the Economic and Social History of the Orient* 18 (1975): 53–114.

Joy, Jody, 'Reinvigorating Object Biography: Reproducing the Drama of Object Lives', *World Archaeology* 41 (2009): 540–66.

Kafadar, Cemal, 'Self and Others: The Diary of a Dervish in Seventeenth-Century Istanbul and First-Person Narratives in Ottoman Literature', *Studia Islamica* 69 (1989): 121–50.

Kafadar, Cemal, 'Mütereddit bir Mutasavvıf: Asiye Hatun'un Rüya Defteri, 1641–43', *Topkapı Sarayı Yıllığı* 5 (1992): 168–222.

Kafadar, Cemal, 'A Rome of One's Own: Reflections on Cultural Geography and Identity in the Lands of Rum', *Muqarnas* 24 (2007): 7–25.

Kafadar, Cemal, *Kim Var İmiş Biz Yoğ İken: Dört Osmanlı: Yeniçeri, Tüccar, Derviş ve Hatun* (Istanbul: Metis, 2009).

Kafesçioğlu, Çiğdem, *Constantinopolis/Istanbul: Cultural Encounter, Imperial Vision and the Construction of the Ottoman Capital* (Philadelphia, PA: Pennsylvania State University Press, 2010).

Kai Ka'us ibn Iskandar, *A Mirror for Princes: The Qabus-Nama*, trans. Reuben Levy (New York: E. P. Dutton, 1951).

Kai Ka'us ibn Iskandar, *The Book of Advice: The Earliest Old Ottoman Turkish Version of His Kabusname, Text in Fascimile* [sic] *from the Unique 14th Century Manuscript, Together with a Study of the Text and a Select Vocabulary*, transcr. and ed. Eleazar Birnbaum (Cambridge, MA: Harvard University Printing Office, 1981).

Kalay, Yehuda, 'Introduction: Preserving Cultural Heritage through Digital Media', in Yehuda Kalay, Thomas Kvan and Janice Affleck (eds), *New Heritage: New Media and Cultural Heritage* (New York: Routledge, 2008), pp. 1–10.

Kamash, Zena, 'What Lies Beneath? Perceptions of the Ontological Paradox of Water', *World Archaeology* 40 (2008): 224–37.

References

Kandemir, 'Eski Hamamlar', *Yeni Gün* 8, 29 April 1939, pp. 14–15.

Kanetaki, Eleni, 'Ottoman Baths in Greece: A Contribution to the Study of their History and Architecture', in Nina Ergin (ed.), *Bathing Cultures of Anatolian Civilizations: Architecture, History and Imagination* (Louvain: Peeters, 2011), pp. 221–55.

Karagülle, Zeki, 'The Health Effects of Hamams', paper presented at the symposium *Fürdö Hamam Sauna*, Research Center for Anatolian Civilizations, Istanbul, 25–26 April 2009.

Karakaş, Deniz, 'Clay Pipes, Marble Surfaces: The Topographies of Water Supply in Late 17th/Early 18th-Century Ottoman Istanbul', PhD dissertation, SUNY Binghamton, 2012.

Karakaş, Deniz, 'Water Resources Management and Development in Ottoman Istanbul: The 1693 Water Survey and its Aftermath', in Paul Magdalino and Nina Ergin (eds), *Istanbul and Water* (Louvain: Peeters, 2015), pp. 177–204.

Karpat, Kemal, 'The Transformation of the Ottoman State, 1789–1908', *International Journal of Middle Eastern Studies* 3 (1972): 243–81.

Karpat, Kemal (ed.), *Ottoman Past and Today's Turkey* (Leiden: Brill, 2000).

Kasaba, Reşat and Sibel Bozdoğan, 'Turkey at a Crossroads', *Journal of International Affairs* 54 (2000): 1–20.

Katz, Marion, *Body of Text: The Emergence of the Sunni Law of Ritual Purity* (Albany, NY: SUNY Press, 2002).

Katz, Marion, 'The Study of Islamic Ritual and the Meaning of Wudu'', *Der Islam* 82 (2005): 106–45.

Kaya, Güven, 'Türk Edebiyatında Hammâmiyeler', in Günay Kut and Fatma Büyükkarcı Yılmaz (eds), *Şinasi Tekin'in Anısına: Uygurlardan Osmanlıya* (Istanbul: Simurg, 2005), pp. 445–75.

Kaya, Süleyman, *Osmanlı Hukukunda İcareteyn* (Istanbul: Klasik, 2014).

Kayaalp-Aktan, Pınar, 'The Atik Valide Mosque Complex: A Testament of Nurbanu's Prestige, Power and Piety', PhD dissertation, Harvard University, 2005.

Kayaalp-Aktan, Pınar, 'The Atik Valide's Endowment Deed: A Textual Analysis', in Nina Ergin, Christoph K. Neumann and Amy Singer (eds), *Feeding People, Feeding Power: Imarets in the Ottoman Empire* (Istanbul: Eren, 2007), pp. 261–73.

Kentel, Mehmet, 'Assembling "Cosmopolitanism": Making Pera Modern through Infrastructure in Late Ottoman Constantinople', PhD dissertation, University of Washington, Seattle, in progress.

Keyder, Çağlar, 'A Tale of Two Neighborhoods', in Çağlar Keyder (ed.), *Istanbul Between the Global and the Local* (Lanham, MD: Rowman & Littlefield, 1999), pp. 173–86.

Keyder, Çağlar (ed.), *Istanbul Between the Global and the Local* (Lanham, MD: Rowman & Littlefield, 1999).

Khalidi, Tarif, *Arabic Historical Thought in the Classical Period* (Cambridge: Cambridge University Press, 1994).

Khleif, Patricia, '"There Goes the Neighborhood!" Sexuality and Society in Seventeenth-Century Kayseri', *Arab Studies Journal* 6 (1998/9): 128–36.

Khuri, Fuad, *The Body in Islamic Culture* (London: Saqi Books, 2001).

Kınalızade Hasan Çelebi, *Tezkiretü'ş-Şuarâ*, ed. İbrahim Kutluk (Ankara: Türk Tarih Kurumu, 1989).

Kırlı, Cengiz, 'The Struggle over Space: Coffeehouses of Ottoman Istanbul, 1780–1845', PhD dissertation, State University of New York, Binghamton, 2000.

Kırlı, Cengiz, 'A Profile of the Labor Force in Early Nineteenth-Century Istanbul', *International Labor and Working-Class History* 60 (2001): 125–40.

Kırlı, Cengiz, 'Coffeehouses: Public Opinion in the Nineteenth-Century Ottoman Empire', in Armando Salvatore and Dale Eickelmann (eds), *Public Islam and the Common Good* (Leiden: Brill, 2004), pp. 75–97.

Kırlı, Cengiz, *Sultan ve Kamuoy: Osmanlı Modernleşme Sürecinde 'Havadis Jurnalleri', 1840–1844* (Istanbul: İş Bankası, 2009).

Kırlı, Cengiz, 'Coffeehouses: Leisure and Sociability in Ottoman Istanbul', in Peter Nigel Borsay and Jan Hein Furnée (eds), *Leisure Cultures in Urban Europe, 1700–1870: A Transnational Perspective* (Manchester: Manchester University Press, 2016), pp. 161–82.

Klinghardt, Karl, *Türkische Bäder* (Stuttgart: Julius Hoffmann, 1927).

Koçu, Reşad Ekrem, 'Çarşı Hamamlarımız', *TTOK Belleten* 155 (1954): 12.

Koçu, Reşad Ekrem, 'Bilicareteyn Tasarruf', *İstA*.

Koçu, Reşad Ekrem, 'Dellak', *İstA*.

Köksal, Duygu and Anastasia Falierou (eds), *A Social History of Late Ottoman Women: New Perspectives* (Leiden: Brill, 2013).

Konyalı, İbrahim Hakkı, 'Bizans ve Osmanlı Hamamları', *Yeni Gün* 1, 11 March 1939, pp. 14–16, 32.

Konyalı, İbrahim Hakkı, *Abideleri ve Kitabeleriyle Üsküdar Tarihi* (Istanbul: Ahmet Sait Matbaası, 1976).

Kopytoff, Igor, 'The Cultural Biography of Things: Commoditization as Process', in Arjun Appadurai (ed.), *The Social Life of Things: Commodities in Cultural Perspective* (Cambridge: Cambridge University Press, 1986), pp. 64–91.

Kreiser, Klaus, 'Icareteyn: Zur "Doppelten Miete" im Osmanischen Stiftungswesen', *Journal of Turkish Studies* 10 (1986): 219–26.

Kritovoulos, *History of Mehmed the Conqueror*, trans. C. T. Riggs (Princeton, NJ: Princeton University Press, 1954).

Kuban, Doğan, *Istanbul, An Urban History: Byzantion, Constantinopolis, Istanbul* (Istanbul: The Economic and Social History Foundation of Turkey, 1996).

Kudret, Cevdet, *Karagöz* (Istanbul: Yapı Kredi Yayınları, 2002).

Kunt, Metin, 'Ethnic-Regional (*cins*) Solidarity in the Seventeenth-Century Ottoman Establishment', *International Journal of Middle East Studies* 5 (1974): 233–9.

Kunter, Halil, 'Türk Vakıfları ve Vakfiyeleri', *Vakıflar Dergisi* 1 (1938): 103–30.

Kuran, Aptullah, *Sinan: The Grand Old Master of Ottoman Architecture* (Washington, DC: Institute of Turkish Studies, 1987).

References

Kuru, Selim Sırrı, 'A Sixteenth-Century Scholar: Deli Birader and his *Dâfi'ü'l-gumûm ve râfi'ü'l-humûm*', PhD dissertation, Harvard University, 2000.

Kut, Günay and Fatma Büyükkarcı Yılmaz (eds), *Şinasi Tekin'in Anısına: Uygurlardan Osmanlıya* (Istanbul: Simurg, 2005).

Kütükoğlu, Mübahat, *Osmanlı'da Narh Müessesi ve 1640 Tarihli Narh Defteri* (Istanbul: Enderun Kitabevi, 1983).

Landrieu, Jérémie, Christian Père, Juliette Rollier-Hanselmann, Stéphanie Castandet and Guillaume Schotté, 'Digital Rebirth of the Greatest Church of Cluny Maior Ecclesia: From Optronic Surveys to Real Time Use of the Digital Mode', *International Archives of the Photogrammetry, Remote Sensing and Spatial Information Sciences* vol. XXXVIII-5/W16, 2011 ISPRS Trento 2011 Workshop, 2–4 March 2011, Trento, Italy.

Lasansky, D. Medina and Brian McLaren (eds), *Architecture and Tourism: Perception, Performance and Place* (Oxford: Berg, 2004).

Laurent, Béatrice St., 'Léon Parvillée: His Role as Restorer of Bursa's Monuments and His Contribution to the Exposition Universelle of 1867', in Hamit Batu and Jean-Louis Bacque-Grammont (eds), *L'Empire ottomane, la République de Turquie, et la France* (Istanbul: Isis Press, 1986), pp. 247–82.

Leisten, Thomas, *Excavation of Samarra, vol. 1: Architecture, Final Report of the First Campaign, 1910–1912, Baghdader Forschungen* 20 (Mainz: von Zabern, 2003).

Levend, Agah Sırrı, *Türk Edebiyatında Şehr-Engizler ve Şehr-Engizlerde İstanbul* (Istanbul: Baha Matbaası, 1958).

Lewis, Bernard, *The Emergence of Modern Turkey* (New York: Oxford University Press, 2002).

Lowenthal, David, *The Past is a Foreign Country* (Cambridge: Cambridge University Press, 1985).

Lubenau, Reinhold, *Beschreibung der Reisen des Reinhold Lubenau*, ed. W. Sahm (Königsberg i. Pr.: Fred Beyers Buchhandlung, 1914).

Lytle-Croutier, Alev, *Harem: The World Behind the Veil* (New York, London, Paris: Abbeville Press, 1989).

MacCannell, Dean. *The Tourist: A New Theory of the Leisure Class* (New York: Schocken Books, 1976; reprinted Berkeley, CA: University of California Press, 1999).

Madran, Emre, 'The Restorer Artisans in the Ottoman Empire', in Nur Akın, Afife Batur and Selçuk Batur (eds), *Seven Centuries of Ottoman Architecture: A Supra-National Heritage* (Istanbul: YEM Yayın, n.d. [2001]), pp. 348–56.

Magdalino, Paul and Nina Ergin (eds), *Istanbul and Water* (Louvain: Peeters, 2015).

Makhlouf Obermeyer, Carla, 'Pluralism and Pragmatism: Knowledge and Practice of Birth in Morocco', *Medical Anthropology Quarterly* 14 (2000): 180–201.

Mandell, Melissa, 'The Public Bath Association of Philadelphia and the "Great Unwashed"', *Pennsylvania Legacies* 7 (2007): 30–1.

Manderscheid, Hubertus, *Bibliographie zum römischen Badewesen: Unter beson-derer Berücksichtigung der öffentlichen Thermen* (Munich, Berlin: Wasmuth, 1988).

Manderscheid, Hubertus, *Ancient Baths and Bathing: A Bibliography for the Years 1988–2001* (Portsmouth: Journal of Roman Archaeology, 2004).

Mantran, Robert, *Istanbul dans la seconde moitié du XVIIe siècle* (Paris: Institut Français d'Archaeologie, 1962).

Mardin, Şerif, 'Super Westernization in Urban Life in the Ottoman Empire in the Last Quarter of the Nineteenth Century', in Peter Benedict (ed.), *Turkey: Geographical and Social Perspectives* (Leiden: Brill, 1974).

Marschner, Joanna and Joanne Marschner, 'Baths and Bathing at the Early Georgian Court', *Furniture History* 31 (1995): 23–8.

Mascuch, Michael, *Origins of the Individualist Self: Autobiography and Self-Identity in England, 1591–1791* (Cambridge: Polity Press, 1997).

Matthews, Owen, 'As Turkey Turns from West, Istanbul's Most Iconic Building is Claimed for Islam', *Newsweek*, 3 June 2015.

Mazlum, Deniz, *1766 İstanbul Depremi: Belgeler Işığında Yapı Onarımları* (Istanbul: İstanbul Araştırmaları Enstitüsü, 2011).

Mehmed Raşid, *Tarih*. Istanbul, 1282 (1865/6).

Meinecke, Michael, 'Probleme der Denkmalpflege und Altstadtsanierung', in Klaus Kreiser et al. (eds), *Ars Turcica: Akten des Internationalen Kongresses für Türkische Kunst, München, von 3. bis 7. September 1979* (Munich: Editio Maris, 1987), pp. 55–72.

Melman, Billie, *Women's Orients: English Women and the Middle East, 1718–1918* (Ann Arbor, MI: University of Michigan Press, 1992).

Mengüç, Murat Cem, 'Interpreting Ottoman Identity with the Historian Neşri', in Christine Isom-Verhaaren and Kent Schull (eds), *Living in the Ottoman Realm: Empire and Identity, 13th to 20th Centuries* (Bloomington, IN: Indiana University Press, 2016), pp. 66–78.

Meredith-Owens, G. M. (ed.), *Meşa'irü üş-şu'ara or Tezkere of 'Aşık Çelebi* (London: Luzac, 1971).

Meriwether, Margaret, *The Kin Who Count: Family and Society in Ottoman Aleppo, 1770–1840* (Austin, TX: University of Texas Press, 1999).

Mikhail, Alan, 'The Heart's Desire: Gender, Urban Space and the Ottoman Coffee House', in Dana Sajdi (ed.), *Ottoman Tulips, Ottoman Coffee: Leisure and Lifestyle in the Eighteenth Century* (London: I. B. Tauris, 2007), pp. 133–70.

Milford, Nancy, 'Bathed in Tradition in Istanbul', *New York Times Magazine: The Sophisticated Traveler*, 27 February 2000, pp. 28, 29, 72–4.

Mills, Amy, *Streets of Memory: Landscape, Tolerance and National Identity in Istanbul* (Athens, GA: University of Georgia Press, 2010).

Mimar Sinan, *Sinan's Autobiographies: Five Sixteenth-Century Texts*, ed. and trans. Howard Crane and Esra Akın, intro. Gülru Necipoğlu (Leiden: Brill, 2006).

Moerman, D. Max, 'The Buddha and the Bathwater: Defilement and Enlightenment in the Onsenji Engi', *Japanese Journal of Religious Studies* 42 (2015): 71–87.

References

Mohammed, K. K., 'Hammams (Baths) in Medieval India', *Islamic Culture* 62 (1988): 37–56.

Mojaddedi, Jawid, *The Biographical Tradition in Sufism: The* Tabaqat *Genre from al-Sulami to Jami* (Richmond: Curzon, 2001).

Morony, Michael, *Iraq after the Muslim Conquest* (Princeton, NJ: Princeton University Press, 1984).

Mottahedeh, Roy and Kristen Stilt, 'Public and Private as Viewed through the Work of the "Muhtasib"', *Social Research* 70 (2003): 735–48.

Muhammad ibn Ismail Bukhari, *The Translation of the Meanings of Sahih al-Bukhari: Arabic–English*, trans. Muhammad Muhsin Khan (Lahore: Kazi, 1983).

Mü'minzâde Seyyid Ahmed Hasîb Efendi, *Ravzatü'l-Küberâ: Tahlil ve Metin*, ed. Mesut Aydıner (Ankara: Türk Tarih Kurumu, 2003).

Murphey, Rhoads, 'Forms of Differentiation and Expression of Individuality in Ottoman Society', *Turcica* 34 (2002): 135–70.

'Muslim group prays in front of Hagia Sophia', *Hürriyet Daily News*, 31 May 2014.

Muslim ibn al-Hajjaj al-Qushayri, *Sahih Muslim, Being Traditions of the Sayings of the Prophet Muhammad as Narrated by his Companions and Compiled under the Title al-Jami' us-Sahih: Rendered into English by Abdul Hamid Siddiqi, with Explanatory Notes and Brief Biographical Sketches of Major Narrators* (Lahore: Muhammad Ashraf, 1971–5).

Mustafa Âli, *Mustafa Âli's Künhül-Ahbar and its Preface According to the Leiden Manuscript*, ed. Jan Schmidt (Istanbul: Netherlandish Historical-Archeological Institute in Istanbul, 1987).

Mustafa Naima, *Tarih-i Naima* (Istanbul: Matbaa-i Âmire, 1281–1283 (1864–1866).

Mustafa Selânikî, *Târîh-i Selânikî*, ed. Mehmet İpşirli (Istanbul: İstanbul Üniversitesi Edebiyat Fakültesi Yayınevi, 1989).

Necipoğlu, Gülru, 'The Life of an Imperial Monument: Hagia Sophia after Byzantium', in Robert Mark and Ahmet Çakmak (eds), *Hagia Sophia: From the Age of Justinian to the Present* (Cambridge: Cambridge University Press, 1992), pp. 195–225.

Necipoğlu, Gülru, 'A Kanun for the State, A Canon for the Arts: Conceptualizing the Classical Synthesis of Ottoman Art and Architecture', in Gilles Veinstein (ed.), *Soliman le Magnifique et son Temps* (Paris: Documentation Francaise, 1992), pp. 194–215.

Necipoğlu, Gülru, 'Framing the Gaze in Ottoman, Safavid and Mughal Palaces', *Ars Orientalis* 23 (1993): 303–42.

Necipoğlu, Gülru, 'Word and Image: The Serial Portraits of Ottoman Sultans in Comparative Perspective', in *The Sultan's Portrait: Picturing the House of Osman* (Istanbul: İşbank, 2000), pp. 22–59.

Necipoğlu, Gülru, *The Age of Sinan: Architectural Culture in the Ottoman Empire* (Princeton, NJ: Princeton University Press, 2005).

Necipoğlu, Gülru, 'Creation of a National Genius: Sinan and the Historiography of 'Classical' Ottoman Architecture', *Muqarnas* 24 (2007), pp. 141–83.

de Nicholay, Nicolas, *The Nauigations, Peregrinations and Voyages, Made into Turkie* (Amsterdam, London: Theatrum Orbis Terrarum, Da Capo Press, 1968).

Niyazioğlu, Aslı, 'Lives of a Sixteenth-Century Ottoman Sheikh: Serhoş Bali Efendi and His Biographers', in Günay Kut and Fatma Büyükkarcı Yılmaz (eds), *Şinasi Tekin'in Anısına: Uygurlardan Osmanlıya* (Istanbul: Simurg, 2005), pp. 607–20.

Northedge, Alasdair, 'An Interpretation of the Palace of the Caliph at Samarra (Dar al-Khilafa or Jaws al-Khaqani)', *Ars Orientalis* 23 (1993): 143–70.

Olson, Robert, 'The Esnaf and the Patrona Halil Rebellion in 1730: A Realignment in Ottoman Politics?' *Journal of the Economic and Social History of the Orient* 17 (1974): 329–44.

Onar, Nora Fisher, 'Echoes of a Universalism Lost: Rival Representations of the Ottomans in Today's Turkey', *Middle Eastern Studies* 45 (2009): 229–41.

Öncü, Ayşe, 'The Politics of Istanbul's Ottoman Heritage in the Era of Globalism: Refractions through the Prism of a Theme Park', in Barbara Drieskens, Heiko Wimmen and Franck Mermier (eds), *Cities in the South: Citizenship and Exclusion in the 21st Century* (London: Saqi Books, 2007), pp. 233–64.

Öncü, Ayşe, 'Narratives of Istanbul's Ottoman Heritage', in Nikiforos Diamandouros, Thalia Dragonas and Çağlar Keyder (eds), *Spatial Conceptions of the Nation: Modernizing Geographies in Greece and Turkey* (London: I. B. Tauris, 2010), pp. 205–28.

Önge, Yılmaz, 'Eski Türk Hamamlarında Aydınlatma', *Vakıflar Dergisi* 12 (1978): 121–35.

Önge, Yılmaz, 'Anadolu Türk Hamamları Hakkında Genel Bilgiler ve Koca Mimar Sinan'ın İnşa Ettiği Hamamlar', in Sadi Bayram (ed.), *Mimarbaşı Koca Sinan Yaşadığı Çağ ve Eserleri* (Istanbul: Vakıflar Genel Müdürlüğü, 1988), vol. 1, pp. 403–28.

Önge, Yılmaz, 'Sinan'ın İnşa Ettiği Hamamlar', *VI. Vakıf Haftası* (Istanbul: Vakıflar Genel Müdürlüğü Yayınları, 1989), pp. 255–72.

Önge, Yılmaz, *Anadolu'da XII.–XIII. Yüzyıl Türk Hamamları* (Ankara: Vakıflar Genel Müdürlüğü Yayınları, 1995).

Orga, İrfan, *Portrait of a Turkish Family* (London: Victor Gollanzc, 1950).

Ormos, Istvan, 'The Theory of Humours in Islam', *Quaderni di Studi Arabi* 5/6 (1987/8): 601–7.

Osman Ağa, *Der Gefangene der Giauren: Die abenteuerlichen Schicksale des Osman Ağa aus Temeschwar, von ihm selbst erzählt*, ed. Richard Kreutel and Otto Spies (Cologne: Verlag Styria, 1962).

Osman Ağa, *Kendi Kalemiyle Temeşvarlı Osman Ağa (Bir Osmanlı Türk Sipahisinin Hayatı ve Esirlik Anıları)*, ed. Harun Tolasa (Konya: Selçuk Üniversitesi, 1986).

Öz, Tahsin, *Fatih Mehmet II Vakfiyeleri* (Ankara: Vakıflar Umum Müdürlüğü, 1938).

References

Özbaran, Salih, 'In Search of Another Identity: The "Rumi" Perception in the Ottoman Realm', *Eurasian Studies* 1 (2002): 115–27.

Özbek, İmre Eren, 'Fatih İlçesinde Ayakapı Hamamı Restorasyon Projesi', MA thesis, Istanbul Technical University, 2000.

Özcan, Abdülkadir, 'Osmanlı Tarih Edebiyatında Biyografi Türünün Ortaya Çıkışı ve Gelişmesi', in Hatice Aynur et al. (eds), *Nazımdan Nesire Edebî Türleri* (Istanbul: Turkuaz, 2009), pp. 124–33.

Öziş, Ünal and Yalçın Arısoy, 'Water Conveyance Systems of the Great Architect Sinan', in Azize Aktaş-Yasa (ed.), *Uluslararası Mimar Sinan Sempozyumu Bildirileri* (Ankara: Türk Tarih Kurumu, 1996), pp. 241–56.

Öztin, Feriha, *10 Temmuz 1894 İstanbul Deprem Raporu* (Ankara: T. C. Bayındırlık ve İskan Bakanlığı Afet İşleri Genel Müdürlüğü Deprem Araştırma Dairesi, 1994).

Öztuna, Yılmaz, *Kanuni Sultan Süleyman* (Ankara: Kültür Bakanlığı, 1989).

Öztürk, Said, *Osmanlı Arşiv Belgelerinde Siyakat Yazısı ve Tarihi Gelişimi* (Istanbul: Osmanlı Araştırmaları Vakfı, 1996).

Ozyegin, Gul (ed.), *Gender and Sexuality in Muslim Cultures* (Farnham: Ashgate, 2015).

Pamuk, Şevket, *İstanbul ve Diğer Kentlerde 500 Yıllık Fiyatlar ve Ücretler (1469–1998)* (Ankara: T. C. Başbakanlık Devlet İstatistik Enstitüsü, 2000).

Paraizo, Rodrigo and Jose Ripper Kos, 'Urban Heritage Representations in Hyperdocuments', in Fiona Cameron and Sarah Kenderdine (eds), *Theorizing Digital Cultural Heritage: A Critical Discourse* (Cambridge, MA: MIT Press, 2007), pp. 417–35.

Pardoe, Julia, *The City of the Sultan and Domestic Manners of the Turks in 1836* (London: Henry Colburn, 1837).

Parker, Claire, 'Improving the Condition of the People: The Health of Britain and the Provision of Public Baths, 1840–1870', *Sports Historian* 20 (2000): 24–42.

Pasin, Burkay, 'A Critical Reading of the Ottoman-Turkish Hamam as a Queered Space', PhD dissertation, Middle East Technical University, 2014.

Pauty, Edmond, *Les hammams du Caire* (Cairo: Institut Français d'archeologie orientale, 1933).

Peirce, Leslie, *The Imperial Harem: Women and Sovereignty in the Ottoman Empire* (Oxford: Oxford University Press, 1993).

Peirce, Leslie, 'Seniority, Sexuality and Social Order: The Vocabulary of Gender in Early Modern Ottoman Society', in Madeline Zilfi (ed.), *Women in the Ottoman Empire: Women in the Early Modern Middle East* (Leiden: Brill, 1997), pp. 169–96.

Peirce, Leslie, '"The Law Shall not Languish": Social Class and Public Conduct in Sixteenth-Century Ottoman Legal Discourse', in Asma Afsaruddin (ed.), *Hermeneutics and Honor: Negotiating Female 'Public' Space in Islamic/ate Societies* (Cambridge, MA: Harvard University Press, 1999), pp. 140–58.

Peirce, Leslie, 'Gender and Sexual Propriety in Ottoman Royal Women's Patronage', in D. Fairchild Ruggles (ed.), *Women, Patronage and Self-Representation in Islamic Societies* (Albany, NY: SUNY Press, 2000), pp. 53–68.

Peirce, Leslie, *Morality Tales: Law and Gender in the Ottoman Court of Aintab* (Berkeley: University of California Press, 2003).

Peirce, Leslie, *The Empress of the East: How a European Slave Girl Became Queen of the Ottoman Empire* (New York: Basic Books, 2017).

Petersen, Andrew, *Dictionary of Islamic Architecture* (London: Routledge, 1999).

Pinon-Demirçivi, Mathilde, 'Le Grand Bazar d'Istanbul et ses environs: formes, fonctions et transformations des han construits entre le début du XVIIIe s. et le milieu du XIXe s', PhD dissertation, Université Paris IV – Sorbonne, 2009.

Pope, Arthur Upham and Phyllis Ackerman, *A Survey of Persian Art from Prehistoric Times to the Present* (London: Oxford University Press, 1964/65).

Potuoğlu-Cook, Öykü, 'Beyond the Glitter: Belly Dance and Neoliberal Gentrification in Istanbul', *Cultural Anthropology* 21 (2006): 633–60.

Potvin, John, 'Vapour and Steam: The Victorian Turkish Bath, Homosocial Health, and Male Bodies on Display', *Journal of Design History* 18 (2005): 319–33.

Pratt, Mary Louise, *Imperial Eyes: Travel Writing and Transculturation* (London: Routledge, 1992).

Prochazka-Eisl, Gisela, *Das Surname-i Hümayun: Die Wiener Handschrift in Transkription, Mit Kommentar und Indices Versehen* (Istanbul: Isis Press, 1995).

Pullan, Richard and Charles Texier, *L'architecture byzantine: Recueil de documents des premiers temps du Christianisme en Orient* (London: De Day et fils, 1864).

Quataert, Donald, 'Janissaries, Artisans, and the Question of Ottoman Decline, 1730–1826', in Donald Quataert, *Workers, Peasants, Economic Change in the Ottoman Empire, 1730–1914* (Istanbul: Isis, 1993), pp. 197–203.

Quataert, Donald, *The Ottoman Empire, 1700–1922* (Cambridge: Cambridge University Press, 2000).

Raymond, André, 'Les bains publics au Caire à la fin du XVIIIe siècle', *Annales Islamologiques* 8 (1969): 129–50.

Raymond, André, 'La localisation des bains publics au Caire au Quinzième Siècle d'après les hitats de Maqrizi', *Bulletin d'Etudes Orientales* 30 (1978): 347–60.

Raymond, André, 'La localisation des bagnes à Tunis aux XVIIe et XVIIIe siècles', *IBLA* 67 (2004): 135–48.

Redhouse, James, *A Turkish and English Lexicon: Shewing in English the Significations of the Turkish Terms*, 2nd edn (Istanbul: Çağrı Yayınları, 2001).

Refik Altınay, Ahmet, 'İstanbul Hamamları', *Akşam Gazetesi*, 29 July 1936.

Refik Altınay, Ahmet, *Onuncu Asr-ı Hicride İstanbul Hayatı* (Istanbul: Kültür ve Eğitim Bakanlığı Yayınları, 1987).

References

Refik Altınay, Ahmet, *Onikinci Asr-ı Hicri'de İstanbul Hayatı (1689–1785)* (Istanbul: Enderun Kitabevi, 1988).

Reinhardt, Kevin, 'Impurity/No Danger', *History of Religion* 30 (1990): 1–24.

Renner, Andrea, 'The Nation that Bathes Together: New York City's Progressive Era Public Baths', *Journal of the Society of Architectural Historians* 67 (2008): 504–31.

Reynolds, Dwight (ed.), *Interpreting the Self: Autobiography in the Arabic Literary Tradition* (Berkeley, CA: University of California Press, 2001).

Rogier, Camille, *La Turquie, moeurs et usages des Orientaux au dix-neuvième siècle. Scènes de leur vie intérieure et publique, harem, bazars, cafés, bains, danses et musique, coutumes levantines, etc., dessinés d'après nature par Camille Rogier, avec une introduction par Théophile Gautier, et un texte descriptif* (published by the author himself, 1846).

Rosenthal, Steven, 'Foreigners and Municipal Reform in Istanbul: 1855–1865', *International Journal of Middle East Studies* 11 (1980): 227–45.

Rozen, Minna and Benjamin Arbel, 'Great Fire in the Metropolis: The Case of the Istanbul Conflagration in 1569 and its Description by Marcantonio Barbaro', in David Wasserstein and Ami Ayalon (eds), *Mamluks and Ottomans: Studies in Honour of Michael Winter* (London: Routledge, 2006), pp. 134–65.

Ruggiu, François-Joseph (ed.), *The Uses of First-Person Writings: Africa, America, Asia, Europe* (Brussels: Peter Lang, 2013).

Ruggles, D. Fairchild (ed.), *Women, Patronage and Self-Representation in Islamic Societies* (Albany: SUNY Press, 2000).

Sabancıoğlu, Müsemma, 'Jacques Pervititch and his Insurance Maps of Istanbul', *Dubrovnik Annals* 7 (2003): 89–98.

Sahillioğlu, Halil, 'Akdeniz'de Korsanlara Esir Düşen Abdi Çelebi'nin Mektubu', *İstanbul Üniversitesi Edebiyat Fakültesi Tarih Dergisi* 13 (1962): 241–56.

Sajdi, Dana, 'Decline, its Discontents and Ottoman Cultural History: By Way of Introduction', in Dana Sajdi (ed.), *Ottoman Tulips, Ottoman Coffee: Leisure and Lifestyle in the Eighteenth Century* (London: I. B. Tauris, 2007), pp. 1–40.

Sajdi, Dana (ed.), *Ottoman Tulips, Ottoman Coffee: Leisure and Lifestyle in the Eighteenth Century* (London: I. B. Tauris, 2007).

Sajdi, Dana, *The Barber of Damascus: Nouveau Literacy in the Eighteenth-Century Ottoman Levant* (Stanford, CA: Stanford University Press, 2015).

Sakin, Orhan, *Tarihsel Kaynaklarıyla İstanbul Depremleri* (Istanbul: Kitabevi, 2002).

Şapolyo, E. B., 'Türk Hamamları', *Önasya* 3 (1968): 10–11.

Sariyannis, Marinos, 'Prostitution in Ottoman Istanbul, Late Sixteenth–Early Eighteenth Century', *Turcica* 40 (2008): 37–65.

Sariyannis, Marinos, 'Time, Work and Pleasure: A Preliminary Approach to Leisure in Ottoman Mentality', in Marino Sariyannis et al. (eds), *New Trends in Ottoman Studies: Papers Presented at the 20th CIEPO Symposium, Rethymno, 27 June–1 July 2012* (Rethymno: University of Crete, 2014), pp. 797–811.

Say, Seda Kula, *Kubbeye Doğru: Erken Dönem Osmanlı Hamamlarında Eğrisel Örtüye Geçiş Sistemleri* (Istanbul: Tarihçi Kitabevi, n.d.).

Schafer, Edward, 'The Development of Bathing Customs in Ancient and Medieval China and the History of the Floriate Clear Palace', *Journal of the American Oriental Society* 76 (1956): 57–82.

Schick, Irvin C., 'Representation of Gender and Sexuality in Ottoman and Turkish Erotic Literature', *Turkish Studies Association Journal* 28 (2004): 81–103.

Schick, Irvin C. and Amila Buturovic (eds), *Women in the Ottoman Balkans: Gender, Culture and History* (London: I. B. Tauris, 2007).

Schmidt, Jan, 'Sünbülzade Vehbi's *Şevk-Engiz*, An Ottoman Pornographic Poem', *Turcica* 25 (1993): 9–37.

Schweigger, Solomon, *Eine neue Reyssbeschreibung aus Teutschland nach Constantinopel und Jerusalem*, reprint (Graz: Akademische Druck- und Verlagsanstalt, 1964).

Scott, Philippa, *Turkish Delights* (London: Thames & Hudson, 2001).

di Segni, Leah, 'The Greek Inscriptions of Hammat Gader', in Yizhar Hirschfeld (ed.), *The Roman Baths of Hammat Gader: Final Report* (Jerusalem: Israel Exploration Society, 1997), pp. 237–40.

Şehitoğlu, Elif, *The Historic Hammams of Bursa* (Istanbul: Türk Tarih Vakfı Yurt Yayınları, n.d.).

Semerdjian, Elyse, 'Naked Anxiety: Bathhouses, Nudity, and the Dhimmi Woman in 18th-Century Aleppo', *International Journal of Middle East Studies* 45 (2013): 651–76.

Semerdjian, Elyse, 'Sexing the Hammam: Gender Crossings in the Ottoman Bathhouse', in Gul Ozyegin (ed.), *Gender and Sexuality in Muslim Cultures* (Farnham: Ashgate, 2015), pp. 253–71.

Seng, Yvonne, 'Invisible Women: Residents of Early Sixteenth-Century Istanbul', in Gavin Hambly (ed.), *Women in the Medieval Islamic World* (New York: St. Martin's Press, 1998), pp. 241–68.

Serdaroğlu, Vildan, 'When Literature and Architecture Meet: Architectural Images of the Beloved and the Lover in Sixteenth-Century Ottoman Poetry', *Muqarnas* 23 (2006): 273–87.

Servet-i Fünun, 6 June 1890.

Settle, Mary Lee, *Turkish Reflections: A Biography of a Place* (New York: Touchstone, 1991).

Sevilen, Muhittin, *Karagöz* (Ankara: Milli Eğitim Bakanlığı, 1969).

Seyyid Muhammed el-Hüseynî el-Edirnevî et-Tabib Emir Çelebi, *Unmuzecü't-Tıb*, Süleymaniye Library, Mihrişah Sultan, 0000342, fol. 19–20.

Sezgin, Banu, 'İstanbul'daki Günümüz Ulaşmış Mimar Sinan Eserleri: Günümüzdeki Durumları ve Genel Gözlemler', MA thesis, Istanbul Technical University, 2001.

Shaw, Wendy, *Possessor and Possessed: Museums, Archaeology, and the Visualization of History in the Late Ottoman Empire* (Berkeley, CA: University of California Press, 2003).

References

Shaw, Wendy, 'Between the Picturesque and the Sublime: Mourning Modernization and the Production of the Orientalist Landscape in Thomas Allom and Reverend Robert Walsh's *Constantinople and the Scenery of the Seven Churches in Asia Minor* (c. 1839)', in Reina Lewis, Mary Roberts and Zeynep İnankur (eds), *The Poetics and Politics of Place: Ottoman Istanbul and British Orientalism* (Seattle and Istanbul: University of Washington Press and Pera Museum, 2011), pp. 114–25.

Sheard, Sally, 'Profit is a Dirty Word: The Development of Public Baths and Washhouses in Britain, 1847–1915', *Social History of Medicine* 13 (2000): 63–85.

Shefer-Mossensohn, Miri, *Ottoman Medicine: Healing and Medical Institutions, 1500–1700* (Albany, NY: SUNY Press, 2009).

Sibley, Magda (ed.), *Special Issue on Traditional Public Baths – Hammams – in the Mediterranean = International Journal of Architectural Research* 2/3 (2008).

Silver, Ira, 'Marketing Authenticity in Third World Countries', *Annals of Tourism Research* 20 (1993): 302–18.

Singer, Amy, *Constructing Ottoman Beneficence: An Imperial Soup Kitchen in Jerusalem* (Albany, NY: SUNY Press, 2002).

Singer, Amy, *Charity in Islamic Societies* (Cambridge: Cambridge University Press, 2009).

Skilliter, Susan, 'The Letters of the Venetian "Sultana" Nurbanu and Her Kira to Venice', in A. Gallotta and U. Marazzi (eds), *Studia Turcologica Memoriae Alexii Bombacii Dicata* (Naples: Herder, 1982), pp. 515–36.

Smith, Virginia, *Clean: A History of Hygiene and Personal Purity* (Oxford: Oxford University Press, 2008).

Sourdel-Thomine, Janine, 'Hammam', *EI2*.

Stavrides, Theoharis, *The Sultan of Vezirs: The Life and Times of the Ottoman Grand Vezir Mahmud Pasha Angelovic (1453–1474)* (Leiden: Brill, 2001).

Stephan, S. H., 'An Endowment Deed of Khasseki Sultan, dated 24th May 1552', *Quarterly of the Department of Antiquities in Palestine* 10 (1944): 170–94.

Stephenson, Paul, *The Serpent Column: A Cultural Biography* (Oxford: Oxford University Press, 2016).

Stewart-Robinson, James, 'The Tezkere Genre in Islam', *Journal of Near Eastern Studies* 23 (1964): 57–65.

Stewart-Robinson, James, 'The Ottoman Biographies of Poets', *Journal of Near Eastern Studies* 24 (1965): 67–72.

Sudar, Balasz, 'Baths in Ottoman Hungary', *Acta Orientalia Academiae Scientiarum Hungaricae* 57 (2004): 391–437.

Süleyman Saadettin Efendi [Müstakimzade], *Tuhfe-i Hattâtîn* (Istanbul: Devlet Matbaası, 1928).

Tamari, Steve, 'Biography, Autobiography, and Identity in Early Modern Damascus', in Mary Ann Fay (ed.), *Auto/Biography and the Construction of Identity and Community in the Middle East* (New York: Palgrave, 2002), pp. 37–49.

Tamdoğan-Abel, Işık, 'Les *han*, ou l'étranger dans la ville ottomane', in François Georgeon and Paul Dumont (eds), *Vivre dans l'Empire ottoman: Sociabilités et relations intercommunitairs (XVIIIe–XXe siècles)* (Paris: L'Harmattan, 1997), pp. 319–34.

Tamdoğan-Abel, Işık, 'Les relations de voisinage d'après les livres de morale ottomans (XVIe–XVIIIe siècles)', *Anatolia Moderna/Yeni Anadolu* 10 (2004): 167–77.

Taneri, Ergun and Adnan Kazmaoğlu, 'Atik Valide Hamamı Yeniden Kullanım Projesi', *Çevre Dergisi* 3 (1979): 40–2.

Tanman, Baha, 'Atik Valide Külliyesi', *DBİA*.

Tanman, Baha, 'Mimar Sinan Hamamı', *DBİA*.

Terret, Thierry, 'Hygienization: Civic Baths and Body Cleanliness in Late Nineteenth Century France', *International Journal of the History of Sport* 10 (1993): 396–408.

Terzioğlu, Derin, 'The Imperial Circumcision Festival of 1582: An Interpretation', *Muqarnas* 12 (1995): 84–100.

Terzioğlu, Derin, 'Tarihi İnsanlı Yazmak: Bir Tarih Anlatı Türü Olarak Biyografi ve Osmanlı Tarih Yazıcılığı', *Cogito* 29 (2001): 284–96.

Terzioğlu, Derin, 'Man in the Image of God in the Image of the Times: Sufi Self-Narratives and the Diary of Niyazi-i Mısri (1618–94)', *Studia Islamica* 94 (2002): 139–65.

Terzioğlu, Derin, 'How to Conceptualize Ottoman Sunnitization: A Historiographical Discussion', *Turcica* 44 (2012/13): 301–38.

Tezcan, Hülya, 'Osmanlı Hamam Tekstilinin Tarihçesi/History of the Ottoman Bath Textiles', in *Eski Hamam, Eski Taş* (Istanbul: Yapı Kredi Kültür Sanat Yayıncılığı, Tofaş Sanat Galerisi, 2009), pp. 112–25.

'The 31 Places to Go in 2010', *The New York Times*, 7 January 2010, http://www.nytimes.com/2010/01/10/travel/10places.html?pagewanted=all&_r=0

The Meaning of The Holy Qur'an, reprint of 10th edn, ed. Abdullah Yusuf Ali (Beltsville, MD: Amana Publications, 2001).

The Sultan's Portrait: Picturing the House of Osman (Istanbul: İşbank, 2000).

Thys-Şenocak, Lucienne, 'The Yeni Valide Mosque Complex of Eminönü, Istanbul (1597–1665): Gender and Vision in Ottoman Architecture', in D. Fairchild Ruggles (ed.), *Women, Patronage and Self-Representation in Islamic Societies* (Albany, NY: SUNY Press, 2000), pp. 69–89.

Thys-Şenocak, Lucienne, *Ottoman Women Builders: The Architectural Patronage of Hadice Turhan Sultan* (Aldershot: Ashgate, 2006).

al-Tikriti, Nabil, 'Ibn-i Kemal's Confessionalism and the Construction of an Ottoman Islam', in Christine Isom-Verhaaren and Kent Schull (eds), *Living in the Ottoman Realm: Empire and Identity, 13th to 20th Centuries* (Bloomington, IN: Indiana University Press, 2016), pp. 95–107.

Tohme, Lara G., 'Out of Antiquity: Umayyad Baths in Context', PhD dissertation, Massachusetts Institute of Technology, 2005.

References

Tohme, Lara G., 'Between Balneum and Hamam: The Role of Umayyad Baths in Syria', in Nina Ergin (ed.), *Bathing Culture of Anatolian Civilizations: Architecture, History and Imagination* (Louvain: Peeters, 2011), pp. 65–73.

Trevor-Roper, Hugh, 'The Invention of Tradition: The Highland Tradition of Scotland', in Eric Hobsbawm and Terence Ranger (eds), *The Invention of Tradition* (Cambridge: Cambridge University Press, 1997), pp. 15–41.

Tscheu, Frances and Dimitrios Buhalis, 'Augmented Reality at Cultural Heritage Sites', in Alessandro Inversini and Roland Schegg (eds), *Information and Communication Technologies in Tourism 2016: Proceedings of the International Conference in Bilbao, Spain, February 2–5, 2016* (New York: Springer, 2016), pp. 607–19.

Tucker, Judith, 'Biography as History: The Exemplary Life of Khayr al-Din al-Ramli', in Mary Ann Fay (ed.), *Auto/Biography and the Construction of Identity and Community in the Middle East* (New York: Palgrave, 2002), pp. 9–12.

Tükel Yavuz, Ayşıl, 'The Baths of Anatolian Seljuk Caravanserais', in Nina Ergin (ed.), *Bathing Culture of Anatolian Civilizations: Architecture, History and Imagination* (Louvain: Peeters, 2011), pp. 77–140.

Türeli, İpek, 'Modeling Citizenship in Turkey's Miniature Park', *Traditional Dwellings and Settlements Review* 17 (2006): 55–69.

Türeli, İpek, 'Heritagisation of the "Ottoman/Turkish House" in the 1970s: Istanbul-based Actors, Associations and their Networks', *European Journal of Turkish Studies* 19 (2014): 1–32.

Tyckaert, Maud, *Hammams: Les Bain Magiciens* (Paris: Dakota, 2000).

Uğur, Ahmet, *Yavuz Sultan Selim* (Kayseri: Erciyes Üniversitesi Sosyal Bilimler Enstitüsü, 1992).

Unat, Faik Reşit (ed.), *1730 Patrona İhtilali Hakkında bir Eser: Abdi Tarihi* (Ankara: Türk Tarih Kurumu Basımevi, 1943).

Ünsal, Behçet, 'Sinan'ın Son Bir Eseri Üsküdar Büyük Hamamın Aslı Şekline Dönüşümü', *Taç Vakfı Dergisi* 1 (1986): 23–7.

Ünver, Ahmet Süheyl, 'Hamamlarımız en Sıhhi Yıkanma Vasıtasıdır', *Kurum Gazetesi*, 10 February 1938.

Ünver, Ahmet Süheyl, 'İstanbul Hamamlarının İstikbali', *Yeni Türk Mecmuası* 84 (1939): 537–8.

Ünver, Ahmet Süheyl, 'İstanbul Yedinci Tepe Hamamları'na dair bazı notlar', *Vakıflar Dergisi* 2 (1942): 245–51.

Ünver, Ahmet Süheyl, 'Türk Hamamları', *Tarih Dünyası* 5 (1950): 198–203.

Ünver, Ahmet Süheyl, 'İstanbul Hamamları', *Milliyet*, 11 September 1952, p. 2.

Ünver, Ahmet Süheyl, 'İstanbul Hamamları, Hali ve İstikbali', *Yeni İstanbul*, 29 July 1972, p. 2.

Ünver, Ahmet Süheyl, 'Anadolu Selçuklarında Sağlık Hizmetleri', *Malazgirt Armağanı* (Ankara: Türk Tarih Kurumu Basımevi, 1972).

Ünver, Ahmet Süheyl, 'Tarihi bir Hamam Halka Açıldı: Çemberlitaş Hamamı', *Hayat Mecmuası* 20, 10 May 1973, p. 23.

Ünver, Ahmet Süheyl, 'Türk Hamamı', *Türk Tarih Kurumu Belleteni* 37 (1973): 89, 92.

Ürekli, Fatma, 'Osmanli Döneminde İstanbul'da Meydana Gelen Âfetlere İlişkin Literatür', *Türkiye Araştırmaları Literatür Dergisi* 8 (2010): 101–30.

Ürer, Harun, *İzmir Hamamları* (Ankara: Kültür Bakanlığı, 2002).

Urry, John, *The Tourist Gaze: Leisure and Travel in Contemporary Society* (London: Sage, 1990).

Urry, John and Scott Lash, *Economies of Signs and Spaces* (London: Sage: 1994).

Ursinus, Michael, '"Der schlechteste Staat": Ahmed Midhat Efendi (1844–1913) on Byzantine Institutions', *Byzantine and Modern Greek Studies* 11 (1987): 237–44.

Üster, Celal, *Once Upon A Time: Istanbul from Empire to Republic, Photographs from National Geographic* (Istanbul: Türkiye İş Bankası, 2000).

Uzun, Mustafa, and Nurettin Albayrak, 'Hamam: Kültür ve Edebiyat', *TDVİA*.

Vahidi, *Vahidi's Menakıb-i Hoca-i Cihan ve Netice-i Can: Critical Edition and Analysis*, ed. Ahmet Karamustafa (Cambridge, MA: Department of Near Eastern Languages and Literatures, Harvard University, 1993).

Vasari, Giorgio, *Vite de' piu eccellenti pittori, scultori e architettorio: Lives of the Painters, Sculptors and Architects*, trans. Gascon du C. de Vere (New York: Knopf; Random House, 1996).

Veinstein, Gilles (ed.), *Syncrétismes et hérésies dans l'Orient seldjoukide et ottoman (XIVe–XVIIIe siècle)* (Paris: Peeters, 2005).

Vigarello, Georges, *Concepts of Cleanliness: Changing Attitudes in France since the Middle Ages* (Cambridge: Cambridge University Press, 2008).

Warner, Nicholas, 'Taking the Plunge: The Development and Use of the Cairene Bathhouse', in J. Edwards (ed.), *Historians in Cairo: Essays in Honor of George Scanlon* (Cairo: I. B. Tauris, 2002), pp. 49–79.

Wehr, Hans, *A Dictionary of Modern Written Arabic (Arabic–English)*, 4th enl. and rev. edn, ed. J. Milton Cowan (Ithaca, NY: Spoken Language Services, 1994).

Weitzman, Arthur, 'Voyeurism and Aesthetics in the Turkish Bath: Lady Mary's School of Female Beauty', *Comparative Literature Studies* 39 (2002): 347–59.

White, Hayden, 'The Historical Text as Literary Artifact', in Geoffrey Roberts (ed.), *The History and Narrative Reader* (London: Routledge, 2001), pp. 221–36.

Whitehouse, David, 'Excavations at Siraf: Fourth Interim Report', *Iran* 9 (1971): 1–19.

Whitehouse, David, 'Excavations at Siraf: Fifth Interim Report', *Iran* 10 (1972): 63–78.

Wilkins, Charles, 'Ibrahim ibn Khidr al-Qaramani: A Merchant and Urban Notable of Early Ottoman Aleppo', in Christine Isom-Verhaaren and Kent Schull (eds), *Living in the Ottoman Realm: Empire and Identity, 13th to 20th Centuries* (Bloomington, IN: Indiana University Press, 2016), pp. 137–49.

References

Williams, Marilyn T., *Washing the 'Great Unwashed': Public Baths in Urban America, 1840–1920* (Columbus, OH: Ohio State University Press, 1991).

Wortley-Montagu, Lady Mary, *The Turkish Embassy Letters*, ed. Malcolm Jack (London: Virago, 1994).

Yaşaroğlu, M. Kamil, 'Hamam: Fıkıh', *TDVİA*.

Yavuz, M. Hakan, 'Turkish Identity and Foreign Policy in Flux: The Rise of Neo-Ottomanism', *Critique* 89 (1998): 19–41.

Yegül, Fikret, *Baths and Bathing in Classical Antiquity* (Cambridge, MA: MIT Press, 1992).

Yegül, Fikret, 'The Roman Baths at Isthmia in Their Mediterranean Context', in Timothy Gregory (ed.), *The Corinthia in the Roman Period: Including the Papers Given at a Symposium Held at the Ohio State University on 7–9 March 1991* (Ann Arbor, MI: Journal of Roman Archeology, 1993), pp. 101–13.

Yegül, Fikret, 'Cilicia at the Crossroads: Transformations of Baths and Bathing Culture in the Roman East', *OLBA* 8 (2003): 55–72.

Yegül, Fikret, 'Baths and Bathing in Roman Antioch', in Christine Kondoleon (ed.), *Antioch: The Lost Ancient City* (Princeton, NJ: Princeton University Press, 2000), pp. 146–51.

Yegül, Fikret, 'Baths of Constantinople: An Urban Symbol in a Changing World', in William Caraher, Linda Hall and Scott Moore (eds), *Archaeology and History in Roman, Medieval and Post-Medieval Greece: Studies on Method and Meaning in Honour of Timothy Gregory* (Aldershot: Ashgate, 2008), pp. 169–95.

Yegül, Fikret, *Bathing in the Roman World* (Cambridge: Cambridge University Press, 2009).

Yérasimos, Stéphane, *Les voyageurs dans l'empire Ottoman (XIVe–XVIe siècles): Bibliographie, itinéraires et inventaire des lieux habités* (Ankara: Société turque d'histoire, 1991).

Yérasimos, Stéphane, 'Dwellings in Sixteenth-Century Istanbul', in Suraiya Faroqhi and Christoph Neumann (eds), *The Illuminated Table, the Prosperous House: Food and Shelter in Ottoman Material Culture* (Würzburg: Ergon, 2003), pp. 275–300.

Yérasimos, Stefanos, *Sultan Sofraları: 15. ve 16. Yüzyılda Osmanlı Sarayı Mutfağı* (Istanbul: Yapı Kredi Yayınları, 2002).

75 Yılda Değişen Kent ve Mimarlık (Istanbul: Türkiye Ekonomik ve Toplumsal Tarih Vakfı, 1998).

Yi, Eunjong, *Guild Dynamics in Seventeenth-Century Istanbul: Fluidity and Leverage* (Leiden: Brill, 2003).

Yıldırım, Onur, 'Ottoman Guilds in the Early Modern Era', *International Review of Social History* 53(S16) (2008): 73–93.

Yılmazkaya, Orhan, *A Light onto a Tradition and Culture: Turkish Baths. A Guide to the Historic Turkish Baths of Istanbul* (Istanbul: Çitlembik, 2003).

Yoldaş-Demircanlı, Yüksel, *İstanbul Mimarisi için Kaynak Olarak Evliya Çelebi Seyahatnamesi* (Istanbul: Türk Dünyası Araştırmaları Vakfı, 1989).

Zacharidou, Elisabeth, 'Co-Existence and Religion', *Archivum Ottomanicum* 15 (1997): 119–29.

Zarinebaf-Shahr, Fariba, 'The Role of Women in the Urban Economy of Istanbul, 1700–1850', *International Labor and Working-Class History* 60 (2001): 141–52.

Zati, *Zati Divanı: Edisyon Kritik ve Transkripsiyon*, ed. Ali Nihat Tarlan, Mehmed Çavuşoğlu and M. Ali Tanyeri. (Istanbul: [n.p.], 1967–87).

Zdatny, Steven, 'The French Hygiene Offensive of the 1950s: A Critical Moment in the History of Manners', *Journal of Modern History* 84 (2012): 897–932.

Ze'evi, Dror, *Producing Desire: Changing Sexual Discourse in the Ottoman Middle East, 1500–1900* (Berkeley, CA: University of California Press, 2006).

Zencirci, Gizem, 'From Property to Civil Society: The Historical Transformation of Vakıfs in Modern Turkey (1923–2013)', *International Journal of Middle Eastern Studies* 47 (2015): 533–54.

Zihli, Tülay (ed.), *Atlas İstanbul Rehberi: Tatlar-Mekanlar, Yaşayan Tarih, İstanbul 2002* (Istanbul: DBR, 2002).

Zilfi, Madeline, 'The Kadizadelis: Discordant Revivalism in Seventeenth-Century Istanbul', *Journal of Near Eastern Studies* 45 (1986): 251–69.

Zilfi, Madeline (ed.), *Women in the Ottoman Empire: Middle Eastern Women in the Early Modern Era* (Leiden: Brill, 1997).

Zürcher, Erik Jan, *Turkey: A Modern History* (London: I. B. Tauris, 2004).

Filmography

Steam, film, directed by Ferzan Özpetek, Italy/Turkey/Spain: Strand, 1997.

The Accidental Spy, film, directed by Teddy Chan, Hong Kong: Golden Harvest, 2001.

Index

References to images are in *italics*; references to notes are indicated by n

Abbasid dynasty, 42–3
Abdülaziz Bey, 122–3, 200
Abdülhamid I, Sultan, 173
Abdülhamid II, Sultan, 185, 199
Abdullah Buhari, 138–9
Abdülmecid, Sultan, 176
ablutions, 47, 105, 108, 117–18,
    199–200
accounting books (*muhasebe defteri*), 11,
    107, 108
    and renovations, 154–5, 157–60, 170
Ahmed I, Sultan, 26, 137
Ahmed III, Sultan, 93
Akçura, Yusuf, 185
AKP *see* Justice and Development Party
Albania, 93, 94, 304n33
Album of Ahmed I, 137, *138*
Âli, Mustafa, 33
    Künhü'l-Ahbâr (*Essence of History*),
    15
Allom, Thomas, 194
Altınay, Ahmet Refik, 193–4
Altınyıldız, Nur, 191
Anatolia, 45–6, 47–8, 304n33
Ancient Greece, 7, 24, 35–6, 180–1
Antioch, 44
archaeology, 7, 18
architecture, 7, 8–9, 19, 186–7, 205
    and Atik Valide, 58–9
    and hamams, 45–7, 48–50
    and health, 144
    and heritage, 189–93
    and mosques, 22
    and Nurbanu Sultan, 27
    and patronage, 25
    and repairs, 169–72
    and tourism, 211
    see also Mimar Sinan

art, 3, *4*, *5*, 12–13, 139–42, 210–11,
    213–15
    and history, 14, 18
Aşık Çelebi
    Meşa'ir üş-Şuara, 14
Atatürk, Mustafa Kemal, 185–6, 190–1
Atik Ali Paşa, 74–5
Atik Valide Hamamı, 66–7, 108–9,
    248–85
Atik Valide Mosque Complex, 31, 53–6,
    57, 58–64, 145–6
    and tourism, 239–40
attendants (*tellakan*), 92–4, 97, 100, 108,
    134
auto-ethnography, 193–5
Aux Gazelles (Vienna), 243, *246*
Avicenna *see* Ibn Sina
Ayşe bint es-Seyyid İsmail, 170, 175
Ayvansarayî, 67, 69–70, 75

Baghdad, 43
Bain Turc, Le (Ingres), *210*, 213–14
bath-gymnasiums, 298n50
Bath, The (Gerôme), *5*, 215
Bather of Valpinçon, The (Ingres), *4*
bathhouses *see* hamams
bathing, 39
bathrooms, 199–200
Bayezid II, Sultan, 74
Bayezid II hamam, 7, 243, *245*
Benkheira, Mohammed Hocine, 8
Big Burning (*İhrak-i Kebir*), 162–3
biographies (*tezkere*), 13–16, 20
Boogen, Maurits von den, 20
bowls, 127, *128*
Brad, 40, 42
Busbecq, Ogier Ghiselin de, 150, 211
business partnerships, 112, 113

Büyük Hamam, 64, 67–8, *69*, 108, 189
Byzantine Empire, 179, 180–1, 195

Cairo, 7
Canon of Medicine (Kanun fi't-Tibb) (Ibn
    Sina), 143
capitalism, 188, 190
caravanserays, 47
Çemberlitaş Hamamı, 1–2, *3*, 20,
    243–5
  and ancestry, 32–3, *34*, 35, 49–51
  and completion date, 89–90
  and customers, 105–7
  and demolitions, 177–9
  and design, 78, 80–3, *84–6*, 87–9
  and digital media, 237–9
  and earthquakes, 165–6, 167
  and employees, 92–7, *98–9*, 100–1,
    102–3, 104–5, 232–3
  and endowment, 54
  and fire, 161–2, 163–4
  and health, 147
  and history, 10–14, 22–3
  and identity, 116, 118–19, 151–2
  and income, 107–15
  and location, 66, 73–5, 78
  and marketing, 229–32
  and modesty, 119–20
  and raid, 122
  and repairs, 153, 154–5, *156*, 157–61,
    167–72, 174–5
  and restoration, 242
  and 'siblings', 71–2
  and Sinan, 31–2
  and survival, 202–6
  and tourism, 209–11
  and water, 90–2
  and website, 227–9, 234–6
Cemil Paşa, 179, 181
Ceylan, Nuri Bilge, 241
charitable foundation, 11, 25; *see also*
    endowment
children, 122–4, 132–3
Christians, 36, 118–19
class, 126–7
cleanliness, 5–6, 36, 116
climate, 6
clogs, 127, *128*
coffee houses, 9–10, 121–2
cold rooms, 42, 45
Commission for Road Improvement
    (*Islahat-ı Turuk Komisyonu*), 177–80,
    181

Committee of Union and Progress (CUP),
    185
communal bathing, 119–20
Constantine's Column, 73, 75, 177
Constantinople *see* Istanbul
contractors (*mutassarrif*), 113–14
Cook, Thomas, 207
Corfu, 24–5
Çorlulu Ali Paşa, 75
Covered Bazaar, 75
Çukur Hamamı, 148
customers, 105–7, 108, 114–15

Dâfi'ü'l-Gumûm ve Râfi'ü'l-Humûm (*The*
    Repeller of Sorrow and Remover of
    Anxiety) (Gazali), 135–6
Damascus, 7
Davud Paşa, 199–200
Deli Birader Gazali, 135–6
Dellakname-i Dilküşa (*The Heart-*
    Breaking Book of Masseurs) (İsmail),
    134
Democrat Party, 192
Dernschwam, Hans, 150
Derviş İsmail, 134
dervish convent (*tekke*), 63
digital media, 234–9
Distant (film), 241
divan poetry, 136
Divan Yolu, 73–5, *77*, 177, 179–80, 181
double rent (*icareteyn*), 174–5, 188–9
dressing rooms, 42, 45, 81–2, 177–8

earthquakes, 11–12, 157, 160, 165–7
Ebussuud Efendi, 130
education, 60–1
Ein Turggisshe Hochzeit (Wyts), 131,
    132–3
Elçi Han, 75, 105
Emir Çelebi, 144–5, 146
employees, 92–7, *98–9*, 100–1, *102–3*,
    104–5
Enderuni Fazıl Hüseyin, 139–40, *141*
endowment, 11, 48, 64, 66–72
  and administration, 173–5
  and Atik Valide, 52–5, 248–85
  and income, 108–12
  and inspectors, 168–9
  and reforms, 188–9
Enmüzecü'l-Tibb (*Summary of Medicine*)
    (Emir Çelebi), 144–5
entrances, 125
Ergin, Osman Nuri, 181

Index

Eski Kaplıca (Bursa), 299n74
ethnicity, 93–4
Europe, 176, 177, 180, 181–4, 243
evil spirits (*jinns*), 132, 310n50
Evliya Çelebi, 63, 64, 97, 100, 151
   and prostitution, 134
   and segregation, 125–6

Fatma Kadın, 158, 159, 160, 174
films, 215–16, 241
fire, 160, 161–4, 174, 177
firewood, 11
First World War, 202–3, 206
food, 62–3, 146, 279–83
Forum of Constantine, 73, 75
France, 27
Fuad Paşa, 181
fuel, 91–2, 153–4
Fuzûlî, 136

Galen, 143, 144
genealogical histories (*silsilenames*), 33,
   34, 35
Genghis Khan, 33
Gerôme, Jean-Léon, 3, *5*, 213, 215
Glück, Heinrich, 9
Gökalp, Ziya, 185
Gortys Bath, 35
Great Britain, 207
Greatest Fire (*Harik-i Ekber*), 163
Greece *see* Ancient Greece
guide books, 219–21
guilds, 93, 94, 96–7, *98–9*, 100–1, *102–4*,
   105

Hagia Sophia, 19, 48, 52, 75, 320n62
   and hamams, 148, 150
   and heritage, 189–90
hamam managers (*hamamcıyan*), 94, 96–7,
   98–9, 101, 104–5, 112–14
   and fees, 108
hamams, 2–7, 19–20, 148–9, 153–4
   and ancestry, 35–7, 39–51
   and artists, 213–15
   and auto-ethnography, 193–5
   and carnal pleasure, 133–7
   and demolitions, 189
   and employees, 304n33
   and endowed, 64, 66–72
   and Europe, 181–4
   and film, 215–16
   and health, 142–7
   and internal tourism, 222–4, 226

and Islam, 118
and kit, 127, *128*, 129, *130*
and models, 96–7, 100, *102–3*
and national pride, 195, 197
and nationalism, 192–3
and nostalgia, 197–8
and the poor, 198–9
and private, 120, *121*
and scholarship, 7–10
and secluded women, 129–32
and secularism, 186–8
and segregation, 124–7
and socialising, 120–2
and splendour, 149–51
and survival, 200–2
and tourism, 211–13, 216–22, 242–3
see also Çemberlitaş Hamamı
Hammat Gader, 40–1
Hanefi Islam *see* Sunni Islam
harem, 25, 27
Haseki Hamamı, 80, 125, *126*, 299n74
Hatice Turhan Sultan, 30
Haussmann, Georges-Eugène, 179, 192
Havuzlu Hamam, 66, 69–71, 108, 112–13,
   189
Hayreddin Barbaros, 24
health, 39, 142–7
heating, 37, *38*, 39, 42, 44, 51
   and Çemberlitaş Hamamı, 88–9
Hevesname (Cafer Çelebi), 150–1
High Council on Immovable Heritage
   Items and Monuments (*Gayrımenkul
   Eski Eserler ve Anıtlar Yüsek
   Kurulu*), 191
Hocapaşa fire, 163–4, 177
homosexuality, 134, 135–7, 212–13
hospitals, 61–2
hot rooms, 43–4, 45, 82–3, *84–6*, 87–8
housing, 199–202
humouralism, 142–3, 146
Hungary, 7
Hürrem Sultan, 25, 26
hygiene, 198–9
hypocausts, 36, 37, *38*, 40, 42, 44, 51

Ibn Khaldun, 292n58
Ibn Sina, 143, 144, 146
Ibrahim I, Sultan, 30
imperial council (*mühimme*), 11
Imperial Rescript, 176
impurity (*cenabet*), 117
India, 6
infants, 122–4

Ingres, Jean-Auguste-Dominique, 3, *4*, 209, *210*, 213–14
inns, 61, 62–3, 74–5, 105–6
insanity, 137
inscriptions, 11, 69–70, 80–1
  and hot room, 83, *86*, 87–8
  and renovations, 155, *156*, 157
Iran, 44–7
Iraq, 43–4
İşigüzel, Şebnem, 216, *217*
Islam, 5–6, 7, 8–9
  and art history, 22
  and bathing, 39–47
  and cleanliness, 116–18
  and endowment, 55
  and medicine, 36
  and monuments, 181, 188–9
  and nationalism, 189–90
  and prayer, 59–60
  see also mosques; secularism
Istanbul, 64, *65*, 66, 73–5
  and development, 147–8
  and maps, 203–5
  and neighbourhoods, 149
  and reforms, 176–81, 191–2
  and tourism, 241–2
  see also earthquakes; fire
Iter factum e Belgico-Gallica, Voyages de Wyts en Turquie (Wyts), 131

Janissaries, 122
Jermyn Street Hammam, 319n32
Jews, 118–19
Jordan, 39–40
Justice and Development Party (AKP), 225, 241, 320n62

Kandemir, 194–5, *196*
Kara Mustafa Paşa, 75
Karapınar, 25
Katipzade, 162–3
Kemalettin, Mimar, 181, 188
Kemalism, 186
Khirbat al-Mafjar, 8, 42
Kılıç Ali Paşa Hamamı, 7, 242, *243*
Kitab al-Hammamat (Abdalhadi), 7
Klinghardt, Karl, 9, 187–8
Koca Sinan Paşa, 75
Koçu, Reşat Ekrem, 198
Konya, 25, 46, 48, 190
Konyalı, İbrahim Hakkı, 195
Köprülü family, 75, 78, *79*
Kopytoff, Igor, 18

Kösem Mahpeyker Sultan, 30, 58
Kritovoulos, 148
Küçük Mustafa Paşa Hamamı, 7, 243, *244*

lanterns, 78
licence system (*gedik*), 105, 112, 170–1
life cycles, 122–4
Lubenau, Reinhold, 150
Lütfi Paşa, 31

Mahmud Paşa Hamamı, 49–50, *51*, 148
male attendants, 11
maps, 203–5
marble basins (*kurna*), 83
marble slab (*göberktaşı*), 83, *84*
market inspector (*muhtesib*), 104–5
marriage, 124
massage, 83, 143, 144
Medici, Catherine de, 27
medicine, 142–7
medrese (religious schools), 60–1
Mehmed II, Sultan, 52, 147–9
Mehmed III, Sultan, 30, 33
Mehmed IV, Sultan, 30
Mehmed the Conqueror, 48, 75
Menderes, Adnan, 192
Milford, Nancy, 216, 218–19, 222
military, the, 112–13, 122
Mimar Sinan, 2, 15–16, 25, 30–2, 190
  and Büyük Hamam, 67–8
  and Çemberlitaş Hamamı, 80, 82, 83
modesty (*avret*), 119–20
Moltke, Helmuth von, 176
mosques, 22, 25, 26, 27
  and endowment, 52–3
  and hamams, 47
  and Mimar Sinan, 31, 32
  see also Atik Valide Mosque Complex
Mu'awiyah, Caliph, 41
Mü'minzâde Seyyid Ahmed Hasîb Efendi, 134
al-Muqtadir, Caliph, 43
Murad III, Sultan, 2, 25, 26, 27, 28, 54
Murad IV, Sultan, 30, 144
Muslims *see* Islam
Mustafa III, Sultan, 154
Mustafa Reşid Paşa, 176
Mustafa Sai, 15–16; *see also* Sai-i Dai
Müstakimzade, 19

nation-states, 171, 180, 184–6, 189–90
national pride, 195, 197

nationalism, 185, 186, 189–90, 192–3
neighbourhoods (*mahalle*), 149
Nicholay, Nicolas de, 150, 211, 212, 214–15
Nigar, 45, *46*
non-Muslims *see* Christians; Jews
nostaligic lament, 197–8
Noyan, Dr Abdülkadir, 202–3
nudity, 8, 104–5, 119–20, 137–9, 216
Nurbanu Sultan, 2, 11, 24–8, *29*, 30
   and Atik Valide, 58, 60–1
   and endowment, 52, 53–4, 55

Orhan, Sultan, 48
Orientalism, 7, 9, 10, 15, 184
Osman II, Sultan, 30
Ottoman Empire, 2–3, 4, 7, 112, 173–4
   and architecture, 19, 23, 32
   and biographies, 13–16, 20
   and family trees, 33
   and hamams, 9–10, 48–50
   and heritage, 179–84, 242
   and identity, 20–2
   and reforms, 175–7
   and royal women, 26–7, 30
   and Turkey, 185, 186
Ottomania, 222–6
Özal, Turgut, 224
Özpetek, Ferzan, 3, 215–16

Palestine, 7, 39–40
Pamuk, Orhan, 225, 241
Pardoe, Julia, 211, 212, 213
Paris, 176, 179
Parvillée, Léon, 182
Patrona Halil rebellion (1730), 93, 122
Pervititch, Jacques, 203–5
photography, 12–13
poetry, 19, 136–7, 150–1
politics, 121–2
Pompeii, 36–7
porticoes, 80
prayer, 118
price register (*narh defteri*), 107–8
processions, 26, 27, 75, 96, 100–1
Prost, Henri, 191, 192
prostitution, 133–5
puppet plays, 137–8, *139*

Qabusnama, 44, 46
Qasr al-Hayr al-Sharqi, 41–2
Qur'an, 59, 61
Qusayr 'Amra, 8, 42

Ratib Ahmed Paşa, 199
Ravzatü'l-Küberâ (*Garden of the Grandees*) (Hasîb Efendi), 134
record-keeping, 93–4
regulations (*nizamname*), 101, 104
religion, 125–6, 129, 151; *see also* Christians; Islam; Jews
repairmen, 169–70, 316n38
Risale-i Garibe (anon.), 134
rituals, 6, 36, 116–18
Roman baths, 36–7, *38*, 39–40, 50–1
Roman Empire, 73
Romano-Byzantine baths, 39–40

Sai-i Dai, 81, 83, 87, 155, 157
Safavid Empire, 93
Safiye Sultan, 30
Sahih al-Bukhari, 117–18
Sahih Muslim, 116–17
Samarra, 43–4, 45
sand cleansing, 118
Sassanian dynasty, 44
Schweigger, Solomon, 150
secularism, 185, 186–8
Sedefkâr Mehmed Ağa, 32
segregation, 120, 124–5, 186
Sehi of Edirne
   Heşt Bihişt (*Eight Gardens*), 14
şehr-engiz poetry, 150–1
Selim II, Sultan, 2, 25, 26, 28, 56, 67
Seljuk dynasty, 45–8
servants (*natıran*), 11, 94, 100, *102–3*, 108
Settle, Mary Lee, 211, 212
Şevk-Engiz (Vehbi), 134
sex, 132, 133–7
slaves, 24, 30
socialising, 120–2, 131–2, 202
Spain, 7
spies, 122
Stabian Bath, 36, *37*
Steam: The Turkish Bath (film), 3, *6*, 215–16
Süleyman the Magnificent, Sultan, 25, 30
Sünbülzade Vehbi, 134
Sunni Islam, 6, 116–18
surgery, 146, 313n101
Surname-i Hümayun (*Book of Imperial Processions*), 96, 100
Syria, 39–40, 41–2, 45, 213, 215

Taban, Ahmet, 194–5, 309n40
Tâcîzâde Cafer Çelebi, 19, 136, 150–1
Tahtakale Hamamı, 48–50

Tanzimat period (1839–76), 2–3, 176–7
taxation, 93, 101, 149
Thermae of Caracalla, 37, *38*
thermae see Roman baths
thermal water, 6
Timurid dynasty, 33
tips, 108
Topkapı Palace, 25, 26, 75
tourism, 1–2, 3–4, 12, 207–10, 216,
    218–22, 239–40
    and internal, 222–4
    and Istanbul, 241–2
    see also travel writers
towel makers (*peştemalcıyan*), 100–1, *104*
towels, 127
trade, 64, 66
traditions of the Prophet (hadith), 116–20
travel magazines, 216, *217*, 218–19, 223–4
travel writers, 6–7, 150, 210–13
travellers, 64, 105–6
Treaty of Lausanne (1923), 186
trustees (*mütevelli*), 168–9
Turkish baths *see* hamams
Turkish Civil Code (*Türk Medeni
    Kanunu*), 188
Turkish Republic, 3, 7, 185–6, 189–93
    and national pride, 195, 197
Turkism, 185–6

Ukhaidir, 42–3
Umayyad desert castles, 8, 41–2
Ünver, Ahmet Süheyl, 9, 197–9
Urquhart, David, 319n32
Üsküdar, 26, 27, 53–6, *57*, 58–64, 189
    and tourism, 239–40

vakif see endowment
vaulted recesses (*iwan*), 44, 45, 46–7

Venice, 24–5, 27
Vezir Han, 105–6, *107*
Vienna, 243, *246*
virtual reality, 236–7

Walid II, Caliph, 8
warm rooms, 42, 45, 82
water, 11, 63–4, 78, *79*
    and Çemberlitaş Hamamı, 88–9, 90–2
    and heating, 37, *38*, 39
    and shortages, 153–4
weddings, 124
Welfare Party, 224
White, Hayden, 13
women, 78, 80, 88, 113, 139–40, *141*, 142
    and childbirth, 122–4, 146
    and dressing room, 177–8
    and employees, 232–3
    and modesty, 120
    and nudity, 137–9
    and seclusion, 129–32
    and secularism, 186
    and segregation, 124–5
    and sons, 132–3
    and tourism, 212
    see also prostitution
World Fairs, 181–4, 193, 208
Wortley-Montagu, Lady Mary, 120, 121,
    211–12, 215
Wyts, Lambert, 131–2

Yenişehirli Beliğ Mehmed Emin, 136–7
Young Turks, 185

Zati, 19
Zenanname (*Book of Women*) (Hüseyin),
    139–40, *141*, 142
Zoroastrianism, 44

Printed in the USA
CPSIA information can be obtained
at www.ICGtesting.com
JSHW011634301023
51114JS00013B/459